ABOUT NOT LOSING

ABOUT NOT LOSING
A high-stakes trial. Life's purpose found.

JAMES S. OGSBURY III, MD

Copyright 2025 James Stanley Ogsbury III, MD. ALL RIGHTS RESERVED.

No part of this book may be reproduced in any form whatsoever, by photography or xerography or by any other means, by broadcast or transmission, by translation into any kind of language, or by recording electronically or otherwise without permission in writing from the author, except by a reviewer who may quote brief passages in critical articles or reviews.

Printed in the United States of America
First Printing: 2025

ISBN: 978-1-954102-30-9 (hardcover)
ISBN: 978-1-954102-31-6 (paperback)
ISBN: 978-1-954102-32-3 (ebook)
Library of Congress Control Number: 2024953045

Edited by Cameron Cowan, Eileen Maddocks, Beth Rule
Cover design by Veronica Coello
Interior design by Amit Dey

Published by:
SOMETHING OR OTHER PUBLISHING LLC
Brooklyn, Wisconsin 53521
For general inquiries: Info@SOOPLLC.com
For bulk orders: Orders@SOOPLLC.com

TABLE OF CONTENTS

Qualifications of a Surgeon ix

Prologue xi
    Dr. James "Jay" Ogsbury *April 2024* xi

Introduction: The First Trial xv
    Jay *November 1989* xv
    Dr. Fran Berman *December 1989* xxviii

Chapter One: Memories of the First Trial 1
    Jay *November 1989* 1
    Fran *December 1989* 4
    Peter Pryor, Counsel for Dr. Ogsbury *December 1989* 7

Chapter Two: Inter-trial Period 11
    Jay *April 1990* 11
    Fran *April 1990* 15

Chapter Three: Pre-trial 21
    Peter Downtown Riverton, Wyoming *Friday, April 27, 1990* . . . 21
    Jay *The Weekend Before Trial* 22
    Fran *Sunday, April 29, 1990* 23

Chapter Four: Day 1 – Voir Dire 25
    Peter *Monday, April 30, 1990, 4:00 a.m.* 25
    Jay *Monday, April 30, 1990* 26
    Fran *Monday, April 30, 1990, 9:00 p.m.* 38

Chapter Five: Day 2 – Voire Dire 39
    Peter *Tuesday, May 1, 1990, 4:03 a.m.* 39
    Jay *May 1, 1990* 40
    Fran *May 1, 1990, 9:00 p.m.* 48
    The Jurors 49

Chapter Six: Day 3 – Opening Statements 53
    Peter *Wednesday, May 2, 1990, 4:00 a.m.* 53
    Jay *Wednesday, May 2, 1990* 55
    Fran *Wednesday, May, 2, 9:00 p.m.* 85

Chapter Seven: Day 4 – The Direct Examination of Frank P. Smith . . 87
    Peter *Thursday, May 3, 1990, 4:00 a.m.* 87
    Jay *Thursday, May 3, 1990* 89
    Fran *Thursday, May 3, 1990, 9:00 p.m.* 99

Chapter Eight: Day 5 – The Cross-examination of Frank P. Smith . . 101
    Peter *Friday, May 4, 1990, 2:30 a.m.* 101
    Jay *Friday, May 4, 1990* 102
    Peter *Friday, May 4, 1990, 6:00 p.m.* 143
    Fran *Friday, May 4, 1990, 9:00 p.m.* 144

Chapter Nine: First Weekend 145
    Peter *Saturday, May 5, 1990* 145
    Jay *Saturday, May 5, 1990* 145

Chapter Ten: Day 6 – The Nurses 149
    Jay *Monday, May 7, 1990* 149

Peter *Monday, May 7, 1990, 6:00 p.m.* *161*

Fran *Monday, May 7, 1990, 9:00 p.m.* *161*

Chapter Eleven: Day 7 – More Nurses & The Direct Examination
    of Lee Krauth 163

Peter *Tuesday, May 8, 1990, 10:00 a.m.* *163*

Jay *Tuesday, May 8, 1990.* *164*

Fran *Tuesday, May 8, 1990, 9:00 p.m.* *198*

Chapter Twelve: Day 8 – The Cross-examination of Lee Krauth . . . 199

Peter *Wednesday, May 5, 1990, 4:00 a.m.* *199*

Jay *Wednesday, May 5, 1990* *200*

Fran *Wednesday, May 5, 1990, 9:00 p.m.* *240*

Chapter Thirteen: Day 9 – Lloyd Cripe & More Lee Krauth 241

Peter *Thursday, May 10, 1990, 4:00 a.m.* *241*

Jay *Thursday, May 10, 1990* *242*

Fran *Thursday, May 10, 1990, 9:00 p.m.* *252*

Chapter Fourteen: Day 10 – Dr. Melvin Greer 253

Peter *Friday, May 11, 1990, 4:00 a.m.* *253*

Jay *Friday, May 11, 1990* *255*

Fran *Friday, May 11, 1990, 9:00 p.m.* *281*

Jay *Friday, May 11, 1990, 11:55 p.m.* *282*

Chapter Fifteen: The Dream 283

Cross-examination of Dr. Greer 283

Defense Case 295

Plaintiffs' Closing Arguments 312

Defense's Closing Arguments 320

Jury Instructions and Deliberations. 326

Chapter Sixteen: Weekend Break from the Trial ... 335
    Jay *Saturday, May 12, 1990, 12:05 a.m.* ... 335
    Peter *Saturday, May 12, 1990* ... 335
    Peter *Sunday, May 13, 1990* ... 337
    Jay *Sunday, May 13, 1990* ... 337
    Fran *Sunday, May 13, 1990* ... 339

Chapter Seventeen: Day 11 – The Settlement ... 341
    Peter *Monday, May 14, 1990, 10:05 a.m.* ... 341
    Jay *Monday, May 14, 1990* ... 343
    Peter *Monday, May 14, 1990* ... 347
    Fran *Monday, May 14, 1990* ... 347

Chapter Eighteen: Post-trial ... 349
    Jay *Tuesday, May 15, 1990* ... 349
    Jay *May 21, 1990*
    One Week Post Trial ... 350
    Peter *September 22, 1992* ... 351
    Fran *November 1992* ... 352
    Jay *January 1993* ... 352
    Fran ... 354

Epilogue ... 355
    Jay *January 2023* ... 355
    Jay *April 2024* ... 360

QUALIFICATIONS OF A SURGEON

The performance of operations predisposes the possession of certain qualities on the part of the surgeon. It is not every man that can become an operator, even presuming he has the requisite knowledge of anatomy and the use of instruments. Courage, which is so indispensable, is possessed by comparatively few; the sight of blood and the idea of inflicting pain were so disagreeable to Haller, that, although he taught surgery with great success for seventeen years, he never, it seems, during all that time, performed a solitary operation upon the living subject. Courage, like poetry, has been said to be a gift of nature and nothing is perhaps more true. ... Celsus, long ago, happily defined the qualities which constitute a good operator. He should possess, says the illustrious Roman, a firm and steady hand, a keen eye, and the most unflinching courage.

But the above are not the only qualities, important though they be, which should be possessed by an operator. If he is not honest in his purposes, or scrupulously determined, in every case, to act only with a single eye to the benefit of the patient, and the glory of his profession, he is not worthy of the name which he bears, or fit for the discharge of the solemn duty which he assumes. ... No operation should ever be undertaken without due deliberation, and without a careful consideration of the various consequences involved in the results. Everything that is done should be done with reference exclusively to the patient; self should not have the slightest weight in the matter.

Samuel D. Gross, Professor of Surgery
Jefferson Medical College of Philadelphia
A System of Surgery
Blanchard & Lee Philadelphia, 1859

PROLOGUE

Dr. James "Jay" Ogsbury
April 2024

As a senior neurosurgeon, I am frequently asked what my advice to others would be seeking a similar career. My advice has always been, "For all of us, doors frequently open, but usually the doors open at an inopportune time; my suggestion is to walk through the door and look to see if what is on other side is better than what had been planned all along." More recently, I have come to realize that there is a corollary which is, "Doors sometimes close, but when one door closes, there is almost always another that opens. One loses only if one fails to walk through the newly opened door."

Throughout my career, I have been fortunate to experience a number of unexpected open doors, each of which led to a path I never could have envisioned. I attended medical school 1965-1969 at the Cornell University Medical College, and while there, decided to apply for a summer job in pulmonary medicine. Somehow, I entered the wrong office to make the application and boldly announced to the secretary that I was applying for the summer job. Given that the secretary worked for Dr. Fred Plum, the famous Professor of Neurology at Cornell, she was clearly surprised as evidently no one had ever applied for a summer job to that office. She politely stepped out, briefly talked to Dr. Plum, then returned and told me that Dr. Plum felt that he could find a place for me. Interestingly, at that point Dr. Plum was studying the neurophysiology of the pulmonary system, and it would be a full three weeks before I realized I was working for a group of famous neurologists (*not* pulmonologists). While there, I was also assigned to work with Dr. Fletcher McDowell, a wonderful senior neurologist at Cornell who was well known for being one of the early developers of the use of L-DOPA in the treatment of Parkinson's Disease. Working for these great men, I soon realized that walking into the wrong office had led to an exciting career in neuroscience.

About one year later, understanding that my personality is more attuned to the surgical aspects of neuroscience than the medical world of neurology, I was fortunate to obtain an elective rotation in the Department of Neurosurgery whose chairman was Dr. Bronson Ray. Dr. Ray was the last resident of the famous Dr. Harvey Cushing, the father of neurosurgery, and was then one of the top neurosurgeons in the world. It was an unbelievable experience to be in that environment with three internationally known attending neurosurgeons, a superlative resident staff, and wonderful nurses, all dedicated to neurosurgical care. The passion exhibited by each person in the department was extraordinary. I frequently was assigned to be a second assistant on Dr. Ray's surgical cases, but, other than one time when he chided me for an improperly tied surgical knot, never once did Dr. Ray speak a word to me. However, one night when Dr. Ray had to take one of his patients back to the operating room to treat a postoperative hemorrhage and no resident was available, he agreed that I could be his first assistant. During the operation, after he had removed the bone flap and the bleeding was profuse, he unexpectedly and briefly put his instruments down, looked up at me with a twinkle in his eye and said, "Are you sure you want to be a neurosurgeon, Doc?" My answer was, of course, "Yes, Sir" and my career as a neurosurgeon was inevitable.

After I completed medical school, one year of internship, and one year of residency at Cornell, I fulfilled my Berry Plan commitment to the military and served in the Air Force for two years. I finished my neurosurgical training in the Department of Neurosurgery at the University of Colorado Medical Center, and thereafter the first years of my practice were largely highly enjoyable and rewarding, both medically and personally.

When this book begins its story, I was the attending physician for a patient for whom there was a request to repair a spinal fluid leak created by an ENT (ear, nose, and throat physician) procedure, and a major complication occurred. The patient was quite sick, likely with meningitis, and two procedures were required to fully close the leak. But just as she was beginning to improve and wake up, and without my permission, she underwent a further procedure performed by an in-hospital physician. From this, she suffered a disastrous complication leading to a severe stroke, from which she never fully recovered. Afterward, I was sufficiently angry that I asked COPIC, my medical malpractice insurance company, to take care of this lady and her family for the rest of her life, and to its credit, the insurance company representative agreed to put forth $1.5 million for their care. Unfortunately, her Native American husband obtained the services of the well-known Native American attorney from Wyoming, Mr. Gerry Spence. A lawsuit was filed by Mr. Spence for $9.7 million against my partner and me, thus closing the door to an honorable settlement to the tragedy.

As a neurosurgeon, I was not well prepared for the experience of being a defendant in a high-stakes malpractice trial. However, before and during the two subsequent trials, I came to know two extraordinary people whose roles were to assist me on the journey. Together, we three tell this story.

The first person of this trio was, of course, my primary malpractice defense attorney, Mr. Peter Pryor. According to the insurance company, he was known to be the best malpractice defense attorney in the region. I had seen him in action in a prior case in which he defended my first partner, and he clearly was an unbelievably skilled attorney. However, in our situation, the passion he devoted to the case was colossal. In addition, because the attempt by Mr. Spence failed to force a settlement and a mistrial was called, Mr. Pryor also suggested that, during the inevitable second trial, I might write about the experience of being a defendant during the trial.

I agreed to document the experience. In addition, I later found out from his team that he keeps a daily diary of his personal experiences during a trial, so I asked him, and he kindly agreed, to contribute his perspective to the writing.

The second extraordinary person whom I came to know well was Dr. Fran Berman. She was a brilliant psychologist who was initially chosen to be the jury selector. However, she also was chosen because she herself is Native American and had spent a full six months training Peter how to face a Native American warrior. Her other role was to support the defense team, and she spent several months attempting to prepare me for the inevitable onslaught. I came to know her well, and when the decision was made to write about the experience, I asked her if she would be willing to include her perspective as part of the project. She too kindly agreed.

The manuscript involves the description of a trial from three separate perspectives written as the trials occurred. For that reason, it might seem at the onset that the focus of the story would be the negative changes which such an experience might force on each of us. In actuality, the story is primarily a description of the response to that trial and to the door being closed to an honorable settlement, initially from my point of view but then also from that of Peter and Fran. It is a story of rediscovery for each of the three of us and thus a story of walking through the doors that open after another door closes.

INTRODUCTION

THE FIRST TRIAL

*Some names of persons have been abbreviated
to protect their identity.*

Jay
November 1989

I first met Sheran R on June 23, 1986, and I liked her immediately. She was a 43-year-old teacher married to a Native American state representative from Wyoming. She had developed a leakage of spinal fluid from her nose following a sinus operation in Wyoming and was sent to St. Anthony Hospital in Denver, Colorado, for its neurosurgical repair.

Her course was difficult. She developed meningitis and required two operations to close the leak. But just when she seemed to turn the corner and started to improve, she suffered an unrecognized complication, a pneumothorax (collapsed lung), from a nonsurgical procedure that I had recommended not be done. She developed massive strokes and despite ultimate improvement far beyond anyone's expectations, she remained, and will remain, severely disabled.

Many physicians were involved in her care including James Barron, otolaryngologist, Susan Mason, infectious disease expert, and Lee

Krauth, my partner, plus two other neurosurgeons, critical care physicians and a general surgeon. However, I remained her attending neurosurgeon throughout and was horrified that this lovely lady had suffered a catastrophic brain injury while under my care. I asked a representative from my malpractice insurance company to accompany me on a trip to Wyoming to check on Sheran's progress. I was pleased to hear that money for her immediate needs had already been paid, and that money for her medical and home care for the rest of her life would be paid by all of the involved insurance companies. However, it soon became evident that the amount, although substantial, was not acceptable. Early in 1987, an offer was received from an attorney representing Sheran and her husband to settle the issue for the staggering sum of 9.7 million dollars which meant that the litigation we had worked so hard to avoid had become inevitable.

On June 23, 1988, a lawsuit was filed on behalf of Sheran R and her husband, Scott R, by Gerry Spence, the well-known Wyoming attorney, in the Denver District Court, naming as Defendants Dr. Lee Krauth and me, as well as one critical care physician, a general surgery resident, and the hospital. Gerry Spence had gained local notoriety for his involvement in the Silkwood and Wyoming Penthouse cases. He was the senior partner of the firm Spence, Schuster, and Moriarity. A response denying all allegations of negligence was made by my attorney, Peter Pryor, a partner at Pryor, Carney and Johnson (PC&J), a Denver law firm with an extensive practice in malpractice defense.

In the first few months after the suit was filed, little occurred that involved me directly. However, the frequent delivery of undecipherable documents to my office indicated that during this period, the attorneys were busy doing whatever it is that attorneys do. Finally, in August of 1989, Drs. Barron, Krauth, and I were scheduled for our depositions, a process involving the attorneys questioning the parties or witnesses under oath before trial. The depositions of Drs. Barron and Krauth were taken by Mr. Robert Schuster and evidently proved "to be long and arduous."

My direct involvement in the case began with my deposition. My deposition was cancelled when Mr. Schuster failed to come to Denver for reasons that were not understandable to me. He then attempted to reschedule the deposition, but this time over two days. I objected to the extra day, emphasizing my (probably naive) view that, since he had caused the delay, it was unreasonable that he asked for extra time. Thus, an offer was made by Ms. Kathy Martel, a young attorney from Mr. Pryor's firm, that I would be available for a deposition which could be completed in one day, lasting as long as he needed, starting in the morning, and interrupted only by a short lunch break and necessary bathroom breaks. I knew I was well prepared for a marathon session (neurosurgeons do not break for lunch in the middle of our sometimes-prolonged procedures), and Drs. Barron and Krauth had told me that, while Mr. Schuster was a slow deposer, he tended to tire after five or six hours. I knew I could last.

The deposition occurred on February 14, 1989. It was certainly memorable. Mr. Schuster proved to be a small, unsmiling man, polite but clearly unfriendly. A medical colleague who knew him from Wyoming had told me that he apparently had a strong dislike for physicians, an observation which was certainly consistent with my experience. He was a piercing deposer and remarkably well prepared. He had even read depositions from previous cases in which I had been an expert witness!

However, his technique of slowly asking questions and then repeating them on multiple occasions (in an attempt to obtain inconsistencies) quickly became clear. This tactic was somewhat annoying to me, more so to the many other attorneys present, and *especially* Ms. Martel. I found I could easily tolerate his nastiness and answer his questions with a clear head. Ms. Martel, on the other hand, was offended by his condescension towards me and to her as well. To my relief, she too held her own in the game of objections and comments. Her main problem during the deposition was with my usual loquaciousness. My legs still bear the marks from her kicks under the table! I felt, however, that I could not give short answers to Mr. Schuster's well-conceived questions. While more information was given to the opposing side than one might wish, never was anything said that did not come directly from my learning or experience, and that therefore might be used against me at trial. I specifically had not done any reading of the literature in preparation for the deposition (give an opposing attorney a favorite article or chapter and he will find a sentence to use out of context against you), and I honestly could not remember exactly what I had read prior to Sheran R's medical care. Mr. Schuster was clearly displeased. I did expect that in trial he would try to imply a lack of preparation.

During the fifteen hours of deposition, from 7:00 a.m. to 10:00 p.m., both Ms. Martel and I were able to maintain our composure. I felt I had held my own when during a brief break, Mr. Schuster remarked that I was a "tough son of a bitch." I then could not resist the opportunity to comment that I found a fifteen-hour deposition much less difficult than a similarly long brain operation. When the deposition transcription, some 500 pages long, was returned for revisions, I was pleased to find no changes of any significance to be necessary. I also noticed that despite her frustration with Mr. Schuster's apparent personal attacks, Ms. Martel had protected me well.

After my deposition, the next event was a strangely unmemorable settlement conference chaired by a former judge, Richard Dana. He seemed perceptive and fair but clearly had a stake in the settlement process. During the conference, this former judge lectured Dr. Krauth that our judicial system and its juries simply cannot deal effectively and fairly with complex issues. These were frightening words from the mouth of a former judge. Dr. Krauth was already upset about his part in the legal action, given the small role he played in Sheran's medical care. These statements did not improve his attitude. Specifically, Judge Dana said that the real issue was not right or wrong, but rather how each side could achieve its goals, the plaintiff some recompense for an injury, and the defendant a release from a tiresome and inconvenient trial, given the apparent strengths and weaknesses of the two respective sides. During the conference he spent time shuttling between the opposing attorneys sequestered in different rooms. He brought offers and counteroffers to the sides, claiming to our side about the intransigence of the other, and I assume similarly to them about us. At one point, he estimated to the defense team that he felt it would take 2.5 million dollars (1 million from the Wyoming ENT physician, 1 million from the neurosurgeons, and $500,000 from the rest) to settle the issue, but the offers from the Plaintiffs were well above this figure and from the defense well below that number. No agreement was in sight at the conference.

In the process of the negotiation, different lawyers took different approaches based on their clients' interest. The attorneys representing the Wyoming otolaryngologist took a very hard position, barely offering to become involved in a settlement, surprising to Ms. Martel given his limited insurance coverage. The attorney for the surgical resident took a similar position, bolstered by a Colorado statute limiting Sheran R's right of recovery against him, as a state employee, to $150,000. The attorney for the critical care physician appeared at least to be open to suggestion. The attorney for the hospital was willing to be helpful within the scope of the hospital's risk. During all this individual gamesmanship, there occurred very little real negotiation and the idea of settlement died an ignominious death.

My only gain was to see Gerry Spence in person for the first time at the beginning of the conference. He was a large, overweight man, wearing ill-fitting western clothing, who seemed to carry an air of haughty condescension to everyone else in the room, including his own team; but he did not utter a word that I could hear. In addition, for the first time, I realized that a trial was truly inevitable.

The period between the settlement conference and the trial was marked by a flurry of depositions of defense witnesses by the Plaintiffs' attorneys. The three neurosurgeons chosen to evaluate my medical care, because of the breadth of their locations and practices, were individually subjected to Mr. Schuster's tedious examinations. All were strongly supportive of the care. Their support was important to me. Had even one been critical of any facet of my medical care, my response would have been to insist on settlement within my insurance limits and not go to trial. But each neurosurgeon advised that I fight the allegations.

While these proceedings were taking place, I read, for the first time, the entire deposition of the Plaintiffs' single neurosurgical expert, Dr. Frank Smith. Dr. Smith was a senior neurosurgeon who, at one time, was of national stature. He had reached that status heading the training program at the University of Rochester in New York, before moving to Monterey, California, in 1974. He had been a plaintiff's expert in two other malpractice actions in the Colorado-Wyoming area in the last several years. We had already crossed paths before as I had been a defense expert in one of the cases in which he had been involved. In each case, the practice standards he proposed were inconsistent with the practice of Colorado neurosurgeons. In addition, he had actually been deposed in one of the cases by Mr. Pryor and reported that he had stopped operating at that time. All of these factors called his credibility into question. Furthermore, his main criticisms of my care did not seem supported by the neurosurgical literature and appeared directly contrary to local standards of practice. Mr. Pryor remarked that he relished the opportunity to go up against Dr. Smith and his opinions again in open court.

We also received the deposition of the Plaintiffs' other expert, Dr. Melvin Greer, the Chief of Neurology at the University of Florida at Gainesville. He too reported a substantial income from testifying in court and reviewing medical/legal matters. Dr. Greer was not a surgeon, and he had a unique opinion on the operation itself. Since Sheran R had worsened following her second craniotomy, a mistake must have been made, implying an expected perfect result in each and every case. The relationship of medical neurologists to neurosurgeons is an interesting one. Neurologists tend to take credit for good results because of their correct diagnosis, yet feel free to criticize neurosurgeons for the bad. A previous professor of mine termed this the "bravado of the noncombatant." In any case, the defense attorneys felt Dr. Greer's opinions were not terribly damaging, especially since he was clearly a "noncombatant."

The next occurrence of Pre-trial preparation meeting during the weekend before trial. Dr. Krauth and I met with Mr. Pryor, Ms. Martel, another attorney at the firm, and his two paralegals, Mary Rose and Sandra

"Sam" Archuleta. We learned that Mr. Pryor, along with Ms. Martel, had spent three weeks in seclusion to prepare for the trial. We also learned that Mr. Pryor had been involved in an extraordinary physical training program for several months to be physically and mentally prepared for the trial. We specifically reviewed, word by word, his opening statement which described his theory of the case. I was somewhat dismayed to learn that not only would we strongly support our care, but we would also focus on the contention that Sheran R's injuries were primarily related to the care delivered in Wyoming (without the CSF leak, there would have been no stroke) and secondarily to blood vessel spasm caused by the meningitis, the opinion of Dr. Krauth and our experts. These opinions ran counter to my feeling that the pneumothorax played a significant role as well. My concern regarding the basic plan of defense involved, of course, the reluctance of one physician to criticize another, particularly in a field other than his own. Mr. Pryor and Ms. Martel were concerned that my opinion regarding the pneumothorax was in conflict with our experts (in fact it was), and I reluctantly agreed to the idea that I could not be sure which of the factors played a major role (again true but with a somewhat different inflection). As part of the intensive trial preparation, Dr. Krauth and I were then each subjected to a mock video tape trial examination.

Prior to trial, Mr. Pryor estimated our chances of winning were only fifty percent, although he thought if we lost it would be highly unlikely for the loss to exceed our insurance coverage. Interestingly, he then granted Mr. Spence an additional twenty percent edge simply for his legal skills. Mr. Pryor noted that this would be the first time in his career that he had been in a trial where he would be considered the legal underdog. That was the moment that I learned this case, for him, represented the trial of a lifetime. We were all to play our parts in his big moment.

The Sunday before trial was spent reviewing the case and my long deposition, and again I was pleased to relearn that I had said nothing, even under Mr. Schuster's prodding, that I would not automatically say again. I was, however, most disturbed to reread the chart and particularly the detailed notes written by the obviously distressed nurse as Sheran deteriorated following her pneumothorax. The horror of finding out about this event later that morning was brought back to me in full detail. The description of the pneumothorax so bothered me that I returned to the law offices (my trial team was, of course, ensconced there) to discuss my concerns with Mr. Pryor. To his credit, he suggested that I had to go with my beliefs, even if in contradiction with our experts. Relieved, I slept surprisingly well the night before the trial.

The first trial, which took place at the Denver District Court, began on November 13, 1989, and the day remains mostly a blur in my memory. The day was reserved for Pre-trial motions. The first motion was to finally (and happily) remove Dr. Barron from the action. Most of the other motions centered on the contention, by the Plaintiffs' attorney, that my malpractice insurance company was coercing its insured to testify in favor of other insureds in malpractice actions.

The first portion of the Plaintiffs' case was presented by Mr. H, a local counsel, member of a prominent local firm, and the past president of the Colorado Plaintiffs Bar. He appeared to be a quiet, competent man. He evidently had frequently opposed Mr. Pryor in malpractice cases in the past. He certainly seemed to have Mr. Pryor's respect as a good, tough, but ethical opponent. I noted, however, that once Gerry Spence took over the Plaintiffs' case on the second day, Mr. H never again smiled. Mr. Branney and Ms. Kudla, partners of Mr. H, were present on the first day, but Mr. Branney was absent thereafter. Ms. Kudla was present throughout, but her only apparent involvement occurred when she suggested, after the declaration of the mistrial, that the Defendants pay eighty percent of the court costs, given that there were four individual Defendants, and that the Plaintiffs pay only twenty percent (this, in spite of the ruling that Mr. Spence had caused the mistrial). Amazingly, the Defense did pay half the bill. Mr. Spence and Mr. Schuster, along with their paralegal, were present on the first day but were not yet memorable.

During arguments on motions, the defense position was presented by Ms. Martel. The attorneys for the other Colorado Defendants and the hospital joined her in most of her motions and made motions of their own with respect to their individual clients. Our two paralegals, early that day and each subsequent day, staked out a seat in the front of the spectator section. The courtroom was packed with attorney spectators from all over the region, there to watch the famed Gerry Spence in action.

Over this large number of prominent attorneys and the large gallery of spectators presided the Honorable District Judge Edward Carelli. He was a small, soft-spoken man. I noticed the obvious stigmata of advanced rheumatoid arthritis. He was known to be scrupulously fair but also reasonably tough and as capable as any possible judge of controlling Mr. Spence and his showmanship. He dispensed with the motions efficiently. Dr. Krauth and I sat at the defense table, both of us uncomfortable with the court's circus-like atmosphere, and we returned to our offices early in the afternoon.

The second day began with the jury selection process, or voir dire. This process started with the introduction of the Plaintiffs, Defendants, and attorneys to the fifty prospective jurors. Sheran R was in the court looking surprisingly well. Mr. Spence introduced her to the jurors, emphasizing her disability with an elaborate double loop of her wheelchair. The other participants were introduced by their attorneys. The process of voir dire started once everyone was seated. Judge Carelli estimated that this process should take one or, at most, two days. The process was not near completion when the mistrial was declared three and a half days later when proceedings ended. The bailiff called the first fourteen potential jurors and eight potential alternates into the jury box. There was lengthy questioning by the attorneys of each party to see if there was any possible bias that might exclude that juror. Each side would then be able to excuse four jurors without explanation, ultimately leaving us with a panel of six with two alternates in case the juror or jurors could not complete the trial. Before the jury selection began Dr. Krauth and I had been given sheets of paper so we could assist in the evaluation of the individual jurors.

Prior to the interviewing by the attorneys of the prospective jurors, Judge Carelli asked the first fourteen prospective jurors if they knew any of the participants. One man reported he knew of Mr. Spence, his reputation, his television appearances, and believed Mr. Spence would not become involved in a trivial matter. His statements seemed like hardly a good start for the Defense. Each side of the case evaluated each juror in turn. The lawyers on the case could quickly assemble a remarkably complete profile of each prospective juror through the interviews and the rapid compilation of such data as political party affiliation.

At lunch on Tuesday, Dr. Krauth and I met with Mr. Pryor, Ms. Martel, the paralegals and a psychologist named Dr. Fran Berman, who had been employed by my legal team to assist in the evaluation of the prospective jurors. Following lunch, Dr. Krauth returned to the office per our plan to not to have him be present in court any more than necessary in part to emphasize his limited role in the care of Sheran R. Following our afternoon session, I too returned to the office to complete a few necessary chores. Dr. Krauth reported that Dr. Berman clearly had another role besides jury evaluation. She also would be responsible for the psychological evaluation and care of the Defendants, not unreasonable given that the psychological functioning of a defendant is an integral part of the defense strategy. She had sought his opinion regarding my family background.

It was not a total surprise when, after lunch on Wednesday during the first week of the trial, the attorneys disappeared and I found myself alone walking with Dr. Berman. I found this to be most uncomfortable, in small part because she is disarmingly attractive, but more so because she already knew more about me than I knew of myself. I resigned myself to her presence, however, because she had an extraordinary ability to evaluate the potential jurors by their body language in connection with their questioning by Mr. Spence.

During the two and a half days of voir dire, Mr. Spence proved to be all that was advertised. Despite frequent objections by Mr. Pryor and occasional admonitions by Judge Carelli, he was able to explain his theories to the jurors, a kind of pre-opening statement. He managed to eliminate twenty-one potential jurors, including five nurses, and, despite repeated warnings by Judge Carelli that specific dollar amounts were not to be mentioned, he managed to expound his theory that justice could be equated with dollars. His theory ran that a little justice meant a little money and that complete justice would mean large amounts of money.

This remarkable man even found a way to pull a chair towards the defense table, adjacent to and facing me, while mentioning the figure of "tens of millions of dollars," to the jury. Those words were quickly objected to by the defense attorneys but instantaneously frozen in the minds of the jurors. Those words caught my attention as well, as they were clearly intended to do. I sat amazed as he initially transfixed the jurors with a combination of skillful oratory (including all the possible nuances of volume, tone, and pace) and body positioning, frequently standing nearly over a prospective juror that he wished to remove. Mr. Pryor told me Mr. Spence's ability to eliminate jurors he didn't like was uncanny, something he never before had seen.

During these first few days, however, the mood of the defense team, but particularly that of Mr. Pryor, clearly changed from one of apparent intimidation to a progressively more optimistic tone. Despite the removal of twenty-one jurors, there remained, in Dr. Berman's opinion, a majority of people on the panel who would be inclined to listen to the issues. If this were true, Mr. Spence would not be able to bury the real issues, which we felt were strongly in our favor, with the one factor strongly on the Plaintiffs' side—the tragic condition of Mrs. R. It was heartening to have one juror speak of clichés when only Mr. Spence had spoken. It was more so when another, interestingly the man who knew of Mr. Spence, spoke eloquently about justice from all perspectives, including the doctors.

Judge Carelli generally remained in control, at one time even warning Mr. Spence not to "quarrel with the Court." Most importantly, Mr. Spence settled into a repetitious style of questioning which seemed predictable. The mood of the defense team improved considerably when each night Mr. Pryor, in private, began to accurately mimic Mr. Spence's style. The way he held his posture over the lectern and his repeated pulling of his sagging non-belted pants up over his protuberant abdomen. He could also do the quick on and off smile toward Judge Carelli each time

Spence addressed the Court. If we recognized these learned poses and gestures, we hoped the jury would see them also. Dr. Berman felt that many of them already had noticed.

In addition to the optimism generated by the realization that Mr. Spence's flamboyant style just might not play well to a Denver jury, the team and I personally began to note a lack of understanding on his part of the real issues involved. For instance, he indicated that non-FDA approved Super Glue, used commonly by neurosurgeons and ENT doctors in the past, was utilized in the first operation on Sheran R. He did not know that its possible use was discussed with Dr. Barron, the idea was discarded, and that a routine surgical adhesive was used instead. That adhesive failed to close the hole and was removed. Also, Mr. Spence charged that the Defense had changed its theory of the cause of Sheran R's injury from hypoxic brain injury, or stroke, to meningitis. He did not seem to understand that we all agreed that she suffered a devastating stroke. We, however, further believed that the stroke was caused by a complex interaction of factors—the meningitis, the trauma of the surgeries, and perhaps the pneumothorax.

Finally, as time went by, I realized that I too had some good instincts and could tolerate this process. The first day of voir dire was a difficult one for me, particularly when the attorneys would discuss matters in the judge's chambers, leaving me sitting alone facing the jurors with absolutely nothing to do except appear guilty. The next day I realized that this was a good time to study my lengthy deposition in preparation for my upcoming testimony. It was not bad to appear studious to a jury that would later be told that I had failed to prepare for my patient's care. I was getting used to the daily process, and I no longer feared simply being in court.

It was therefore with some dismay that, when a motion had to be made for mistrial in an attempt to control Mr. Spence's repeated allusions towards insurance (not permitted in malpractice actions), Judge Carelli granted the mistrial. Although none of the Plaintiffs' attorneys appeared pleased, Mr. Pryor felt Mr. Spence had also realized that the jury selection was not going his way. He engineered the mistrial by putting our side in the position of either accepting his improper conduct, or applying for a mistrial which might have to be granted, even though the Defendants didn't want one. A physician finds a system strange that allows an attorney, by clever lawyering, if things are not going well, to simply start over—and the other side has to pay half the court's bill.

The Defense handled the obvious letdown by retiring to a nearby restaurant, sharing war stories over drinks. Mr. Pryor, while obviously disappointed, was remarkably humorous in his description of the past events and was now totally optimistic about the next round, regardless of whether or not Mr. Spence returned. He also reported that he had received a death threat on his answering machine the night before, perhaps related to a strange call I received the same day. Ms. Rose was bubbling over her unplanned "no way" to Ms. Kudla's suggestion that the Defense pay eighty percent of the cost. After this untimely wrap-up, I returned to the safety of my office, and, over the next two weeks, I tried to resume the routine practice of neurosurgery.

During this time, the necessity of being prepared to make a decision became apparent. It seemed obvious to the defense team that Mr. Spence did not really wish to try this case. The loss of a case involving a tragically injured patient and her politician husband from his own state would surely shatter his aura of invincibility. In our Pre-trial preparations, Mr. Pryor's team predicted that an attempt at intimidation would be made during the already scheduled three days of my cross-examination. If the intimidation worked, the trial would proceed. If it didn't work, an offer of settlement would be forthcoming, the size depending on my performance.

As the opportunity for intimidation was forestalled by the mistrial, it was not clear when the offer would come again. However, the events of the trial had made me no longer automatically receptive to an offer that I would have previously considered reasonable. I decided, with the agreement of Mr. Pryor, to enlist the aid of Dr. Berman in this decision. In a later conversation, Mr. Pryor suggested that, if I decided to take the issue to trial or if no settlement offer was made, I document my experiences as they occurred for the benefit of any future participant in a similar action. I quickly realized that I lacked the verbal skills to report my feelings and emotions in the most trying of circumstances, and I surprised Dr. Berman with the request that she share her considerable talents with me in this project—and she surprised me with her gracious acceptance. In addition, Mr. Pryor agreed to allow us to include his feelings recorded in his daily journal as a third perspective of this process. Whether we had another trial or a settlement, we would create a permanent record. Our collaboration would begin in four months just before a possible new trial.

Dr. Fran Berman
December 1989

When does anything begin? My entry point to this case was at Peter Pryor's Denver office. Peter and two of his paralegals were filling me in on the Plaintiffs' lawyer, Gerry Spence. The name and the man meant nothing to me. Peter's dissertation regarding this man's brilliant history as a trial lawyer still left me disinterested and bored. Sam murmured something about a file of recent news articles. In moments, Mary put them in front of me. As I shuffled through the papers, listening to Peter's ongoing description of the MDs (medical doctors) involved, I was stunned by a photograph of Gerry Spence. He was a Native American Indian.

Peter's voice faded as I was drawn into the meaning of this man's face, his stance, his eyes. I know him. Not personally, but I know him. Having a Native American father, growing up in rural Oklahoma, and hearing stories of my ancestors, not from history books but from my family, I knew him. I saw the same burning intensity in his eyes in the photograph of my four-generations-ago father who was also a great attorney. He was about truth, and I knew it immediately. I was trembling inside. My objectivity was lost.

"He's Indian, Peter, why didn't you tell me he was Indian?" Peter, Sam, and Mary had no idea why this concerned me. My mind was racing, thoughts of what this meant shattered the reality of sitting in the war room analyzing this case. Peter at that moment became a stranger to me.

I questioned his Euro-cultural motives. I questioned my trust in him as an ethical man with integrity and, more than anything, I hated my countertransference with a vengeance. My impulse was to follow my allegiance, go find this spirit, and work for him.

Gerry Spence had become juxtaposed with the native Oklahoma prairie I loved with a passion. I was going to have to deal with my own Indian history in relation to assisting with this trial. My doubts ran deep. And with this association, I felt a deep caring for Gerry Spence, as well as a sense of betrayal continuing with this trial on the side of the defendant in the days to come. I submerged myself in all the information I could get my hands on about Spence—his books, news articles, audio tapes of opening and closing trial statements. I had to know him apart from my ancestors. I had to know him and his tribal lineage to pull myself back to the trial at hand. His tribe had known the war path; my tribal ancestors would rather die than leave the peace path.

His ancestors' rage exploded, mine imploded—both being a different choice of death. This all felt so crazy to even consider that any of this was relevant. Studying Gerry Spence, I let go of the images of sticky, hot summer evenings populated by June bugs and fireflies. The smell of Lake Texoma and stories of my ancestors re-established their places in the past. Guilt from rejecting Indian lovers because they were not "white" enough haunted me. Regrets and sorrow of my own betrayals again experienced loosened the shackles enough for me to continue with this trial. I understood his thinking, his direction, and his passion. There was no longer a conflict raging, just smoldering memories I knew I could never completely extinguish.

The trial prep continued, but with a different focus. Peter, the brilliant, articulate lawyer, was now a curious student learning the ways of the Indian. I gave him sage and herbs to burn. He read books written by Native American Indians. I showed him Jerome Tiger prints and told him the stories behind them. Peter was grasping the way another culture thought and experienced time and events. He was understanding the meaning of the responsibility of being a warrior.

He was becoming a warrior, slowly developing an inner strength that he would need to survive in a courtroom with a seasoned, wise, twentieth century warrior. Peter's beliefs about Indian people were changing. As his awareness grew, so did his respect for Spence, not his fear and ridicule of him. He reluctantly accepted that Spence's talents were well-honed personality traits and not tricks and gimmicks he had mastered over the years. Whether he accepted this completely or not, I never knew. Peter Pryor became adept at masking his true thoughts in my presence, knowing he would get a disapproving look if his comments exceeded beyond the attitude I was trying to instill in him. I smiled to myself many times, watching Peter curb an impulsive comment that would have provoked my wrath. Peter was finding his own balance with this trial. I respected this in him. He wasn't going to play a part in a staged performance. Peter was determined that he, as a human being, was going to be in that courtroom to face Spence and the jurors.

Where I was spending hours scrutinizing the nuances of this trial, Peter was spending days and nights. His energy was undiminishable. Peter played out the permutations of possibilities as a child with tinker toys, creating structure after structure, until he was satisfied with the strongest form and relationship among the parts and pieces of this trial. The starkness of the gray, drab war room drastically contrasted with the rich dark paneling and spotlighted oil paintings in his office. An outsider looking in on the war room would never suspect the gravity of intent. The rainbow colors on the white board displayed equally colorful remarks and drawings.

Peter's Fisher-Price radio with microphone attached was positioned within arm's reach. Never mind the phone or intercom. Jan, his secretary, tolerated this altered approach. From the end of the majestic hall, hearing Peter's booming voice calling her through the Fisher-Price radio, she magically appeared with the dignity that matched this room's exterior.

Our eyes met, smiled silently, with mutual acknowledgment. This scene was bizarre.

Sam and Mary were Peter's constant companions, decked out in jeans or gym clothes, hands full of an endless supply of documents highlighted in yellow, pink, and blue. They deposited these critical parcels in the war room with the speed and demeanor of a UPS delivery. They each carried an endless supply of yellow sticky notes on which they would scrawl one word, then strategically position it within Peter's working range. The communication was cryptic, yet they understood each other completely.

Jay Ogsbury was the final item on the agenda, an undercurrent running through Peter's mind and influencing every degree of movement he made in putting this defense together. Jay was a thread not so easily woven into the elaborate, tight weave textile of this trial. An associate in the firm, Kathy Martel had been meeting with Jay, reviewing the minutia, and prepping him to communicate with only one possible interpretation.

Peter and I agreed that it's good to have a neurosurgeon when you need one. It's not good to have a neurosurgeon going to trial. We laughed at this ludicrous picture. Peter would be trying to sell a goldfish who looked like a shark. At best, Jay could be visually warmed up and softened by getting him out of his three-piece "power" suits. It would take hours of coaching to modify his facial expressions and body movements. Kathy, setting aside her legal skills, became Jay's coach.

The enormous difficulty with any defendant or plaintiff is to get them to reveal true feelings and emotions. This is a struggle for any man or woman under less stressful circumstances. It is vital that the jurors know each person in any trial. No juror is a machine. No juror can stay with the facts. They want to know why. They are, like all of us who are still alive, curious. So in getting to know the defendants' thoughts and feelings, the juror has the glue to put together the facts. Telling them the roots go down and the stem goes up isn't enough. Telling them about the sun and its effects on the stem cells closes the loop. In this particular situation, as with any significant threat to one's personhood or livelihood, both inextricably connected for most physicians, the developed picture looks like anger and hostility.

Unfortunate it is for humans, when the primitive "fight or flight" response kicks in, we look and act like monsters. I am reminded of the wounded animals throughout life I approached to help, only to be met with a ferociousness that sent me reeling back. Their excruciating pain presents with flattened ears, slit eyes, bared teeth—they can and will rip you apart. Jay was the wounded animal; Peter worked as the director, agonizingly frustrated with the play practice performances right up to the first trial. I am always surprised when I see Peter that he has any hair left on his head at all.

With the completed canvas, it was time to determine the best possible viewers, the jurors. The legal system fractures justice with the limitations it places on the presentation of truth and voir dire, the process where the lawyers pick the jurors. I have always been baffled by the oath, "Do you swear to tell the truth, the whole truth, and nothing but the truth, so help you God?" How can we see the whole truth when the truth has already been severely distorted by preliminary motions ruled by the judge as to what can and cannot be used as evidence or what can or cannot be talked about in the jurors' presence? Lawyers tell me I just don't understand. The problem is, I do understand. This system plays a game with peoples' lives and pretends it isn't a game. It is the most schizophrenogenic system in our country. The person who said that the relationship between law and justice is incidental was right.

At some level I admire trial attorneys for their willingness to make a living playing this game and playing within this arena. This is a playing field where destruction is the only guaranteed outcome. It is understandable why winning means so much to them. Coming out on top of a lunatic system is a remarkable feat. The win or the loss always extracts a price.

The attorneys spar with the letter of the law. The judge is in a sense a referee. It is the only situation I have ever seen where the referee is robed and empowered with wisdom. I am reminded of sitting in front of a TV with my father as a child, watching Friday Night at the Fights. The short, stocky, balding fellow who walks around the boxers, ensuring they fight according to preset rules, would be much more palatable to jurors, I think. It fits with what is happening in front of them. The jury decides; it is their collective wisdom and judgment, not the judge's. How quickly I forget—the courtroom is the magic room, a place where illusions survive and thrive. If the attorneys deal with the letter of the law, then the jury represents and embodies the spirit of the law.

The jurors in this case, and as in any case, must have access to their hearts, ears, and their heads. They can't be impulsive decision-makers. They have to tolerate lengthy periods of evidence presentation from one side, interspersed with "I object, Your Honor," and maintain a willingness to suspend judgment until the entire story was told. A tough job for the best of us—one that is grossly underpaid. On the other hand, if jurors who made decisions from their heart were selected, Peter was in serious trouble. The trial was going to be emotionally loaded, not to mention the time of year. It was near Christmas, and lawyers are shy about trying these kinds of cases, fearing that even the most levelheaded juror will transform into Santa Claus and get overly generous, regardless of the facts.

Consulting with me, Peter tossed out the familiar parameters of jury selection and set out to create another measure. A person's linear history with medicine, with Indians, with minorities, with relationship to authority were all critical issues. Gerry Spence was a spellbinding storyteller, one of the oldest forms of teaching that hooks the innocent child in all of us. In my view, this made him a master hypnotist. Listening to audiotapes of opening and closing statements, he embeds metaphors, distracts the left brain, and works with the right brain like any pro-hypnotherapist I have ever observed. In simple terms, he was Indian Chief material. Picking jurors not easily entranced became one of the critical variables in the juror profile.

In test construction, there is something called the line-of-best-fit. This is what we set out to generate. We took all the critical variables we could consider at once, maximized the fit between Peter, case presentation, and the juror while minimizing the fit between Spence and his presentation. Nightly I asked myself, was this worth it? Was I making this too difficult and complicated? My response was a consistent and resounding no. To bring to consciousness anything that is unconscious is difficult, tedious, and worth every ounce of energy it takes. If this wasn't done, the course of the trial would be left to Peter outmaneuvering Gerry.

The perfect juror profile began taking shape. We needed independent-thinking rebels with a heart. Spence, the Ram, needed sheep. It was a dismal, disheartening reality. There are statistically more sheep out there than there are independent thinkers, much less with the sensitive rebel attached to the identity. The odds of Spence getting the kind of jury he needed were tilting in his favor. This unnerved Peter. A sense of hopelessness and despair permeated our meetings. I wasn't offering positiveness or optimism, just bleak reality. Peter's task would become two-fold: wrestling with Gerry and jolting the jurors out of their trance. A formidable task, but doable for Peter.

I was going into this wondering where justice fit into the machinery of law? Would there be justice at all for the family? Would there be justice for Dr. Ogsbury and his wife, Kathy? The Plaintiffs and Defendants had the financial means to secure the best attorneys. Yet I still felt troubled. The process of therapy I trusted intrinsically. The process of the legal system, regardless of the caliber of the players, left me with a feeling of dread. I did not like what I was beginning to know. Peter wanted to hit a home run. I assumed Gerry Spence wanted to hit a home run. This was looking more and more like surgical procedures. Numbers of procedures and accuracy of procedures become the bottom line. The bead is aimed at the job done, regardless of what it takes to do it. And in doing the job, injuries, too insignificant to be noticed, are incurred. Neither medicine nor law consider the psyche, much less the soul. Once a long time ago they did. And so, in an ignorant yet innocent manner, the doctors and lawyers practice their skills, riding on the integrity of the professional ancestors. It is not out of choice, but out of the necessity of surviving within a system that is just as cold and cruel to them as it is to the people they serve. There are no real home runs here, only illusions of home runs.

The jurors are the only possible vehicle for justice. They will watch a drama, a re-enactment of a past experience, not from the players themselves but from actors and actresses. It's showtime. Hours and hours of planning, organizing, strategizing—exhibits masterfully produced are ready to be viewed by a select few. The trial begins. Pre-trial motions are argued before the judge. The final pieces are set in place, giving both sides cause for concern and elation.

Judge Carelli, a benevolent godfather figure, doesn't take kindly to either Pryor or Spence. Neither attorney seems to know how to win this man's favor. Judge Carelli allows them to play out their quibbling, then jumps in the middle sending them both back to their respective sandbox corners, without any hint of what they need to do differently in relation to him. They are confused. Not only do they have to deal with their facts and the jury, but they also have to figure out how this particular judge on this particular day wants to be treated. Spence responds with continued but somewhat cautious pushing. Pryor takes a step back and tries to figure out a more successful approach. I wondered if this was how they dealt with their fathers. I chuckled as I watched them fret in their own way. This was not going to be easy.

In stature, Peter was dwarfed by Gerry. Both men had an air of arrogance about them, like two Merlins meeting for the first time. I liked Gerry Spence immediately. A pang of guilt shot through me. For a moment, I regretted having any part of this trial. He presented himself well. He was who I thought he would be. I shook off my romanticizing trance with effort.

This was my first opportunity to see Dr. Krauth and Dr. Ogsbury. They sat off to the side from the defense table, thumbing through their medical journals, as if they were in a waiting room. The courtroom was packed with observers. Trial attorneys and law students were here to see the pros, especially the legendary Gerry Spence. I moved closer to Sam and Mary, the paralegals, and asked which one was Dr. Ogsbury. Mary pointed him out to me, and I began studying the man we had been preparing all of this for. Peter was right in being concerned about Jay and his three-piece suits. I wanted to cover my face with my hands and occasionally peak at him between my fingers.

Dr. Ogsbury was a distinguished-looking man. His salt and pepper hair was more salt than pepper. He sat holding his lean frame erect as he thumbed through his journal. He was anything but relaxed. Dr. Krauth had a similar tense demeanor about him. I wondered if they were even seeing the words on the journal pages, and I decided they were. Surgeons seem to find a way to be productive in any situation. They seem to keep moving, even when the best thing to do would be to keep still and just take in what's in front of them.

At last, we broke for lunch. We met at Peter's usual restaurant where he huddles with his team during the break. The location and the food were incidental. Critical insights and fine tuning the defense were the substance of nourishment.

The short break from the courtroom was enlightening and troublesome. First, I was not in agreement with any of the jurors they were finding adequate and second, there seemed to be a need to create Spence as the enemy. True, in a sense he was. However, I was aware that this being "bound up" in putting energy into Spence as the opponent was as spellbinding and dangerous as my earlier romanticizing trance. I interjected a positive comment about Spence and was unmercifully met with a barrage of "friendly fire." Peter got it. He saw what was happening and redirected the focus back to the jurors. Most of my responses regarding the appropriateness of a particular juror were "don't know" or "Let's wait and get more data from this person." I knew intuitively some of these favored jurors would be trouble, yet I had no words. I knew no one at that table would accept with comfort, "They just don't feel right," so I kept my peace and hedged as much as possible. Somewhere from an hour to twenty-four hours the words would come defining the "just don't feel right," then I could effectively communicate my observations.

I sat between Mary and Dr. Jay Ogsbury. Lee was sitting on Jay's other side. Journals had vanished and they were actively involved in the flurry of issues and perceptions. The two figures I had observed this morning were coming to life as I listened to their voices and words. They were both wound as tight as they looked. Rapid fire, staccato responses to questions in voices both sharp and pained. Compassion and gentleness were buried deep within them, put away for the exam room where they were safe with their patients. I knew if I was having difficulty finding the smoother, softer edges in these men, it would be virtually impossible for a juror. Peter can show his compassion and vulnerability without compromising his strength. Peter was a man comfortable with the earth moving under his feet. Peter would have to be the medium through which the jurors know Dr. Ogsbury. It just wouldn't work any other way.

I deliberately walked back to the courthouse with Dr. Krauth, asking him personal questions all the way about himself and Dr. Ogsbury. He was uncomfortable but cooperative. A steely man who kept his work world separate from his home with wife and children. I assumed he had developed a separate personality for each place. He seemed pleased and comfortable with this arrangement. What happens in one world isn't supposed to touch the other world. I couldn't tell which world was his sacred one. Was it one, both, or neither? The partnership with Dr. Ogsbury was an arrangement of convenience and opportunity. The trial for him was an interruption and insult to the arrangement. Our discussion ended at the courthouse doors with me feeling frustrated but therapeutically tolerant. I suppressed a rather primitive urge to scream at his sterile arrangements. Dr. Krauth moved toward Kathy, dismissing me with his action. They walked on down the hall together. I wondered if Dr. Ogsbury was invulnerable, as inaccessible as Dr. Krauth. I wondered if I was crazy and maybe I should have more arrangements in my own life.

Back again for two more rounds of jury selection. I'm impatient. I'm ready to do my work. What's happening to Spence? He's here, but I don't feel his presence like yesterday. He says, "I'm a little paranoid." He's changed his posture. His move into the jurors' space is different. He says, "Here's the show." He's beginning his storytelling about how insurance companies hide behind the attractive faces of young attorneys and the nun from St. Anthony. The jurors are not responding, except the most obsequious ones. I wondered what was happening simultaneously with his private life or with his other cases. He's preoccupied with something else. He's not completely here. My mind's wandering, drifting to more interesting thoughts about Peter and Jay.

Jury selection is droning on, eliminating one juror after another for cause or for conflicting personal responsibilities. I felt a sense of being worn down, like arm wrestling with someone who sustains only the strength needed to keep you exerting force. After time in this arm lock, the light goes on and you know what's going to happen next. It's inevitable; you know your loss is imminent.

Spence is patient. He knows the power in waiting something out. His intent is still there. He tracks wild game, and he knows how to tire them without injury. He knows how to lure them into a sense of safety. I can't allow myself to even think he is not completely present. He's good.

The following day, I resumed my practice seeing clients. A day back in familiar surroundings was needed. Peter would let me know when the defense would have their time for voir dire. Then, the phone call from Jan, Peter's secretary, informing me of the mistrial. The trial was over before it began. I cried, I think for all of us, tears of great sadness and loss. What pain. Who, someone tell me, has victory in their hip pocket?

CHAPTER ONE

MEMORIES OF THE FIRST TRIAL

Jay
November 1989

The image of Sheri as I first knew her remains before me. I have tried to maintain some semblance of a medical practice during this period between the two trials, yet the tragedy that has befallen this lady permeates every action, each decision, and allows me to continue only on the most basic of levels. I have been asked what was so special about her? What did she mean to me? Why of all other patients, some of whom with equally sad neurologic outcomes, did she affect me so? Dr. Berman, the team psychologist, was unrelenting on this question, telling me to dig deeper. I kept coming up with "I don't know"—an unacceptable answer. I did know, she insisted.

Neurosurgeons—because of the nature of our specialty—are trained, or quickly learn, to distance ourselves from our patients. To do otherwise would render us incapable of carrying out that which we need to do. There is no training for not taking a lawsuit personally. It is personal.

Why was she different? I can still picture Sheran's quiet beauty, not exotic, sophisticated or aloof, but outdoorsy, warm, and friendly. She was intelligent and understanding yet never condescending, strong but not overbearing, optimistic in the face of an already complicated medical course. Most of all she was trusting, once appropriate questions had been answered, but clearly also understanding the magnitude of the risk she was facing. I remember obtaining the operative consent for her first surgery. For obvious reasons, consents for neurosurgical procedures are particularly detailed, listing all reasonable options and complications. When we finished, she looked directly at me and, with a hint of hurt in her voice, said that I was treating her as an enemy, not a friend—that she knew it was a difficult matter and that I would do my best. How ironic that this consent form proved to be an important part of our defense in the lawsuit filed by her family against us.

Much of Sheran's wonderful trusting happiness remains after her horrible neurologic injury. This was ascribed by the experts in their depositions to be solely the result of frontal lobe dysfunction. They were wrong. This core personality was there before and remained so after her injury. The memory of her warm and honest smile, which she gave me when I talked to her after she awoke from her coma, and which even occurred during the first trial, remains important to me. My difficulty in maintaining a medical perspective between the time of the two malpractice trials was also heightened by the memory of the attorney combatants.

We were opposed by Gerry Spence, the well-known Native American Wyoming attorney involved in the Silkwood and Wyoming Penthouse cases. He is a large man wearing a fringed light brown suede leather jacket. His shirt had Native American tribal symbols. His bolo tie was snug against his buttoned-up shirt. A cream cowboy hat sat on his longish hair. He wore tan pants, with a belt hanging below his large abdomen, and worn cowboy boots. His striking appearance was matched by his unlimited skill at storytelling and connection with potential jurors while looking directly at me with his piercing steely blue-grey eyes. During the time between the trials, I found it nearly impossible to pay proper attention to patient complaints of chronic pain while thinking of Mr. Spence's approach with the prospective jurors and attempted intimidation of me.

The defense attorney team was led by Peter Pryor, a small man but with skill fully matching that of Mr. Spence. He had a smile that spread across his face from ear to ear, and eyes that were both dead serious and mischievous. He also was remarkably adept at understanding the emotional condition of his defendants, me in particular. The intimidation of Gerry Spence was only countered by the safety I felt with Peter Pryor. Even his appearance was reassuring. Usually wearing a baseball cap stating "Me and My Team," he looked like the boy next door. At one point after a difficult trial day, he raised the spirits of the intimidated defense team by appearing wearing clothes identical to those of Mr. Spence, with his belt hanging below a pillow under his shirt, and mimicking Mr. Spence's practiced theatrics. He could be the clown, a remarkable gift during anxious times.

The other primary member of the defense team was Dr. Fran Berman. She is a psychologist who was chosen primarily because of her extraordinary ability to pick a jury, but also because she herself is Native American and able to prepare Peter on how to face a Native American warrior such as Mr. Spence. As a psychologist, her other obvious role was to be part of the support system for the Defendants. For me, Dr. Berman herself proved to be a woman of polar extremes. During sessions I had with her, she was at times warm and reassuring, and at others cold and intimidating. She varied from open to aloof, from passionate to calculating, even from strongly maternal to quietly alluring. I didn't connect how her seemingly unpredictable approach was part of my trial training. Her discussion of tribal ways and her own heritage, although useful for me to understand the nature of our adversaries, also revealed a deep and disturbing ambivalence about her own role in the proceedings. While she felt strongly about the merits of our case in the legal assault upon me, she did share that she felt uneasy opposing in any way one of her own, even when she disagreed with his positions. She knew it was difficult for me, a white man, to grasp how to think like a sly or trapped animal. At moments, it felt like Mr. Spence had an unknown but unwitting ally in our camp.

Fran
December 1989

A call from Peter's secretary that day informed me of the mistrial. I was shocked and confused. Why had I chosen to return to the office that day to see clients instead of returning to court? I was angry at not anticipating the real possibility of this event. There had been three days of Pre-trial motions and voir dire on the part of the Plaintiffs' attorney. It had been tedious and psychologically exhausting for all involved, regardless that my inquiries into their well-being were responded to by, "I'm fine." What was I expecting? For them to drop their obsessing and gush anguish? Sometimes my stupidity amazes me. I knew that if I was having feelings of confusion and mixed emotions, they must be feeling something other than "fine."

I called Peter at his home and left a message on his machine to call as soon as he felt like talking about what had happened. I wondered about Jay. Was he doing all right? My impulse to call his office was deterred by not wanting to be intrusive. I had felt some distance from him during the trial. There was clearly a boundary around him that I knew I couldn't or wouldn't cross without either his invitation or permission. I was left to fill in the blanks with my own fantasies about how he was dealing with this abortion. My guess was that he would return to his surgeries and skills that he knew so well and find comfort and reprieve in familiarity. For him, I thought, this would soon become a nightmare that with time would lose its destructive potential. He would fully recover to Pre-trial functioning. He knew me and my profession to the extent one can let in information under these horrid conditions. I would wait for a call from him.

Peter and I had talked on the phone two nights before. He had shared with me a death threat left on his answering machine. I listened as he played it back. We were both convinced, not in fact, but with joint intuition that this threat to him and his family was related to this trial. We discussed procedures any professional should follow when getting a threat such as this one. I felt afraid for him and selfishly was glad I was positioned far in the background.

Peter returned my call the following day after the mistrial. He described briefly the events that led up to the mistrial. He indicated that he had spent some time with Jay afterwards and that Jay would probably be calling. I was interested in both the events and Jay's call. How could two attorneys of the caliber of Gerry and Peter end up in mistrial? My only conclusion was that these warriors in the courtroom agreed at some level to stop. Gerry, the Plaintiffs' attorney, played a hand that forced Peter into calling a mistrial. For the moment, the death threat was defused.

This weekend: I wasn't surprised when Jay called. We established a time when we were both free from our usual responsibilities. What did surprise me was the proposal to write this book. I couldn't imagine anything more dreary than binding a public document. I had fallen asleep more than once reading depositions. A trial document would be dry as a bone. The only possibility here I saw was a sure-fire cure for insomniacs. Jay kept on talking while my mind wandered through all the reasons this was doomed for failure. "I want people to know what doctors go through emotionally," he announced emphatically." Sequel, my beloved Kittyhawk's replacement, climbed Jay's pant leg. Picking the stuck claws from his leg, Jay went on, "It's important. People just think we get sued and that's it. No one knows what it's like to be challenged this way, to have the finger pointed at you and be accused of practicing bad medicine when you know you did more than was called for." Sequel was curled in Jay's lap purring like crazy. Sometimes, it's nice being a therapist. Nobody really expects you to say anything. You just sit there and listen. The pink orange of the sunset filled the room as Jay talked on about the importance of this book. I looked at him in his dark three-piece suit, manicured nails and military haircut. He wanted to take the part of the self we all desperately try to hide and share it. I was awed and humbled. He was cradling this kitten in his lap like a mother would a sleeping child across her lap. Somehow, wherever the child is touching you, your anatomy just detaches and protectively wraps around the child. The rest of your body proceeds as usual.

This surgeon has a heart. His body has some nice primitive, unconscious responses. I wondered if he had ever let anyone really know him. My guess was that only his wife and a select few others really knew him.

My first response was: this is Jay's story, not mine. At this point he believes he needs someone to describe, put into words or record in some kind of recognizable form, his journey through unknown territory. Maybe this is true for the moment. I know it won't be true in some future moment.

I accepted, not in the role of therapist, but with the experience of a therapist and the tools of the therapist. I can't act as a guide or a mirror in this case. I can't use my tools. I can only stand back and close at the same time—observe, record, and be silent in a sense. This world, his world, will no longer be what he has always known it to be. I have said to him, "Don't do it. Settle. End this for yourself." He ignores me in his strange way of politely listening, nodding, and proceeding on with his words.

I am afraid for him, sad for him, yet excited for him. This is a journey most wouldn't choose. Those who have before him are somewhere silent. Lawsuits fall into the category of unmentionable diseases. You can have it, the lawsuit or disease, and no one will talk to you about it. You don't get to talk about it either, because it makes others too uncomfortable and then they *really* avoid you if you try to talk about it. The only other comparable awkwardness I have seen in people is when someone's child dies.

In his decision to proceed with this trial, Jay was metaphorically leaving point A. The jury verdict, point B, is his destination. It is this existential space, not the linear time, between these two points that can create the new that shakes the very core of our being. There is no turning back once this process is in motion. To turn back would be tantamount to making blood flow backwards. Those tiny little flaps in the blood vessels just won't allow it. Some of life is just like this. Unseen tiny little flaps propel us at times in directions with unknowable destinations.

Jay's story has nothing to do with the material world we innocently think is on the line for a physician being sued. It is not about winning. It is about not losing.

Peter Pryor, Counsel for Dr. Ogsbury
December 1989

I'm still in a state of shock as I can't let go of my feelings about the first trial. A thousand disjointed thoughts are tumbling through my mind, relief from the excruciating physical and mental strain, continued bewilderment and fear about the death threat to me and my children, disappointment and anger at Spence who'd decided he didn't like the odds and then, masterfully but unfairly, engineered a mistrial.

That first trial was an experience I'll never forget. Face to face, eyeball to eyeball with a legend, big of stature, huge of ego, a man of oratorical skills I couldn't hope to match in a lifetime. Spence is a man on a mission of intimidation and persuasion, an irresistible force in the courtroom, the self-described lawyer for the little man.

For days I watched him try to bring the jurors to his knees during a drawn out and acrimonious jury selection process. He wanted them to agree with *his* view of this system, Mr. or Ms. Juror—otherwise you're history. Sitting there helpless with the sense, one way or another, he was going to get rid of any prospective juror he didn't like.

Day after day of jury selection was marred by numerous objections and trips to the judge's chambers where the judge did his best to keep this powerful man under control. I was fearful some prospective jurors were already thinking the trial only had to do with how much money Sheran R deserved. When was I going to get my turn to talk to the jury panel, to let them meet me, for me to be able to portray myself as a David against this Goliath? Jay Ogsbury, Sheran R, they'd been lost in this clash of legal wills and egos—pawns to an epic struggle between lawyers. Each morning, he would swoop into the courtroom removing his huge cowboy hat to be placed ceremoniously on a rack with his flowing white knee length jacket adorned with a huge emblem on the back. Each day I quietly entered the courtroom carrying a cardboard box, a big, happy smile on my face, a red baseball cap on my head which said "Me and My Kids, What a Team," and an old leather jacket which didn't quite cover my sport coat.

There was no one there but him and me. Sheran R, a woman physically and psychologically destroyed by a series of events Jay could not remedy. A woman no longer capable of decision making; in a fog—yet someone who flashed me a 21 carat smile every time I looked at her, which was often. She had no idea who I was, poor thing. And poor Jay, even he had dropped from my mind as I zeroed in on my target—destroy this man. Our clients, like chess pieces on a board, a mental physical dual, me against him.

As the days went by, I lost my fear. Spence was visibly tired, didn't seem to know the case—didn't really care about his so-called "little people" who, after all, were no different than all those "little people" sitting in the jury box. I strained forward in my chair, watching in utter fascination as he showed little interest in, scant respect for these people in the jury box. His view of jurors was that they were to be the instruments of his will. He talked down to them, even badgered certain jurors who had the audacity to disagree with him.

As my fear departed me, an amazing transformation began to take place. "I am a better person than he, I care more about people and am physically and emotionally healthier. I can more than hold my own with this legend except in the arena of impassioned rhetoric where he is unequaled. I will match his rhetoric with preparation, his melodrama with my passion, his mock indignance with my sincerity, his down-home folksiness with my sense of humor."

Tuesday night after the courtroom had cleared, Jay, some of my staff, and I stayed behind, as always, to reflect on the day and give each other strength. Without thinking, I moved to the podium and began to do an imitation of Spence "hunkerin" down "hitchin" his pants before placing his hands together, palms open, to begin his sermon of the moment. I had him down to a T, speech and all—within minutes we were hysterically laughing, tears in our eyes; without knowing, we knew—things were going to be okay. We were in control.

By Wednesday, the third day of the trial, a subtle shift of power was taking place. The jurors weren't buying Spence. They were collectively resisting him. The judge was openly frustrated and with my help, battling to keep him under control.

Late Wednesday Spence asked one juror, a CPA, a question about having liability insurance to "protect the victim," a question he knew was patently improper and grounds for a mistrial. I objected but let it go since Spence was faltering and things weren't going well for him. The next morning the other defense lawyers approached me saying they wanted to move for a mistrial "for the record." At first, I said no, I wouldn't join in, fearful that the judge might grant it. But I was ultimately persuaded. All defendants had to be united, and I agreed that while I wouldn't make the motion, I would say "me too." To my complete shock, the judge declared a mistrial, maybe out of his weariness and frustration with Spence.

As I sat there in chambers, a light came on—my legend didn't like his odds and had wanted and found a way to get out. As we filed out of the judge's chambers I suddenly knew—and told one of the other lawyers—"we will never see Spence again."

I returned to the courtroom—Jay was shocked at the news; my God, he was even disappointed. My doctor, my client, my pawn was about to become my ally and friend. As we sat there in the courtroom glaring across the room at the back of this man, I told Jay that Spence would never be back. And, in that moment, in the ashes of trial number one, Dr. Jay Ogsbury began to find his cause. No lawyer, even the likes of Gerry Spence, was going to intimidate or defeat him. He was in this for the duration—for medicine and himself. As a legacy of Gerry Spence's departure, Jay began reaching within and, for the first time since I'd met him, started to come in touch with his passion. Within this cerebral and dispassionate client, through whose veins blood flowed like cold water on a stream, I see a fire beginning to burn.

CHAPTER TWO

INTER-TRIAL PERIOD

Jay
April 1990

During the four months between the trials, I attempted to return to some semblance of a medical practice, but during this time I could never really be a doctor because I was never completely free of activities of the trial to come.

On December 4, 1989, Mr. Spence requested that Judge Carelli disqualify himself as a trial judge, asserting the appearance of partiality. On December 13, 1989, much to Peter's surprise, Judge Carelli capitulated and recused himself. It appeared that Mr. Spence had again succeeded in getting things his way. However, on December 12, 1989, the Defense learned that the Honorable Judge Connie Peterson had been appointed to succeed Judge Carelli, and that the trial would take place from April 30 to June 23, 1990.

Judge Peterson is known to be tough, fair, unbiased, and more importantly, she is always in firm control of her court and its participants. There was some satisfaction within the defense team that Mr. Spence, in getting rid of Judge Carelli, this time may have shot himself in the foot. In addition, on January 18, 1990, we were also happy to learn that the malpractice case against the Wyoming physician had settled for a substantial sum, a settlement that would be offset against any verdict in the Rs' (Sheran and her husband) favor in the Colorado case.

At Christmas, I received a simple card from Sheran R's sister-in-law. During the many months of Sheran R's prolonged medical care and partial recovery, she had devoted an extraordinary amount of time and energy to her care, functioning as therapist, nurse, and emotional supporter when needed. She frequently called with reports and questions about Sheran's condition and treatment. Somehow it was reassuring to think that at least one member of the family still apparently understood and respected our efforts. Yet it was also depressing to have to ask my attorney for his permission to simply answer a Christmas card.

In contrast to the pleasant surprise of the Christmas card, two occurrences involving the firm of the local attorneys representing Sheran R were disturbing. In January, I received a request from another attorney in the firm we had faced in the first trial, that I assist them in a different case. When I declined because of the lawsuit, he, through his secretary, reported that he himself was not directly involved in our lawsuit, and that it was reasonable that I work with him. It is inconceivable to me to think that one member of a law firm could happily utilize me as an expert while, at the same time, another was holding me out to be guilty of negligence.

At about this time, a new detail put things in a different perspective. I learned that Ms. Kudla, who had recommended that we bear the court costs from the first trial, is a nurse, as well as a senior partner in her law firm. Somehow, the disclosure that a nurse, who had spent a significant period of time learning medicine and the system of patient care, would leave that system and enter into the adversarial legal system as a malpractice plaintiffs' attorney was remarkably depressing. I will have trouble looking at her when the trial occurs.

During this time, Peter, Lee, and I underwent surgical procedures of our own. Lee and I underwent nose operations by Dr. Barron, both the same operation as undergone by Sheran R, except, happily, through an endoscope. The operations went well and barely interfered with our practices and later trial preparation. Peter's ear operation in early April did not go as well as had been hoped, and the discomfort limited his physical conditioning.

As the trial approached, the Defense again had the impression that Mr. Spence was reluctant to try the case. The hints of settlement possibilities, delivered through Judge Dana (who remained active in his attempts to settle the case), became progressively lower to dollar amounts that I would have authorized at the time of the first settlement conference, thus once again challenging my decision not to settle for any significant amount. I felt impelled to reiterate to Peter and to my insurance company my strong disinclination to settle.

Finally, Mr. Spence outdid even our estimation of him when, on February 7, 1990, the announcement was made that Mr. Spence had agreed to lead the defense of Imelda Marcos in connection with federal racketeering charges. That trial, scheduled to start on March 20, and projected to last at least three months, would clearly conflict with ours. It seemed neither solution to the apparent conflict—that Judge Peterson would allow a continuance of our trial, or that Sheran's husband would allow another attorney to try the case—was likely to occur.

However, Mr. Spence demonstrated once and for all that he could work his own agenda when the defense team learned that Mr. H and Mr. Branney in the same law firm would try the case, rather than Mr. Spence. How Mr. Spence convinced Mr. R that it was acceptable for him to drop out, having miss-tried the first case, is beyond my comprehension. (Mr. R repeatedly spoke glowingly of Mr. Spence during the negotiations with my insurance company.) To me, it seemed that Mr. Spence initially felt he could walk all over the Defense on his reputation and oratory alone, then simply had run for cover when we were more resolute than expected.

Strangely, the departure of Mr. Spence had a depressing effect on the defense attorneys, and on me. If nothing else, Mr. Spence possessed an energy and aura that captivated and energized all around him, especially his adversaries. I particularly felt the loss of the focus which came from the intense dislike I felt for this man, a feeling which could have been channeled into the necessary passion for the battle ahead. In addition, as Mr. Pryor succinctly stated, "If you're going to work in a circus, you might as well play the center ring."

Any possibility that Mr. Spence might make a surprise cameo appearance was dispelled by the ruling of Judge Peterson on April 23 that, while she would allow Mr. Spence to try the case, he would be on a short leash, since she felt he had deliberately miss-tried the first case. While this ruling stood as part of a strong condemnation of Mr. Spence's conduct in the first trial, and thus at first glance seemed a positive factor for the Defense, it may have eased what Mr. Spence wished all along—his removal from the trial.

There was also a change on our side. Kathy Martel, our original second attorney, left the firm to accept a job with the government. She graciously informed me of her decision so I would not hear of the news secondhand. From my standpoint, her departure created an emotional void, as I had gotten to know her well. Scott Nixon, an appealing and evidently very good young attorney, joined the defense team in Kathy Martell's place.

All of the above, particularly the departure of our famous adversary, and especially Mr. Pryor's continuing trouble with his ear, led to a serious emotional downturn about two weeks before trial. However, shortly before trial, our spirits finally began to rise. Dr. Berman was able to convince all of us, the attorneys, and particularly me, that the main issue was medicine and our defense of it, not Mr. Spence. Peter wrote in a letter, "Judge Peterson's blasting of his (Spence's) trial behavior in the mistrial is final assurance that we won't be seeing the great Mr. Spence again."

Peter's ear improved to the point that he could start working out, and the improvement in his spirits affected all of us. During the week before the trial, Peter took the deposition of the Wyoming otolaryngologist, and induced him to accept responsibility for the cerebrospinal fluid (CSF) leak, and to admit possible negligence—a stunning turn of events. Finally, on Friday, just three days before the start of the trial, we learned that the hospital and physicians involved in the pneumothorax settled their litigation, leaving only Dr. Lee Krauth and me as Defendants, along with our professional corporation. This settlement simplified the Defense immensely. Not only would we not be lumped with the other Defendants, but we now would be able to explain my care without fear of finger-pointing by the other Defendants. And, while not being told the exact dollar amounts, the jury would surely be told about the Wyoming and Colorado settlements and would just as surely understand that Sheran R had already been paid far more money than should be necessary for her care. We hoped that the jury would ultimately conclude that awarding future amounts against me would be punishment money; thus, the strategy of portraying me as a second victim of the tragedy became clear.

Fran
April 1990

Tuesdays at 2:00 p.m. became a time and space separate from anything I'd known before. Two strangers agreeing to do something together they'd never done before.

What's left when you take away your professional identity, your cars, your address, your money, your spouse, your children? Week by week, like adolescents, we played psychological strip poker, until finally, there was nothing left to discard. Knowing each other through things, projections, images, and fantasies is limiting. Safe, but limiting and about as appealing as last night's leftovers. The images dropped away and we faced each other as aliens—surprised, shocked, angry, disappointed, and scared.

It's me, Jay, Snapping Turtle, the Indian and deepest part of me. It's O.K. I promise I won't bite you unless I get very angry. He didn't like this part of me or at least was very uncomfortable. His discomfort and fear were tolerable. In time, the shock would subside. He had courage and curiosity to move him through.

A long line of Snapping Turtles precedes me. As a small child I would sneak off to Oklahoma Presbyterian College, sit in Great Aunt Anne's office and wait for her between the classes she taught. She always had a gift for me—a feather penny, an Indian head nickel, or a story about our crazy Indian family. She would laugh and say your father is a Snapping Turtle. I never knew which stories were true. As a child I believed them all. In later years when I would confide in her, she would sometimes shake her head and say you are a Snapping Turtle too. I never knew if this was a blessing or curse. I would flinch, feeling both the excitement and dread of this identity. Snapping Turtle grew up for the most part outside my awareness. It took me by surprise as much as it did whoever came across it. A Snapping Turtle, when it bites, doesn't let go until it thunders.

Was any shred of trust possible between us? Steel was meeting flint. When this happens, sparks fly. As in every honest relationship we have, these little sparks of light can alienate with the fire of destruction, or as the stars, guide the way to connecting and understanding. The choice in every moment of this time together was to destroy or trust.

I felt it unfortunate he had no name for this historical, cultural self. Jay was born and raised on the east coast, the son of generations of wealth. His genealogy was benchmarked with fortune, prestigious schools, and Catholicism. My genealogy ledger balanced his, showing the red of loss, genocide, and a religion banished from the main until 1979. Since this part of Jay was virtually unknown to him, at least in the sense of how it plays with who he is today, I was constantly bumping into this shadow, in the dark. Although Jay's time in Thailand gave him some feel for a culture viewing life differently, it was not enough to keep us out of strong, conflicting moments. Alcohol ran through his family and mine, the only difference was his family's ability to cover the destruction to the soul. In my family, we watched each other bleed out. I have since learned it is better to go chew on a piece of rye grass than to drink Jack Daniels.

It was easier in some ways for me to move into Jay's organized pattern of the world than it was for him to enter mine. Indians have been expected to do this in the name of God for generations. I see the red highlights in my hair too much some mornings and am reminded there was an Irish missionary back there somewhere who was going to set my ancestors straight. Stories of the nuns at the Indian Orphanage beating my father to near death and refusing to administer to him when he was ill, leaving him to die, still live in my mind. And his brother Buddy, raped repeatedly by the older boys with no protection, still brings a pain that too easily transforms into rage. Beautiful little souls, little Snapping Turtles, renamed heathens, and with that, flipped these precious little turtles on their backs forever. What Hitler was to the Jews, missionaries were to the Indians. How did white people know the only way to kill us was to destroy our religion?

As I heard more of his childhood, I understood how his personality had crystalized, like many other physicians I have personally known or have seen in therapy. He is, like many physicians, a warm loner. He can be close and vulnerable only as long as there is emotional distance, which makes him the ideal physician prototype for the insurance companies.

He keeps others at a distance by giving to them. In return, he simply wants his space and peace. If someone complains, he assumes he needs to give more until the complaining stops. He, like others, never quite figures out it is the distance that is so infuriating and feeds the complaining. Listening to him speak of his friends and wife, I hear how enormously grateful he is for their tolerance regarding who he is and what he needs, that is to be understood and known from a distance. The truth is that no one gets that part of the physician, and he has it for himself only in brief fleeting moments of solitude. This tortures him as much as anyone else. And he silently pleads forgiveness, knowing full well he doesn't know what to do but give more of what's not asked for. Silly white men, silly doctors, no wonder you get divorced and sued.

I was not good friend material for Jay, and I was not going to write this with a stranger. Many times, I violated his distance rules because I just can't breathe through my intellect or know anything with all this distance. Indians have always known that space between anything brings confusion and bad feelings. We clashed and raged at each other only to return to Tuesdays at 2:00 to resume work. Our pathology matched up around commitment. Regardless of the fear and the anger, we could consistently return to what had to be done. His word was good. My trust cycled like the phase of the moon.

Despite his punctuality, impeccable dress, and sanguine demeanor, Jay was game to work amid the teeming life of my living room. He became quite adept at sitting on the floor and working while the cats and dog took turns getting back rubs from him and kids with homework questions darted in and out. He had a warmth to him that was easily accessible to animals, children, and, I supposed, his patients.

The trial had a profound impact on Jay. On the surface, nothing appears to get him down. Yet scratch the veneer and his anger at Spence still raged, "I can't look him in the eye and say you're wrong. He challenged me and I don't get to respond." Jay needed a target for his anger, and with Spence leaving he was unraveled. The volcanic anger he felt, the frustration that disorganized his otherwise purposeful and preservative behavior, would have to give way to another form of expression. He was not going through this second trial numbed out. If he tried, I was throwing in the towel, calling off all bets and signing no more treaties with him.

Jay couldn't comprehend what was happening to him, to his life. He was either putting more distance between himself and his wife or becoming acutely aware of the distance that already existed in their marriage. His relationships at work were strained. He couldn't say what had changed or was changing but things were different. He ached to have contact with something in his life that was familiar, but he couldn't find it. His life had become an unknown to him. He didn't like it and stayed ambivalent between isolating and confirming that everything had in fact changed. Grim choices. Least of all, he didn't want his peers, his friends, to respond ambivalently toward him. Yet that is what he saw and felt with each exchange. He needed a solid pat on the back from a friend and colleague saying, *I'm here with you and we're going to talk about what is happening with all of this.* I saw and he saw that professional camaraderie is for the most part limited to the good times.

His wife, I know, tried and tried to reach out to him, yet with no real success. The distance between them was too great for her to bridge alone. He refused to go get help with her.

He stayed isolated. When a physician or any other professional, whose work is a part of their identity, is rejected by their peers, you can guarantee a severe drop in self-worth. This in and of itself keeps them from responding. Humiliation, remorse, bitterness, and self-doubt became his pithy bedfellows disrupting even the most needed sleep. His circle of trust had shrunk, encompassing Peter, me, and Scott, one of Peter's partners who would try the second case, as friends with conditions. We were the only ones he could be sure of, and at times he had his doubts about me. His stubborn pride was untouched by this ego-stripping experience we were all going through with this trial.

CHAPTER THREE

PRE-TRIAL

Peter
Downtown Riverton, Wyoming
Friday, April 27, 1990

I'm on the trial assembly line and just being carried along from day-to-day. Trial is like being caught up in a powerful current. It carries you along with your having nothing to do with your destiny. I feel like Lucy in the Chocolate Factory in terms of it being the last week before trial and there being so much to do. I feel overwhelmed, on the one hand, while on the other, I just want to get started, to get into the pressure cooker so I get used to the environment.

My biggest concern in this trial has been my emotional and physical well-being as well as the effect my ear surgery has had on my preparation. I think I dislike having to admit that at 50, I am not as strong and resilient as I used to be, that the surgery, anesthesia, pain, bleeding, and lack of exercise took far more out of me than I had bargained for. I guess I am around seventy percent of normal strength going into a five- or six-week trial, and I am fearful of the physical toll of trial. Part of my fear is having to acknowledge the aging process and the fact that I'm not going to be 100 percent for trial.

Jay
The Weekend Before Trial

The weekend before trial was characterized at last by the buzz of enthusiasm and intensity that I had come to expect during the first trial. Peter encouraged me to take a more active role in trial preparation, a prospect I relished. In addition, the tactics of the trial were changed by the elimination of the hospital and the other Defendants. We would now have to present the evidence critical of their care while the Plaintiffs' lawyer, originally critical of the other care, would now be downplaying the contribution of everyone but Lee Krauth and me.

The issues were tackled head on. It seemed clear from the depositions that less emphasis was being placed by the Plaintiffs on the criticisms of the actual medical care, the timing and techniques of the surgeries, and more on the peripheral matters. The use of Super Glue keeps recurring, yet it's hard to feel it will be difficult to defend given that it was not used; and if we were to be criticized for even considering Super Glue, its use is well supported in an article by eminent neurosurgeons advocating its use. We hope that their emphasis on such minor issues will reveal the underlying weakness of the Plaintiffs' case.

The Sunday before trial was reserved primarily for the preparation of Peter and the team for voir dire. Dr. Berman prepared a list of questions which were designed to point out potential jurors who would or would not have personality characteristics which would be favorable to our position and particularly our personalities. The psychology of jury selection is frightening and again unrelated whatsoever to justice. Dr. Berman's talents were by this time no longer surprising to me. I would be terrified to find her on an opposing side. The upbeat feeling of the preparation was tempered by Dr. Berman's insistence that we take all possible measures to ensure Peter's safety during the trial. Given that it was their joint opinion that the death threat that he received during the first trial was probably related to the trial itself, the danger, of course, could still exist, a chilling thought to begin an already unhappy event.

Fran
Sunday, April 29, 1990

The war room, one of my favorite places. The play, the bantering, the creative energy pulls me into the whirlwind of trial prep generated by Peter. Factors have changed since December. Spence is gone, just as Peter predicted the day of the mistrial six months ago. Settlements have been made with the other doctors and hospital. It's a new trial now and a much cleaner one. The jurors needed for this trial will have a different profile. This time around we need jurors who can stay open for five weeks of tedious listening and not make up their minds quickly. Is there anyone on the planet like this? Peter and I ran through the questions, rephrased some of them to fit Peter's style and to stay as best as we could within the limits what the judge would allow him to discuss in jury selection. We agreed on the jurors we were looking for, and hopefully they would show up at the courthouse. If not, we were left with matching communication styles.

Peter was hurting. He was concerned about his ability to see this trial through. His surgery recovery has been slower than expected. He was down, I could hear it in his voice. I could only remind him to nurture himself. He holds himself responsible for pushing himself and everyone else across the finish line. He'll do it, somehow, he'll do it.

Jay arrived and Peter shifted to an animated, positive mode. Jay was included as an integral part of the trial planning. This was clearly what Jay needed. He became a valuable contributing part of the team in his own defense. The bonds among us were growing stronger.

By the end of the afternoon Peter had taken everyone's spirits to the mountain top. We left, going our separate ways, with the feeling we were going to a picnic tomorrow.

I burrow into my bed knowing Peter won't go near his tonight.

CHAPTER FOUR

DAY 1
VOIR DIRE

Editor's Note:
The highlights of voir dire follow. Unspoken commentary
from Jay is in brackets.

Peter
Monday, April 30, 1990, 4:00 a.m.

It seems so long ago that I was dealing with the issues of the great Gerry Spence and Ogsbury, when he chickened out and threw the match. This time feels, and is, so different. It's much more difficult to stay focused, to find the heat or emotional energy which drives you through fear and exhaustion into your creative, heroic being. As a warrior, I find myself relatively peaceful and relaxed and wondering whether I just don't have the drive, or the case has changed so much, it no longer frightens me and, in the process, no longer fuels my creative juices.

Everyone has settled but Jay Ogsbury and Lee Krauth in this case against Sheran R and her family. Mr. Branney and Mr. H will be at the helm for the other side (instead of the evil forces of Spence and his good but intensely unlikeable little sidekick, Schuster the Rooster). While trial will be a war, it will be a civilized war. As a warrior, I am physically, and thus emotionally and intellectually, weakened. As a warrior, I must recognize that I can, and may, call upon the power of my mind and spirit to nurture my body which, while surgically weakened and undermined by lack of exercise, must be cared for and preserved. Because of surgery and complications (how ironic that the medicine I have strived so mightily to defend has wounded and weakened me for this battle), I must be wily, cunning, perceptive, and attuned to all that goes on around me—like a wounded animal in the forest seeking to evade his hunter.

I find myself unprepared as to the Colorado medicine, first being felled by surgery and then having to spend a week to kill Dr. N, the Wyoming doctor who started all of this. Now I must deal only with a few witnesses and issues and possibly, over next weekend, I can come to speed and relearn the entire case. In the meantime, I must not let my ego and my compulsivity force me to weaken myself by overpreparing to the detriment of sleep, exercise, connection, and self-protection of my limited reservoir of emotional strength. I have only so much energy now to give to Jay and the others and must be careful to nurture my supply. To use it all now in such a long trial would be a disaster. We can and will prevail. I will see to that. But it will take strength, courage, cunning, self-love, and conviction. I reach within while asking for love and support from without; this case, as justice so earnestly calls for, will be ours.

Jay
Monday, April 30, 1990

I awoke on the morning of the first day of the second trial considerably later than usual. I had decided to sleep in, drink coffee and leisurely read the paper, all activities foreign to me on work mornings. Unfortunately, my feeble attempt at power relaxation served only to create the anxiety that I might actually be late for the first day of my own trial.

However, as I approached downtown Denver and realized that, even with a late start, I had plenty of time, I finally noticed that there was a white coat of snow on the ground, a good omen for one who had grown up on skis in Vermont. Finding the Denver District Court was not difficult as I had testified there on numerous Worker's Compensation and personal injury cases. The security at the entrance was more stringent than I remembered, but happily so given Dr. Berman's concern for Peter's safety. I located Courtroom 9 on the third floor and was relieved to find Peter and Scott already there.

Upon entering Courtroom 9 for the first time, I was struck by the difference between this courtroom and the dominion of Judge Carelli. Courtroom 9 is perhaps a bit smaller but seems much more spacious; the section for spectators is indeed much smaller—but without Mr. Spence there would be no crush of gawking lawyers overfilling the gallery—while the section for the participants seems not only much more roomy but also more orderly. Each table has the same number of the same kinds of chairs and the juror chairs are in perfect rows.

At precisely 9:00 a.m., the Bailiff announced, "All rise," and I had my first introduction to the Honorable Connie Peterson. She is tall, blond, graceful, and strikingly beautiful, meticulous in appearance, wearing slacks under her judicial robe. She immediately demonstrated her concern for the decorum of her court by rearranging two juror chairs that had arms different from the others. She greeted the attorneys, seemingly warm and open.

The teams are different this time. The Plaintiffs' table is marked by the absence of Mr. Spence, and also Mr. Branney, who has reportedly come up with some pressing matter elsewhere. Still behind the Plaintiffs' table are Mr. H, Ms. Kudla, Mr. Schuster (all in blue suits), plus Mr. Fitzgerald and Sheran R and Mr. R. The defense team has likewise changed. Sitting, at Peter's instructions, in front of the defense table are only Peter, Scott and me (the first subtle message to the jury that we are proud to be here). Lee Krauth, as planned, will remain away from the trial and at work except when needed to testify.

The first segment of the morning was reserved for motions made by each of the attorneys. The scope of the motions was limited as many of the issues had been argued and ruled upon in the first trial. Mr. H did request a delay of one week be made in order to reschedule his witnesses and to allow Sheran to return to Riverton for her care. Peter asked for only one day. Judge Peterson stated she did not wish to waste this week and ruled that there would be one day off this week and then some the following weeks.

Next, Scott moved that Super Glue be removed from consideration. Mr. H said that I had used Super Glue and that it was relevant to the question of meningitis. The motion was denied. I wondered with his repeating Mr. Spence's charge that I had lied (when I stated I had not used Super Glue), whether I could now generate a useful dislike for him.

Mr. H next stated that the economic damages exceeded 5.4 million and asked about stating specific amounts, a contested issue in the first trial. Judge Peterson ruled that he could only say large amounts or even possibly millions, but not specific amounts. Next Peter asked that Super Glue not be addressed in voir dire, and Judge Peterson agreed stating, "Let's not let Super Glue take over this case."

Peter answered, "I'd love that."

Mr. H countered, "I'm sure."

Finally, Peter asked about telling the jurors about the length of the trial, estimated to be five-plus weeks. Judge Peterson said, "I will tell them, and you will see their ears lay back." I already like her. She seems to like this case and her presence, warm personality, wonderful smile, and sense of humor cut into the oppressive formality characteristic of most courtrooms.

There being no more motions, the morning recess was called. During the morning recess, both Mr. H and Ms. Kudla made a point to come up to me to introduce themselves. Mr. H said that he had met me before in my office and hoped I understood it was nothing personal. Amazingly, I believe him. I will indeed have a difficult time disliking him. On the other hand, I found myself reluctant even to shake Ms. Kudla's hand.

On returning to the courtroom, I noted that the fifty potential jurors had been assembled for the first time. I also noticed, reassuringly, that Dr. Berman was in the gallery. The second session of the morning began the process of voir dire, or jury selection, a seemingly innocuous process which I realize, from Peter's words and particularly from Mr. Spence's actions at the first trial, to be one of the single most important parts of any trial.

The process began with Judge Peterson saying a few words to the potential jurors. She said, "We are going to have to get to know you in a very short period of time. I know that jury duty of any kind, whether it be one or two days or one day or one week or four weeks or four months, is an inconvenience. We will ask you to interrupt your regular life, come in and serve as jurors. We appreciate that service. I know in some cases it is a greater hardship than others, and we will ask you about that and we will try to work out these considerations in our selection of the jury."

She then instructed the Bailiff to call the first fourteen possible jurors and alternates. Their names were drawn from a box containing the names of all fifty potential jurors. My initial impression as they were called was that this was not a bad start, and, except for one strange looking man who later said his main interest was "spreading the word of Jesus," the group seemed like mainline America.

Judge Peterson instructed the Bailiff to raise a large card of basic questions involving names, addresses, marital status, education, work status, interests, association with law enforcement, and previous jury duty. The process started with each of the jurors answering these questions. Each of us at the defense table (as well as the paralegals) filled out this information on large sheets blocked off in the appropriate spaces for the twenty positions. I noted that the attorneys at the Plaintiffs' table were doing the same thing.

Mr. H then walked to the podium facing the jury panel. He began his portion of voir dire with a low key, brief description of the nature of the case, though I did note that he did slip in the point that brain injury occurred with each surgery. He first turned to a lady with an association with four or five doctors, obtained an agreement that she could be biased, and asked for her removal for cause. Peter was asked if he had any questions and, while it seemed obvious that she surely did deserve to be excused, Peter stated that he did have a few questions. For the first time,

I saw him in action, beginning to lay the foundation of our case. To his questions as to whether she could get beyond the emotion of the tragedy, listen to the facts and issues, and render a fair verdict, she reiterated she could possibly favor one side. She also said she would try to return a fair verdict, but did not know, for sure, if she could return a fair verdict. Peter graciously granted her removal but had been clever and successful in instructing the rest of the jurors while presenting a generous and reasonable stance.

Mr. H resumed by addressing a woman with a history of dental training who had worked for two dentists, one whom she considered great, and the other bad. She noted that good and bad medicine occurred and that doctors can make mistakes. In addition, Mr. H discovered the fact that a friend of hers had had a back operation complicated by an infection, and therefore she had a little bias for each side. I expect she will be considered dangerous by both the plaintiff and defense attorneys.

Several other jurors with possible relevant factors in their histories (one with dental training and another as an insurance sales agent) stated that they had no biases. Mr. H then asked several jurors their opinion of the right to sue, particularly a doctor. One said, "It would certainly have to depend on the circumstances" and "I don't think they should be expected to be perfect," but that he would have no trouble deciding against the physician if the rules were broken. A second who had filed a worker's compensation claim six to seven months before said, "Doctors are human, too. We are all entitled to mistakes."

A third whose company had had a worker's compensation case filed against it said she, too, could be fair. Finally, in the last moments before noon, Mr. H talked to two other jurors who had had contact with medicine. One, a delightful 69-year-old lady, had a son who had undergone brain surgery several months before and was seemingly recovering well. She noted her husband had unexpectedly died of a massive heart attack, but she could not blame the doctors as he had had a normal electrocardiogram not long before his heart attack. A second had had a close friend paralyzed in an auto accident fifteen years before, and she had spent many hours with him at Craig Rehabilitation Hospital. She had no particular bias as "every case is different."

We went to the Radisson Hotel for lunch as had been the case each day at the first trial. Peter and Dr. Berman largely controlled the conversation about the jurors. The religious man was "gone" as one could not predict how he might react. Because of him, a church pastor, and several others who were interested in gospel music, Peter joked that this would have been a great jury for Mr. Spence. Peter was also concerned over the number of jurors with athletic interests, who might overly identify with Sheran's loss. We talked about each of our opinions regarding the jurors. I noted I generally agreed with Dr. Berman.

On returning to court, Mr. Fitzgerald talked amiably to me in the men's room about the weather. After the court was called back into session, the attorneys and I went into Judge Peterson's chambers. The attorneys sat on either side of a large table stretching from Judge Peterson's desk; I sat demurely in the corner. Peter and Mr. H agreed one juror could be excused because of an unavoidable conflict with a final exam. Scott also pointed out that he had had a previous contact with another juror, the pastor, and both sides shared their concern with the unpredictability of any ultra-religious juror and eagerly agreed to let him go. Even Judge Peterson noted that he was not her favorite as she could "just hear him saying Amen to my instructions." We returned to the courtroom, and the two jurors were excused.

Mr. H resumed his voir dire. He first introduced the three daughters of Sheran and her husband. I already knew them well, but I had noted that, even at the time of the first trial, they seemed at least open to me. However, they were now completely cool as I caught their eyes. In addition, Mr. H revealed a bit about Sheran R's husband, his background, and his job.

Mr. H then turned to the man with the "very strong Christian convictions" and asked "if while sitting in judgment, monetary compensation used for injury was acceptable" to him—another major point straight from Mr. Spence. He asked another man whether the standards were as clear as the rules of the road. He noted that in a civil case the rules involve "the preponderance of evidence" in contrast to "beyond a reasonable doubt" applicable in criminal cases. He further noted that on "the scale of justice," the slightest tipping is to be considered "preponderance of evidence." These were identical words to those used by Mr. Spence, and I wondered if they were learned from him, or simply widespread plaintiff jargon used to convince jurors to make difficult decisions in favor of their clients. This juror was asked further if not having an absolute was a problem. He responded, "Two doctors who supposedly know the way to go and they disagree, that's a tough job." But he would follow instructions as far as he knew them. Several other jurors were asked if they could be impartial with the above factors, and they reported they could. One, an attorney, said it would be her obligation to be impartial. Another, the man who had faced the worker's comp case, said, "You've got to check the evidence."

Mr. H turned back to the man who expressed the obvious difficulty in choosing when experts on each side disagree. He asked the juror if he had seen the advertisement taken out by the insurance companies regarding lawsuit abuse and would this affect his thinking. Was this another major Spence theme? He said, "We read so much about the people suing for everything all the time, and for frivolous suits, that you get tired of that. But when they are legitimate—something that has got to be settled—someone has got to do it, I guess." The juror commented, in response to questions, that he had heard about "ridiculously high" verdicts but had also heard about "ridiculously low" verdicts as well. It seemed Mr. H was a bit surprised with the latter statement. I smiled at the small point for us. He should know not to ask the question if you don't want the answer.

Several of this group were also asked by Mr. H again about financial compensation for injury. One agreed that over thirty years, "millions of dollars" might be a reasonable compensation. Another said that "many millions of dollars" in compensation was okay. Another, when asked, "If he had any problem with the concept of awarding for things like disfigurement, deformity, physical impairment, mental impairment," said he had no problem with "putting a price on something that isn't able to be—." All of these comments were of course within the guidelines set in the early motions and had none of the impact on me that Mr. Spence's comment "tens of millions of dollars," while looking directly at me, had had at the previous trial.

Of course, the questioning certainly again planted the idea of a large verdict clearly in the minds of the jurors here. After questioning the remaining two jurors about these points in general, Mr. H stated, "I would pass this group for cause." A brief recess was called. The fourth juror, the man with the "strong Christian convictions," was excused.

At the end of the recess, Peter came to the podium and began his voir dire. "If it please the Court, ladies and gentlemen. My name is Peter Pryor. It's my pleasure to represent Dr. Ogsbury and Dr. Krauth." He then introduced Kathy, my wife, in the gallery. She was surprised and a little bit embarrassed, but the counterpoint to the introduction of Mr. R and the daughters was made.

He then addressed the jury as a whole and asked if there were any concerns that troubled them coming in. He said, "You tell me your feelings and honest heartfelt beliefs, and I will respect those. It's all right to tell me you're scared."

Peter turned to the man who expressed his reasonable concerns about making choices when experts disagree and asked if people can learn.

The man replied, "I quit buying green bananas." Another juror noted that it was scary, "We're just not involved in this type of thing every day."

Peter then asked, "Do you all understand that this is a part of your civic duty? Is anyone mad at anybody right now?"

The delightful older lady said she was not angry but then asked, "Do you think I'm too old to be a juror?"

Peter asked, "Does this sound like an exciting challenge to you?"

When she said it did, Peter answered, "So you've got everything it takes to be a good juror—you've got a sharp mind and a sense of enthusiasm about life. And there's no age constraint on that. You could be 87 as far as I'm concerned or 27, okay—and that's simply not an issue, since that does not necessarily get linked in with whether you're 21 or 81."

She obviously likes Peter. He then went on to say, "I've watched you people and I've never learned how to read minds yet. Sheran R went into a hospital on June 15, 1986, walked in with a runny nose, and left St. Anthony Hospital in a wheelchair. Now it's going to be emotional in the courtroom. That's fine, okay? That's fine to feel emotion. It's okay to feel the empathy. It's okay to react to what's going on. There may be tears—some of those tears may be yours and that's fine with me."

Peter moved through introducing us in a personal way. He seemed to be getting friendlier with the people who were left.

He asked one juror, "Are you an emotionally responsible person?" To another, a penal officer, he asked, "Are you steeled to it or does it affect you mildly from time to time?" To a third, "Do you think you could set fact and emotions on two different shelves?" He said, "We have what we call a fault system of justice. You have to do something wrong, first, before you have to answer in damages." To still another he suggested, "While Mrs. R was a victim and while she's entitled to compensation, it's not from Jay Ogsbury, it's not from Lee Krauth." [Personalizing us for the first time.] "Did you ever hear the expression, 'Pointing the finger'?"

Peter asked, "Could you find the man who stayed behind to protect his name and stand up for his care didn't do it?" (In contrast to those who settled.) "If you find Dr. Ogsbury was zero percent responsible—even if you thought her damages were millions of dollars—would you have any hesitancy in finding in favor of Dr. Ogsbury?" The juror said, "If you could prove it." [And I felt transfixed.] He asked if it was okay to have a little humor and, "not belittle Mrs. R." He then asked, "Had anyone known someone who had come out of medical care worse than he or she went in?" Several jurors had, but felt they could be objective.

Peter then began to ask Dr. Berman's questions, though each, of course, was contained in a discussion relevant to bias. Did each juror want to be thought of as a "person with feelings or a reasonable person?" Several questioned jurors wished to be reasonable. He then asked, "Does anybody have trouble making decisions about important issues where it involves other people's lives?" None did. He asked the attorney who was a weightlifter, "Would this be a problem putting yourself in Mrs. R's situation?" Before the answer, the afternoon break was called.

The break was simply time for a quick cup of coffee, and we returned to court. We were called into Chambers. Mr. H complained, not inappropriately, that Peter was giving statements rather than asking questions. Judge Peterson agreed that Peter was indeed stretching voir dire and suggested "a more traditional approach."

Upon returning to the courtroom, Peter returned to Dr. Berman's questions. He asked one juror, would he put himself "on an emotional extreme or a factual category" in his work? Did he "like to lay it out as you go and get all organized or do you pretty much like to just get into it and see what happens, take it as it comes?" Did he feel the ideal supervisor would be "kind or fair?" Most of the jurors were more factual than emotional, had jobs which were more "take it as it comes" than pre-planned and wished supervisors to be fair. Several, however, liked routines rather than organized situations. Peter then asked several jurors, "Do you like someone who is coming up with new ideas continually, even if they are not good, or do you like the type of person who is just solid and has his feet on the ground?" Most liked new ideas, although one noted, "It depended what job they're in." Peter then asked one juror, the one who had filed a worker's comp claim, about his being unemployed. He said he was a musician waiting for a gig and described his musical style as "thrash-hardcore." He was asked about playing at night and being at court all day. He said, "I ain't draining out no physical energy or nothin'. It's kind of saving it." [I love this guy.]

Peter turned to several others and asked about responsibility. One had wrongly taken blame and felt terrible. Peter asked if he were sued, would he take the blame? He and others agreed no. He asked another question, "If Dr. Ogsbury feels he is being blamed for something he didn't do, how do you feel about giving up a month of your time to let him bring that issue and let a jury of his peers decide whether his position is right or wrong?" He, of course, agreed there was "no problem with that."

Peter then asked, was it okay that Dr. Krauth was not here but "back in the office taking care of patients?" And then asked, "Could they all make a promise they would keep their minds open regarding the issue of Super Glue?" Next, he asked were there any other questions. The older lady asked whether the doctor's license was being questioned here and was assured it wasn't. He finally asked one juror whether the power inherent in a jury was "scary" and the juror noted that the responsibility was overwhelming. Peter turned to the jury and asked, "If you're picked regardless of any feelings or emotions or you might have for or against Dr. Ogsbury, for or against Sheran R, would you base your verdict on the law and the evidence? Can all of you right now honestly from your heart answer that question, yes?" The jurors nodded in the affirmative. Peter agreed with the removal of one further juror, an insurance agent. The Judge agreed, and Peter sat down.

Six new individuals were then picked and called to fill the places of those excused, and the process began again. Mr. H began his questioning and several of the potential jurors indicated the possibility of bias. Interestingly, during this time Mr. H frequently alluded to Peter's questions, a good sign that Mr. H was worried. Finally, 5:00 p.m. came, and the court was adjourned.

Following the adjournment, the defense team stayed in the courtroom discussing the day's events. We did not appear to be doing badly in voir dire. Peter stated that he was not yet fully prepared for the opening statements scheduled the following day but planned to stay in the courtroom for a while. I drove home, worked out, ate a quick supper, and went through my notes. I had noted Mr. H had introduced many of his ideas, among them that jurors would sit in judgment, could deliver monetary compensation for injury, would decide the issue by preponderance of evidence, that the jury might have been affected by the advertising campaign regarding lawsuit abuse, and that millions of dollars was reasonable over thirty years.

On the other hand, Peter had introduced many of Mr. H's ideas as well. His summary simply granted Mrs. R's terrible injury. He then cleverly told the jury that it was okay to have emotions but that fact and emotions would be on different shelves; he stated that there must be fault to award damages; he personalized the doctors; he described me as the man who stayed behind to defend his care; he said it was okay to have humor in the court even in the face of this tragedy; he told them that they would have to differentiate between opposite opinions; he challenged the tendency to put oneself in Mrs. R's situation; he asked them to keep their minds open regarding Super Glue; and he acknowledged the responsibility that went with power of the juror. At the same time, he managed to ask nearly all the jurors Dr. Berman's three critical questions: emotional versus factual, lay it out or see how it goes, and ideas that were solid or new.

On reflecting about day one, I felt that we were picking a jury that was not great but was not bad either; that Mr. H, while organized, seemed detached, almost like he did not have any belief in the situation; that the jurors were not responding well to him; that Peter, jumping around from juror to juror in his questioning, promptly woke the jurors; that Peter and Judge Peterson seemed to play well off each other; and that Judge Peterson was a striking figure totally on top of things and appeared to like the case. Furthermore, I feel I too will work well with Judge Peterson. Dr. Berman tells me that I do better one-on-one than before a group and suggested that I talk to Judge Peterson and then to the jurors who will sit behind the judge from where I will sit. Thus, Judge Peterson may provide the focus that was lost for me when Mr. Spence refused to return for Trial Two. I will tell her my story in her courtroom.

However, I do have a serious concern that Peter will not be prepared for the opening statement. He talks about just letting it happen, that's indeed what he does best. However, I am worried that he does not yet have a full understanding of the facts. He is not a physician, and I have an obligation to ensure that he gets the medicine right. I do not want to have to apologize for my attorney if I lose.

Fran
Monday, April 30, 1990, 9:00 p.m.

The second beginning. First day trial jitters, moving into a rhythm that will sustain us. Everyone's watching everyone else. The opposing counsel strut and preen. Scott looks solid. May and Sam are watchful for the slightest indication of anything going wrong.

Peter has presence. His emotions, his fears, his apprehensions don't move him off his intent. Everything appears to his liking, whether it is or isn't. He is communicating but taking in twice as much. Peter has learned to listen with all of his senses—his eyes, his skin, his heart. He hasn't forgotten anything. He remains a warrior, here with singularity of purpose.

Jay is different this time. This time his blood flows and his emotions pulse. Quite a transformation. He is clearly no longer a victim frozen with fear. He doesn't hope the jurors will understand. He knows they will. His conviction runs deeper. I look at Jay and Peter. I feel these two vastly different men have come together.

CHAPTER FIVE

DAY 2
VOIRE DIRE

Peter
Tuesday, May 1, 1990, 4:03 a.m.

I'm three minutes late for my 4:00 a.m. arrival at "La Club," the White Spot on 6th and Broadway where I have trial prepped for years, amidst the street people, gays, and night people who frequent all-night restaurants in out-of-the-way parts of town. I am shocked to find someone at my table, the table I have toiled away at for up to six hours a night, away from the distractions and loneliness I feel at home during trial.

Trial Day Two and we are still picking a jury. I am pulling all the stops emotionally, using the tricks and nuances learned over twenty-four years, in an effort to deliver to Jay the confirmation he deserves. I'm wearing warm colors and non-threatening sports clothes rather than authority suits.

Sitting out there in front of the jury, Jay and I are alone against the four of these strangely quiet and unemotional "suits" on the other side. Their ardor is no doubt dampened by the huge sums (close to 1.8 million) they have gotten for their clients over the past several months, their enthusiasm tempered by the oh-so-many holes in their case created by a settlement with everyone but Jay and Lee. Strange, but there just doesn't seem to be any heat or passion in these people, and, like a prize fighter who senses fear in his opponent, I have chosen to heat up the courtroom with my passion for Jay's cause. "We are here, people, for one reason. These doctors, my doctors, Jay Ogsbury, my doctor, who stands here alone, didn't do anything to hurt this woman and he wants you to tell him that." Not so subtle fires of passion burn and Plaintiffs' counsel objects in chambers to my "ingratiating" style of relating to the jury.

The Judge smiles knowingly and asks if I could question in a more "traditional" manner. I lamely protest that, in voir dire, communication is an art form and that, like an artist with his painting, I should not be bound to the traditional. "I'm just selling a few basic points here ladies and gentlemen of the jury, points I want you to sense without my really telling you; we're the underdogs, the David, the courageous, compassionate doctor taking a last stand. Over there are the faces of evil. I care more about Sheran than her mouthpieces sitting at her side. We are driven by conviction and courage, not by the quest of money." What will the jury think when they hear Dr. N was sued and settled; everyone else in Denver was sued and settled? I'm a little frazzled but feel that this will be an okay jury, hopefully good enough to see the holes in the Plaintiffs' case.

Mr. H is dying to settle. He hints in passing in meetings in the hall; he asked the Judge for a week's continuance, then two days, but gets one. I sense their heart isn't quite in it, that they are not ready and need more time, that deep down they wish they weren't here. And even though I have to drive myself to the ends of my surgery-weakened endurance, I pushed the court to go on. I send out all my energy to the jury and to Jay, reach within for the strength. The spoor of their fear and defeat is faintly present. Can I kill this case before it gets off the ground, not only in the hearts of the opposition, but in the hearts and minds of the jury? Back to work.

Jay
May 1, 1990

The morning of the second day of the trial was a little more organized than the first. I left home at a reasonable time and noted with disappointment that the snow had melted. I ran into Sam, Peter's paralegal, in my usual parking lot, and it felt reassuring to walk to the courtroom with her. The team—Peter, Scott, Mary, Sam, Dr. Berman, and I—met at 8:15 a.m. in the cafeteria and discussed voir dire. Noting the variety of personalities of the jurors, Dr. Berman recounted the parable of the elephant and the blind men and how each blind man interpreted what he felt of the elephant in a different way.

All in all we thought we were working with a good jury panel. We felt good as well about the difficulty Mr. H was having, and would have, being forced to change his theory of the case so he could now target just the care of the neurosurgeons and not that of the other Defendants. Mary told Peter that he would have to learn to juggle and sing the song, "First you say you will and then you won't," for his final argument.

We left for the courtroom in an upbeat mood. Upon arriving in Courtroom 9 we found that Frick and Frack, our names for Mr. H's paralegals, had seated themselves on the bench immediately behind the Defense, possibly to better hear the defense discussions. At the first trial Mary and Sam had learned to arrive early to protect our turf. Today Mary simply sat down beside them, Kathy sat behind them, and ultimately Frick and Frack moved to the Plaintiffs' side of the gallery.

Promptly at 9:00 a.m., we were called into Judge Peterson's chambers. While in chambers, Mr. H attempted to have the thoughtful juror (who had expressed reservations about making the choices) excused. Peter objected to his removal and Judge Peterson ruled that Mr. H could talk to him further. An attempt was made to schedule Lee Krauth's examination by Mr. H. Judge Peterson was obviously annoyed that Lee had surgical and office commitments conflicting with the days Mr. H wished. She said, "Dr. Krauth has other people to accommodate, and I have other people to accommodate too." Peter emphasized that it was the convenience and plans of the patients, particularly those scheduled for surgery, that were in question; the Defense agreed to try to make arrangements with Lee.

We returned to the courtroom, and I noted all of the Plaintiffs' attorneys, except Mr. Fitzgerald, had joined Peter and Scott in wearing friendly sport coats rather than their previous dark suits.

Mr. H then resumed his voir dire. He asked if any of the new jurors had had any relationship with COPIC, the Defendant's malpractice insurance company, or medicine. One reported that he knew a doctor but that this would not affect him.

Mr. H then turned back to the "thoughtful juror" and found that he was an unwilling participant, had become sick with breakfast, and would probably be physically ill during the duration of the trial. He then turned to one of the new jurors and asked, "If a building downtown here was knocked down, destroyed, due to the negligence of someone and you sat in the jury, and you found that the building had been destroyed due to the negligence of someone, would you have any hesitancy in awarding to the owner of that building the face value of the building even though it may be millions of dollars?"

He went on [I thought here we go again with more words directly from Mr. Spence] and asked [of course], "If instead of a building the damage is to a human being and you sit on a jury and you find—and I emphasize this—that there was negligence by someone, and that negligence caused the damage to this human being, do you agree that human being ought to be compensated for the full loss that that human being suffered just like the building?" The juror said, "Again if it is proven, you know negligence and—sure—I agree."

Mr. H said, "Now if I was going to show you the loss of that building, I would bring in photographs of that building and prove to you what the building looked like before and after, and I may do that in this case with Sheran R and some may suggest that I am trying to play on the emotions of the jury—sympathy." Mr. H turned to another new lady and noted, "Do you understand that Sheran R is not in the courtroom for sympathy? She can get all the sympathy she needs elsewhere." The juror said Mrs. R could get sympathy "in the street." Mr. H obtained permission from the jurors for Sheran to be absent, just as Peter had done with Lee, and sat down.

Peter began his questioning of the new jurors. He first said he understood they felt like they were "students in a classroom where you don't want to be in school" but assured them that this would be a rewarding experience. He turned to the lady who had been asked the questions about sympathy. He asked her about the loss of her husband to a heart attack when she was 34. They also discussed her love of antiques and gourmet cooking.

Finally, he elicited the statement that she wished to be fair, but firm as well as kind, would try to deal with the facts not emotions, and felt she would be a good juror. [I like her, she is a very disciplined lady.] He talked to two men, an accountant and an investment broker, about taking time off from work. He first talked to the accountant who had worked on several political campaigns, asked him when he had last taken time from work. The juror noted he had last taken a vacation two years ago but still thought he could be a good juror. The investment counselor, on the other hand, said that his mind would be elsewhere and that, "I feel like I'm victimized" [join the crowd].

Peter talked again to the "thoughtful juror" with the anxiety making him sick and induced the agreement that the juror would listen to the evidence and make a decision on it even if he became sick every morning. Peter then passed on these jurors for cause and approached the bench. The anxious man who was sick and the investment counselor were excused.

Four new jurors were called, and they answered the standard questions. Mr. H talked to the new jurors. One had had a kidney transplant and a recent urinary tract infection. She obviously had a good reason to be excused. The second was a licensed optician but was working currently as a checkout supervisor at Woolworths. She strangely was not asked about a splint on her arm. A third had a friend who had suffered a gunshot wound to the leg and nerve damage. The patient had undergone surgery, and the juror under questioning implied there were problems with the medical care. The fourth stated that he had a sister who was a physician in our area [I know her] and when asked about doctors, said that the "medical profession attracts a certain amount of greediness. It turns me off."

The last two men were taken back into chambers. Mr. H now obviously wished to keep the man who had felt his friend had experienced bad medical care and tried to mitigate his admission of bias. Noting that this case had nothing to do with the friend, Mr. H asked could he not, "listen to the facts of this case—and make an independent judgment about the propriety of the care that was given in this case?" The juror said he would try but that he was "an opinionated person." He also noted that he had a problem with Lee not being there [all the right answers to get him excused].

Peter then completed his removal by asking, "So you're allowing, in your mind, then, the possibility that you have a little bias against Dr. Ogsbury and Dr. Krauth?" [words usually from the Plaintiffs' attorney] and the juror agreed.

Judge Peterson turned to the other juror and, obviously annoyed by his blatant attempt to be removed, asked, "You said there's some greed in the medical profession. Where is the greed? Who has it?"

He answered, "Generally I think doctors make a lot of money." Mr. H then asked questions attempting to keep him as well. "You don't know anything about Dr. Ogsbury or Dr. Krauth, do you?" He answered, "No," but added he felt his feelings about doctors would cloud his judgment. Both of these jurors were obviously excused along with the lady who had the transplant. It appeared to me that Mr. H again had asked questions which induced answers he did not want.

Three more jurors were called, answered the stock questions, and Mr. H was on his feet again. The first was a man in his sixties who was retired, had had previous medical care which was good, but would have no preconceived feelings. He said he intended to listen to all the information in making up his mind. He said, "That's the idea of a trial, to find out who is right and who is wrong." "No assumptions made?" "No, I've got to hear it all." I liked him but suspected the Plaintiffs' attorneys would not. The second juror was a lady who worked at Albertsons, felt the trial was scary, but could keep an open mind. The third was an attractive young girl who had nonrefundable airline tickets for a previously scheduled trip. She was strikingly articulate but, upon learning she had helped care for a young friend with multiple sclerosis and would have strong feelings for Sheran R, I was happy to see her excused. On her walk from the courtroom, she appeared to talk briefly with Sheran. We appeared close to having a jury.

The noon recess was called and, before we left, we were called into chambers. One of the original jurors, a lady who was willing to work at night to fulfill her responsibilities at work, reported that she was now expected to be involved in a special product conference during the trial and her absence would be a real hardship to her work. Both sides—and the Judge—agreed that she would have made an excellent juror, that she had really made an attempt to be a juror (in contrast to some of the others), but that it was reasonable to let her be excused. There were therefore two more chairs to fill. At lunch we rated the jurors. The choice was felt to be a little difficult as the Plaintiffs may want a lot of the same qualities that we do.

We returned from lunch and the trial was called back to order. Judge Peterson obviously had on her work face. Two more jurors were called. Mr. H began with a man who was a picket captain from King Soopers. He clearly wanted off. "I think I would have some bias" and started to explain. Mr. H then suggested we take up the matter in chambers. The juror said that he had had reconstructive surgery on his nose and, although his breathing was improved by the surgery, he was unhappy with the result. In addition, he had had three unsuccessful hernia operations. For that reason, he said he was biased with no trust for doctors. He felt the word practitioners indicated that doctors were practicing and that doctors were "experimenting" on people. He continued that his father went downhill after the removal of an ostomy bag, and he felt he couldn't put aside his bias. Judge Peterson ordered that he be removed.

Mr. H then asked about the other man, a banker whose inclusion in the trial would be an inconvenience for the bank. To my surprise, Judge Peterson demonstrated her annoyance by denying his removal at that point. We returned and another juror, a lady, was called. Mr. H turned to the banker. He admitted he wished off, but, as a combat medic for thirty-two years in the Reserves and having a current close working association with doctors, his assertion of possible bias seemed reasonable, and his removal was requested. Mr. H then talked to the lady. She had worked for her father's appliance distribution company which had been recently sold leaving her currently unemployed. She was a high school graduate but had a manner of speech and physical presence of someone with far more education. I immediately liked her. She obviously expressed no areas of concern for Mr. H and his questioning was brief.

Peter then took over. He asked the retired man, "Do you have a sense, right now, that there was a problem with this man's care?" He answered appropriately, "I can't tell until I'm given all of the information—I would have to hear it all." He then talked to the optician who worked at Woolworths. He first asked her about her cast (which was for tendinitis). She seemed pleased with Peter's concern. She reported that she left her job with an eye doctor to have a child and took a temporary job at Woolworths which continues to the present. She said she would be fair and seemed to be both intelligent and warm. I happened to notice Dr. Berman signaling Peter to stop his questions so the other side would not eliminate her. Peter did stop and talked to the lady who worked at Albertsons. She agreed she was a warm and caring person but that the tragedy would not get in the way of wrestling with the hard facts. He turned to the newly unemployed lady. She was not mad at her family for causing her current unemployment. She noted she was a fan of country music, "music of the heart," and rated herself as emotionally caring. She admitted her mouth was still numb from having a wisdom tooth removed but could keep the promise to keep that unhappiness out of her thinking.

Peter turned to the last juror, a lady who admitted she might have a bias because of the condition of Sheran R. He asked, "Would you allow for the possibility in your mind that that bias might interfere with your ability to be fair to Dr. Ogsbury and Dr. Krauth?" She answered, "I want to be fair but I'm not sure I could be." Mr. H then reversed the question and asked whether she could "make a decision on whether Dr. Ogsbury was negligent and whether the negligence caused the injury without letting sympathy get in the way of these decisions?" She answered, she "would try." Mr. H then asked, "Do you think you could do that?" She obliged, "I think I could." Mr. H requested she be included in the panel. Judge Peterson agreed and the juror remained.

With that decision twenty possible jurors and alternates had passed challenges for cause. Judge Peterson turned to the panel and said, "I want to thank you for all your time and attention and coming back after our recesses. We should probably call this jury 'unselection' because that is really what we do—we start with a huge group and unselect people and end up with six jurors and two alternates. Currently, we're going to make the first cut. The first cut is everybody in the audience. Thank you very much for your time. You are excused. For the rest of you, what we have to do is get down to eight from this group. That means each side will excuse six people leaving eight people. That will take a little bit of time. It's done by a very high-tech process; they have a piece of paper, and they pass it back and forth and scratch your names off, until they have eight people left."

She then excused herself from the room, and the process of preemptory challenges was begun just as she described. A paper was presented with the names of fourteen possible jurors and six possible alternates which was passed first to the Plaintiffs' team, one name crossed off by them, and then passed to the Defense, one name crossed off by us, and so on until the names of the four jurors and two alternates had been removed by each side leaving a panel of six jurors and two alternates. Our team was well prepared, and Peter was pleased to be able to immediately choose the juror to be removed while the Plaintiffs' team required minutes to make their decision. When the process was completed, Peter took great delight in showing Mr. H that, not only did he know which of the jurors the Defense wished removed, he had successfully predicted the jurors the Plaintiffs wished to remove as well.

With the preemptory challenges completed, Judge Peterson returned. The jurors were recalled, the names of the final jury was called and seated, and the rest excused. Judge Peterson then turned to the new jury and discussed the upcoming trial briefly with them. She first asked that they keep the same chairs during the trial. "It's a little like school. If you sit in the wrong chair we may call you by the wrong name."

She then noted that a trial is composed of seven steps—voir dire, opening statements by the attorneys, the presentation of evidence, closing arguments, the reading of instructions, deliberations of the jury, and the verdict. She added that the purpose of the trial was to find and determine the facts, that the jurors were the sole judge of the credibility of the witnesses, and that the jurors had to follow the law. She discussed the process of opening arguments, witnesses, and closing arguments.

She reported to the jurors that Dr. N as well as the other Colorado doctors and the hospital had settled with the family. While she said, "You will not be told nor should you speculate concerning the amount of the settlement," the jurors clearly must understand the settlements were large, given the nature of Sheran's condition. Peter is pleased. Scott said, "She said the word. We are un-lumped. The care before and after us is lumped together." With that, the court was adjourned with opening statements scheduled the next day.

As we had done on the first day, the defense team stayed around to talk over the day's events. We noted a new attitude from Mr. H; he had finally found "the feeling religion" and actually appeared to care. I noted further that Judge Peterson was more firm and less friendly to either side than before. I will defer my judgment of her. The jury panel that will decide our fate has finally been chosen.

Fran
May 1, 1990, 9:00 p.m.

Fifty jurors. All the good jurors we had to let go. All the jurors we were glad to let go, with some you wonder how they make it through the day. Peter went second in jury selection. He had the peacefulness that makes it all look so easy. He dropped the ball twice but recovered. The first error was a common one, continuing to question a juror who clearly had all the characteristics he was looking for in a juror.

We were losing time in questioning jurors we still had insufficient information about, and I hated taking shots in the dark. I was dependent on Peter to get the information I needed. The second error occurred when he stepped on a juror's toes to make a connection with her around similar experiences. He went back and repaired the damage. I was sweating when I handed Mary the juror list prioritized from most wanted to least wanted.

Visually, they were quite a crew. Four were Peter's dream come true and two were what he asked for. And whether Jay knew it or not, he had a jury of his peers. Peter referred to this jury as his "buttercup" jury (picking jurors only because he liked them and they liked him), and I am reminded of the saying, "He is happiest who hath the power to gather wisdom from a flower." Just wait Peter, these guys are dynamite. Peter chuckles and says, "Look Mr. H, we picked your jury too!"

Jay stays firm, more excited than frightened. He's in this like he's in surgery. He's back to defend medicine, to defend himself. His rage has transformed into a force of determinism. The picture's changing; now we have Peter the warrior, and Jay the lawyer.

The Jurors

Juror – Sally Romero

Sally Romero is a 33-year-old baker at Albertsons. She is a high school graduate but said she is four hours away from a psychology degree. She was raised on a farm and her mother was a secretary for a tri-county health center. She is divorced and has three children. She revealed that her first husband had died of a ruptured cerebral aneurysm when both were 21. Her reaction to that immense tragedy, "It was an Act of God, he died of natural causes."

During voir dire, she said that being on the jury was "scary," but she could be fair. We all liked her.

Juror – Jacqueline Holmes

Jacqueline Holmes is a 34-year-old married checker/supervisor at Woolworths. She has a B.A. in Education and did some student teaching. She is also a licensed optician who had worked for an ophthalmologist but had left that job two and a half years ago to deliver her daughter and then took the temporary job with Woolworths. We found out, in addition to her own relationship to medicine, her husband is a phlebotomist who had started premed, and her brother had had meningitis. She said she would not let her medical background sway her. She had once before served in a jury involving two DUI's—"boring." During voir dire, she described herself as a kind person.

Juror – Narcisco Martinez

Narcisco Martinez is a 21-year-old self-described heavy metal thrasher, a rock musician, who at the time of the trial was unemployed waiting for a gig. He is a lead guitarist in a group that had been together for three years although he had played the guitar ever since elementary school. He had the equivalent of a high school education but said he went a different route, the ROTC. He had suffered an on-the-job injury to his hand but took a small settlement rather than going to trial.

During voir dire, he was a favorite of our team with his description of his rock music, "hard core," his acceptance of his injury and the judicial system, and particularly his feeling about being a juror, "You got to check the evidence." Narcisco said he grew up on "the other side of Denver," that "people don't get to liking me too much." He jokingly described his mother as "mean." I'm 22 years old and I can't smoke in her house. I have to go outside." He said his dad was in the Marines, "some kind of general or something," who was "not around," but was "always a supplier." He came back on a pass, grabbed my hair and cut it." He told us he had been in jail on several occasions—usually he just happened to be in the neighborhood when the police were investigating a crime. "That's the way it's always been. Some days I get sucked up into something; they stop me for nothing at all."

Juror – Clara Huey

Clara Huey is a 39-year-old divorced housewife with three children. She had had no experience with medicine that might create a bias. She did admit to Peter during voir dire that because of her feeling for Sheran R her "meter was tipping toward Sheran R," that there was indeed a bias. She then, however, responded to Mr. H's questions by stating she thought "she could get past that issue." Our team was somewhat concerned.

Juror – Carl Saline

Carl Saline was a 62-year-old maintenance foreman of Parks and Recreation for the City of Minneapolis who retired at age 48 after thirty years of service. He had a high school education. He has been married for forty-three years and has five children, the oldest of which is 42.

He was a favorite of our team after he said he had had good doctors and that "doctors are human too." He said he would have no preconceived feelings, that "I've got to hear it all," and "that's what a trial is for, who is right and who is wrong." When asked whether he could be a juror for both Dr. Ogsbury and Sheran R, he said, "Absolutely," and we felt he would be able to see through their witnesses. But expressing his responsibility of juror he said, "If the doctor was negligent, that was what we had to do. If you're negligent, I think she shouldn't have to go into the poorhouse because she came to you."

Juror – Vicky Petit

Vicky Petit is a 35-year-old unemployed high school graduate. She was married with no children but three stepchildren, ages 19, 22, and 25. She had worked for four and a half years in her father's appliance distribution business and, along with other members of her family, lost her job when her father sold the business. She was not angry with him as it "added fifteen years to her life." She reported she had had wisdom teeth removed and her mouth was still numb and said she now wished she had not had it done, but "could keep the promise to keep that out" of her thinking.

During voir dire she described herself as emotional and caring. We liked her for this, for her measured response to her unfortunate medical and job experiences, but particularly for her almost professional demeanor and speech that indicated she would be willing and able to listen to the complex issues.

Alternate Juror – Lloyd Quintana

Lloyd Quintana is a 34-year-old special security officer at Stapleton International Airport. He is married and has a 2-year-old child. During voir dire, he said he had no problem looking at causation, "not at all," but being a juror was "scary. Am I going to do the job right?" He also reported he once wrongly took the blame and "felt terrible." We found out to our surprise he had an Indian background. "My mother was an Indian. It goes back into my heritage. I noticed Mr. R wore Indian medicine on him. I felt sorry for him, but I couldn't. He is an Indian. I felt obligated to him. Being that he was an Indian, I had hard feelings for him because of what happened, but I wasn't going to let that interrupt what was going on here. We want to find out who's right and who's wrong."

Alternate Juror – Jody Garcia

Jody Garcia is a 21-year-old, single hairstylist. She admitted she might have a bias because of the condition of Sheran R, but, when asked, stated she thought she could get beyond her sympathy for Sheran R.

CHAPTER SIX

DAY 3
OPENING STATEMENTS

Editor's Note:
The opening statements have been included in their entirely.
Again, unspoken commentary from Jay is in brackets.

Peter
Wednesday, May 2, 1990, 4:00 a.m.

Riding into La Club in the black of night is one of the few peaceful times of the day. Listening to the Subdudes and feeling safe; enshrouded in the cold, dark night. There is still no anxiety and I allow my thoughts to wander to other things. But suddenly I am here in a booth in the restaurant; in my head hearing the whir of the machinery in my brain starting up as I am about to go live again—another fourteen to sixteen hours of reading, planning, preparing, plotting, thinking, debating, dueling both mentally and physically.

In a blink of an eye, the day will be done. On the way home, my energy will have been sucked out of my body, and I'll be thinking about a little rest or connection, so I'll have the strength to start all over again tomorrow. Always with that little burning knot in your gut that will never go away, never let you forget you are in a war.

The first day of jury selection was disappointing to the minions on the other side. They seem flat, disorganized, surprised that Jay didn't buckle and want to settle. I worked on the jury (or tried to in little ways): sports clothes with warm colors, body language, humor, compassion, listening and talking to them. Search for the link, to let them know I am a compassionate, likable man defending a super surgeon with the guts to take a stand.

Yesterday Mr. H fought back. He showed up in sports clothes instead of his power suit. Suddenly he was out from behind the podium, trying to humanize himself in response to the fact that I had shown far more compassion and empathy to Sheran's plight than he the day before. This jury is far less sophisticated and discerning—a Gerry Spence jury I dare say—than the one we had in the trial Spence threw. It is far more to the Plaintiffs' liking where, of necessity, I am forced to select a jury by the "buttercup" fashion ("love me, love me not"). I am trying to connect emotionally with these people, to let them know me well enough to like me. The process is simple—I'm looking for warm, feeling people who will ultimately end up liking Jay and me.

By the end of Day Two, the other side is more juiced up. Mr. H has tuned up his style a little and the jury seems a little more to their liking. Our jurors are a rather uninspiring bunch from outward appearances. There are three people, Mr. Saline, and Madams Holmes and Pettit, that I must bring this case home to. I am not overwhelmed by this jury but have to let it go and move on. Fears and doubts arise—will all this subtle and not too subtle psychological positioning work? (During jury selection, Jay and I sat alone in front of the table, right out in front of the jury for all to see). I'm spending lots of time with Jay and Kathy, giving them my strength, my conviction, boosting her emotionally in the hopes she will have energy for him in return. Once again, I have been sucked dry emotionally and wondering what shall I do to get it back again?

Jay
Wednesday, May 2, 1990

On awakening, I noted the weather was clear. I chose a gray-black sport coat with black pants, a pink shirt, and gray and pink tie, hoping to impress our opponents, and perhaps myself, with the appearance of strength and confidence. The drive in seemed better. During the ride, I came to realize that first, by law the captain does not have to go down with the ship, unless he is responsible for the sinking; and second, we will now have to point a finger at the others, but Mr. H would have pointed the same finger had there not been settlements made involving the other doctors and the hospital.

I arrived at the courthouse and Courtroom 9. Kathy arrived somewhat after me and promptly took the seat behind the Defense. Frick and Frack, plus a new tall blond girl, evidently a Spence paralegal, were forced to go to the Plaintiffs' side.

Mr. H walked in alone, away from the other attorneys on his team. His face was grim. Mr. H, Ms. Kudla, and Mr. Schuster were back in suits. Mr. Fitzgerald was, as usual, out of sync in a sport coat. Peter seemed anxious as well, talking less than usual. Obviously, today begins the serious business.

The Court was called into session and the jurors were brought in for their first day. Judge Peterson explained to the jury that opening statements would be made by the attorneys in the morning and that a recess would be had for the rest of the day to reschedule the witnesses. She turned to Mr. H, "Opening statements for the Plaintiffs?" Mr. H answered, "Thank you, Your Honor," came to the podium and began his case.

"Good morning. As Your Honor indicated, this is the part of the trial called opening statements, so what we say here is not evidence. The evidence has to come from the witness stand. You undoubtedly will hear two different versions of what we anticipate the case will show—if Mr. Pryor and I agreed on everything, we wouldn't be here. So, you are going to hear two advocates give their impression of what we think their evidence is going to show in this case. I am going to try and tell you what we think the case is all about. If, at the end of the case, the evidence conflicts with what I have said, then obviously you go with the evidence; you don't look back and say, 'Mr. H said that it was going to be this'—that's not the evidence. You go with your recollection of what you heard and what you understood from the exhibits and the witnesses." [He seemed to be starting out as Mr. Nice Guy.]

"This suit is about a tragedy to Sheran R who was a vibrant, active wife and mother of three who went into St. Anthony Hospital here in Denver in June 1986 in excellent health [omitting, of course, her CSF leak]. In September 1986, she came out of that hospital essentially comatose, unable to walk, unable to talk, paralyzed—in a more or less vegetative state, with extreme brain damage. That is a tragedy in itself.

"But the evidence will indicate that the real tragedy is that it shouldn't have happened—and wouldn't have happened if Dr. Ogsbury and Dr. Krauth had been careful, had been patient, had not involved themselves—at least Dr. Ogsbury involved himself—in a fashion of experimentation during the surgery. And, if Dr. Ogsbury had been up on the way this problem that she came in with should be treated, if he had been familiar with the methods of treatments available and the characteristics of the problem, it could have been, and should have been, avoided.

"It is a tragedy, the evidence will indicate, because her mind and body were devastated as a result of what took place during that hospitalization in June 1986. The testimony will be that her health cannot be given back to her; it is permanent. Her physical loss cannot be given back to her, and her mental loss. It is going to be with her the rest of her life and I believe that is undisputed.

"The evidence will be that Dr. Ogsbury and Dr. Krauth were negligent. They deviated from what are called standards of care and, because of that, the brain damage to Sheran R occurred. You will hear from nationally-recognized doctors who have no axe to grind, who have no interest in this case, who don't even know Dr. Ogsbury or Dr. Krauth, who reviewed the facts of this case and will come and sit on this witness stand and give their opinions about what occurred and whether the conduct, the treatment, was appropriate, and, equally important, what caused the brain damage to Sheran R. These doctors will testify that doctors—neurosurgeons included—are not in a position where they can do as they want in treating their patients without some restrictions.

"The first restriction is standards of care. There are standards of conduct in the medical profession—and particularly within various specialties, including neurosurgery—that if your conduct falls below what is considered acceptable under the circumstances, *that* is negligence. These doctors will sit here and tell you that's what happened in several instances in this case.

"Another restriction on the freedom of a doctor to do what he wants, as far as treatment of a patient, is that a patient is entitled to make that decision, the patient is entitled to be informed of all the necessary information to make an intelligent decision about what happens and what is done to the patient. It is the duty—as these doctors will indicate—of the treating physician to adequately inform the patient so that intelligent decisions can be made. That not only includes the risks involved of, say, doing surgery or not doing surgery, but it also includes what options are available to the patient and the risks associated with those—so the patient can make a decision, with counsel from the doctor about what is to be done to that patient.

"You will hear that the first rule taught to doctors is 'physician do no harm.' It's in the Hippocratic Oath—physician do no harm—first rule. That rule was disregarded in this particular case.

"You will hear from Dr. Frank Smith, a neurosurgeon currently practicing in Monterey, California. Dr. Smith is a distinguished neurosurgeon in this country. He is a former President of the Neurosurgical Society of America; he is a former President of the Neurosurgical Society in the State of New York; he is a former President of the Neurosurgical Society of the State of California.

"You will hear from Dr. Melvin Greer, a neurologist. Dr. Greer is currently Professor and Chief of the Department of Neurology of the University of Florida. He is also former President of the Academy of Neurology for this country—the National Academy of Neurology.

"You will hear from Dr. Barry Pressman, who is a neuroradiologist. Dr. Pressman is Chief of Radiology of Cedar-Sinai Hospital in Los Angeles, California.

"You will hear from all of these individuals who will be called by the Plaintiff. They will testify that Drs. Ogsbury and Krauth were negligent in this case, and all three of them will testify that the negligent conduct of Drs. Ogsbury and Krauth is what caused the brain damage.

"Why have I emphasized causation? A substantial portion of the Defense in this case is to point the finger at other people or other things as the cause of this brain damage. There were other physicians involved in the care and treatment of Sheran R. Part of the Defense in this case is to say they were negligent; they caused the damage. There was, has been, an allegation by the Defense, particularly after the case was filed, that she had a disease called meningitis and that is what caused the brain damage. So, there is going to be a lot of evidence about what caused the brain damage to this lady.

"You heard last night that Sheran R and Mr. R have settled claims with Dr. N in Wyoming, against Drs. D and M, who were physicians who treated Sheran R at St. Anthony after or during the time Dr. Ogsbury and Dr. Krauth were treating her, and also St. Anthony Hospital itself. And you heard the Court instruct you last night that you were not to allow the fact that there has been some type of settlement enter into your consideration, that you are to listen to all of the evidence, and at the end of the case, determine if there has been negligence. And you will be given the opportunity to apportion that negligence and then to determine the total dollar value loss that you feel Mr. and Mrs. R (Sheran R) have suffered, and then the Court will take whatever prior settlements have occurred and do that matter herself.

"As I said, you are going to hear from a number of doctors and there will be doctors, as I said, called by the Plaintiff; there will be doctors called by the Defense. One of the things that Her Honor read to you last night, also, was an instruction about credibility of witnesses. And that instruction indicated that you should look for potential bias, reason for testifying in a certain way. I believe that you will see that the doctors who are called to the witness stand by the Defense all have relationships with either Dr. Ogsbury, Dr. Krauth, or Mr. Pryor, and that should be taken into consideration in why they are sitting on the witness stand and saying the things they are saying, whereas the doctors I named to you, as I indicated, have absolutely no reason to testify one way or the other, except for their objective opinions in this case."

Mr. H paused, then began to discuss the case.

"On June 16, 1986, Sheran R went into a hospital in Lander, Wyoming, to have nasal surgery. It was called an ethmoidectomy." He showed a picture of the sinuses, ethmoid air cells and cribriform plate and continued, "This white part right here is called the cribriform plate that separates the sinus cavity from the cranium where the brain resides, and it is a very thin bony plate.

"What happened when Dr. N was doing this surgery was that, apparently, an instrument punctured through this cribriform plate. There is no evidence that it did any damage to the brain or anything like that. It just punctured a little hole through that… [I knew that was wrong because there was definite evidence of brain injury at the time of the first operation].

"Now around the brain, there circulates a substance called cerebrospinal fluid that is kind of a cushion for the brain—it is a watery substance that circulates around and through the brain, and it is in a little space called the subarachnoid space that, again, surrounds the brain. But, as a consequence of this little hole punctured through here, it was believed Sheran R had some leakage of this spinal fluid, and it was down into the sinus, down into her nose.

"Now the cribriform plate is really divided into left and right. The puncture here occurred on the right side. She was getting drainage or leakage into her nose on the right side—not on the left side. This is sometimes called rhinorrhea. Now, Dr. N, when he realized that this had occurred, ran a test, and that test was to see if there was any infection because when you get a cerebrospinal fluid leak, you get concerned with infection, and particularly the infection that you would be concerned with in the cerebrospinal fluid is meningitis.

"What is meningitis? Meningitis is just infection of the meninges, and the meninges are the lining of the brain. And so he did this test, and the test, basically, is that you get a sample of cerebrospinal fluid through a lumbar puncture. They take a needle, they go into the spinal canal, they draw out spinal fluid, and they send that to the laboratory. In the laboratory, they have tests: they look at it on a slide and they also put it into a Petri dish and culture it to see if any organisms grow. And, if organisms grow—bacteria grow—you have got an infection. And, if organisms don't grow, that is an indication, at least, that you don't have an infection. But there are also some other factors you look at—and you will hear about protein and glucose, but those are things that they look at to try and get a feel whether there is any infection.

"Well, the test came back in Wyoming that she didn't have any infection. It didn't grow any bacteria. It did show two white cells, but I think even the Defendants will admit that it didn't indicate infection, that it was just typically a postoperative kind of thing. Dr. N decided to transfer her to Denver to Dr. Ogsbury. He did not know Dr. Ogsbury but was given Dr. Ogsbury's name by someone else, and when she left Wyoming, it was undisputed that she was neurologically normal.

"When she got to St. Anthony Hospital, Dr. Ogsbury did a physical examination on her. And you will hear he found she was in excellent health and neurologically normal. She could walk, talk—everything was fine—alert, mentally right, brain not hurt, and no infection. There still wasn't any evidence of infection. Now, at discharge over here, in September, the picture was quite the opposite of what she came in on the 23rd.

"Now, this type of puncture that occurred with the cribriform plate, you will hear, is something that is foreseeable and that neurosurgeons like Dr. Ogsbury occasionally have to treat, and they treat punctures in this area not only after surgeries, but they treat punctures in this area after trauma, automobile accidents. You will hear that spinal fluid leaks in this area are very treatable. There is nothing about them that is unusual or that should create any special problems, and that they should be able to be taken care of without a problem.

"Within forty-eight hours of her arriving at St. Anthony Hospital on the 23rd, Dr. Ogsbury is operating on her—June 25, 1986, first craniotomy. He drilled holes in the skull, took a saw apparatus and cut a larger hole in the front of the skull, and went in with retractors, and pulled back the brain to find this little hole. Now important, he only worked on the right side—that is the side the hole was cut on.

"He found a little hole in that cribriform plate, and he took some muscle tissue and laid it over the top of it—didn't suture it down, just laid it on top, put the brain back, and sewed her up. Now, out of that procedure came documented brain damage to the area where he was working, and it was limited to the area where he was working, and the area was the frontal lobe. He had taken the frontal lobe on the right side, retracted it back and worked on the little hole in the cribriform plate underneath it.

"His patch that he laid down didn't hold, didn't stay there, because it wasn't anchored, it wasn't sutured in any way. The patch moved, and, as you will hear, the leak recurred, necessitating yet a second surgery which caused profound brain damage—much worse than the brain damage that just occurred to the right frontal lobe after the first surgery.

"I want to talk about first the decision to do the surgery on June 25, 1986. You are going to hear testimony that the majority of these kinds of leaks heal by themselves; in fact, the medical literature indicates as high as 85 percent of these, if you will leave them alone, will heal by themselves. You have to give them time. It is particularly true if it is a small leak, and this was a small leak.

"In fact, Dr. Ogsbury did what is called a cisternogram. They put dye in and then they look at it on an X-ray to find the hole where it is coming out. And that didn't depict any leak at all—it was that small of a hole.

"Dr. Ogsbury describes himself as an aggressive surgeon; he indicates that he was taught to be an aggressive surgeon. He didn't wait but went in and did this craniotomy surgery. And the evidence will indicate to you that he didn't adequately inform the Rs of the options available to them and the risks involved with these options. He did the most dangerous, extensive surgery possible for this type of problem; it is called a craniotomy. Now, there were other surgeries available to patch this hole that involved much less risk, did not even involve going inside the skull, did not involve touching the brain; they are called extracranial rather than intracranial.

"Dr. Ogsbury doesn't do these surgeries [which, of course, is not true as I along with other modern neurosurgeons routinely approach the nearby pituitary gland by an extracranial approach]. Some neurosurgeons do, ENT doctors do, but he doesn't. The evidence will be that he was aware of these surgeries, that he considered them very lightly and did not discuss them at all with the Rs.

"With the craniotomy, the risk is extreme because you are opening the skull, exposing it to infection. You are actually taking retractors and manipulating the brain, pulling it back; you are contacting blood vessels. The evidence will be that he did the craniotomy in a negligent manner in this case. He had never repaired a cribriform plate resulting from a surgical procedure of this nature. He didn't know how to do it; his partner, Dr. Krauth, who did know how to do it, was on vacation and was returning two days later on the 27th. Dr. Ogsbury didn't wait but went ahead and did the procedure on his own. He didn't take the time to read the literature on the procedure the way it should be done, not even from his own professor who had written on the very situation that we are talking about. He laid the muscle over the hole. The fluid inside the brain floats in that, allowing the little patch to move, and, as we learned later, that is what happened. There is no stitching down, contrary to what is recommended by his own professor in the article, and there is no attempt to plug the hole in the little thin bone.

"The proper procedure for taking care of this is to take some muscle and to go in and plug the hole firmly, push material down in the hole and plug it so it doesn't leak. What Dr. Ogsbury did was not plug the hole but to take this patch, put the patch down on it, but the stuff wouldn't go down and plug the hole, as obviously happened. This procedure that I told you about—firmly plugging the hole—Dr. Ogsbury didn't learn about until later. You will hear Dr. Ogsbury called it a new trick that Dr. Krauth told him about when they had to go in and operate on her the second time. The 'new trick' had been recorded in the medical literature for years.

"Instead of suturing, he did an experiment. He tried to use glue to hold the patch down—not just any glue, Super Glue, Crazy Glue—and Dr. Ogsbury will indicate that the Super Glue that we are talking about is the kind you may go and buy at Mini Mart. He may deny that he used Super Glue, but you will hear testimony from a nurse who was present that that is exactly what was used in this surgery.

"Why is that significant? First of all, it is not approved by the Food and Drug Administration. Dr. Krauth, Dr. Ogsbury's partner, will testify that it was illegal to use that type of glue in a procedure like this. Dr. N, the doctor in Wyoming, will testify that if he had had any idea that Dr. Ogsbury was going to use this kind of material and this procedure, he would have never sent his patient down here.

"And why is it illegal? It's a toxic substance to put in the brain tissue. It can cause all kinds of problems including infection. Now, the evidence will indicate that this is important because, after a lawsuit was filed, this meningitis has become a big issue. This glue has been associated, in the medical literature, with causing meningitis, and if there was meningitis, this is where it started—in this surgery, right here on June 25, 1986.

"Dr. Ogsbury got in with the glue and realized that it wouldn't stick, and so he tried to wipe it out, and he will admit he couldn't get it off. It stayed there; the experiment didn't work. Now, in addition to that, the retraction that I talk about, where he took the retractors and pulled the brain back, you are going to hear evidence that the retraction was clearly excessive, caused trauma to the frontal lobe on the right side of the brain, and that caused her brain damage in this surgery right here.

"The evidence will be that immediately after the surgery, there was evidence of edema—swelling, bruising, hemorrhage to her brain, right where this work had been done, no place else, right there—in what is called infarction of a portion of her brain—that infarction being right where he was working. Infarction means death—death of the brain; no evidence of swelling, edema, or anything else on the left side of the brain. This is important because the experts will indicate to you that if meningitis causes this, as opposed to surgical manipulation, with meningitis you expect what is called diffuse swelling of the brain. That isn't what occurred—it was only right here where the work had been done. In fact, the swelling on the right actually pushed the midline toward the left. So, there was no swelling on the left; there was swelling on the right.

"What happened was that *that* swelling on the right did damage or compress the nerve called the third cranial nerve. She started having symptoms with her right eye; the right pupil got larger than the left. She started having a problem where one eye started going closed—the right eye. So you have, following the first craniotomy, some decrease in neurological condition. It is not normal—it is below normal, there is some damage.

"Now enters Dr. Krauth and he comes back from vacation. He is more experienced with these types of surgeries, and they now realize there is trouble. And Dr. Krauth and Dr. Ogsbury decide to go in and operate again. One of the things that occurs, though, is that about in two days—the spinal fluid leak stops for about two days, and then it starts up again, but, again, instead of waiting to see if it will stop—they decide to go in and operate again. The testimony will be that the decision was negligent, where you already have an injured brain.

"They not only go back in and do another surgery, but they do a bigger surgery, a more aggressive surgery bilaterally. This time, both sides.

The evidence will be there was no reason to go in on the left side of this woman's brain. They knew the leak was on the right side—that is where it had been before. He had patched it, it had healed for about two days and then it had started leaking again. There is no evidence that there was a leak on the left side of her brain. Dr. Ogsbury, in his preop note, says he intends to go in and use the unapproved illegal glue in this surgery. So, they drill more holes in the left side, saw further across the skull, and they go in and they retract. They retract the left side all the way back to what is called the tuberculum sellae which is clear back here in the middle. The frontal lobe on the left side is retracted with those retractors back that far. Then they go over to the right side and retract that back and discover, sure enough, that is where their leak is occurring; the patch didn't hold. So, Dr. Krauth now advises Dr. Ogsbury the proper method of doing this, and they plug the hole this time, then again, go back over to the left side, retract the brain back—no hole, no leak—and just take a piece of muscle and put it there anyway and lay the brain back down on top of it and close her up.

"She never wakes up, essentially, from this surgery for months. She is awake obviously now, but she never woke up, essentially, from that surgery before she left that hospital. You will see CAT scans that will show the extensive damage that was done to the left side of the brain. The right side, you will see how that was further damaged. Now, both frontal lobes of her brain are severely damaged right where she was working. Now, infarction takes over both anterior cerebral arteries: both sides—left and right—in the frontal lobe. That portion of her brain dies. That portion of her brain has to do with control of the legs, has to do with judgement, higher cortical function, to some degree use of her arms and hands, all fitting perfectly with what she wound up with.

"After this surgery, she is intubated and put on a respirator. Her pupils get to a point where they won't react at all. They screw a bolt into her head to measure the intracranial pressure in her head because of the swelling that is taking place. She becomes unresponsive to painful stimuli—people trying to poke her with a pin or what have you. She loses her hand grasp totally and began to do what is called posturing where she becomes rigid, and her hands curl up and her legs go out straight in rigid positions.

"Now during this time she has IVs running, into her arms, for antibiotics. They have her on antibiotics just in case she has meningitis. But, back on 2nd July, right before the surgery, there is a nursing service called IV service where they do IVs in patients, and they are called to come down to the surgery and take care of the IVs on Sheran R. They get down there and they can't get a vein. They write a note to Dr. Ogsbury in the chart, 'Please consider a central line.' Central line is a mechanism where you can take a long needle, you go into the subclavian artery under the collar bone, and you run a tube into that. It's an extremely dangerous procedure to do. The reason that it is dangerous is that it is right by the lung. And surrounding that lung is the pleura. If you puncture the pleura the right lung collapses. It is called a pneumothorax.

"Well, on the night of July 3, about 10:30, Dr. Ogsbury is in the hospital, and the Nurse Caring for Sheran R actually chases him down the hall as he is leaving the hospital and says, 'Doctor, please give me permission to do the central line.' Dr. Ogsbury said—well, what he said depends on who you listen to. The nurse will say, 'Yes, okay, call the Critical Care Department. [I never would have said that.] Dr. Ogsbury said, 'Yes, you can do it but only if there is no other access.' [That is what I may have said but would have said to call me if you do.] And, Dr. Krauth will say that Dr. Ogsbury told him after all of his happened, 'I told the nurse, don't do it.' [That may be true as well.]

"The nurse told him, 'Doctor, the lab people were up to draw blood earlier and they couldn't get a vein,' and she told him her vein is about to blow. Dr. Ogsbury, if you believe him, said 'okay,' at 10:30 at night, 'go ahead' [no way I would have said that] and at 2:00 in the morning the Nurse Called and asked that a central line be put in because sure enough the vein collapses.

"Dr. D is a critical care physician. He comes in and tries a number of times, and he can't find the vein. So, he called a surgical resident by the name of Dr. M. Dr. M comes in and gets the needle into the vein. Dr. M orders an X-ray and reads the X-ray. There is no radiologist—Dr. M reads the X-ray and reads it wrong. And sure enough, there is a pneumothorax (collapsed lung), but he doesn't recognize it, and she lays there during the night with this one collapsed lung.

"About 8:00 the next morning, another doctor, Dr. Mason, comes in and recognizes what is going on, gets an X-ray, recognizes the pneumothorax and treats it and Sheran R is saved.

"Now, the Defense—one of their defenses is that this brain damage was caused by hypoxia, shortage of oxygen into the brain—and that this hypoxia comes from the pneumothorax. The testimony will be there was no hypoxia. You will see from the nursing notes there is absolutely no change from the second surgery—July 2—through the whole pneumothorax situation. [Ignoring the many ups and downs she had in the interim—I cannot believe how many episodes are turned around to try to make me look bad.]

"Meningitis—let me mention this because it is one of the defenses. Dr. Ogsbury and Dr. Krauth, both are now saying, 'Well, she had meningitis and that contributed to this.' During the time she was there they were doing these cultures and sensitivities and not once did she grow any bacteria. Some experts may say, 'Well, she was on antibiotics and that covers up culture growth and you won't see any growth because of antibiotics.' The experts will tell you also, though, that if the antibiotics are working that well that you can't grow one little bacteria because of them, there is no way that the meningitis that she supposedly had would be able to be strong enough, in light of that antibiotic, to be causing brain damage like occurred to Sheran R. The CAT scan evidence we will show you is not consistent with meningitis. If it was meningitis—if meningitis was present, assuming that—Dr. Ogsbury was negligent from the very beginning because before the first surgery, he called in an infectious disease doctor, Dr. Mason, and Dr. Mason said, 'I don't think there is meningitis, but you ought to do a culture.' It was never done. [I agree, he did find the one mistake. The test was supposed to be done by the radiologist at the time of the cisternogram to have information in case she later developed meningitis but was inexplicably not carried out—my responsibility, my fault.]

"The evidence will also be that if they suspected meningitis at all before they went in and did this bilateral craniotomy, they should have waited, treated the meningitis with antibiotics—it is a treatable disease—and then gone in and done the surgery. Surgery is contraindicated in the face of meningitis. [Usually but not always true.]

"Okay, she lay on this breathing machine for two weeks; they did a tracheostomy next. Dr. Ogsbury wanted to put in a shunt to relieve pressure. He called in a consultant, Dr. Fried. Dr. Fried said, 'Look the damage is done, there is no reason to take the risk and the chance of doing it. Don't do it.' Dr. Ogsbury wrote him a thank you note and within a few days later, there was a shunt inside her.

"Part of Sheran's brain today, and then, was clearly dead. She was unconscious. Her feet began to twist and turn. They had to call an orthopedic surgeon in who did surgery on both feet to try to cut and lengthen the tendons, because her feet and ankles were starting to contract. They sent her home almost three months to the day of admission, in September, sent her back to Wyoming, unresponsive, on her back, with casts on both of her legs.

"She stayed in Riverton for three months where she got therapy until December 1986. Then they sent her to Craig Hospital here in Denver. She was discharged from there in March 1987.

"She developed the ability to talk but her thinking process is still impaired. She has regained some of the use of her arms, but it is still limited. She has more hospitalizations to look forward to, or she did have.

"In August 1987 she returned to Craig; in September 1987 she went to Craig for another month. In 1988 she returned to Craig again for evaluation. She has future hospitalizations and treatment to look forward to, intensive therapy—physical therapy, speech, psychological. She also needs daily therapy at home. The therapy she is getting now is primarily maintenance therapy. She needs surgery on her legs. She needs surgery on her kidneys. She will need continued urologic care for the rest of her life.

"She has to have constant care with her all the time. She is totally dependent on others. She cannot control her bladder. She is up numerous times during the night where her husband has to get up and help her. She cannot control her bowels. She cannot clean herself after a bowel movement. She has to wear a diaper to bed at night. She cannot dress herself. She cannot do her personal hygiene. She cannot get her own glass of water. She cannot drive. She cannot get a driver's license.

"She cannot smell, because when they went in on the bilateral surgery, they necessarily cut the olfactory nerves. Intellectually she is dependent on others. She has impaired judgment, will do inappropriate things at various times. She has impaired ability to relate to others. She has impaired memory. She will never walk again. She has no feeling in her legs below her knees. She wears leg braces constantly.

"She has one leg that sticks out and one leg that curls under—she has named one of them 'bashful' and one of them 'ornery.' That is the situation she will be in the rest of her life. Before this happened, she was a healthy, active, vibrant woman. She loved the outdoors. She grew up on a ranch in Wyoming—Wheatland, Wyoming. She grew up riding horses. She loves to ride horses—or did love to ride horses—it is impossible now. She worked as a secretary in an elementary school in Wyoming. She will never be employed again. She was a devoted mother. She has been married to Mr. R for twenty-eight years. She is a grandmother having three daughters and can't today play with her grandchildren like she would like to and that bothers her very much.

"There are two Plaintiffs in this case. The other one is Mr. R, and his claim is called lost consortium. And basically, that is the impact on their marriage, on their relationship. There is no sexual relationship between Sheran and Mr. R. Sheran has an inability to relate emotionally. Her personality now is flat, where before it was very bubbly—fiery, she has been described. They can't share activities together anymore. She is in constant pain.

"You will hear Dr. David Rollins, a rehabilitation specialist, and he will describe for you her needs in the future—including they are going to have to have a different house.

"You will hear Dr. Jerome Sherman, an economist, who will calculate the economic loss, both past and future. Very quickly I am going to show you what his calculations are. Past medical bills: $475,650; $505,473: construction of the home to accommodate the needs of what she has; special accommodations would be $145,355; and the cost of future care is $4,288,789. The total of all of that is $5,415,267.

"Ladies and gentlemen, thank you very much. Let me be clear: we are not here for sympathy. You can only award this if you find negligence and if you find causation. We will prove negligence. We will prove the injuries that she has were caused by the brain surgeries, not by the pneumothorax, not by Dr. N, but by the actions of Dr. Ogsbury and Dr. Krauth.

"Thank you very much."

Mr. H sat down, Judge Peterson said, "Thank you Mr. H," and she called a brief recess. When Mr. H finished, I noticed several of the jurors crying. Indeed, there was hardly a dry eye in the courtroom, including mine. While Mr. H had subtly altered many of the medical facts, he had truly and accurately described the horror of her current and permanent situation. Little was said by our worried team during the break.

Peter remained in the courtroom alone with his thoughts and notes. Clear to all of us was the need to neutralize the obvious impact of Mr. H's opening.

After the jury was recalled, Peter solemnly took the podium.

Judge Peterson said, "Opening statements for the Defendants, Mr. Pryor?" and Peter calmly began.

"If it please the Court, Counsel, Mr. R and Sheran R. That was a pretty horrible description of what happened to—a good description of a horrible experience, let's put it that way." He walked toward Mr. H and his eyes and face changed to an expression of anger.

"I need to bring you back to the facts of the case. Her Honor told you, and Mr. H mentioned during his opening statements, that he expected the Defendants, Drs. Ogsbury and Krauth, to change their position, and that they had changed their position as to what went on at St. Anthony Hospital and what had caused this tragedy.

"I am going to tell you right now, in terms of this evidence in this case, of what it will show in finger pointing, that the evidence will show that in the Wyoming lawsuit where only Dr. N was the Defendant, that the fingers were pointed straight from this table and these Plaintiffs and these very same sets of attorneys, who, through some of the same experts who will appear in this case, we will show you, pointed the finger and attempted to lay entire responsibility in Dr. N's case on this outcome.

"The evidence will show that as to the settlement and payment of monies by Drs. D and M and the hospital, that, until recently, the fingers were pointed by this attorney and his compatriots and Plaintiffs in this very lawsuit, by some of the same experts who were called and endorsed and who will come as experts against my clients. The evidence will show you, and we will show you, that in attempting to prove the negligence, what you will come to conclude was probably gross negligence, that we took a position and take a position no different than the Plaintiffs did in the Wyoming lawsuit, until the settlement for money of that claim. And that in attempting to prove—which is my responsibility and obligation—under the evidence we will show you, using some of the very same experts that the Plaintiffs used in both cases, that we are pointing fingers where because of a settlement and payment of money, and the absence of these parties from this case, is now convenient for Plaintiffs to point the finger solely at Dr. Ogsbury." [Peter was obviously already effectively working off Mr. H.]

Peter paused, his face softened, and he continued. "Now, let's go back. Once upon a time, a long time ago, in 1986, there was a very nice lady who lived in Lander, Wyoming—married, good person, generally good health, children, job. She had some allergies; she had rhinorrhea.

"Rhinorrhea is a runny nose; she had some congestion in her lungs. And she fell under the care and spell, medically, as you will hear from the evidence, of a small-time specialist named Dr. N. And under that spell her brain was punctured by a surgical instrument in connection with a surgery that was absolutely unnecessary. When Dr. N four days later finally figured that she had a CSF leak or leakage of this brain—cerebrospinal fluid—into the nose and it is a potentially deadly, lethal complication, he sent her to Dr. Ogsbury.

"And Dr. Ogsbury accepted a lady in distress, with this hole into her brain, who with every breath she took, in terms of bacteria getting into her brain, was at risk for a potentially deadly disease called meningitis.

"And Dr. Ogsbury rode forth and did everything he could to repair the damage done by somebody else in another state for an unnecessary procedure. And just when it looked like he was saving this woman in distress, another doctor—for whom he was not responsible, as you will hear from the evidence, two other doctors poked a hole in her lungs—her right lung totally changed and destroyed the breathing pattern in terms of getting oxygen to her brain.

"And as a combination of the meningitis that this doctor didn't cause but he couldn't arrest and the pneumothorax, and peripherally some controlled insult to her brain—which had to be done in his efforts to prevent what the Wyoming doctor had done—Sheran R became a victim.

"Now, strong words. Let's see if we can trace chronologically what happened in this case.

"Now, our tale takes us back to May. Dr. N saw Sheran R the first time on May 7. Dr. N performed an exam. He looked into the nose, and what he saw there was two things. Now, the sinuses, you will hear, are kind of an air purification system in the body. Every time you breathe in, we bring in minute particles, bacteria, dust, things of that nature. The sinuses are part of that filtration system where they have a mucosal lining, and the particles are caught within the nose. Now, what did he see? He saw a thickening of some of the bony ridges inside of the nose. He saw some thickening—mucosal thickening of that lining—this lining that lines the sinuses on the turbinates. And he also saw something called a polyp. A polyp is just a little piece of tissue, and that was pretty much all he saw.

"Now that's pretty much the first visit and he writes on the bottom of his notes, 'CT scans, X-rays.' And what he wanted, at this point, is to get some special computerized serial cuts—this is the first X-ray. This is an X-ray he ordered about two weeks later. You will see over here, these kind of black, kind of look like liberty bells, in the right-hand picture. These are the maxillary sinuses, you see the gray cloudiness. That is evidence—and nobody disputes that—that we have maxillary sinus, mild chronic maxillary sinus mucosal thickening. That is, the lining has thickened up.

"Now you see we are going a little higher to the cribriform area of the ethmoid sinuses. And you will see, and the experts will tell you, there isn't any evidence of disease in this area. Another study is taken on June 15 which is a specialized surgical study. Again, 'no ethmoid involvement.' [I looked at the jury. Mrs. Pettit and Mr. Saline do not appear to be impressed at all.]

"Okay, about eight or nine days go by, and he calls her on the phone and recommends surgery. Now he recommends four-part surgery, not just a single procedure.

"What he wants to do is go in and curet out the polyps. And nobody is critical of that. I mean, that was an appropriate decision. He also, because of this—the bony turbinate swelling and overgrowth—he wants to resect part of that just to allow ventilation into her interior nose.

"Now, the operation—the operation that we are concerned about is the—something known as an ethmoidectomy. An ectomy means remove. So, every time we hear the word ectomy we are cutting something out or off. He wants to stick an instrument up here—which is a quasi-blind procedure. You can't see what you are doing; you go in part by limited vision. He wants to snip away these little structures to provide additional air and ventilation. Now the risk of this operation is that the top of the ethmoid bone, or cribriform plate, is the bottom of the brain, but it will be called 'paper sack thin.' It's like a honeycomb.

"Three things are a problem here. Number one, the bone is paper thin; number two, the dural lining is plastered down on top of the cribriform plate like glue. If anything happens to the cribriform plate, that's potentially a problem for the dura. And, for some reason, in this particular area, the dura is thinner—it is not as thick and tough as it is in the rest of the brain, so we have a particularly vulnerable spot right here.

"Now the risk then is when you are doing this operation, you can punch a surgical instrument through the cribriform plate right through the dura. What happens then is this fluid starts to run down into the nose and the back of the throat. Now that doesn't sound very scary, and the running down—that will cause headaches and problems. That is not, as you will hear, the scary part. What happens, if there is an opening between the subarachnoid fluid, every time you breathe in a breath, bacterial contaminants have the potential of going back into the brain and affecting these meninges, thus, the name meningitis. And many times, you can give people—you can give them numerous antibiotics—enough to float them away on a ship—and unless you can get that leak closed, they just keep recontaminating and reinfecting. And if it gets ahold of a human body, first you have a runny nose and you get headaches and get a fever, and then you get convulsions, and your blood vessels go into spasms. If it gets bad enough and it is uncontrolled, you go into a coma and people die. Somewhere—depending on the literature you read—ten percent to twenty-five percent of people who suffer this type of problem develop meningitis. So, the moment he poked a hole into the brain there was between a one and ten and perhaps twenty-five percent chance that she would develop meningitis.

"So, Sheran R finds herself in the hospital on June 15, 1986. The surgery is a four-part process. He goes ahead and does all four parts of the surgery. Then he is doing the ethmoidectomy—and now he is up here with an instrument in a blind or semi-blind procedure—up around this danger area. He is way back up in the back of her nose, near the brain, with these kind of Pac-Man-like forceps biting away at this honeycomb. And all of a sudden there is some bleeding. You will hear again that unilateral—one-sided—bleeding on something like this is a classic red flag for this type of injury.

"So, what happens then is on the 16th and the 19th she has some terrible headaches—frontal headaches—classic warning sign of the cerebrospinal fluid leak. She is throwing up and vomiting. Finally, on June 19, in comes his partner and says, 'I think she has a cerebrospinal fluid leak' and he is right.

"So, we have the surgery now on June 16. Okay, so 16, 17, 18, 19 and 20—now we are five and then six days out, and she is still having headaches, and she is still having leakage.

"So a neurologist and Dr. N get together on June 22 and they talk to the family about repairing from the outside—which we have been criticized for not doing—or repairing intracranially, where you go in and open the skull and repair from the inside. That is, an intracranial versus intranasal or outside repair. Dr. N is going to tell you, 'I recommended as the most optimum treatment, that we do this inside now. The testimony is going to be that when you do an intranasal repair, you are going up through the nose and put a patch. Now, the explanation you will hear is that some people prefer to do it this way because you don't have to deal with the brain, that is, you don't have to go in and operate around the brain or retract the brain—which has risks that are different from the other operation. But the problem is, if you go and do it from the outside, it is like you went out with a radial tire with no tube inside and got a flat tire and you would get your kit and slap your patch on the outside of the tire. All the pressure of the tire is forcing the patch away. You can't suture in this area because this is so delicate, the dura. So, what happens—you will hear from numerous people—that while the intranasal approach works sometimes, as many as fifty percent of them fail good doctor, good surgeon, excellent technique. It is the limitation of the human beings in this condition. Up to half of them don't work because you are patching from the outside.

"Now, on the brain-injured side, in the intracranial, there is still a twenty to thirty percent chance that a patch will fail. So, for every ten that we do—superior neurosurgeon, superior technique, ideal conditions—statistically there is a two to three chance out of ten that it won't take.

"The other thing is that if you come in intracranially, you can see what has happened. You can see the dura. You can see the size of the hole. You can see what is going on—you can see if there is bleeding or anything else that needs to be corrected.

"Now, the disadvantage is that, while you get a higher percentage rate of success, and you can determine the other structures and abnormality of what is going on, there is a slightly enhanced risk of injury to the brain, classic area of decision, medical decision making.

"Now, if you patch from the inside, as you will hear from the doctor, if she is lying on her back, the brain is gently folded and retracted back, and so we can see this. Once it is patched and she is repositioned, the brain, the brain falls and lies back down over the patch. So, number one, Dr. N recommends that this be done intracranially.

"I want to show you something else, too, before I leave Wyoming completely. This is another CAT scan. Do you see these little black spots in various places in these four studies? Air, on X-ray, typically shows up as black.

And what we have, as early as June 20, is evidence of air. And that is nowhere to be seen on the films before surgery. There is only one place air can come and that is up through—and she is breathing up through—this hole up into her brain, and that air is contaminated. And while not every breath you take infects you, every breath that you take and gets into your brain, in terms of air pockets, creates a potential of meningitis infection.

"Now, the next film, this is a study done at St. Anthony on June 24, 1986. Dr. Ogsbury sees her as soon as she gets here. She has cerebrospinal fluid leaking out of her nose. And it doesn't drain like water out of a faucet: it is drops rather than a flush. So, she has got CSF draining out of her right nose.

"Now, right away, Dr. Ogsbury is concerned because if we start counting days—we are June 16 now, we have the 16th, 17th, 18th, 19th, 20th, 21st, 22nd, 23rd—we are eight days post-op and it is still leaking CSF.

"Now, he brings in a fine, fine infectious disease expert by the name of Marilyn [actually Susan] Mason. We are going to bring Dr. Mason in here and let you hear her opinions and her testimony about her involvement and care. She sees Sheran R on the 24th—and right there she does not think she has meningitis, she says it right in her consult note. But she says, 'I think she is at horrible risk for meningitis,' and you can see right here in her note that she anticipates that Dr. Ogsbury is going to repair this leak, because of the risk of meningitis.

"Now, Dr. Ogsbury takes his X-ray and the significance of this X-ray. Now you see two new black spots on the right side of the film. This is new air. This is not the air that was here—that air has long since been absorbed. This isn't left over from air on June 20. This is other air that she has breathed into her brain in the interval period between June 20 and 24.

"Now, there is a new player and you are going to meet this man too, Dr. James Barron. Dr. Barron is an ENT doctor; he is like Dr. N—an otolaryngologist. So, now Dr. Ogsbury is reaching out within his hospital to involve the very best people. And he had a neuroradiologist, Dr. Siegel, who says, 'we have got pneumocephalus'—air in the brain—'and though I can't see a frank leak, she has got a rent in her brain and she is getting air into the brain from outside.' Now, Dr. Barron can do the approach that Plaintiffs' nationally recognized experts claim Dr. Ogsbury was negligent in considering. They talk it over, and because it involves a fracture of this cribriform plate, and because it is now nine days and it hasn't sealed off, and because with every passing day and every breath that Sheran R takes there is risk of meningitis, Dr. Ogsbury feels that surgical closure is indicated.

"Now, as to the decision to repair at that point, the textbooks will show that you must close surgically a cribriform injury of this type. The literature will tell you, in an article since this case, that if you go beyond seven days, that you close because it isn't going to close, and it doesn't even close when they try to patch it, and yet a big criticism is that we didn't close it. Three of the neurosurgeons—and leading neurosurgeons, in this case—will tell you that it was an appropriate decision.

"There will be overwhelming evidence from ENTs, from neurosurgeons, from Dr. Ogsbury, and from medical literature that applies to his practice and sets guidelines for this practice, that his decisions made with respect to salvage of this woman were appropriate and within the standard of care.

"Did he do a negligent job at surgery? We will show you this Super Glue issue is a giant red herring. Dr. Ogsbury thought about using Super Glue. Dr. Ogsbury talked to Mr. R about using Super Glue before the first operation. Dr. Ogsbury wrote in the chart that he was thinking about using Super Glue. And the reason he was thinking about that is, because knowing that twenty to thirty percent of these patches won't hold even if you do your darndest, he was looking for some type of an adhesive that might work. You are going to hear that it ain't experimental and you are going to hear that lots of things doctors do in medicine aren't FDA approved. And that is the way medicine moves forward. And you are going to hear that some of the doctors in this case use Super Glue. You are going to hear from not one person in this case that Super Glue had anything to do with the patient's outcome. Not one of the experts in this case is going to say that this anterior cerebral artery infarction or clogging off was caused by the alleged—and Dr. Ogsbury will tell you he didn't use it—use of Super Glue.

"One nurse, and you can judge her credibility and her ability to recall under the circumstances in which she recalled, will talk about Super Glue and that's it. Super Glue, as you will hear, had nothing to do with the outcome of this case.

"Now, patching. You will hear that Dr. Ogsbury followed the textbook system of patching in this repair. He gave her—preoperatively—a drug called Mannitol. Mannitol is a drug that draws fluid out of the brain and then causes the brain to become smaller and relax. Now, when she lays back on her head, then the brain tends to be slack or loose and tends to fall back. You will see the description that the brain was slack at the time of surgery.

"Now we have the patient on her back. Now on the issue of retraction, you draw your own conclusions as to whether there was even retraction with an instrument. But, in order to operate on the brain, sometimes you have to use an instrument. Then you use cotton wipes or something to place between the brain and the structure. And you very gently move that back—now we are working on this side. All that is happening at this point is that we are exposing the leak area.

"Now, what does Dr. Ogsbury see? Dr. Ogsbury sees a couple of things. He sees a 4- to 5-millimeter hole. It is not very big in terms of our lives, but it is huge in terms of damage of this type. He sees a round hole to suggest to him that an instrument has come through the hole, and he also sees some matting of blood. It is like if you cut something with a large instrument, you will see blood around that area of the instrument, or any kind of blow—there. He sees what is called subpial—or just under the pia, which is the innermost lining of the brain—some blood, all of which suggests to him that he has an instrument puncture.

"Now, Dr. Barron is assisting him. This is microscopic. It is fascinating stuff—microscopic surgery. She is draped except for a hole this big, and they have got a microscope. Now, they are in there and Dr. Barron, who can do the operation the other way but feels this is the way to do it, Dr. Ogsbury wants him there because, if this doesn't take for some reason, and they decide to come from a different direction, he wants Dr. Barron to know what the anatomy is inside the brain. I mean, that is how cautious and careful he is being at this point.

"Now, they lay a little surgical material called Marsolex [actually, Surgicel] and then they take a piece of fascia—which is the tough fibrous lining next to the muscle—and some muscle. I think they take it right up from the temple area. And, they take a substance known as Gelfoam. Now, you can't sew in this area because there is a hole. There is nothing to sew, number one, and number two, this dura is so thin and so delicate that if you try to sew you will tear it. So, he does classically what he learned during his training.

"And we will show you the literature and training that he followed. You pack this little muscle on top of the Marsolex, down into the hole. If you pack too hard you poke it right through. It is like tissue paper. So, if he just stomps it in with his foot or sticks his finger down there, he has a great big hole. So, he is making a surgical assessment of how to pack. He lays this down at this point, working only on the right side.

"And then the retraction. Now, you will hear that there is no meter to tell you how much retraction is too much retraction. I mean you just do it by sophisticated touch and feel. And in this case, it was not too much, and the brain is laid back, the patient closed, and the procedure is ended.

"You are going to hear from just excellent, superb people that this care was appropriate. While there was some insult to the brain—whenever you touch a structure like the brain there is some bruising—but it is called controlled injury or insult. And that is exactly what happened here, and it didn't have a darn thing to do with what happened to Sheran R and that is why we are here.

"Now, it doesn't work. Sheran R is one of those twenty to thirty percent of patients—and the very next day, on June 26, she is leaking. Now, even before this was done—he had this huge conversation with Mr. R and Sheran R and talked about all the things that could go bad, including brain injury and damage, and memory impairment and options and everything like that. He writes it right out in his own handwriting in the chart. He has Mr. R and Sheran R sign it acknowledging that he has taken them through this. He is extraordinarily careful and thorough about informing his patients about surgical risks and options.

"Now, when the leak starts again, he is distressed. His job had been to repair this leak. So, he says, 'Well, I've got three options—one of them is that I can go back in and repair with Super Glue; one of them was to drain off the cerebrospinal fluid to relieve the pressure to see if that would allow this to heal; and the third option was, let's just reposition in bed, Sheran R, to minimize this amount of pressure to see if this will help facilitate this healing without having to go back in again.

"Now, she becomes progressively sicker. By June 28 she has meningitis. Now, I want to jump forward a little bit. And I hope, if I don't address every single point that Mr. H raised in terms of what our evidence will show that you will understand, we wouldn't be here if we agreed.

"Okay, she is a pretty sick lady by June 28. They put her in the intensive care unit. She has a white blood count which measures the number of white blood cells. Those are the cells that the body produces to fight infection. This is consistent with meningitis. Now, Dr. Mason is following this patient. Dr. Ogsbury is following the patient, and Dr. Barron is involved in the care of this patient. He goes out and involves another neurosurgeon. He is not a partner, just another neurosurgeon practicing out of the hospital. He says, 'I think she has meningitis. I think we should hold off a little on surgery and wait and see.' So, Dr. Ogsbury talks this over with the family. Every decision he made is cleared through the family, *every* treatment decision that he made. So, they reposition her and she starts to do a little better and they bring her out of the intensive care unit. And Dr. Mason comes in on June 29 and Dr. Mason evaluates her and notes in her record that her lab and her findings are 'consistent with meningitis'—which to an internal medicine specialist is the diagnosis of meningitis. And Dr. Mason will be here to tell you that she believed this patient had meningitis as early as June 28, 1986. I will tell you right now there is lab evidence confirming the presence of—laboratory documentation of—meningitis. The reason she didn't grow out in the culture disk is she was so loaded up with antibiotics that it wouldn't grow out; but every temperature, her white count, her neurologic course, her sinking condition—this woman is now in a struggle and getting sicker.

"This man is now confronted with a decision: do I operate and stop this recontamination, recontamination and recontamination?—because every time she breathes in, even if she has got it, she is recontaminated. He is bringing in the best people he can think of to help him and advise him, talking over all of his options with the family. And now, critical, there is this huge thing about operating on the left side in the second operation. Dr. Mason comes in and she mentions for the first time, a history of severe left-sided headaches and left-sided pain, periorbital—on the left side of her head pain. The nursing notes during the same period of time document repeated complaints of left-sided headaches, something new.

There is a note of left-sided drainage of CSF through the nose. And Dr. Barron comes in on June 30 and he notes 'severe left-sided headache, will discuss with Dr. Ogsbury.'

"So, on July 1, Sheran R is critically sick and Dr. Ogsbury is in a classic, surgical dilemma. Do you operate in the face of meningitis—which is something that no doctor desires to do, but if you don't, do you just let her die? So, he discusses the options with the family, and he explains all of the options, including the thought that they may have to use Super Glue, because he thinks this is the last time he is going to be in there because she is so terribly ill. He knows each time he does a surgery there is an issue of insult to the brain.

"There is a film you will see that is important—July 1, which is the date which he is discussing options with the family. A couple of things. There is the air again. See the air? It is gone on June 27. Now we have air on the left side. Now we have got the possibility of, even though all indications are that we are dealing with a single leak, there is air on the left side of the brain.

"So, Dr. Krauth is consulted, and he sees Sheran R. Dr. Krauth will tell you that his practice in training is always to examine both sides even if there is no evidence of a leak on the other side. We have left-sided headaches, left-sided drainage, left-sided air. And he will tell you he examines both sides because he has had patients with holes on both sides following an ethmoidectomy.

"You will hear Dr. Ogsbury is not inexperienced in dealing with this kind of problem because you don't have to repair this kind of surgically-induced injury. Smith has not had one in fifty years. I mean, this isn't something you get every day. He is not inexperienced; luckily no one has a great amount of experience.

"This operation was appropriately performed and, because I don't want to carry you into the lunch hour, I want to talk for a second about the pneumothorax. I will just tell you that, again, with respect to the surgery and the surgery decisions, the very limited role of Dr. Krauth, who said, 'I recommend we go both sides,' and Dr. Barron came in right after Dr. Krauth has written his recommendation and the ENT doctor said, 'I concur.'

"Now, she did get better for a while, not terribly better but she did she wake up some after the surgery and started to improve. No nurse ever came running down the hall to Dr. Ogsbury asking him, 'can we put in a central line?'

"On the morning of July 4, about 4:30 a.m., Dr. Ogsbury got a call from the nurse, and she said that the patient was lightening and seemed to be doing better. What she didn't tell him was what had happened two hours before. Now, this line, which was for antibiotics, is designed to allow the patient to get medication. It is not in an artery, it is in a vein, and Mr. H did a pretty good job of describing how they put a great big needle into it—or tried to.

"Now, you will hear that Dr. D, who is a young critical care doctor, made with this huge, great needle—and it is right next to the lung—poked her five to six different times all around in a little area like this, trying to get the needle in and he couldn't get it in. So, he called Dr. M—Dr. M makes the pass on the very first attempt."

Peter then put up two X-rays of the chest and continued.

"Now here is a study from July 4, 1986, and here is a study from July 3, 1986. This is a picture of the lung. Now, this is a study that is taken at about 8:00 in the morning and this is a study that was taken at 3:00 in the morning."

At this point Judge Peterson turned to Peter and said, "Mr. Pryor, we are running out of time." Mr. Pryor asked, "Can I just finish this one point?" The Court agreed and Peter resumed.

"Now, you can see from this study, this is all filled up with air. It has pushed the diaphragm down toward the abdomen and pushed the heart closer over to the other side, and Dr. M missed the pneumothorax, and he will tell you that neither he nor the doctors, they didn't call Dr. Ogsbury—Dr. Ogsbury wouldn't have allowed this to happen, didn't know it happened, wasn't involved in it.

"And what happened was, for the next five hours, she has now got one lung. Her autoregulatory system—which normally makes sure if you have got inadequate oxygen, inadequate blood, that the first place that the blood and oxygen go to is the brain—is now shut down because she is so sick. So, two, three, four, five, six blood pressure drops. By 6:00 in the morning, her blood pressure is 60/0. She has no resting blood pressure. Her pulse is so weak that they can't even find it at the wrist—they have to go down here and find it in the femoral pulse. We will see a record by 6:30 or so in the morning, they couldn't find a pulse. Nobody called anybody for help. She is found by accident by Dr. Mason, and they save her life.

"And, the pneumothorax tipped the scale, in terms of all of these other things that are happening and had been going on to cause this devastation and injury.

"Dr. Ogsbury is a hero. Dr. Ogsbury was supposed to save this woman's life and he did. Dr. Ogsbury's care was above the standard of care. And when this is all done, I will ask that there not be any more victims."

Peter sat down and Judge Peterson called a recess until the following morning.

When opening statements were completed, I was exhausted. It was wearing to hear a whole morning of criticism of my care. Mr. H was organized and well prepared, his understated style perfect for his dramatic material. But for me, his ordered presentation of first generalities and then specifics became more tolerable as he proceeded because I could see, with each issue, the fallacy or untruth involved. But seeing several jurors crying following his accurate description of her condition was very difficult to take. Peter's opening was actually harder on me than Mr. H's. I was uneasy with his talking about the other physicians. He really hit hard on Dr. N, and I noted that the jury seemed closed during this time, particularly Mr. Saline. I felt better when, at the end, Peter talked about my care and the jury finally seemed to listen. He did give a few specifics and in essence he said, "Here are a few answers; we will have the others as well." All in all, I felt that we were okay, that Peter had reasonably neutralized Mr. H's obvious advantage at the time of his opening.

The afternoon was spent back in the war room of PC&J helping Peter prepare for his cross-examination of Dr. Frank Smith, the Plaintiffs' single neurosurgical witness. Once again, we were struck by Dr. Smith's angry attitude toward me and by his myriad of criticisms. However, we felt confident that we could demonstrate his limited recent experience in the treatment of cerebrospinal fluid leaks and in neurosurgical practice. Comforting to me was his apparent lack of understanding of the case, despite his claimed twenty-five to thirty hours of preparation for his deposition. We remain guardedly optimistic.

Fran
Wednesday, May, 2, 9:00 p.m.

Opening statements. Mr. H did a good job. The jurors were shocked and in pain. They appear to be emotional, but they basically aren't. They were given permission to express their feelings by Peter in voir dire. Judge Peterson adds to the safety to express your feelings in her courtroom. They are alive, thinking, feeling human beings, open to listening and taking it all in. If they hadn't responded this way, I would have been disturbed. There were no toe-tagged jurors here.

Peter saw the distress on Jay's and Kathy's faces in response to Mr. H's brutal opening. He kept the levity saying something like, "Gee, Jay, if you're really that bad, I'm signing off this case." Some of the jurors overhead his comment and giggled. If Peter was faltering, he wasn't going to let anyone know it. He knows the power in healing humor.

Jay was a mix of feelings. It was hard to fight back the self-doubts. He struggled with it but managed to work it through and come back with conviction. Mr. H's opening statement landed a blow that was needed. Peter's adrenals kicked in, unleashing the passion sepulchered in his surgically wounded body. Unknown to Mr. H, his opening statement gave Peter the pin-hole passage he needed to volley back and neutralize the damage Mr. H had done.

CHAPTER SEVEN

DAY 4
THE DIRECT EXAMINATION
OF FRANK P. SMITH

Editor's Note: The testimony of witnesses in this case has been edited for length and clarity. The main points of their testimony are included with commentary from Jay in brackets.

Peter
Thursday, May 3, 1990, 4:00 a.m.

Riding in to work with a million thoughts jumbling through my mind. Usually, in the dark of the van, with just the sound of music and no one else about, there are a few moments of serenity, a time of quiet and isolation. Away from the anxiety and the need to think, think, think, talk, argue, plan, and strategize. This crazy process of emotional, psychological, physical, and intellectual warfare we call trial by jury. As the first week draws on and I begin to feel the physical drain, my feelings and emotions surface and become raw. So many thoughts, feelings; so much to do and think and worry and fret about. The last blood sport—only you can't see the bleeding. It's only internal; the wounds are to your psyche and emotional state. And just like the warrior, the boxer, the gladiator, when wounded or hurt, I cannot show or give in to my fear lest the battle be lost. There is the legitimate stage and the legal stage. We are, above all, actors in the arena of legal truth. Rarely does our legal system reach metaphysical truth, if such an absolute exists. Instead, we legitimately and necessarily manipulate, seduce, and condition jurors with our words, our bodies, and our expressions in any and every way possible, to convince them to see the case as we perceive it to be. Our, my, view of this woman's tragic plight first becomes my legal truth and ultimately, if everything falls into place, the jury's legal truth as well.

The other side came roaring back yesterday. They seemed to have gotten back their momentum, buoyed, no doubt, by their perception that our jury is not particularly sophisticated in this complicated case, a "feeling" jury that may not be able to separate itself from this poor woman's devastation.

Mr. H is good—nice looking, articulate, well prepared and convincing, a technically skilled artist whose single weakness may be his inability to connect with the jurors emotionally. That's possibly our hole card. Have we ended up with a bunch of "shit happens" people who are warm and caring but who will ultimately connect and hopefully care about Jay and me? Mr. H's opening was powerful, especially his almost droning (beautifully understated) description of the myriad of changes Sheran has gone through and the countless ways the stroke has changed her life. The jurors were moved—almost every one of them had hands to mouth. I heard later that several had cried in the hall. When we were all done for the day, my stomach was rolling and I felt bad, first because I thought I had not done a good job, then because I remembered that this is a war. With devastation so great, can a jury walk away from it without allocating Jay some responsibility, without telling this innocent woman that she didn't need to go through this ordeal we call trial for nothing? Can I through words, and letting these people know me and Jay and the righteousness of his care, bracketed within grossly incompetent care, overcome the siren's call of Sheran's injuries? Or, will we see yet another victim?

Jay
Thursday, May 3, 1990

Day four began with a fight with Kathy over some trivial matter. My words to her, "This is not a social event," were probably as inappropriate for her as they were for me—her anger over the apparent unfairness of it all has always been, if anything, greater than mine, and my words probably hurt deeply. The reflections of Author Sarah Charles (another doctor who wrote of her experience in trial) about the destructive nature of a trial certainly are proving true.

We arrived at the court and waited. Motions in another case involving the removal of an attorney from that case were argued for over an hour. Peter asked how I was doing. I said okay. Kathy disagreed.

After the court was called back into session, Mr. H asked if he could move a chair. Judge Peterson allowed him to move it only to the other side of the table. He then said that he had made a small reference to the settlement issue, but that Mr. Pryor had talked about it substantially. He said, "I am trying to get some direction from the Court on that issue." Peter then asked that the witness be sequestered from the courtroom. He explained that Dr. Smith had reviewed the care of Dr. N and had testified in deposition that Dr. N had "set the whole thing in motion" and "that the pneumothorax may well have aggravated the brain insult and injury which was present at that point." He said if Dr. Smith "changes his positions, adds to his opinions, modifies his opinions in any way, shape, or form, his knowledge of the settlement would be relevant on the issue of bias and credibility, and is relevant to the issue of impeachment." Judge Peterson ruled, "Let's not bring it up until we have any reason to do so." To some extent I agree with Mr. Pryor that if there is a change of opinion or inconsistency of focus, that that may be relevant for impeachment.

The jury was brought in carrying notebooks. Mr. H went out and brought in Dr. Frank Pie Smith, their initial witness. He is a tall, slender man with an apparent grandfatherly appearance. I am worried that a jury might be antagonized by a hard-hitting approach by the Defense. Dr. Smith was given the oath and Mr. H embarked on his identification.

"Name?"

"Frank P. Smith, MD."

"Current practice?"

"I closed my office on September 1, 1989."

"Specialty field?"

"Neurological surgery."

Mr. H went through his training from college through medical school, military service, completion of training, initial career in California, and then his move to the University of Rochester which "recruited me." He stayed there for thirty-eight years of which he was Chairman for twenty years. He recounted his extensive experience as Chief of Service performing three to five cases per day, three days per week. When asked what type of cases were involved, he reported that he did the first shunts for hydrocephalis; he was involved in head trauma, frequently getting up at night to go to the Emergency Room [not my experience with professors]; he also performed operations for the relief of pain. Mr. H asked if he had managed patients such as Sheran R. He answered, "Oh yes," and then described his experiences with CSF leaks. He described the mechanism in automobile accidents [not differentiating those caused by surgical instruments from those caused by auto accidents] and noted that seventy-five percent clear with a few days [I agree] and the rest certainly "within ten to fourteen days" [I disagree].

Mr. H asked, "Did you have occasion to teach other doctors how to manage patients that had had cerebrospinal fluid leaks?"

He answered, "Oh I suppose I did." Mr. H stopped him when it became obvious, to me at least, that the management of CSF leaks was not a major feature of the Rochester program.

Mr. H then asked about his national activities in neurosurgery. Dr. Smith discussed at great length his involvement in neurosurgical societies including the important American Association of Neurologic Surgeons. He noted he was President of the Neurosurgical Society of

America in 1969 but admitted that this was a small group [I have not heard of it]. He was President of the Upstate Neurosurgical Society of New York in 1960 and 1961 and President of the California Neurosurgical Society in 1986.

"Have you had the occasion to write articles?"

"Yes."

"Are you currently in the process of writing a book on the field of neurosurgery?"

"Yes."

He asked about his move to California. Dr. Smith admitted he was not doing as many cases because of the smaller drawing area.

When asked was he still doing intracranial cases, he said, "Oh, yes." Mr. H then asked whether he had been asked to evaluate other neurosurgeons.

Dr. Smith said, "Yes" and that "peer review is killing all of us." He stated that he did not know me and that he saw cases for both Plaintiff and Defense—in personal injury cases primarily for the Defense and in malpractice cases for the Plaintiff.

Mr. H then asked, "Is it difficult for an injured plaintiff to get a neurosurgeon to testify against another neurosurgeon?"

Peter immediately objected. The jury was excused. Judge Peterson asked, "What's the reason for your objection?"

Peter said, "This is a conspiracy of silence issue; he is not endorsed to testify in that regard."

Mr. H countered that Peter had said that Dr. Smith was going from state to state "testifying against doctors" and that he should have the right to "let him talk about his observations and the reasons that he would be willing to review cases."

Judge Peterson sustained the objection, to my surprise.

The jury was brought back into the courtroom and Mr. H resumed. He said, "When you agreed to review the performance of Dr. Ogsbury and Dr. Krauth, do you have some sense of responsibility to look at cases like that to see if they're meritorious as a prominent member of your profession?"

He answered, "The whole move is the medical profession should be willing to review problems that develop within the practice of medicine and surgery. It has not been a big part of my practice." He admitted he was paid for his work but insisted that it was "not lucrative" for a neurosurgeon and that it was done strictly because of his duty. [I wondered how the jurors would feel when they saw just how much money he would make from this.]

Mr. H asked about the number of hours involved in the preparation of his review. Dr. Smith said, "I wish you'd asked me that earlier. I certainly have notes, all of the bills that my office has submitted. He said the opinions were all his own. Under further questioning he said he was 74 years old, in good health (a senior handball champion), and mentally sharp. He commented that he still goes to meetings and tries to keep up and is not only Board Certified but has served as an examiner. He asserted that the standards were the same in California as in Colorado. [I wondered about the strange opinions in his depositions.] With that Mr. H. submitted him as an expert in neurosurgery.

Peter stated that he did not object to his qualifications.

Mr. H placed the hospital record in front of Dr. Smith and returned to the lectern.

"Doctor, have you formed some opinions that the care delivered by Dr. Ogsbury and Dr. Krauth fell below the standard of care?"

Dr. Smith said, "Yes" [chilling words for any professional, particularly if it is one's first experience with this type of criticism].

"Have you formulated an opinion, within a reasonable degree of medical probability, that their actions caused the brain damage?"

"Yes."

"What is that opinion?"

"You go back to the Hippocratic Oath of 2500 years ago, that principle is not doing harm to the patient, and I think that the craniotomy—the first one and the second one—produced irreversible harm to the patient in terms of brain damage."

"Have you formulated an opinion as to whether or not Dr. N in Wyoming caused any of the brain damage to Sheran R?"

"Yes, my opinion is that he did not cause any of the brain damage. The patient could have cleared without the brain damage if Dr. Ogsbury had performed what I consider to have been the proper operation."

"Have you formulated an opinion as to whether or not the pneumothorax caused any of the brain damage?"

"Yes. I don't think it really had a big contribution. I think it was just one of those side issues that can be brought in. I think the real damage was done before the pneumothorax."

"Have you formulated an opinion as to whether Sheran R had an infection, meningitis, bacterial meningitis?"

"Yes. My opinion is that she didn't have a bacterial meningitis." [I thought, how can he possibly say this?]

"Have you formulated an opinion whether or not bacterial meningitis caused any part of the brain damage?"

"Yes, it's my opinion that the alleged meningitis did not contribute to her brain damage. I can demonstrate this."

Mr. H asked Dr. Smith to take the opportunity to explain the anatomy. He answered, "We have some excellent drawings." [I thought it interesting that he apparently thinks of himself as part of the Plaintiff team rather than an expert whose views are being utilized.] He gave what seemed to me to be a rambling and confusing explanation of the anatomy of the base of the skull, the fractures that occur there, strokes, the cerebrospinal fluid, and its infection—meningitis. He noted that still "too many people die" because of meningitis. [Yes, this is why we treat CSF leaks.]

Mr. H resumed, "Did you formulate an opinion as to physiologically what happened in Mrs. R's brain?"

"Yes. I think that the first surgery produced mainly injury from retraction, compression, compaction of the right frontal lobe. The second surgery did the same for both lobes."

"Have you formulated an opinion as to whether this retraction was excessive?"

"Yes. My opinion is that it was excessive, and I don't know of anything else that would produce the changes so early and so definitely."

"Do you have an opinion as to whether or not excessive retraction that you believe occurred was below the standard of care for a neurosurgeon in 1986?"

"Yes. My opinion is that it was below the standard of care, even at a minimal standard."

With questioning from Mr. H, Dr. Smith discussed Mrs. R's condition when she arrived at St. Anthony. Her exam was normal except for clear fluid in the right nostril [I agree].

At this point the noon break was called. We talked for a few minutes in the court. I felt Dr. Smith was longwinded and boring; I had difficulty maintaining concentration despite the obvious importance of what he was saying. His use of circular reasoning and adversarial thinking seemed obvious, at least to me. I had lunch with Kathy, Scott, and Sam, again at the Art Museum. I was able to get down a small bowl of soup. While I had already lost six pounds, I would not recommend this experience as a strategy for weight loss. When we returned to the courtroom, I nearly inadvertently tripped Ms. Kudla as she walked by [nice try, subconscious].

The court was called back into session. The jury was brought in, and Mr. H resumed his questioning. His answers were, at least initially, much more concise than they had been. The Plaintiffs' attorneys had obviously worked with him over the lunch hour. In addition, however, he now displayed a sinister expression and a nasty demeanor that was not obvious earlier.

He reported the radiologist had interpreted the test showing simply "no leak."

Mr. H asked, "What does that mean to you?"

Dr. Smith answered, "It means to me the leak has stopped" and that any fluid in the nose is not CSF but rather "a reaction of the sinus."

At that point Scott wrote me a note asking, "How could he say that in good faith?" I agree.

Mr. H then asked about the cultures which Dr. Mason requested be done at the time of the cisternogram. He said that none were drawn. [I agree. I had expected that a culture would be sent to the lab by the radiologist who performed the cisternogram. The protocol with any spinal tap at the hospital had always been, at least to the best of my knowledge, to have all CSF samples sent for culture. Why one was not done, I do not know. Fortunately, the omission did not change her course as we felt that with the absence of clinical meningitis in a patient on prophylactic antibiotics, we should proceed with the surgery before the forty-eight to seventy-two-hour period that any bacteria would require to grow if it did grow at all. We thought about but elected not to do another spinal tap at that point.]

Mr. H asked whether the failure to obtain the CSF was below the standard of care. Dr. Smith stated it was [and I guess I would have to reluctantly agree even with the above circumstances]. Dr. Smith added one should never operate in the presence of meningitis. [While one could wish to never be in the position of operating in the face of meningitis, other circumstances will occasionally override even that strong consideration.]

Mr. H asked if antibiotics could hide an infection. Dr. Smith reported that antibiotics can prevent culture growth although if you concentrate the sample by spinning it you can occasionally see bacterial rods or cocci on gram staining. He added if the antibiotics were sufficient to prevent the culture growth, they should be sufficient to control the infection and prevent any brain injury [another disagreement].

Mr. H then questioned Dr. Smith about the first operation and the operative report. I was astonished to hear that he had never heard of a standard procedure called "dural tenting" nor did he know of the intracranial use of Surgicel [a cellulose derivative made into strips that are routinely used on small bleeders by all neurosurgeons I know to induce clotting]. He felt we should have employed preoperative spinal drainage [I strongly disagree]. He stated a microscope is not necessary [a strange opinion for a modern neurosurgeon]. He said that the bone flap was too small, and the brain must have been retracted backward and upward against the bone [wrong again, as the brain is retracted primarily to the side and not backward].

Finally, after an objection by Mr. Pryor was overruled by Judge Peterson, he discussed the use of the surgical adhesive, obviously equating hardware store Super Glue [which I considered using but didn't] and an FDA-approved surgical adhesive [which I did use]. He claimed I should have a permit to use Super Glue or any non-FDA-approved product [which is ludicrous as many research-tested but not formally FDA-approved products are used widely, and specifically Super Glue has been used by neurosurgeons and otologists in special circumstances for years]. He noted that the glue did not stick [an obvious point to me that it was not Super Glue] and that it was removed.

Mr. H asked, "Were there other procedures available to be used to try and repair the leak in the summer of 1986?"

Dr. Smith said, "Yes," and described the extracranial approach. He stated you go back through the nose, "put a pack in there, and hold it, and pack it, and voila." He emphasized the low risk with that operation. [But, of course, neglected to report the generally high failure rate.]

He said furthermore the standard would have been to discuss the options with the patient [I would agree—all the reasonable options; Dr. Barron and I did not feel that an extracranial approach was remotely reasonable in this situation.]

He said that even the performance of the craniotomy was "below the minimal standard of practice," that the patch used to close the hole should either have been sutured in place [which is quite difficult in that location] or packed into the hole [it was].

He equated a trick which Dr. Krauth showed me in the second operation [which involved actually enlarging the hole and packing from above the ethmoid sinus which lies below] with packing the hole and, as I referred to this as a new trick, felt that my knowledge was below the standard of knowledge. He said additionally that had I sutured or packed the wound, she would have recovered with some infirmity. Mr. H asked whether Super Glue could have caused any of the brain damage. Dr. Smith who in deposition stated the glue had played no role, said, "During the deposition I sort of freaked out." Peter objected and the matter was dropped.

Dr. Smith then returned to the view box and reviewed the tests that occurred between the two procedures. I followed Peter to a position near the jurors to better see Dr. Smith's demonstration. Peter feels that it is important for the jurors to see me taking an active role (unlike any Perry Mason defendant that they have seen before on television). Even from close proximity, I had difficulty following his points. The jury must be terribly confused.

Finally, the afternoon recess was called. We went downstairs to the cafeteria for coffee, actually laughing about the opinions which seemed extraordinary to us and should be easily challenged in cross-examination.

After the court was called back into session, Mr. H resumed, "If Dr. Ogsbury had not negligently retracted and manipulated the brain in the right frontal lobe in the first surgery, would you expect to see the damage you pointed out on the CAT scans?"

Dr. Smith answered, "No," that the injury was "the result of too much compression of the right frontal lobe causing injury to the deep blood vessels, capillary structures deep in the right frontal lobe that were broken, were injured, and led to the infarction that we see on the scan" [another interesting theory].

Mr. H asked about the pupillary change that occurred after the first surgery. Dr. Smith felt it was secondary to pressure of the temporal lobe against the third nerve [again interesting because none of us saw evidence of sufficient shifting of the brain for this to occur].

Mr. H asked about the second operation. Dr. Smith explained that the leak did recur but that the CAT scan on 6/28 showed no air, indicating the leak had abated. "The next day she underwent exploration—a second surgery."

Mr. H asked, "Was there any consideration being given to the possibility of meningitis? What did you say earlier today when I asked you, in the face of meningitis, whether a surgical procedure—an intracranial procedure—should be done?"

"I said it should not be done in the presence of meningitis. I think that's injury upon injury."

"Was it below the standard of care for both Dr. Krauth and Dr. Ogsbury, on July 2, 1986, to go back in and open this lady's skull back up and do further exploration?"

At this point Peter objected vehemently with respect to Dr. Krauth. The objection was overruled.

Mr. H therefore asked, "Do you have an opinion that it was below the standard of care for Dr. Ogsbury and Dr. Krauth to decide to go back in and surgically reexplore this lady's area in her brain on July 2, 1986?"

Dr. Smith said, "I do, I do, it was much more of a major procedure. It involved taking down a flap not only on the left side but one former on the right side—both of them. It was too aggressive."

Mr. H asked, "Was there any reason for them to believe there was a leak on the left?"

Dr. Smith said that neither the new left-sided headache nor the air on the left on the CAT scan of 7/1 was sufficient justification for doing a bilateral craniotomy. He said it was below the "even minimum standard of care" to do the bilateral craniotomy on July 2, 1986, and further suggested that to explore the left side when the patch was found to have moved on the right was "below the standard of care" as well.

Dr. Smith then described his evaluation of her course following the second operation. He said she showed some evidence of prompt severe damage [ignoring that she initially woke up reasonably well and then deteriorated]. He accurately described the follow-up tests including the CAT scan that demonstrated the bilateral infarction of the anterior cerebral arteries, the "dual picture of damage that destroyed, in my humble opinion, the brain function of this lady."

Mr. H asked once again, "Do you have an opinion that excessive retraction and manipulation after the second surgery caused the damage?"

Dr. Smith answered, "Yes. Without any question, it's a well-known condition resulting from excessive retraction in that area. It was below the standard of medical practice."

Mr. H started to ask about intravenous fluids, but Judge Peterson decided to call a recess for the evening.

After Dr. Smith and the Plaintiffs' attorneys had left the court, Peter put his arm around me. Indeed, he had felt obliged to support me all day after Kathy's comment about my not doing well in the morning. He showed us what he'd written in his diary that morning. He then told me to go home and find the ten best "zingers" to counteract Dr. Smith.

Surprisingly, at the end of the day I did not feel particularly bad. Dr. Smith was clearly not a simple, nice, senior professor. He was angry and nasty, sometimes even to Mr. H. His anatomic demonstrations were confusing, and he seemed always eager to expound his many criticisms. I would think his adversarial positions would be as obvious to the jurors as they are to us. Even then, I did go home and feverishly poured over my notes of the day. I found fifty-four separate points which might be useful. The points varied from the realization that I had as many achievements in my professional resume as Dr. Smith (a factor which might be useful in countering any extra credibility because of Dr. Smith's purported stature), to points of medicine which I believe were unequivocally wrong. I went to bed awaiting Peter's first real test, the cross-examination of Dr. Smith.

Fran
Thursday, May 3, 1990, 9:00 p.m.

Jay's moods are swinging from irritable impatience with everything to frenetic enthusiasm. He's moving and maneuvering like an F-16 pilot. I try to tap him on the shoulder and let him know I'm not in the back seat, in fact no one is in that back seat. He doesn't seem to care. Another wall, and he doesn't even know it. I hadn't come upon this one before. I mentally check all pathways to him. Every path is blocked and closed. Now, I'm irritated with him and moving toward irrational. Geezus, I just want him to leave.

Dr. Smith had been on the stand all day. Jay had taken meticulous notes and had a gold mine of academic/medical errors made by Dr. Smith. He was prepared, and his ammunition packed and ready to deliver to Peter. I wondered if it had occurred to Kathy to just send this man right on to the White Spot!

I suggested taking a break from this work, starting tonight. We could resume Monday with our end-of-the-day 9:00 meetings. That did it. He was hurt and angry at me. I had made things worse and knew at this point any kind of break over the weekend with things as they were at this moment would be a tormented break. He left, still angry. Great, just what he needs. I sat down and thought, remembering "you are what disturbs you." I have always hated that thought. I remembered, reluctantly, the times in my life when I left others in my own tornadic wake.

CHAPTER EIGHT

DAY 5
THE CROSS-EXAMINATION
OF FRANK P. SMITH

Peter
Friday, May 4, 1990, 2:30 a.m.

Friday, glorious Friday, up again at an ungodly hour to prepare for Plaintiffs' big gun, Frank Pie Smith. Hard at work by 2:30 a.m. with some low-level anxiety that I won't be able to chop him hard enough to keep us even or will be so tired I will have the material but lack the mental wherewithal to deliver.

Dr. Smith was on all day starting out as a kind of "gramps" type (insisted on taking his coat off, all smiles and anecdotes and long-winded digressions typical of those steeped in the past and self-admiration), but as the day progressed and he got into the care (and had been coached into cooling his garrulousness jets over lunch, no doubt), he hardened.

Although disclaiming any tendency to nitpick the care, Smith managed to come up with a mere seventeen criticisms of the care, the vast majority completely spurious. Still, his simplistic, but easy-to-understand, explanation of how overly aggressive traction devastated Sheran's brain left me uncomfortable and the jury taking notes like crazy. I could see the pain and uncertainty in Jay's face and knew he was afraid—fearful that the jury would take this over-the-hill blowhard's opinions to heart, maybe even a little afraid that there was some truth to something he said. My job—kill the bastard, gently, softly, but kill him. If we can get back to even with the jury after the first week then things will be okay, at least for now.

Jay
Friday, May 4, 1990

Day five broke clear, the first since the trial began. Hopefully Peter and I will be able to ride our bikes together today after trial. I joined Peter and Scott at the White Spot at 7:00 a.m. Peter was deeply engrossed in his preparation for the cross-examination of Dr. Smith but took time to listen to my suggestions from last night. To my surprise, he liked a number of them, even the admitting to writing this narrative as a counteractive parallel to Dr. Smith's book. He said I am beginning to think like a lawyer—that is a scary thought. As expected, Peter is wired.

We returned to Court and the jury was brought in. Judge Peterson asked Dr. Smith how he was feeling. He said, "Fine," but we'll see after Peter gets his hands on him. I noted Mr. H was in a sport coat.

Mr. H resumed his direct examination of Dr. Smith. He said, "I have a few things to go over. In your neurosurgical career, have you ever had to go back in for a second surgery to correct a repair for a cerebrospinal fluid leak?" He didn't "recall" having to do that [not surprising to me since he has not done many].

"Is the dura that lays next to the bone of the skull too thick to suture?"

He admitted, "Some people may not tolerate a stitch so you might have to flap over some of the dura."

"In a lady the age of Sheran R would you expect the dura to be too thin to put a suture in the dura there?"

"I wouldn't expect that as a problem."

"We talked some throughout your testimony about meningitis and you pointed out you did not see any evidence of meningitis. From your review of all of the CT scans, are you able to formulate an opinion, based upon a reasonable degree of medical probability, as to whether or not Sheran R ever had bacterial meningitis during any of this treatment?"

He answered, "Yes, my opinion is that she never really had a clinical problem of bacterial meningitis. The cultures were all negative. She had nothing of a clinical nature that was shown on CAT scans, the peripheral, the surface of the brain changes. And the big thing is that, if there were meningitis, did it actually cause the problem? The pathology that I demonstrated—the localization, the timing, the whole matter—definitely is related to injury."

"You mentioned localization. What did you mean?"

He answered, "The changes in the right frontal lobe, quite promptly after the operation, were so localized. The only thing I know that can cause those were retraction. If it were meningitis, it wouldn't be localized such as you have here."

"In your opinion, were the CAT scans consistent with bacterial meningitis?"

"No."

"When you reviewed the care, was there mention made whether or not there was meningitis?"

He answered there was an "elevated temperature off and on, some stiffness of her neck, a spinal tap around the 28th of June where there was a cellular count of red cells and white cells, a clinical concern written by Dr. Mason worried about the possibility of meningitis, a case like this you always worry about it."

"Was there meningitis that produced the real problem of the patient?"

"I would be less than honest if I were to make a flat bold statement [what an advocate], but it never reached a clinical problem and it certainly did not cause the damage that took place in this case."

Mr. H said, "I have no further questions."

Peter rose and asked, "Dr. Smith, if I were to tell you that Dr. Ogsbury is the President of the State Neurosurgical Association for the State of Colorado, do you feel that that would lend any more credence to his opinions or testimony in this case?" [I thought my God, he used my opening.]

Dr. Smith answered, "Well, I don't see why."

Peter continued, "Okay, very good. If I were to tell you that he was a member or past President of the Clinical Neuroscience Society, would that lend any more credence to his testimony or any opinions that he might express?"

Dr. Smith answered, "Well, I don't—I think I would certainly give him full recognition as to whatever comes up—I think he just—I think each issue as you know you don't get any change in clinical status because of the offices you hold."

"Okay, and if I were to tell you that Dr. Ogsbury is currently writing a book about the clinical practice of neurosurgery, do you feel that would lend any additional credence to his opinion or testimony?"

"Well, it depends on what came up."

"And if I were to tell you that Dr. Ogsbury has been involved in peer review throughout his professional career, has that view, and has even been sued as a result of his peer review, do you think that lends any additional credence, or should, to his testimony or any opinions he might have in this case?"

"Well, I would just say that each case, each opinion, would have to be judged on its own. You don't accept or disavow an opinion because of a reputation. You judge an opinion by the facts brought up."

"Okay, okay, I think we're getting somewhere. So if I understand you, what you're telling the members of the jury is that as far as Dr. Ogsbury being President of the Medical Society and the past president of another organization, that doesn't really lend credence to his opinion, that's something the jury has to judge in this case?"

"Exactly."

"And the same applies to you?"

"President of the United States, even he could be impeached."

"Could you answer my question? The same would apply to you."

"Exactly."

"So, the fact that Mr. H spent quite a bit of time dealing with the fact that you are president of various organizations, that does not lend credence or additional weight to your opinions, do you agree?"

"I would think you're exactly right" [and I felt we had eliminated the whole issue of his national stature].

Peter continued, "Now you have obviously formed certain opinions about standard of care, and I think you've told the jury that the standards of care are pretty much the same throughout the United States."

"Either are or should be."

"Now if I were to tell you that the standard of care in Denver by board-certified neurosurgeons in this community as concurred by board-certified ear, nose, and throat specialists is to repair this kind of cribriform plate leak by an intracranial approach, are you saying that's not the standard of care here or that the entire community in practicing that standard is beneath the national standard of care?"

Dr. Smith looked uncomfortable, Mr. H objected, and the attorneys went to the bench.

After their discussions, Peter continued, "Doctor, you told the jury that you believe you have knowledge based on your background, training, and skill, and experience of certain national standards of care to relate to management of this type of surgical problem. Is that correct?"

"Yes, I assume so."

"You consulted with no neurosurgeons—these are your opinions?"

"Yes."

"And that remains true today?"

"Yes."

"And so, your sense of what the national standard is, since you've been retained or hired in this case, is essentially your opinion as you've told Mr. H and the jury in direct response to his questions, correct?"

"Based on my experience, and also, I think you probably know that a full Bible of criteria for cases, problems, and standards that should be maintained at a national level."

"Do you, through conversations with any local neurosurgeons, have any actual knowledge of standards in Denver relative to surgical repair of this type of problem?"

Mr. H objected saying the question implies a difference nationally as against locally. The objection was sustained.

Peter went on, "You mentioned the Hippocratic oath and the concept 'do no harm.' Would you acknowledge that for a physician or surgeon to do nothing in the face of certain situations may do more harm than to do surgery?"

Dr. Smith agreed that it's possible.

"And that sometimes the surgeon is between a rock and a hard place, is he not?"

"That is conceivable."

"And sometimes it is a choice of not particularly good choices to begin with, and that's occurred to you, has it not, in your long career?"

Dr. Smith, of course, agreed and the foundation of our case was laid.

Peter paused briefly, "Now, if I say something that you did not say, will you correct me? I took some notes but sometimes I misinterpret or mishear what you say." [Peter is going somewhere strong.]

"Do you remember the term 'Surgicel'? What is it?"

"Well, Surgicel, I believe, I'm not exactly sure. It is a form of cellulose used to advance coagulation."

"And I believe you told the ladies and gentlemen of the jury that you had never heard of Surgicel being used in the brain."

"It could be. It's my opinion."

"On the brain surface?"

"Yes, that's correct."

"Then you used the term dural tenting. You told the jury that you had never heard of the term."

"I'm not familiar with the use of that term." [Where has this man been the last ten years??!]

"You've done intracranial operations in the last ten years and assisted in intracranial operations? You would agree the primary surgeon is responsible for the actual technique and decision making, the assistant is there for consultative advice and to retract and to do things of this nature?"

Dr. Smith agreed. [Okay, Lee Krauth.]

"Now, and again, please help me out. You said yesterday that you had never heard of any kind of surgical adhesives being used in surgery of the brain?"

"For this particular problem. And I think that the use of it is greatly decreased."

"Do you recall talking about that in your deposition?"

"Oh yes."

"Now, nobody's told anybody yet what a deposition is. So maybe I'll use you. You've given a number of depositions before, have you not? And this was a procedure where, after you were listed as a witness in this case, a large group of people came out to California to your office, and you were placed under oath."

"It wasn't actually my office. It was a local hotel."

"Mr. Schuster was there for the family (of Sheran R), and he was the man who hired you in the first place."

"You could call it that I suppose."

"So, this gave us an opportunity to find out your background and to get your opinions in this case? And, a booklet was sent to you, and you got to make any corrections that you wished to, knowing that if you departed from that substantially, that could be called to your attention at trial."

"I suppose so."

"Now among other discussions was the fact that you noticed Dr. Ogsbury, in operation number one, tried to use a 'surgical adhesive,' remember that? And do you recall at that time expressing an opinion or a statement that 'I've never heard of surgical adhesives being used in this type of operation'?"

Mr. H objected. Judge Peterson agreed, stating, "You must give the doctor the deposition."

Peter continued, "All right, at that time did you testify you never heard of a surgical adhesive being used in closing a cerebrospinal fluid leak?"

Dr. Smith glanced at his deposition and answered, "No I had not. I'm familiar with it having been reported for use around large skull fractures to repair a defect at the floor of the skull, but I had never read of a simple cerebrospinal fluid leak of this nature. I've never heard of Surgicel being used."

"You've never heard of a surgical adhesive being used in the repair of a CSF leak? Of the cribriform plate?"

"No, I never have." [He evidently doesn't know of the literature advocating its use for this.]

Peter then asked, "Now when you were talking about that surgical adhesive, and I would take it today that, in your opinion, that was not a major issue in this case either in preventing the leak or in doing anything else. Isn't that correct?" [Using his words in the deposition.]

"I think that is possible."

"Oh, by the way, is this where you freaked out in your deposition?"

Mr. H, of course, objected, and Judge Peterson instructed Peter to move on.

"Did you read your deposition before you came to trial yesterday?"

"Yes."

"You talked to the jury about the trans-nasal ethmoid repair. You said there was a new procedure where you used an endoscope?"

"The endoscope is a magnifying instrument. It gives you visual contact."

"So, you don't do this operation do you? That's something normally ENT specialists do."

"Neurosurgeons trained for hypophysectomies by this route would do this."

"You don't do this operation, and you haven't been trained in it, and you've never assisted on one, and you've never seen one?"

"I've seen films of them, training films, going to neurosurgical meetings—people have films of this procedure for demonstration purposes." [And this is an expert?]

"When you were first retained, you were practicing out of a community hospital in Monterey. How many beds?"

"Two hundred beds. But it's a gem of a hospital."

"And this is not a teaching hospital, is it?"

"No, but we do accept students from Stanford, and we have a lot of conferences from Stanford—professors and so forth."

"The jury is going to need to know something of your background in the repair of these kinds of problems. Have you ever written a paper, a learned paper, on cerebrospinal fluid leak repair, whether physician-caused or trauma-caused?"

"No."

"You have not written about any cranial surgery of any kind? "

"Well, I suppose back—that's probably true."

"Have you ever written about the issue of extracranial versus intracranial repair of CSF leak of this type?"

"No."

"Have you ever done a talk or made a presentation on the repair of cerebrospinal fluid leaks?"

"That comes up in any lecture or teaching of head injury in general. I think you're out of order in that question."

"Look at page 153 of your deposition."

Dr. Smith reviewed his deposition. His answer then to the same question was, "Not specifically that I recall."

"Any talks that you gave to residents would have been back in 1974 or before?"

Dr. Smith agreed.

"You've never been asked to speak at a national meeting concerning the issues in this case?"

"Not on cerebrospinal fluid leaks."

"And neurosurgeons don't come to you, and haven't come to you, as a super specialist with special knowledge of cerebrospinal fluid problems?"

"I have had difficult cases referred to me."

"And as a neurosurgeon, difficult cases are part of the turf, aren't they?"

"That's a difficult field. Especially in a university center."

"Now will you tell the ladies and gentlemen of the jury and agree that in terms of surgical/neurosurgical decisions and management and evaluation of cerebrospinal fluid leaks of this type, that by way of research or background or training or experience that you have no more than the skill and ability of an ordinary, well-trained neurosurgeon?"

"I would think that's true."

"Doctor, in terms of your actual surgical experience with this procedure, how many CSF leaks, either produced by another surgeon or an accident, did you manage or surgically repair?" [Peter writing on the blackboard.]

"I know I didn't surgically repair any. I think maybe I've seen one or two since then."

"In the period of '80 to '85, how many repairs did you do?"

"Well, I don't—I don't recall having an actual repair since arriving in California in 1974."

"Okay, then we'll just go back to 1974. So from '74 until today—actually you've never done this operation? In fact you've never done this operation involving a cribriform plate fracture in your entire professional career? You've never done what Dr. Ogsbury was attempting to do, right?"

"Correct."

"Is there any chance that you have fallen out-of-date?"

"No."

"Do you agree that the Youman's text of neurological surgery is considered generally reliable and authoritative? Now I'm going to represent that this was the edition in effect of Dr. Ogsbury's treatment, the second edition."

"The one you have there is 1982. We have given that away."

"This is the 1990—Is this the one you've got?"

"It hasn't arrived yet."

"Chapter 65, Volume 4 talks about dural fistulas needing repair. I want to refer you to page 2212 and there is a comment here under location of posttraumatic fistuli. Now fistula is a medical word for hole or perforation, and it says, 'The fragility of the cribriform plate and the juxtaposition of the arachnoid investment to the bone where the first cranial nerve perforates the skull makes this area of the skull the most common site of a dural fistula.' Do you agree with that?"

"Yes."

"'So fragile is the cribriform plate that it is the pathway for most high-pressure fluid leaks.' Do you agree with that?"

"Well, yes."

"Now we have two issues, do we not? One issue is if you have a hole and a CSF leak. One of these issues is whether that's going to seal off on its own accord with the passage of time, right? In medicine the term you use is spontaneously, and then another issue is this, as long as the hole is present, there is the risk of infection through contamination coming into the brain and into the arachnoid, into the CSF, and causing a meningeal infection of various types?"

Dr. Smith agreed, "You said that seventy-five to eighty percent of them seal spontaneously, normally within the first few days based on the factors of the site, the cause, the magnitude, the health of the patient. But if the hole doesn't heal right away within the first few days, and especially if you get to a week or beyond, doesn't the orders of spontaneous closure go down?"

"Certainly, if you get out to ten days, to twelve days, two weeks."

"We were at nine days when the operation was done, and you thought a couple of more days that he should have waited."

"Yes."

"And as the hole stays open, the longer it stays open, the risk of infection goes up?" [During this time Peter was drawing the time course of each on the blackboard.]

Even Dr. Smith briefly seemed to like this. He smiled and said, "I don't know where you got this concept, it's good," then went back to his advocacy and said, "It's a little misleading—this is legalistic, I don't know that it's medical. Each case is different."

Peter continued to read on page 2213, "The reported incidence of meningitis in patients with post-traumatic fistula varies from three to fifty percent. The infection rate tends to be higher if the cerebrospinal fluid leak lasts longer than seven days."

Dr. Smith answered, "If you don't use antibiotics."

Peter continued on pages 2220 and 2222. "The article listed the advantages of the intracranial approach: 'Direct visualization. Inspection of the cortex adjacent to the defect. In addition, a graft placed intracranially over the dural defect is tamponaded in place by the overlying brain.'"

Dr. Smith said, "Well I don't agree with that. I think that's wrong." [I love it. He disagrees with the eminent authors of this very good book.]

Peter continued from Youman's, "The disadvantages of the extracranial approach are that it's impossible to visualize the associated brain damage, and it is difficult from the outside to plug the dural defect against the pressure of the brain.'"

Dr. Smith responded, "I think this article is outdated," and a break was called.

During the break, we discussed Peter's cross of Dr. Smith. The jury was listening, all of them, and while Peter had hit hard at Dr. Smith, he had not antagonized him or the jury. Peter will continue on the attack. I was particularly pleased that Peter had used my opening and several other ideas. We reconvened.

Mr. H objected to the 1990 version of Yeoman's and requested that he be allowed to see it if it were used. Peter refused, stating its use was simply in response to Dr. Smith's statement that the 1982 version was out-of-date.

Judge Peterson overruled the objection to my surprise. I have simply not been able to predict her rulings.

Peter resumed his cross-examination of Dr. Smith.

"One of your major criticisms of both these operations, choosing an intracranial approach over the extracranial approach?"

"I don't think my major criticisms here have been the procedure that was used. My main objections have been the details of the craniotomy."

"Doctor, we made a list of criticisms that you gave this jury yesterday. Did you tell the jury yesterday that it is beneath the standard of care, in response to Mr. H's questions, to do an intracranial operation rather than an extracranial, the first procedure? Did you tell Mr. H, in connection with the second procedure, that it was beneath the standard of care to do an intracranial versus an extracranial if you were going to do it?"

"Yes."

He then asked, "Based on your review of the literature, does extracranial patching of repair fail? What are the reported percentages?"

"I don't know of any time that extracranial patching of that type of defect has failed [another convenient lack of knowledge]. These cases don't get put into the literature because they're all problems of lawsuits."

Peter then read on from Youman's. "'Optimal management requires that the neurosurgeon consider both approaches in choosing the appropriate procedure for any individual patient. A tuberculum sella leak is probably treated more effectively by using an extracranial approach [I agree] whereas a cribriform plate leak requires an intracranial approach.' That's what it says, so you disagree?"

"Yes, I think that's not what they were talking about."

"So, you think Dr. Spetzler [one of the authors of this chapter] would go extracranially?"

"I would think so."

Peter read on further, "'Here the use of an operating microscope is mandatory.' Do you see that?"

"Yes."

"The fact is that any well-trained neurosurgeon not only looks for the obvious but looks in the surrounding area for other micro-perforations or injury to the floor of the dura?"

"He may use magnifying loops other than a microscope, but some magnification."

"So, you would agree that an operating microscope is mandatory? Right?"

"Yes. You would use the operating microscope as needed."

Peter said, "Okay. Now, let's go back for a second and talk about surgical adhesives." He continued from Youman's, "'Sticking the graft to the dura can be performed with many small sutures, or the graft can be secured by the judicious use of small amounts of tissue adhesives.' And yet you had never heard of it?"

"I think I never heard of it being currently used." [Another cop-out but the point is well taken].

Peter continued, "May I have the doctor step down so they can see what we're talking about. We will call it a flow sheet." He showed the jury the identical flow sheets from the two editions. "Look, as of 1990, if we put these down, side by side, if you have a cribriform plate lesion, the same recommendation, direct intracranial repair."

"I don't think this is comprehensive."

Peter took off the stickers and gave the 1990 version to Mr. H. [What a great move, the jurors seemed to love it.] "I'm just going to ask you a question. Are you willing to withdraw your criticism of Dr. Ogsbury on the issue of intracranial versus extracranial repair for a cribriform plate fracture?"

"Well I wouldn't bring up the personality standpoint. It's not one person against the other. The diagram that you showed is not comprehensive. The main thrust of my testimony is not meant to go against the decision to use a craniotomy; the main thrust is a craniotomy can be very injurious to the brain."

"But, along with your main criticism, did you not put in about a dozen other criticisms?"

"I don't think so."

"Now I'm going to ask for...the answer to this question. Now hypothetically, if an intracranial approach were an acceptable choice to Dr. Ogsbury, that would place him surgically into the brain and thus create the possibility of damage to brain structures. Isn't one of your arguments that the reason he shouldn't have gone this way is because there should be no risk of brain injury?"

"I didn't mean to imply that. There is always a risk of brain injury if you have an opening of the skull and exploration of brain, a lot less with the extracranial approach."

"Acknowledging that Dr. Spetzler, in the 1982 edition and in the 1990 edition advocates an intracranial approach for a cribriform plate fracture, are you still telling the jury, in your opinion, this is beneath the standard of care?"

"Well, I think that that article is beneath the standard of current literature."

"So now the article is below the standard of care, right?"

"I, well I think it's below the standard of literature." [I can't believe I'm hearing this.]

Peter paused, appearing to have great difficulty containing himself. "So if somebody like Jay Ogsbury or Lee Krauth, or any other neurosurgeon around here, were to have looked at Youman's and looked at the Spetzler article and made a decision in part based upon that recommendation, would that surgeon be beneath the standard of care in relying upon that flow sheet and article?"

"I can't get into quibbling. I did—what I saw in one article—I certainly have never operated—a neurosurgery—and I'm not going to be the—I think that's going to be up to the jury to decide."

With a smile Peter said, "All right, let's go on to something else."

"You said yesterday, you were very uncomfortable being here. You have been in Court frequently."

Dr. Smith answered, "I would say I have been in Court infrequently."

"You have looked at about 125 malpractice cases in the last ten years?"

"Not that many—personal injury cases, maybe. It's the obligation of every neurosurgeon to be available for that type of case."

"You did that out of a sense of obligation?"

"Well, whatever you want to call it … it's part of the practice."

"Well doctor, let me ask you another question. Have you testified in Court at least thirty times in the last ten years?"

"I don't think it would be thirty times. I think I said it might be as many as three times in one year or some years none, but it certainly wouldn't be that many times."

"Now you feel a duty to review cases as I've heard you say twice. Consistent with that duty, do you charge for your time?"

"Oh yes."

"Does the money you receive make the carrying out of your duty less painful?"

"I never touch it. My secretaries have always taken care of everything. I just tell her the hours and she makes the billing."

"How much an hour do you charge?"

"Well, that's been a changing thing. I believe the most recent was about $300 an hour."

"Do you remember me from—I mean other than the beginning of the week—do you remember having another lawsuit with me out here in Colorado?"

"I remember there was another lawsuit here in Colorado that I was a potential expert in."

Peter then described another case he tried in which Dr. Smith testified against doctors (including a neurosurgeon friend of mine) in Denver. "All right. Do you remember me?"

"Yes."

"Now if I were to suggest at that time you were charging $250 an hour for your time would that be about right?"

"It's a country-wide scale that seems to go up every so often."

"Now you've mentioned twenty-five to thirty hours that you've put into this case reviewing records and depositions. Do you recall that?"

"I don't recall."

"But you're paid for time, aren't you?"

"Yes, but it's not that lucrative."

"Okay, but if you charge your $300 an hour, it would be $7,500 to $9,000?"

"Yes, but that's not very large in terms of surgical fees or surgical practice." [I wonder if the jury would agree.]

"You're going to be reimbursed for your travel expenses and your lodging expenses?"

"I would hope so."

"What do you charge when you're to go to Court?"

"I think it's $500 for a half a day in Court or $1,000 for a full day in Court for any person accepted as an expert witness."

"Okay, Doctor, we may be talking $15,000?"

"Well, you do as you see fit."

"You have billed and then we came out and took your deposition, didn't we, and you charged for your deposition at $300 an hour for eight hours?"

"I can't tell you."

"Then there was a deposition all day; didn't Mr. Schuster come out before your deposition and meet with you the day before on that evening?"

"That evening, I believe."

"Okay. $15,000 to $20,000, maybe?"

"I think it's a relatively small fraction of all that's involved in this case." [I can imagine how someone making average wages would feel about that.]

"Now, would you think that as part of your duty in reviewing the case, that you would be objective and non-adversarial in reviewing records? Do you think that's part of your responsibility?"

"Well, I would certainly hope so."

"Okay. I mean, you used the term "we" a couple of times yesterday. Were you trying to identify yourself with one side or the other?"

"I'd have to know how you—you try to use the collective plural when I'm speaking of myself, but it could be as you said." [Am I surprised?]

"Do you want the jury to find against my client?"

"I want the issues to be fully explained and ventilated, and hopefully this type of process will not happen again. It's in the nature of a deterrent." [Amazing, he wishes to punish.]

"Now, Doctor, just in terms of your impartiality, did you at any point in this case talk about Dr. Ogsbury's first surgery in terms of a big fat neurosurgical fee?"

"If I said it, there would probably be some reason for it." [Oh my.]

Peter paused and continued further, "Well let's look at a whole bunch of exhibits attached to the back of your deposition. It says, 'There seems to be no question that when Dr. Ogsbury proceeded with open craniotomy the following day, he opened himself to a very major issue of medical malpractice. If he had been successful in closing the problem without recurrence, he might have gotten away with a big surgical fee.'"

"Yes. I didn't use the term 'fat.'"

"Well, I take back the word fat."

"Now, have you ever talked about, under oath, his being dishonest with his attorneys?"

"I understand you need to have a play on words. I did not feel that the operating surgeon had fairly informed his attorney on all issues, as I understand it, if a client has an attorney. I think he is supposed to be truthful and tell him how much is involved, and did he swipe the diamond ring and pawn it, or did he do this or do that. And maybe there are just reasons for it, but I don't think Dr. Ogsbury has been less than truthful."

"And then Mr. Schuster took a break? And then you went out in the hall and talked about this very issue? Didn't you?"

"If you say so."

"Do you remember being cautioned that's pretty stern in strong language to be accusing a surgeon of dishonesty or lack of truthfulness? Didn't that happen in the hall after you started into that discussion, Doctor?"

"I'm not sure he said that. I think he might have said something like 'don't get involved with personalities.'"

"Now let me ask you just with respect to that report that you wrote on February 7, 1989. Didn't you use the following terms to describe Dr. Ogsbury at various points—inexperienced, aggressive, premature, uninformed, impulsive, immature, and, what we talked about, in search of a big surgical fee?"

"It's possible. I must have had pretty good reasons for using those terms."

"Now I'm going to ask you a couple of other questions about the personal opinions you hold. Are you of the view that many times the word complication is just a ploy doctors use to protect themselves against malpractice?"

"I haven't any ideas on that."

"Your answer was, 'Well Mr. Downs, the statement that you made about this frequency potential has been the blanket of insulation that we surgeons have used for years and years and years to protect ourselves against malpractice. We have sold it to you, and we have sold it to everybody.' Did you say that?"

"Yes, I think that will get down in history as a pretty good statement."

At that point Judge Peterson said, "Let's stop at this point."

The team was up at lunch, telling jokes, each more obscene than the one proceeding it. Indeed, little strategy was discussed. Peter was on a roll, why change a good thing? Indeed, he admitted he slept in that morning (which meant until 1:00 a.m.).

When the Court was called back into session, Peter picked up where he had left off.

"Doctor, now going back for just a second, the 1990 edition of Youman's chapter on neurofistula repair is written by Dr. Spetzler and Dr. Wilson, right? These are two of the biggest names in neurosurgery, are they not, and the most respected?"

"Yes. Both good friends of mine."

"Now I wanted to ask you one other thing about this negligent flowsheet in the two Youman's."

"I didn't say it was negligence."

"You didn't?"

"No. I said it was not all-inclusive and was outdated, maybe outmoded, but it didn't take into consideration what they now have in the latest edition."

"Did you have a chance to read that over lunch?"

"Yes, not over lunch but over the interval."

"Well, let's go. Here we are. Remember you said yesterday you didn't want to nitpick and then you listed a series of criticisms?"

"Could be."

"Now in many of these cases we have an issue of somebody doing or not doing something and so we have an issue of whether they're negligent. And then we have a question of whether that contributed to the ultimate outcome?"

"Those issues are there."

"Now as far as doing a CSF analysis before the craniotomy, you're saying that from the time of admission, 6/23 to 6/25, this wasn't done? Right?"

"Right."

"But you also told the jury that she didn't have meningitis at that time. Isn't that, right?"

"She didn't have any clinical bacterial meningitis."

"So, here's my point. If this test had been done, you're not going to tell this jury that this was going to produce some evidence that she had meningitis, are you? If it had been done, it wouldn't have shown anything to a reasonable medical probability. Isn't that right?"

"Well, I can understand you saying that, but I—I'm not here to vague ifs, ands, whats, or buts."

"I'm going to ask you to answer this question now. Even though it wasn't done, had it been done, it wouldn't have shown meningitis. Isn't that true?"

"I think that's speculative."

"Well, I thought you told this jury that there was no evidence of meningitis in this hospitalization?"

"I don't think I said quite that. I remember patently there is a vague meningeal reaction without clinical meningitis."

"But I want you to look at your deposition, page 51, again. Okay, now, question line 19, 'Was there any evidence of meningitis throughout the hospitalization at St. Anthony?' Answer, 'Not that I know of.'"

"Was that your testimony?"

"Of clinical bacteriologic meningitis, yes."

"Well, I'm going to ask you, I'm going to ask you a hard question, Doctor. "Did she, to a reasonable medical probability, have signs and symptoms of clinical meningitis prior to the time of the first surgery?"

"I think it would be speculative prior to the first craniotomy."

"So, she may have, is that what you're saying?"

"No, we don't know. It might have been a phase that would have shown up. I just don't know."

"Now on June 28, she's got—she's got, except for the culture—and we'll talk about that in a minute—she's got a picture that is classic for, a picture consistent with meningitis clinically, correct?"

"Well—I think—I talked about that. I think there's a simmering meningeal reaction. It seems to me you want meningitis at one time and not at the other. I don't understand." [Peter is doing a great job exposing Dr. Smith's advocacy.]

"Let's ask another direct question. On 6/28, to a reasonable medical probability, did Sheran R have meningitis?"

"Well, I feel that we've gone into that enough, and I think I know—my concept, and I don't think she had what we call a clinical bacterial meningitis. I don't see where we are really very far apart on this."

"Okay. To a reasonable medical probability, did she have bacteriologic meningitis as of June 28, 1986?"

"Just like dermatitis, that's an irritation of the skin, that doesn't mean it's a gross infection."

"Well, all right. Sheran R had relative meningitis. You tell me the word, and I'll write it there." Peter stood at his blackboard poised to write down the word.

"What I said, meningeal inflammatory reaction."

"From a bacteria?"

"I think a few gram-negative rods were found in some smears. She had some glue in there. She had air in there. She had red cells."

"This indicates bacteria. Gram negative rods indicate bacteria, right?"

"Right."

"Now gram-negative rods are evidence of bacteria, correct?"

"Yes, but they may have been dead. There may have been a few bacteria that already have been neutralized by the antibiotics."

"This indicates bacteria, doesn't it? Whether dead or alive?"

"Right."

"Okay we'll talk about this bacterial infection issue in a minute. Now, you wrote your notes on February 7. And then you wrote your analysis notes within four days? So in these notes, I don't believe there's any mention of operating in the face of meningitis in the first surgery or failure to get a spinal fluid analysis in connection with the cisternogram or any issue whatever about the size of the flap in terms of the retraction?"

"Well obviously no."

"Now in the second operation in connection with your report, you thought initially that the operation was done on the left side and then the right?

"Well, the actual treatment was on the left side first and the actual treatment was then on the right side."

"Okay, Doctor, did you testify in your deposition?"

Mr. H shot up, "Excuse me, Your Honor, I object. It's improper use of the deposition." Judge Peterson answered, "I agree. The objection is sustained."

Peter started again, "Now in your deposition—"

Mr. H again objected, "Your Honor, I'm going to object to this line of questioning. It is an improper use of the deposition."

Judge Peterson stated, "I thought we just went through that, Mr. Pryor."

Peter answered, "I'll do it a different way, thank you."

"Throughout the entire day of your deposition, do you have any recollection of ever talking about the size of the bone flaps?"

Mr. H rose to his feet again, "Your Honor, I object again." Peter answered, "It's not in the deposition, so I can't point it out to him, Your Honor."

Judge Peterson ruled once more, "That's not the problem. The objection is sustained."

Peter tried once again, "Have you ever expressed any opinion in your notes or anywhere considering the size of bone flaps until this morning or yesterday morning and if so, can you point that out?"

No objection was made to that approach, and Dr. Smith answered, "I don't think that issue has come up for ventilation."

"And it never came up by you?"

"I don't recall it, no. These things develop in stages."

"Now when did that first occur to you that the bone flap was too small? And that the top of the brain was retracted into the anterior part of the cranial wall?"

"I must have noticed it when I looked over the CT scans in July."

"Now can you explain to me—I don't understand how this in fact works. And as I understand it, the brain was being lifted in, and, because the bone wasn't cut far enough back, that caused the pressure on the top of the brain?"

"Yes, no, it caused pressure on the brain. The inner tissue of the right frontal lobe first and then the inner tissue of both lobes as shown clearly on the brain scan. It caused confinement of the frontal lobe. The blood vessels of the brain terminate in very fine capillary vents that nourish neurological tissue. And if you compress them, you close them. When they are closed, often the next stage would be clotting or thrombosis."

"That means clot off permanently?"

"Well, there can be, depending on the size of the blood vessels."

"How about anterior cerebral arteries?"

"Yes, I think they're closed permanently."

"And so, when these blood vessels clot off for a significant period of time, the oxygen supply to the brain tissue stops and whatever distribution, that is the tissue supplied by that, dies?"

"No, it is an infarction." [Peter attempted to write the sequence on the board but Dr. Smith's unique theory of infarction makes no sense to me.]

"Now was it pulling too hard, the pulling up or the lifting up of the instrument that caused this? Or the fact when it was lifted up, it was lifted into the top of the cranial vault and pressure was transmitted to the brain, or was it both?"

"Both."

"As a result, there's pressure on the brain from two directions? That is your explanation and theory to a reasonable medical probability as to what happened to Sheran R?"

"Yes."

"That letter you got from Mr. Schuster, do you have it in front of you? Doctor, look on the bottom on paragraph 1 of page 1 on June 25, 1986. Do you see the description of a quick overview of the Wyoming care? [with strikingly similar wording] Did you find that helpful and did you use and consider that in terms of that and the information provided to you in arriving at opinions in this case?"

"Well, I don't—I doubt that it had nothing to do with the opinion. I think it just summarized it."

Peter then switched to Dr. N's care, attempting to use the opinion of Dr. Smith [who prior to the settlement had been endorsed by Plaintiffs to speak against Dr. N]. Mr. H objected.

Judge Peterson stated, "You can't talk about that now. You will have to subpoena him to do that."

Peter did ask whether an instrument in Wyoming could cause the problem. Referring Dr. Smith to his deposition, he read, "It does look to me there was a definite plunge of an instrument."

"Yes." [By God he knows the word.]

"And throughout your deposition do you have any recollection of ever describing the injury or wound in Wyoming as other than a plunge [said loudly] of the instrument through the dura of the cribriform plate?"

"All I can tell you is I think the instrument caused the fistula or the spinal fluid leak—I didn't know for sure whether the instrument fractured the bone which tore the dura or whether the instrument went through the bone and through the dura. How could I know?"

"All right. All right. Now, Doctor, was there a period where you stopped doing surgery as a primary surgeon sometime in the '80s?"

"It was probably in '84 or '85 when I got very busy, a national level chairman of the committee of neurosurgical manpower, and I was traveling a lot. Do you want to hear anymore? Just very busy, and I didn't want to operate and leave town. I didn't stop practice. I didn't stop assisting."

"Did your age have anything to do with that?"

"No—in '87 I was in the national squash racquet tournament. I was in top physical shape."

Peter continued again, "Doctor at the time of your deposition in this case, do you remember if you were aware that there was even a neurosurgical consultant request by Dr. Ogsbury?"

"I saw nothing in the records that identified a neurosurgical consultant. Since then I've learned that Dr. Shogan is a highly respected neurosurgeon—it didn't show in the record, I didn't happen to know that."

"Was one of your criticisms initially in this case that Dr. Ogsbury did not get an ENT consultation?"

"It could have been."

"All right. Now look at the record. See in the progress notes here? Who's that?"

"That's Dr. Barron. It doesn't look like much of a consultation. You know, if I didn't write it, I didn't say it."

"Why did you think he wanted an ENT consult? Do you recall the purpose of the consultation?"

"I'm sure he had a good one." [Fric, one of the paralegals, came to the rescue and brought Dr. Barron's deposition.]

"Okay, here's Dr. Barron's deposition. Do you recall reading in Dr. Barron's deposition that one of the reasons he was asked to look at Sheran R was to see if possibly they could come in through this extracranial route? Does that refresh your recollection in reading Dr. Barron's deposition?"

"Yes."

"Or one of the purposes that he was asked to come in was, from an ENT standpoint, to see if this was amenable to the extracranial repair? And do you now recall his testimony that he did not think it was?"

"I wouldn't quarrel with that."

"All I'm getting at, Doctor, when you gave your deposition, you criticized this man?"

"It wasn't a big issue."

"Well, you criticized him as a little issue as being negligent in not getting an ENT."

"Then I apologize."

"Doctor, did you read Dr. Ogsbury's deposition?"

"Yes."

"And do you recall Dr. Ogsbury testifying that another reason he had Dr. Barron was that if he ever had to do an extracranial repair, that Barron would be familiar with the interior aspect of the brain? Do you recall that testimony?"

"Vaguely but I don't know what, if you're going to be doing it from below, I don't know why you need to see it from the other side."

"Okay. Did you know one way or the other whether there was a discussion in Wyoming of the options of intracranial?"

"I think that does appear in Dr. N's deposition."

"I want you to look at Exhibit B3. Dr. N has identified this as his note, and I will represent that he will testify that after these discussions took place, he sat down with the family, discussed alternatives with patient and family at length, reclosure of ethmoidectomy would offer reasonable chance of effecting closure, but neurosurgical approach would offer optimal results. Now with respect to that, would that not be appropriate within the standard of care?"

"All I can tell you is that how you state tomato or tomahto and how you approach the family could be quite different from what may or may not have taken place. I think it's a very vague area."

"Now another thing. Do you remember at the time of your deposition that you were concerned that the doctor had not documented his discussions with the family? Since re-reading the records that determine that there are numerous discussions of options. That afterward there are two separate discussions documented in the progress notes as to options of bedrest versus drainage versus additional surgery. And finally, prior to the third operation that there was a lengthy discussion and documentation of going in both sides of Sheran R and an explanation that if he did that, that was a much more significant surgery and there were much greater risks associated with that?"

"I don't look upon that as being a big key or major issue in my testimony. I think it's all a matter of record.

"Okay. Now you said the first surgery was premature, right? That he shouldn't have opted for surgery—he should have waited. That was one of the criticisms that you gave yesterday. So instead of performing surgery on 6/25, he should have waited a few more days, right?"

"Is this about the fifth time we've gone through this?"

"No, this is the first time. How far out was she on the day of surgery? How long had this leak been open?"

"I think it was performed on the 16th."

"Right. Nine days."

"And you said the radiologist said it was negative?"

"Right."

"Now I want to ask you a question because this is important. Is this negative for a separation of bone?"

"I didn't see anything that would be called a fracture."

Peter showed him the X-ray report. "'Impression: abnormal cisternography with abnormal air collection within the subarachnoid space on the right and questionable dehiscence.' That means separation, right, of the bone in the right cribriform plate region?"

"I won't buy that. You can buy it but I know that no two cribriform plates are completely symmetric." [Will he ever admit to a point?]

The break was called, and the team remained in good spirits.

After the Court was called again into session, Mr. H came to the bench and objected to Mr. Pryor using Dr. Smith against Dr. N stating it was improper to use a neurosurgeon against an ENT.

Peter answered, "Your Honor, one, we designated Dr. N as a nonparty so we have an obligation and a right to establish his negligence. Number two, the doctor reviewed the record, indicated in his deposition that he has been hired to review all of the care indicated, that he was aware of the January 1990 trial date in Wyoming, that he was available as a witness in that matter, and at the time of the deposition, he felt he was competent to testify about indications for surgery. We then in August of 1989 endorsed Dr. Smith."

Judge Peterson ruled Peter should hold and lay the foundation for his expertise by phone and bring him back if a foundation were laid.

Peter resumed, "Doctor, we're now dealing with the issue of waiting a few more days for this leak to heal. Want to ask you first. Do you have an opinion to a reasonable medical probability—if Dr. Ogsbury hadn't done the operation on June 25, would the leak have healed?"

"I think that—it could have. I would have wanted another two or three days."

"But in your opinion are you telling the jury that if the operation hadn't been done on June 25 and they had just let it alone, that more likely than not this would have healed on its own without surgery?"

"No. I think you're going to be speculating. I don't have a definite opinion. I would say it could have."

"It's possible, but not probable?"

"Yes."

"All right, we also know some things about this leak, don't we? He put a pledget in the hole. And yet even with the pledget in the hole, even with the brain laying over the pledget, and even with the pressure of the brain, two days later she's leaking? Are you telling the jury then, that in trying to fix the leak on June 25, that he caused the leak?"

"I'm just saying that the instrumentation tends to disturb the situation. That's what happened, and then you start the process all over again." [Now is he saying I actually caused the leak?]

You don't have any reason to believe that it was ethmoid surgery drainage from nine days or eight days before, do you?"

"No." [My goodness he backed off on one.]

"Now let me show you a couple of things in this operative report. Dr. Ogsbury will ultimately testify that this subpial blood, if in fact there was significant subpial blood, wouldn't that be consistent with a direct trauma from an instrument? Would you agree that this is consistent with an instrument plunging through the dura?"

"I would rely on his observation."

"Now he goes on to say below that at which point there was an obvious rent in the dura and some blood about it. Would that be consistent with an instrument plunging through the plate and into the dura?"

"It could."

"If you look at the operative report, he indicates not that the pledget was laid over the hole, does he, but he says it was placed in the hole? So as opposed to just sitting over it like this, at least by the operative report, there's some indication that it's down inside or in the hole or at least part of it?"

"Yes."

"Okay, now I need to talk to you about the Super Glue issue. You have made some assumptions based upon some questions given to you by

Mr. H about the use of Super Glue, and you see no evidence in the record, I take it, that it was ever used, in terms of the hospital chart. There is not indicated anywhere that Super Glue was used, isn't that, right?"

"No, I didn't see any definite record in the hospital record."

"And Dr. Ogsbury said in the operative report that he used a surgical adhesive. Now if Dr. Ogsbury testifies—and I want you to assume he used a surgical adhesive rather than Super Glue or Crazy Glue, would you agree that based upon Youman's text and your knowledge of standard approaches, that that is acceptable within standards of care?"

"Not in the way he describes its use because it doesn't conform to the usage described in Youman's text."

"Do you know Ludwig Kemp?"

"Yes, I knew him for years."

"Do you recall reading this article where he used these compounds at Walter Reed Hospital many years ago? They weren't just experimenting—there were actual patient treatments, isn't that correct?"

"Yes."

"And the upshot of this report, there is a literature, albeit old, that indicates that the use of cyanacrylic isobutyl is safe and effective?"

"Oh yes, yes."

"Now back to meningitis for a minute. I'm not going to try to sneak up on you. [I had trouble not smiling on that one.] Remember you were talking about this kind of like good or less dangerous like pneumococcal bacteria?"

"Yes."

"And there are gram negative bacteria. Those are the virulent (and potentially deadly) bacteria. If you get a full-blown gram-negative meningitis—that did cause a person to become vegetative or kill them, right?"

"This is serious—it can be a serious situation."

"So, when you see evidence of a gram negative infection, even if it's just in its beginning stages, that is potentially a serious, even a deadly situation?"

"It could be." [He admitted to another one.]

"Now let's talk a little bit about the culture. You said the culture didn't grow anything out. And you talked about whether that's because it's being suppressed by all these antibiotics she's getting and you're well aware of the literature on prophylactic antibiotics?"

"Yes."

"But the problem with prophylactic antibiotics is that they don't always successfully prevent a meningeal and bacterial meningitis, do they?"

"Right."

"When you said that they took it and spun it down in a machine, then you put those on the plate, and your gram stain. It will stain in a certain fashion that will tell you what you're looking at under a microscope?"

"Hopefully yes."

"In this particular case, when they did that with respect to the lumbar puncture on June 28, they found a few gram negative rods?"

"Right."

"That's right in Dr. Mason's note, right? There's a progress note on 6/25 that says a few gram-negative rods, right?"

"Right."

"And if you had a gram stain showing a few gram-negative rods, that would be absolutely laboratory-wise consistent with meningitis, would it not?"

"I think I've testified to that, and I can just tell you I don't think she had clinical meningitis."

"Well, she had a stiff neck?"

"She was on the operating table for four hours—that would give anybody a stiff neck."

"Okay, is she running a temperature. Is that consistent with meningitis?"

"Yes."

"And she had a white blood count of, what, 26, 27?"

"It was 17,000 and went up to about 23,000."

"So that can be indicative of an infectious process in the body?"

"It's a response of the body to some problem."

"Now she had a lumbar or CSF fluid analysis, which we've already talked about that, and that is certainly consistent with meningitis, is it not?"

"Well, I think the craniotomy ruins your programming, because I think just the manipulation of the brain in a craniotomy could be throwing off 2,300 whites and 2,760 red cells."

"Does Dr. Shogan think she has meningitis?"

"I think he thought she did have."

"So that was a reasonable decision within the standard of care to come to that assumption and opinion?"

"If he so chose, that's fine, yes."

"So that was a reasonable decision within the standard of care to come to that decision and opinion?"

"Well, I don't—I wouldn't agree to that, but I think they have a right to their opinion."

"Doctor, you've had all kinds of opinions and criticisms about all kinds of his care, and I'm asking you to give an opinion based upon a reasonable degree of medical probability as to whether it was reasonable for Dr. Ogsbury to conclude on June 28 that she had meningitis."

"Well, I think it was very reasonable for him to give his opinion. I don't think I have to agree or say that she did have meningitis."

"My next question is, is it consistent and reasonable within the standard of care to come to that opinion that she had meningitis?"

"Well, I don't think it's right for you to stir up some big personality conflict here because I don't think that's necessary."

Peter turned to the Court for help. Judge Peterson instructed him to answer the question.

Peter asked again, "Okay I'll repeat it one more time. Assuming as of June 29 that Dr. Ogsbury was of the opinion, based upon the information I have covered with you, that Sheran R had a bacterial meningitis. Was coming to and forming that particular opinion within the standard of care for a board-certified neurosurgeon?"

"Well, it could have been."

"No. Was it, or wasn't it?"

Judge Peterson interjected, "Okay, Doctor, Doctor…"

Dr. Smith asked the court, "Do I have to say yes or no?"

Judge Peterson said, "Yes."

Dr. Smith said, "I can't—I'm not able to—I really don't know the answer to that question."

Peter tried again, "Okay. Doctor, you gave an opinion yesterday that the surgery was beneath the standard of care to be intracranial. So, you were able to talk about intracranial versus extracranial, right?"

"Oh yes."

"And you thought the surgery was premature?"

"Yes."

"You talked about the technique of surgery?"

"Right."

"You talked about retraction you were able to form an opinion about that?"

"Right."

"You gave an opinion about glue?"

"Right."

"And you were able to form an opinion about his obligation to discuss various risks of surgery and informed consent, right?"

"Informed consent, yes."

"And you were able to form—you said it was below the—where you talked about the retraction, right?"

"That's in the technique, I believe."

"Also, the technique in terms of not stuffing the pledget down in the hole or suturing?"

"Yes."

"Then the retraction, right? And then you talked about the failure to get a CSF analysis before the first operation and you were more than willing and able to express opinions as to whether each of these were in or outside the standard of care, right?"

"Well whatever questions were asked along that line."

"And offered opinion about the cisternogram showing no leak?"

"Right."

"And you talked about the bone flap not being big enough? "

"Right."

"And you raised the issue of operating potentially in the face of meningitis?"

"Yes."

"See that's one of the problems I want to talk about. So just in connection with the first surgery you offered opinions in ten different areas did you not?"

"But in all the areas the questions were strictly neurosurgical matters."

"And then you offered another three or four opinions about the second surgery in terms of indications, the flap size, bone size, retraction. So why are you so afraid to give me your opinion about whether she had meningitis or not?"

"I can assure you if I had an honest opinion on that matter, I would give it."

"Is there any chance that you don't want to give an opinion because in looking back you think it will hurt the Plaintiffs' case?"

"I don't know how it can hurt it because one minute you say meningitis, the next minute you say no meningitis. I'm just trying to give you an opinion in a way that I don't ruin my other opinions."

"So, you're trying to protect your other opinions?"

"I'm trying to protect my honesty, my dedication to be willing to say what I think." [Wow!]

"Do you know Bronson Ray?"

"Oh yes."

"In reading Dr. Ogsbury's professional resume, you know that he trained with Bronson Ray?"

"I think he spent a brief time there at the New York hospital."

"Now is Dr. Bronson Ray internationally known for his transcranial hypophysectomy? And of the 1,600 cases that he has had, how many anterior cerebral artery infarctions has he had?"

"I presume none because he doesn't lift both lobes of the brain."

"Now, Doctor, have you ever had the complication of anterior cerebral artery infarction secondary to your surgical retractions?"

"No."

"Would you agree that the most common cause of this bilateral anterior cerebral artery infarction is aneurysm surgery of the arteries? And an aneurysm is kind of like—just for lay understanding—a blister or something in a hose where it's thinned out so that surgery involved direct manipulation of the arteries themselves, does it not?"

"It may."

"And if you have to retract all the way—back to the tuberculum, then you have to retract hard enough to get back there?"

"Well, I wouldn't go along with that. I'm afraid that's what happened here but I think it was wrong, and I think I can't go along with your line of questioning."

"Okay. Doctor, there's no way to tell with a brain how much, in advance, how much is too much, is there?"

"It's an issue of touch and feel and judgment and experience where the doctor uses his best judgment of—how much traction is appropriate in a given situation."

"Is there any test that you can do on someone to tell how much traction you can do in advance?"

"Well hopefully this will be a striking example." [He still wishes to punish.]

"Okay. Now Dr. Krauth—can I talk to you just a second about him? Dr. Krauth indicates that he recommends that bilateral approach. Is it ultimately the primary surgeon's responsibility whether to accept or reject the advice of his consultants or recommendations?"

"The ultimate decision? You mean the final decision?"

"Right."

"And that's his sole and ultimate responsibility, you agree, as the treating physician?"

"Yes."

"Then your sole criticism, I take it, of Dr. Krauth, is that you don't think he should have recommended a bilateral approach in the first place of any surgery?"

"I believe that would summarize it."

"Now who else looked at the patient on the same day with respect to the issue of surgery?"

"I believe the primary people are Dr. Krauth and Dr. Mason and Dr. Shogan before the second craniotomy."

"Did you know that Dr. Barron came in right after Dr. Krauth where he says, 'Recommend bilateral exploration,' and said quote, 'I concur with the above'?"

"I don't recall that."

"But Dr. Krauth—was negligent for making that recommendation?"

"I don't think they should have gone and done the second craniotomy at that time."

"In your opinion, in making the recommendation, did Dr. Krauth fall below the standard of care?"

"I would have to say yes."

"Now you're critical of Dr. Krauth even though the man who had been following him all along, the ENT doctor, came right in and said, 'I agree with, exactly with, Dr. Krauth—should be done'?"

"Well. I have no qualms with that, because I'm not sure that was within the scope of his practice." [If he had conceded that point, Lee would have been let off.]

"Now you told Mr. H that, if only Dr. Ogsbury would have gotten a patch the first time, that Sheran R would have ended up with much less severe and maybe even nil right-sided damage?"

"Yes."

"And you testified that you didn't think the Wyoming doctors caused any harm neurologically?"

"Never any identified."

"But isn't it true, Doctor, that in the same analysis that if Dr. Ogsbury had just gotten the June 25 operation right, there would have been mild to minimal symptoms, that if Dr. N hadn't done the operation at all, that none of this would have happened?"

"Well, you could say that. I would assume you don't need an expert to tell you that."

"To a reasonable medical probability?"

I can certainly say he caused the CSF leak. I don't think he can take responsibility for everything thereafter."

"Now you also talked about the pneumothorax. The lung was punctured and it collapsed and she is now being perfused by one lung, that she's getting her oxygen supply from one lung, correct?"

"The right lung was impaired, but the blood gases were all within normal limits."

"Well just bear with me. So, here's a woman who is very ill at this point, isn't she? She's in critical care? How long did she go with this pneumothorax before it was recognized?"

"Well, it was put in probably 2:00 or 3:00 o'clock in the morning."

"And so, between 3:00 in the morning and 8:00 or 8:30 in the morning, isn't it true that as far as you know, her collapsed lung condition was unnoticed and untreated?"

"Yes."

"With respect to that issue, from your careful review of the records, did you notice that her blood pressure dropped in the early hours of the morning to 60/0? Were you aware of that?"

"I can't answer it because I don't remember that part of it."

"Well assume that her blood pressure was 60/0. Then assume that her pulse did really weaken, assume that her pulse was so weak that by the very early morning hours that the only place they could find any pulse was in the femoral artery. Assume further that by sometime shortly prior to 8:00, they can't find a pulse, what does that mean to you? Arterial collapse potentially?"

"When you talk about arterial collapse, it's probably really decreasing cardiac output."

"But there weren't any blood gases at all were there, during the time frame?"

"Not during that critical period."

"A woman who was morbidly critically ill, a woman who was dying, in your opinion, to a reasonable degree of medical probability."

"I didn't see that, but go ahead."

"A woman where when Dr. Mason found this, she called a Cor zero, correct? A Cor zero in a hospital means 'everyone hit the decks, we have a potential life and death situation,' correct?

"We have no argument on the care."

"And the first time the blood gas was ever done was in the morning, and by then they placed the chest tube, and her lung was reinflated. So we don't know from blood gases that were taken at the time that she was lying there in critical or intensive care for six hours, what the blood gases would have shown, do we?"

"Well, I've explained certainly there was no CT evidence of signs of cerebral anoxia. In other words, if she had been severely hypoxic, the CT brain scan taken subsequently would have shown classical changes. Maybe a few cells around there didn't get quite as much oxygen as they would have hadn't there been a pneumothorax, but I don't think it was a big, significant aggravation of the primary condition."

Doctor, to a reasonable degree of medical probability, would you agree that the final insult was this woman having her lung collapse and her blood pressure dropping to a nonexistent level for five or six hours?" [his exact words on deposition]

Mr. H objected. Peter had touched on the issue of opinions which seem to have changed following the settlements. The objection was sustained.

Peter tried once more "To a reasonable medical probability, was there some aggravation of her preexisting condition?"

"In my opinion, no."

"Did you discuss this issue with the attorneys for the Plaintiffs, since you've been here, and your opinions in this regard?"

"No, I don't recall any suggestion of what I should say."

His point made, Peter asked Scott and me if there were any further questions. We agreed there were not. "No further questions, Your Honor."

Mr. H took the stand. He looked tired. "Doctor I'm going to hand you the nursing note from the early morning of July 4 just to orient you that there's a note at 6:30 a.m. Does it indicate that somebody was called because of the blood pressure dropping?"

"Yes. Dr. Krauth."

"And at 7:00 a.m. in the morning, the Nurse Changed shifts and turned her over to another nurse, and by the time she left, what does it indicate as far as whether Dr. Krauth had responded to that call at 6:30 a.m.?"

"It says, 'no call back from Dr. Krauth.'"

"Just let me ask you, have you had an opportunity to look at the neurologic status the way the nurse keeps it in the chart? Did you look at the patient's neurologic score before the second surgery? And did you look at the neurologic score immediately after the second surgery?"

"Yes."

"What did you notice about the difference before and after the surgery?"

"There was a dramatic change—the worse."

"Did you look at the neurologic score during the period of time to see if there was any difference from before the pneumothorax?"

"Yes."

"And was there any difference in the neurologic score during the pneumothorax episode?"

"No, she was in very serious trouble before that, before the pneumothorax, and stayed that way, didn't change."

"And did you see clinically any indication of a change neurologically from before the pneumothorax and after the pneumothorax?"

"No."

"Mr. Pryor talked about Dr. Krauth and made a point that Dr. Ogsbury was the primary physician. Let me show you the front page of the operative report for the first surgery, June 25. Dr. Ogsbury, what is he titled?"

"Surgeon."

"And Dr. Barron is titled what? "

"Assistant."

"Now let me show the operative report for the operation that Dr. Krauth was involved in. You see the words 'surgeons'? And whose names are there?"

"James Ogsbury and Lee E. Krauth."

"And is anybody identified as an assistant in that surgery?"

"No."

"Mr. Pryor talked about retraction with the surgery that was done in the case to repair a cerebrospinal fluid leak. Should that retraction be able to occur without the kind of brain damage that occurred in Sheran R?"

"Yes. Under the proper mechanical arrangements."

"Doctor, in the presence of meningitis, when a doctor is considering whether to go in and do a craniotomy, what does the standard of care require, as far as what is done first in the management of that patient if the patient had meningitis?"

"Cure the meningitis before any surgery."

"And you do that how?"

"Oh, with antibiotics, a general care."

"And if one antibiotic isn't working, what do you try?"

"You should really get a culture and line up the bacteria with sensitivity testing and know which bacteria responds to which antibiotic."

"Doctor, if you have the bacteriology results there, do you see the one slip that talks about the few gram-negative rods? It was on 6/28, is that correct?"

"Right."

"Would you look and see if you can find the culture from June 28?"

"I cannot find any related to June 28th."

"Are you aware, Doctor, of any time other than July 1—when a few gram-negative rods were found—any other time when any other bacteria dead or alive were identified?"

"No."

"Mr. Pryor made reference to a stiff neck on the 28th. Can you find Dr. Shogan's consult? Does it indicate that he did a physical exam? "

"Yes."

"Now if Dr. Shogan suspected meningitis, would you imagine that he would zero in on physical findings on an exam that would be consistent with meningitis? Tell me if you see any indication of a stiff neck on the 28th by—"

"No, he doesn't mention any stiff neck."

"She had gone through a craniotomy on the 25th. What kind of support is there on the back or neck or the head?"

"There are all different kinds of supports, but the fact of being in one position under anesthesia and so forth, it's very common after a craniotomy for the patient to complain of a stiff neck."

"Doctor, Mr. Pryor asked you a question about the placement of the patch, and he talked about the operative report indicating the patch was put in the hole. Do you remember that in your review of this material—did you review the deposition of Dr. Ogsbury?"

"Yes."

"What was Dr. Ogsbury's explanation of how he placed the patch?"

"Well, he said then you sort of push it down so that hopefully a little of the muscle may get into the hole."

"Is that kind of pushing into the hole the kind of packing that occurred during the second surgery?"

"No."

Mr. H then continued, "Doctor I'm going to hand you the text that was referred to earlier, Neurological Surgery second edition, page 2221. Would you read that?"

"'Optimal management requires that the neurosurgeon consider both approaches in choosing the appropriate procedure for any individual patient.'"

"And by both approaches, he's talking about the intracranial and extracranial approaches, is that correct?"

"Right" [ignoring the emphasis in Youman's of the extracranial approach for sphenoid leaks and intracranial for ethmoid leaks].

"Doctor, turn the page for one last reference for this article, on page 2224, 'When the transsphenoidal approach is used'—do you see that? What does that indicate, Doctor? Would you read it?"

"If a patient has rhinorrhea—that's leakage of fluid—a patient has rhinorrhea following the transsphenoidal operation, then a trial of conservative management is in order."

"Doctor, let's go to the cerebrospinal fluid sample that Mr. Pryor talked about. You talked about white cells, and red cells, and about protein and glucose?"

"Yes."

"I think he asked you if that was consistent with meningitis. Is it consistent with meningitis?"

"I presume it's consistent, as long as you have something else to go with it."

"Doctor, are increased white cells and red cells and their value of the protein and glucose consistent with other things besides meningitis?"

"Very definitely."

"Doctor, last topic."

"You were questioned at length about your experience testifying. Doctor, would you give us an idea of the number of medical malpractice cases you've reviewed or been involved in over the last ten years, medical malpractice cases?"

"Yes. The last ten years I would say around fifteen, possibly a few more."

"So, you've averaged about a case and a half a year over the past ten years?"

"Yes."

"If you wanted to, Doctor, if you were in it for the money, could you do this full-time?"

"I could be doing it now. I won't do it."

"If you wanted to do it full-time, could you stay busy doing it?"

"Oh yes."

"Could you advertise it?"

"Well, I never have, but I could."

"Is there a demand for members of your profession to review cases for injured people?"

"Well—I think—I'd say yes."

"Are you under any contractual obligation at the present time that requires you to cooperate with defense lawyers and not cooperate with plaintiffs' lawyers?"

"No."

"Doctor, would you tell the jury why you agreed to review medical cases on the average of one and one-half or even two a year?"

"Well, it's just that I personally feel it's an obligation for any neurosurgeon, especially as sort of at the zenith of his career, if you will, to help out in sorting out a problem."

"Doctor, do you belong to any of the professional societies that have established any databases concerning doctors who have been identified as testifying against other doctors?"

"I don't anymore. I did for ten years."

"One last question. A point was made that you're paid for your time?"

"Yes."

"In your county where you live and where you were practicing, are there guidelines or are there customary charges for neurosurgeons that they charge when they have to go into the courtroom and get involved in something like this?"

"Yes."

"And where does your $300 fit in your accounting with those guidelines?"

"That's a relatively—below average."

"Are you here because of the money?"

"No."

"Do you have anything against Dr. Ogsbury or Dr. Krauth?"

"No."

Mr. H conferred with his colleagues and then stated, "I have no further questions."

Judge Peterson asked, "Anything new Mr. Pryor?"

Peter answered, "No, Your Honor. Thank you, Dr. Smith."

Judge Peterson said, "Thank you, Doctor. Nine o'clock Monday morning. Have a nice weekend. It's Miller time."

After the jury left, Mr. H came up and amicably congratulated Peter on his rebuttal. Peter congratulated Mr. H on his opening statements. These are the same men who were serious combatants with the jury in the room. It seems like the Super Bowl for my career. I talked with Peter and his mother, who evidently comes to many of his trials. He asked her how it went. She said two things: Dr. Smith knows every word except yes and no, and Peter killed him.

I generally feel pretty good. We came out of Dr. Smith at least neck-and-neck. The jury seemed very impressed with Peter's points. Mrs. Pettit and Mr. Saline often appeared to have specific personal questions that were answered.

I also learned that my neurosurgical colleague and friend came to see Dr. Smith. Several years ago, Dr. Smith testified in deposition that my colleague had been negligent in giving a second opinion (which I know to have been appropriate) in a case that later turned out poorly, not a small factor in my colleague's retirement. I hope my colleague took some solace in Dr. Smith's obvious discomfort today. I walked out of the Court and again it was raining. When will we get to ride?

Peter
Friday, May 4, 1990, 6:00 p.m.

Today went swimmingly with the morning cross of Smith being especially good. I just flowed with instinct, no sense of time or anything above or around me, except Dr. Smith and me. I was miles ahead of him all the way, carving him into tiny little pieces to the open amusement of several jurors. By noon, which arrived seemingly within seconds of 9:15 a.m. when we started this morning, Smith seemed an outdated, arrogant, scatological, old man, intent only on keeping his ego intact at all costs.

At one point I asked him if he wanted the Plaintiffs to prevail and, after listening to his predictable "I'm on the side of justice" response, I launched into what had been clearly a personal attack on Jay during Smith's deposition. At one point when I bopped him over the head with a famous neurosurgical text which refuted many of his opinions, he accused the author of negligent writing.

Although the afternoon session wasn't nearly so sharp, we got into an amazing discussion where the man simply would not answer my question whether it was reasonable by June 29, 1986, for Jay to assume that Sheran had meningitis, even after thirty minutes of dodging, ducking, and maybes, and the Judge twice ordering him to answer the question "yes" or "no." Smith didn't hurt. Dr. Dinosaur is dead.

Fran
Friday, May 4, 1990, 9:00 p.m.

No meeting this evening—a needed break from the heat and intensity of this trial. I'm beat. Between my practice, my kids, this trial, and the book, it all feels overwhelming. I wish I had a wife or something to that effect.

Where is the friction coming from? I'm not flowing with anything. I'm angry with Jay. He feels like a swollen, raging river in a storm. There is no safe place to step in a raging river, and I was stupid enough to try it.

I have regrets. I know to sit by a raging river and wait for the peaceful waters to return. The tears fall, sad for myself that I cannot remember my lessons, sad that I didn't trust the peaceful waters to return, sad that my narcissism prevailed, sad that his trust is now shaken.

CHAPTER NINE

FIRST WEEKEND

Peter
Saturday, May 5, 1990

A day with the boys, running errands, doing things for them. I tried to connect with them, which normally comes so naturally and spontaneously, but the physical exhaustion and preoccupation with the trial kept me at a distance. It was fun but not close and therefore a little painful, especially Saturday night when I went out to a fancy black tie affair and had to leave them home. I bailed out at 10:00 p.m. to come home. I think the biggest sacrifice of trial, aside from my body, is my relationship with my boys. While there are the calls, the little two-hour get-togethers (mini-vignettes) serve mostly to remind me of how distant and unconnected I become during trial, a process which weakens me.

Jay
Saturday, May 5, 1990

Taking Peter's advice, I did not go to a performance of Opera Colorado on Friday evening. Dr. Barron and I have been supporters of Opera Colorado since its inception, and our families attend the performances together. This night I cannot be seen with him since he is an important witness in my trial. Angry that all facets of my life were being held prisoner to the trial, I returned home and reviewed my notes until midnight. Kathy and the Barrons went without me. I took call Friday through Sunday since Lee was covering weekdays during the trial. Saturday morning, I ran a clinic of recent post-op patients. Most of the patients were doing well, and I realized then how much medicine has consumed my life, and yet, in some strange way, has sustained me as well. It also felt good again to see my medical team, and I appreciated their willingness to allow me a few moments of reprieve despite their obvious interest in the proceedings of the past week.

The improvement in mood did not persist and, on Saturday afternoon, I found myself simply lying on the bed until Peter called suggesting a bike ride the next day. While I had been looking forward to the ride for a week, I did not feel good about the overall situation. I had faced my challenge by another neurosurgeon, one of at least some previous prominence, with significant trepidation. But Frank Smith seemed clearly adversarial, an expert whose opinions were for hire.

And while, prior to the trial, there was always the underlying question that he might have some valid criticisms despite his obvious bias, the answer was a ringing **no**. I no longer had to face Dr. Smith, but I also no longer had the motivation of his challenge. In addition, the nightly meetings with Fran did not seem to be going well. The narrative and Fran have helped sustain me so far; I wonder how it will feel if the project falls through.

That night I did not sleep at all. I realized that with the challenge of facing Dr. Smith having passed and the support of Fran and our project in jeopardy, I was, for the first time, considering ending the fight. I reviewed my motivations for being here. The defense of my medicine seems to be going well. My colleagues know it; Dr. Smith knows it; the attorneys know it (both ours and I think even theirs); and, following my encounter with Dr. Smith, I know it. Our response to the legal challenge has been strong but controlled. My team feels we have chased Mr. Spence clear out of Colorado, and he is no longer an issue even to me. The project of describing this experience to my colleagues, friends, and adversaries is still ongoing, but I am worried whether Fran can or will stay really involved. The responsibility to my professional colleagues is still a factor, and finally the feeling of frustration and helplessness expressed by almost every malpractice defendant that I know ("but I am a good guy") is still very real.

I spent the night mulling over my motives and almost decided to throw in the towel. By morning I decided to proceed for at least another week; ambivalence is not a comfortable experience for me, I like myself being sharp, clear, concise, and decisive. I rose early for the ride with Peter. We ride well together. I am used to the safety and comfort of an inner life surrounded by self-constructed walls, but his openness about himself provokes me to be more open with him. We share feelings, experiences, and relationships as only do comrades in war. I realize I am forming a friendship with a lawyer, and I find it amusing to think of the animosity that is supposed to exist between all physicians and lawyers.

We returned to the war room of PC&J. The afternoon was spent assisting Lee and Scott prepare for Lee's testimony on Tuesday and Peter for his encounter with Nurse B tomorrow. I went home, ate dinner, laid down, and finally fell asleep.

CHAPTER TEN

DAY 6
THE NURSES

Jay
Monday, May 7, 1990

I did not sleep well again. The dominoes still seem to be crumbling under me, and if the narrative fails, I'm not sure the defense of my medicine will be sufficient reason to continue. Even now I am questioning, was I 'a good guy'? I will give it one more week.

Driving in felt terrible. Kathy was very polite but had to schedule a manicure from the car phone. Somehow her call seemed out of place, but life goes on, I guess. In front of a little house I pass each day, I promised myself I will never do this again. I had joked earlier in the week that I would not volunteer again for this duty, but going to trial is no joke. I don't care what it takes—settling, changing practice, leaving medicine, even suicide (probably not), but there is no way I will ever be caught defending myself in a courthouse again.

We met Mary and Sam in the front of the courtroom, and they had already staked out the front row bench. It is amazing how reassuring the presence of these two people is to me—somehow more than my colleagues and friends. They, along with Peter and Fran, are my trial family. Today, Scott, Peter's second attorney who had been helping with the trial but had yet to do anything in the courtroom, would be taking point today in the cross-examination of the nurses.

Once in court, Kathy asked Mr. H to turn the tall exhibits on their side so the gallery could see. He graciously agreed to do so. It is difficult to have such a good man opposing us. He is obviously a skilled and, perish the thought from a doctor, ethical attorney doing his job. I want to dislike him, but I simply cannot. Mr. Spence, on the other hand, I could have easily disliked.

Mr. H is in a sport coat; Ms. Kudla is in a dark suit. Peter is wearing a light sport coat, Scott a dark coat. It appears to be a power day for the second attorneys. The court was reconvened. Judge Peterson appeared much more relaxed. Peter began by making several motions, again attempting to show that a witness, this time Dr. Smith, had changed his position specifically now that Dr. N had settled.

Dr. Smith would become an "un-expert" regarding Dr. N's care and the issues of meningitis. Hopefully Dr. Smith was to be used by our side to show the contribution of Dr. N. Mr. H denied that there was any change in Dr. Smith's testimony.

Judge Peterson ruled that there was no specific evidence of a change in testimony. Peter has repeatedly attempted to introduce the issue of change in testimony by witnesses since the settlements. Judge Peterson obviously finds outrageous the idea that these witnesses have been coached to redirect their total criticism toward me, rather than toward the other Defendants, and simply will not allow the issue to be considered. The motions completed, the jury was called.

Today four nurses will be called, and I have difficulty remembering the first three. It is interesting that not one of the superlative senior members of the neuro-rehab or ICU teams at the hospital were called. It is particularly striking that the Plaintiffs failed to call the magnificent nurse who was Mrs. R's primary nurse on the neuro-rehab floor for most of her stay at St. Anthony and who twice traveled with me to assist Sheran in her care in Wyoming.

Ms. Kudla came to the lectern. Nurse Y was called and sworn in. Even after seeing her, I only vaguely remember her. Ms. Kudla went through her background. She was an RN since 1985, working at St. Anthony since 1981. In June of 1986, she was working on 2 East, the Neuro floor, and was the nurse for the first evening of Mrs. R's hospitalization. She stated at 11:00 p.m. she observed drainage of fluid from Mrs. R's nose which tested positive for glucose, an indication of cerebrospinal fluid. She remembered the quantity to be a few drops.

Nurse Y stated she then oversaw an LPN's care on 6/27. At that point, Sheran R had undergone surgery, was unable to open her right eye completely, and her right pupil was large and not reactive to light. Ms. Kudla attempted to ask the relationship of the difficulty of the eye opening to the surgery. Scott objected as, of course, the nurse is not a clinical neurologist. Judge Peterson sustained the objection.

Nurse Y stated she again took care of Sheran R on 6/30 when she was "pretty much the same." When asked did she take care of her again, she noted she had but was not sure when. When questioned about her condition, she said it was a lot different, with a tracheostomy, feeding tube—not very responsive.

Scott stood up and immediately, and almost angrily, asked did Nurse Y have an independent recollection of the hospitalization that occurred four years ago. She stated she had only vague memories. He also attempted to have Nurse Y explain the significance of emesis or vomiting and its relevance to the failure of the operation. Ms. Kudla objected, and Judge Peterson smiled and said, "The same objection that you had, Mr. Nixon. Fair is fair," and sustained the objection [she doesn't miss a trick]. Scott had no further questions.

Scott had scared me at first. However, it quickly became apparent that his initial angry demeanor was a measure of his own anxiety. As his questioning proceeded, he became more calm and soon exhibited the same quiet style as Peter when Peter wishes simply to discredit but not antagonize a witness.

Ms. Kudla next called Nurse CK She is a big, strong, Germanic-appearing woman. I do not remember her at all. She reported that she had been an RN at St. Anthony since 1980.

She reported she came on at 2:45 and was told that Sheran R had undergone a craniotomy for a CSF leak one to one and one-half hours before; her vital signs were stable. She described her assessment as, "basically pretty sleepy from surgery, she was following commands like 'squeeze my hands, move your toes.'"

At that point a break was called. During the break, I noted that Dr. Mason's husband, an attorney, was in the court. He asked me how we were doing. I then wondered whether I should have talked to him at all. Scott said it was okay as long as I did not talk to Dr. Mason. Incredible! One must get permission to talk to one's friends.

I also thought about Nurse CK. She often grimaced as she talked, and I had a funny feeling that she had a chip on her shoulder against me, but she didn't say anything particularly damaging or untrue.

Peter reminded me that all of the nurses had been coached on what to say by the St. Anthony Hospital attorney when the hospital was a defendant. That their statements now seem a bit antagonistic toward me is not therefore surprising.

After the court was recalled, Nurse CK described Mrs. R's continued deterioration over the next few hours. Another CAT scan was ordered and completed at 9:50. Her condition at 10:30 was that of no verbal response, pupil's unequal, and following simple commands with extreme difficulty.

Ms. Kudla then turned to the need for IVs during this period. Nurse CK reported, "The IVs were running fine at the time, but the lab was having difficulty drawing the blood for tests. Borderline to me as being cruel—multiple pokes, with continuous digging and poking trying to find it."

Scott started his cross-examination by asking about Sheran R's condition during these hours. Nurse CK agreed that all parameters, except her verbal response, remained the same, and that her general overall assessment was pretty good. He then attempted to counter Nurse CK's apparent implication that she had difficulty contacting me. She admitted that after that, she didn't contact me as it was not necessary since I was usually in attendance.

Ms. Kudla then resumed her direct examination. Nurse CK added that Sheran R's condition at 4:00 p.m. was "fairly good" but that she was "extremely concerned" about her at 11:00 p.m. Her testimony finished, Nurse CK also left the stand without looking at me.

Nurse MK was then called to the stand by Ms. Kudla. She had been an RN since 1981 at St. Anthony and in the ICU since 1983 or 1984. She described Sheran R's condition when she came on duty at 3:15 p.m. on July 3. She was not following commands; her pupils were asymmetric; she withdrew from painful stimuli. Her condition was clearly worse than the condition as described on July 2.

She also noted that by 6:00 p.m., Sheran R was showing some evidence of reflex movement called posturing, clearly further worsening. Finally, she noted I called to order blood and urine tests [to confirm the cause of the decreased urine output] and that the first technician was unable to get the blood. Someone else from the lab came back and "did so with difficulty." At this point the lunch break was called.

At lunch we discussed the strange morning. Despite having my career on the line, I was bored with the tedious questioning posed by Ms. Kudla and the drolling testimony of these nurses and almost went to sleep. We talked about the later testimony of nurses regarding the CVP (Central Venous Pressure) line. Nurse MK had said in deposition she asked whether it could be placed [which I guess is possible but do not believe happened] and Nurse C had said she told me about it [there is no way that could have happened]. Finally, we also laughed about the difference in attorney interactions on the two teams. Peter frequently passed tactical hints to Scott during his cross-examination. Mr. H did less of this. Humorously to us, Mr. Schuster frequently wrote notes to Mr. H who put them down with none passed to Ms. Kudla.

After court was reconvened, Ms. Kudla asked further about Mrs. R's condition and the need for IVs. Nurse MK said again she was concerned that the urine output was below nursing guidelines. She said Sheran R's condition was stable from 7:00 to 9:00 p.m. and reported further that I came in at 9:00 p.m., examined Sheran R, and spoke at length with the family. She noted that she received orders to insert an NG tube and to call the critical care inhouse service if the urine output was decreased.

She also said she wished to talk to me, actually ran down the hall after me, asked if it was okay to put in a central line, and I said it was okay. [Wrong, I never would have said this though I might have agreed to have it placed if no other route could be found and then only if I was called.] Nurse MK then stated she gave report to Nurse C describing her condition, noting that I said it was okay if she needed a CVP line, and told her to watch the IVs which she thought would not last.

Nurse MK stated that she next saw Mr. R on July 4 at 3:00 p.m. She was told by the nurse on the day shift that Sheran R "had crumped and had to go down for a CAT scan, and she also developed a pneumothorax (collapsed lung) and they had to put a chest tube in."

She read from the day nurse's notes at 8:00 a.m. Her blood pressure was "80/90, pulse 102, and respirations 14. At 8:45 her "color extremely poor, level of consciousness down, not moving to pain as did earlier, blood pressure zero with Doppler, femoral pulse barely palpable, Dr. Mason here, Dr. Worley (a senior hospital doctor) called stat. Plasmanate increased—it's wide open." She reported that there was little change during her shift except admitting the possible elevated intracranial pressure. She said specifically when she completed her shift Sheran R was the same. At that point Scott showed me her deposition in which she had said, "There was a drastic change," an obvious change in her testimony, and he took the stand.

Scott asked about the deterioration that occurred between 8:00 and 8:45 on July 4. He noted that at the shift change her blood pressure was 88/0 and was not that something to be concerned about?

She answered, "Yes, in my opinion, yes."

He then asked, "And at that time isn't it true that in your opinion as a nurse her level of consciousness had deteriorated from the prior night?"

She answered, "No."

Scott then asked for the deposition and said that she took an oath, Mr. Schuster had asked a lot of questions [I bet he did], referred her to page 89 lines 6-14, and asked her if the deposition refreshed her recollection.

She again answered, "No."

He therefore said, "Well, well, is it true that at that time you were asked the following questions and gave the following answers: 'Question: Would it be fair to say that the condition of this patient when you came on for your shift on July 4 as radically different than when you left her on July 3? Answer: Yes. Question: In particular how was her condition changed from your perspective now? Answer: Her level of consciousness and her neurologic status had deteriorated.' Were those your answers to questions posed at that time?"

Nurse MK said, "Yes."

"So, her condition had deteriorated?"

"Her condition had deteriorated because she had a chest tube and—"

"Just a moment—I didn't ask you why—I just asked if it isn't true that her condition deteriorated?"

"Yes."

"And you had a chance to review those records before your deposition was taken, I believe, didn't you?"

"Yes."

"So, her care was fairly fresh in your mind at that time based on your review of the records?"

"Yes."

Scott paused, I think smiled, and resumed his questions.

"Now you consider yourself a good nurse, don't you?"

"Yes, I do."

"And most of the patients you see in the surgical intensive care unit are critically ill, aren't they?"

"The majority of them, yes."

"Now one of the most important aspects of your job in the surgical intensive care unit is to make notes concerning what's occurring with the patients, correct?"

"Correct."

"And that's part of your custom, habit, and routine, as an ICU nurse?"

"Yes, it is."

"Well, let me ask you, based on your charting that night and the fact that there's no report of any collapsed vein, there's no note of any difficulty infusing in her IV sites, there's no note of the need for a central line, there are noted orders at 10:00 and you recall asking him about something just after 10:00, and there was a note at 10:05 concerning the nasogastric tube and the urinary output. Don't you agree that it's more likely than not that you chased Dr. Ogsbury out of the room to get the order concerning the nasogastric tube and not the central line?"

"No."

"You don't think that's even a remote possibility, do you?"

"No."

"Well, if he did give an order, you didn't record it?"

"I didn't ask for an order for a central line. I asked him if he minded if we put one in."

"Isn't that the same as asking permission, the same as asking for an order from the doctor?"

"No."

"It's not?"

"No."

"When you asked Dr. Ogsbury for permission about the nasogastric tube, you wrote that in the chart, didn't you?"

"That's because that was something I could do."

"And when you asked him about the central line, you asked him for permission to place the central line, but you didn't write that in the orders and sign it, did you?"

"I asked him if it was all right with him if we got a central line placed if we ran out of places to start IVs, and he said he didn't care. That, to me, is not an order. I asked him if he cared, and he said no, he didn't care." [Wow! This is outrageous.]

"You would not as a nurse, without permission from Dr. Ogsbury as a primary treating physician, in this case, of Sheran R, initiate the placement of a central line without his permission, would you?"

"No."

"In fact, sitting here today, you really don't have any idea of why you didn't record that note in the chart, do you?"

"In retrospect, no I don't."

"And there's no chance that the chart on this patient which was prepared at the time—approximately three and one-half years ago—reflecting an order for a nasogastric tube at 10:05, is a more accurate reflection of what you talked to him about as you chased him out of the door than your independent memory?"

At that point Judge Peterson turned to Scott and said, "Mr. Nixon, let's not repeat questions, we've been over this, it's the same question."

Scott resumed. "Ms. MK, did you ask Dr. Ogsbury about this at any time between when he arrived at 9:00 p.m. and before he left shortly after 10:00 p.m.?"

"I remember that I told him that I wanted to specifically ask him—I had some questions that I specifically wanted to ask and the one I wanted to ask him, to my recollection, was to see if he minded if we needed a central line put in if we could get one put in."

"Do you think you should have recorded that in the chart as an order from Dr. Ogsbury?"

"In hindsight, I can say yes."

"Do you make any record in your final note of your report to Nurse C that Dr. Ogsbury had given you permission to place a central line?"

"It's something I passed on verbally to her."

"Did you make any note of it in the chart at the time of your last entry?"

"No."

Scott then talked to Judge Peterson, again trying to note the change in testimony since the other settlements. She again refused to allow that point to be made.

Ms. Kudla took the podium for her redirect and asked Nurse MK if she would ever go against doctors' orders, would she pass on an order if it were not given. She said of course not. She also asked if permission for a CVP line had been refused, would she have noted it. The answer was of course yes.

Ms. Kudla asked about Sheran R's condition. Nurse MK again said there was no change from July 3 to July 4, again omitting the improvement which occurred on July 4.

Nurse MK was excused, and the afternoon break was called.

The team was happy during the break. Scott did a great job. Nurse MK was so rattled that she never did say that nurses do not need orders to pass information on to physicians—not relevant but a small point for the good guys. Scott is Peter's clone, the same quiet, nasty demeanor. Nurse MK was pale and quivering as he asked her about the failure to write the order. She clearly realized, as she was being repeatedly complimented, that the cobra would strike, and he did. We also once again noted that Judge Peterson will simply not hear of the idea of any change in testimony since the settlements.

Nurse C was next called to testify. She is a nice lady I have known for a long time, indeed the only nurse I remember well. She looks terrified.

She reported she had been an RN since 1985. She was working in the ICU in 1986.

Under Ms. Kudla's questioning, Nurse C reported she first met Sheran R on the evening of July 2. She took report from Nurse MK that Mrs. R would follow simple commands only with strong arousal. She further reported that her breathing was labored, her color was poor, and by 2:00 a.m. she was less responsive, no longer following commands. She drew blood gases and called Dr. Krauth who was on call that night. Dr. Krauth instructed her to call the critical care service. The critical care doctor came and replaced the endotracheal tube. Sheran R's condition improved some.

After that, she responded that she called me [another error, I actually called in to find out her condition and ordered a CAT scan]. Nurse C reported that, after the CAT scan, I came in and placed an intracranial pressure monitor. Ms. Kudla finally had Nurse C summarize Sheran R's condition that night. When she came on duty, Sheran R was following commands; by the end of her shift, Sheran R needed painful stimulus to elicit any response.

Nurse C reported she next came on duty at 10:45 a.m. on July 3, received her report from Nurse MK including my permission to call the critical care physician to place a CVP line if a peripheral IV needed to be restarted. She further said that reports had indicated that Sheran R had further worsened, but her exam by midnight indicated a slight amount of improvement in that she was no longer stiffening. With the IV not working, she called the critical care physician. Ms. Kudla asked would she have done this without permission. She said no, that she told Dr. D, the critical care doctor, that I had asked that the CVP line be placed.

Nurse C described in detail that Dr. D tried to place this line five times. She then asked Dr. D. if he wished her to call the surgical resident who was in the house. Dr. M (the resident) came in and placed the CVP line on the first attempt and a chest X-ray was ordered.

Nurse C was asked whether she was trained to read the X-ray. She said no, but she was given the information by the people at the desk that the X-ray was okay. Ms. Kudla then asked about Sheran R's condition following the placement of the line. Nurse C said Sheran R was "a little more awake, I got her to squeeze my hand once, so she followed a simple command once." Otherwise, there was no change.

Nurse C reported that at 4:00 a.m., Sheran R did not follow commands, but she did note a clear substance in Sheran R's nose and called me [not mentioning she called me directly at home, not through the answering service]. She reported the CSF in the nose [which is common from residual spinal fluid in the sinuses], reported her neurologic status, and said she reported the nasogastric tube placement. She stated I had asked for another CT but made no comment regarding the CVP line. [I would have been up and into the hospital like a shot had I heard about that.] Scott turned to me and said, "She appears coached."

Nurse C reported that by then, Mrs. R was again doing some abnormal posturing, indicating her condition was worse than it had been at 4:00 and 5:00 a.m. when both times Mrs. R squeezed her hand to command [different than her testimony only a few moments earlier]. When Ms. Kudla asked, "For those two hours, did she seem just a little bit better to you?"

Nurse C said, "Yes, because she would squeeze my hand again, and then I had charted that I had asked her twice to do it over again and she did it." [I believe the terrible tragedy is that, at that moment, Sheran still had the potential to have made a good neurologic recovery had the pneumothorax been promptly discovered and treated.]

Ms. Kudla asked if Nurse C had cared for Sheran R the next day. She reported she had received report from Nurse MK about the events which had occurred after she had left at about 8:00 a.m. July 4. She said her exam that evening, the evening of 7/4, showed her to be stiffening her arms and legs without any purposeful movement, and that she was basically the same as when she left her on the morning of the 4th of July. Ms. Kudla had no further questions.

Scott asked Judge Peterson if he could start his cross-examination tomorrow since it was 4:50. Judge Peterson, true to form, insisted that he complete the day. Peter told Scott, with a smile, to "swirl in the water."

Scott complied, asking questions about the nurse's notes on July 2, about the breath sounds and their significance as well as the call to Dr. Krauth and the return call from me. These discussions easily took the necessary ten minutes, and the evening recess was called.

As was usual we remained in the courtroom after the recess and discussed the day's events. Peter felt they had made some important points.

I know of none of significance. I have said all along that I wished the CVP line placed only if there were no other alternatives; the nurses turned this into a strong approval. And while Nurse C is a nice lady, it is difficult to imagine she did not pick up the possibility of a pneumothorax if she truly listened to the breath sounds on the morning of July 4 as she said she did. We will await her cross-examination. I expect she will be taken apart. Peter has had a day off and is loaded for bear.

Peter
Monday, May 7, 1990, 6:00 p.m.

Blah! Took a Dalmane (sleeping pill) last night to ensure plenty of z's (eight hours) and felt relatively stuporous when I awoke. Plodded through the day emotionally and physically and couldn't get in touch with my energy source. Everyone was flat—the Judge, jurors, Jay—as Plaintiffs paraded a series of nurses to the stand to show that Sheran R was really sick after the second surgery and didn't seem any different after her pneumothorax.

The irony of this legal chess match—Plaintiffs are now trying to suggest the pneumothorax didn't really count, a cool $790,000 lining their pockets from their settlement with the pneumothorax people. Now, we must listen to nurses' recall (favorably to Plaintiffs) unrecorded, undocumented incidents where Jay supposedly gave permission in the first place to place the line in the wee hours of the night (he didn't). After listening to a flat-out lie by Nurse MK, I again found the fire, and my competitive juices are flowing.

Fran
Monday, May 7, 1990, 9:00 p.m.

The tenor has changed. The levity, the enthusiasm gone. In its place, a solemnness and resolve to never do this again. "I could be so right and yet I'll never do this again. I don't know what this means, but I can guarantee you, I'll never get caught in a courthouse again." Grim reality sets in. Jay can't be angry with Mr. H. He can't be angry with his wife. He can't be angry with his practice. He's numb. He related the day, listing facts, quotes, impressions all very surgically related.

Time to talk. Time to review the last few days. Time to put the cards on the table. We were cracking under the stress of documenting the daily destruction and planning tomorrow's scenario. Resolve to keep moving forward with this. How labile, how fragile.

CHAPTER ELEVEN

DAY 7
MORE NURSES &
THE DIRECT EXAMINATION
OF LEE KRAUTH

Peter
Tuesday, May 8, 1990, 10:00 a.m.

Rode in early today—not enough sleep (which seems to work better) and my mind floating between trial and personal issues. I thought about Jay and his ambivalence about settling since Spence is gone, and I literally destroyed their only neurosurgical expert, Harry Pie Smith. Rarely do I get caught up in my own performance, but the surgical cross I performed on that sad excuse for an expert was at times high art. This is what trial lawyers live for, the special moment when you go into a trance, the entire world goes still around you, and you attack and parry from the soul. All the tedium, anxiety, stress, fear—for a few technical hours you become totally focused, a verbal assassin, guided by cunning and instinct on your mission to intellectually kill a witness.

Poor Dr. Smith (no he's not "poor" because he's egocentric and intellectually dishonest). He is so light mentally. He was probably the only one in the room who didn't appreciate his destruction. Oh well, enough back patting—'tis another daytime to reach within and find the energy, enthusiasm, and strength to carry my crew.

Scott is up with Nurse C where Plaintiffs were dumb enough to produce and show the jury the sword-like needle used to perform a central line placement, in this case to kill off Mrs. R's right lung. And good old Nurse C listened to this lung with a stethoscope twice (after the lung collapsed) and the lung sounded normal. Hah! Lucky Scott has this woman and the opportunity to be a showman and jump his trial skills up about five notches. He says that is not him; I say it is. He has that ability within him, and it is time for him to take a few chances. Should be a good one today as we also have "Ms. Super Glue."

Earlier this morning Lee, Jay, Scott, and I sat around the White Spot and got to giggling hysterically about "Dr. Fossil"—our nickname for the ubiquitous Dr. Smith. Craziness and laughter are the time-honored outlet for this incredibly stressful business.

Jay
Tuesday, May 8, 1990

I slept fitfully, but today my resolve feels a little bit better. The meeting last night with Dr. Berman went more smoothly, but the project still seems iffy.

I drove in early to meet with Peter, Scott and Lee. Peter had been here all night as usual. Scott was preparing Lee for his testimony. Peter was preparing himself for his encounter with Nurse B The memories of Dr. Smith kept intruding on the seriousness of preparation. Peter dubbed him, "Dr. Fossil" for his opinions, clearly locker room humor and perhaps inappropriate at such a moment; however, he will be Dr. Fossil to all of us from this moment on.

We arrived at Court and once there, Lee tried to call Dr. Spetzler, the author of the textbook article on CSF repairs. We wondered if the standard of care today would be recent enough for Dr. Smith and his opinion of the intracranial approach. I asked Lee about his current thoughts about the timing for the repair of CSF leaks. He reported he still repairs iatrogenic (doctor-caused) CSF leaks immediately, and posttraumatic leaks after eight to ten days.

When we arrived at the courtroom, Kathy was already seated. Joneen, Lee's wife, was home per his request. I understand his preference for keeping her out of this although that approach proved difficult for Kathy.

Peter and Scott are both coiled, and I know this could be an eventful day. This is also the first time the jurors will see the elusive Dr. Krauth. Judge Peterson was strangely late in getting started. The Bailiff said that one of the jurors was late. It was Narcisco, as we all suspected; he probably had had a big gig.

Scott went to the podium and resumed his cross-examination of Nurse C. He asked about charting responsibilities. "It's part of your responsibility as a nurse in the Surgical Intensive Care Unit to chart on every patient on every shift, isn't it?"

"Yes."

"And that's part of your training as a nurse?"

"Yes."

"You've been taught, it has been your practice, to chart a number of different things over the course of a shift, including significant observations that you make of a patient during your shift. and any changes in conditions that you note?"

"Yes."

"When you're in the ICU, in addition to charting, you're acting sort of as a doctor's eyes and ears because the doctor is not there to see the patient the entire time, and that's especially important when you have a patient who's as critically ill as Sheran R was, isn't it?"

"Yes."

Peter leaned over to me and said, "He is setting her up beautifully."

"Would you look at the physician's orders portion, please? It should be tabbed—you see that Ms. MK has recorded that at 10:05 in the evening, that Dr. Ogsbury gave her verbal okay to put in the tube? Do you see that?"

"Yes."

"I think you told the jury yesterday that if you thought a central line was necessary during the shift and had not been told by Nurse MK that Dr. Ogsbury gave his okay, that you would have telephoned Dr. Ogsbury and asked him about it before you did anything, correct?"

"Correct."

Scott continued, "Were you aware there was permission from Dr. Ogsbury in the chart, as noted by Nurse MK, to place an NG tube?"

"No."

"Did you become aware that Nurse MK had noted in her chart permission from Dr. Ogsbury to call Critical Care if the urinary output went down?"

"Yes."

"She also told you about the placement of a central line, right?"

"Yes."

"But the actual act of placing the central line is a more significant thing than the calling of a critical care doctor, isn't it?"

"I don't understand."

"There was no documented permission from Dr. Ogsbury in the chart about the placement of a central line, was there?"

"No."

"Now, as you noted on the shift, you'd agree that you made fairly extensive notes during that evening?"

"Yes."

"For instance, at 1:00 a.m. you were charting that the ICP reading hadn't changed, and you noted at 3:00 a.m., I believe, that you had suctioned the patient? Can you read your note about the checking of the breath sounds at that time?"

"Breath sounds coarse with rhonchi middle and upper lobes."

Scott wrote, "Breath sounds" on the blackboard. "You used a stethoscope to check it, by placing it on the lungs, correct?"

"On the chest of the patient where the lungs are."

"Do you also listen from the backside of the patient?"

"Yes."

"So that would be on the front and back, correct?"

"Yes."

"What are you listening for when you're listening to the breath sounds?"

"You listen to see if you hear sounds on both sides—each lung. You also listen for sounds that indicate the patient might need suctioning."

"Can you describe for us what a normal breath sound sounds like to you through a stethoscope?"

"The breath sound is a fairly clear sound, it's just a 'whoosh'—inhale, exhale, where you can feel yourself breathing in and out, as opposed to if you felt congested. You could hear the congestion as you are breathing."

"So, a normal sound would be a clear rush of air, basically?"

"Basically."

"When you checked Sheran R's breath sounds at about midnight, you noted that she had coarse breathing, what does that describe?"

"It's like when you have a cold, and you have—you cough and you have secretions. It's a rattly kind of sound."

"It's something different than a clear rush of air?"

"Yes."

"What do you identify with the sound of a collapsed lung through a stethoscope?"

"The absence of a breath sound."

"Is a collapsed lung the same thing as a pneumothorax—layman's terms?"

"Yes."

"Now you said one of the complications of placing a central line can be the puncture of that lung space, correct?"

"Yes."

"So, you'd agree that once a patient has a central line placed, it's very important to check breath sounds carefully for that particular complication?"

"Yes."

Scott next turned to the procedure done by Dr. D. He mentioned the kit and moved for the admission of Plaintiffs' Exhibit 108. "May I ask the witness to come down and help explain the procedure?"

Ms. Kudla objected, saying that the witness had not done the procedure.

Judge Peterson said, "I think if we're going to have a demonstration in front of the jury, we should have the witness that did the procedure."

Peter motioned for Scott to come over and told Scott, "Ask her what she saw."

Scott tried again. "Ms. C, you were there when Dr. D placed the central line and I believe, as you testified, you observed everything that he did in relation to attempting to place the line. Did you observe what needle was used by Dr. D at that time? You observed the needle in his hand, I presume. And you observed the catheter that was used. And the guidewire? "

"Yes." [I think he got by the objection.]

"Is there a shot of Xylocaine or some type of numbing medicine that's given to the patient beforehand?"

"Yes."

"After this kit is opened, there's a needle that he uses attached to a syringe, correct?"

"Yes."

"The first thing the doctor does is to place the needle into the patient and locate the vein, correct?"

"Yes."

"Where is the subclavian area, if you could show the jury?"

"Right here between the clavicle."

"So, it would be just below your collarbone?"

"Yes."

Ms. Kudla objected to Mr. Nixon demonstrating the procedure.

Judge Peterson said, "Approach the bench" and I heard her say, "Mr. Nixon, Mr. Nixon." She was obviously lecturing him. I looked at the jurors. Mr. Saline and Mrs. Petit were just waiting.

Scott tried again." The first time you observed Dr. D. insert the needle, what is the next thing he does in the procedure that you observed on the first attempt?"

Judge Peterson again told him to "approach the bench." This time she told him to ask what happened.

Scott started once more. This time, by asking for her description of what did happen, Scott was finally able to graphically demonstrate the attempted CVP line placement. "Didn't he pull the needle out of Sheran R's chest on five separate occasions so that he had to reinsert and make five separate sticks?"

"Yes."

"Did you start getting worried about after the time he couldn't find the vein on the second or third or fourth time?"

"No."

"You actually suggested to Dr. D. that perhaps he might try to call the surgical resident to come up and try, right?"

"Yes."

Turning to the blackboard Mr. Nixon said, "There are several things that you testified to yesterday that I want to go over with you again. The first is that Nurse MK told you that Dr. Ogsbury said a central line was, okay?"

"Yes."

"One of the other things was that you told Dr. Ogsbury, later on that evening, about the placement of the central line, correct?"

"Yes."

"And last was that after placement of the central line, you had checked Mrs. R's breath sounds and they were normal, correct?"

"Yes."

"Will you please read to the jury your notes where you listened to her breath sounds after the placement of her central line?"

"There isn't anything in my notes."

"You would have been listening specifically for a potential collapsed lung, wouldn't you?"

"Yes."

"If you had heard abnormal breath sounds, you would have called the doctor, wouldn't you?"

"Yes."

"Now working backwards. Can you read to the jury where on the chart you documented you told Dr. Ogsbury about placement of the central line?"

"There isn't a place in the notes."

"Now you've told us about your note at the end of the shift where you called Dr. Krauth, and it's your testimony you called Dr. Krauth because of the decrease in blood pressure taken sometime between 6:30 and 7:00 a.m.?"

"Yes."

"And you called the answering service, didn't you? You didn't call Dr. Krauth personally?"

"No."

"You don't know if Dr. Krauth—or Dr. Ogsbury, either—received a message that you had called?"

"No."

"After you elevated the head of the bed, after noting the blood pressure, you immediately took it after that, and it was at '0' ... correct? Is there anything in the chart where you note taking her blood pressure again?"

"No."

"You didn't call Dr. Krauth's or Dr. Ogsbury's answering service a second time, did you? You didn't make any request of the oncoming nurse to call Dr. Ogsbury's or Dr. Krauth's answering service a second time, did you?"

"I notified her that the doctor had not called back."

"With a blood pressure of 88/Doppler, did you have a concern that Mrs. R might be going into shock?"

"No."

"Now prior to the time that you requested critical care to come up and place a central line, you made a note, at 1:30, that her right IV was infiltrated?"

"Yes."

"She also had an IV going into her left arm. There's nothing noted that there was anything wrong with that IV, is there? That IV wasn't infiltrated, was it?"

"No."

"Leg veins are frequently used to infuse IV fluid when arms are infiltrated, aren't they?"

"Not frequently."

"Did you ever consider whether Dr. Ogsbury might want IV lines placed in any of the other veins other than the subclavial, before you called critical care?"

"No."

Scott spoke briefly with Peter, "Nothing else, thank you."

Ms. Kudla took the stand for her redirect. "Mr. Nixon just asked you about various other IV sites. Do you have any reason to believe that if you were unable to get good peripheral IV access in her arms that the doctors would have been able to start a central line in her arms?"

"No."

"From your experience as a nurse, are there inherent dangers in putting IVs in somebody's legs? Is it especially dangerous for patients who are lying in bed and pretty immobile?"

"Yes."

"Can you tell the jury what these dangers are?"

"Very high risk of phlebitis—of blood clots in the legs. And—a better chance of infiltration in the legs that cause the cellulitis inflammation of the cell—a lot of risk for IVs in the legs."

"If you get blood clots in the legs from IV sites, what can happen to those blood clots?"

"A blood clot has a real high incidence of dislodging from that area, and it could travel to their brain or their lungs and cause them serious damage."

"You testified a minute ago in response to Mr. Nixon that there was nothing wrong at that time with her left arm IV, is that correct? Was one IV enough to provide her all the antibiotics, all the medications, all the fluids she needed to sustain her life that night?"

"No."

"What time did you actually leave Sheran R?"

"I don't remember exactly what time I left."

"From the time you placed the call to Dr. D's answering service at 6:30 in the morning to the time you left at 7:15 or 7:30, did Dr. Krauth call back?"

"No."

"At 6:30 in the morning on July 4, did you ever call the answering service of Dr. Ogsbury and Dr. Krauth and have them not respond to the phone call, other than 6:30 in the morning."

"No."

"Do you have any information or any reason to believe that the answering service, at 6:30 in the morning of July 4, would not have given the message to Dr. Krauth?"

"No."

"You discussed that the placement of the central line in a critically ill patient is a standard procedure. Do you customarily call the attending physician and say: 'We did it'?"

"Not just a call that would say that. We would have mentioned it if we called him for other things."

"And, as a matter of course, to fully inform him of what had gone on since he had last seen her, you advised him the central line had been placed?"

"Yes."

"During the time that you were taking care of Sheran R after the central line was placed, she was still on the ventilator, wasn't she, and she was receiving oxygen? And you listened but did not detect any change from what you heard earlier?"

"No."

"You stated you were in the room when you were told by a nurse outside at the central desk area—that the line placement was okay. Was receiving information that way, something that ordinarily occurred in the Intensive Care Unit?"

"Yes."

"And why was it that you were in the room rather than out at the nurse's desk?"

"Because she was a very sick lady."

"Mrs. C, have you ever heard anything to the contrary that the placement of the line wasn't okay? To the best of your knowledge, was the placement of the line okay?"

"Yes."

"Although we discussed that there was no written order from Dr. Ogsbury for the placement of the central line, Mrs. MK did tell you about that when she gave you report. Was there any reason for you to doubt that the information Mrs. MK gave you was accurate?"

"No."

Would you describe your nurse's notes fairly extensive and complete?"

"Yes."

"Is it possible for you, as a nurse, to write every single thing that you do and every single thing you observe on a patient who is critically ill?"

"No."

"Although you have used your notes and told us about what happened on your shift with Sheran R from your notes, do you also have some recollection of what went on?"

"Yes."

"You do remember Sheran R?"

"Yes."

Ms. Kudla paused and said, "I have nothing further."

Nurse B was next called and took the stand. I remember liking her. It is sad that this situation turns friends into adversaries. Ms. Kudla asked her to describe her background. She had been an RN since 1976 and had worked in the Operating Room since 1985.

In June of 1986 she was a relief circulating nurse and reported that she observed a craniotomy going on. She reported that when she entered, she got a report and was told the patient had a CFS leak, that the patient was awake, alert, and oriented. Ms. Kudla turned to Nurse B and asked,

"After you arrived and started performing as a circulating nurse, did Dr. Ogsbury request you to get anything for him?"

"Yes."

"What was that?"

"Glue."

"What kind of glue?"

"Super Glue."

"When you say, 'Super Glue,' are you talking about Super Glue that one can buy at a hardware store or grocery store?"

"Yes."

"Did you go and obtain the Super Glue for Dr. Ogsbury?"

"Yes."

"Where did you get it?"

"The instrument room."

"Would you describe for us how it was packaged?"

"It was sterile packaged, doubly sealed."

"And when you opened it and it falls forwards such that the sterile part lands on what's sterile in the operating room?"

"Yes."

"Did you see Dr. Ogsbury actually use the Super Glue?"

"Yes."

"What did he do when the Super Glue appeared not to work?"

"He removed it."

"How did he remove the Super Glue?"

"With wipe and irrigation."

"After the Super Glue was removed by Dr. Ogsbury did he ask for any other glue?"

"No."

Ms. Kudla then said she had no further questions.

The break was called. Lee called Dr. Spetzler. He said he agreed with the intracranial approach in the repair of CSF leaks in this area and said he would support us in any way he could.

Lee went into the bathroom and inadvertently flushed his watch down the urinal. We called the office—all quiet on the home front. When we returned to the courtroom, Peter was already on his feet for the cross of Nurse B. He is up for this.

He asked, "Can I show you what I think is your operating record?"

"Yes."

"Can you just tell us, first, what portions are completed by you?"

"Operation in time, patient out time, my signature as the circulator, specimen #1, and I sign as circulating nurse on the count."

It appears she is very wary; she should be.

Peter continued, "You said that you were asked to get Super Glue, right?"

"Yes."

"You said that Dr. Ogsbury said that it didn't work."

"Wasn't doing anything."

"Are you going from memory on this?"

"Yes."

"You're an RN and you've been practicing nursing for ten years, roughly?"

"Correct."

"Okay, is this a four by four?"

"Yes, it is a four by four."

"So, you told the jury when this wasn't doing anything he wiped it with a four-by-four?"

"To the best of my knowledge."

"Had you ever used Super Glue, pretty sticky stuff?"

"Yes."

"Before this surgery?"

"Yes."

"Did the four-by-four stick to the bottom of the brain?"

"No."

"It just came up on the cloth, as far as you could tell?"

"Some of it."

"Okay, so your testimony would be that he tried to remove it all; he may have removed it all; he may not have; I simply cannot tell you?"

"That's correct."

"Now you were standing there fairly close to Dr. Ogsbury watching him do this. How far were you away when you watched him do this?"

"About eighteen inches, two feet."

Peter then went on to draw on the blackboard the placement of the surgeon, the assistant, Dr. Barron, and the scrub nurse, as well as the anesthesiologist at the head of the table along with his machines. He then asked, "Now, will you tell the ladies and gentlemen where you were when you watched him wipe up the Super Glue?"

"I can't specifically remember where, but just—approximately, that I could see—to the right."

"You with your eyes looked out and saw him first put in the glue and then wipe it up later on at some point?"

"He didn't put the glue in the brain. He put it on a piece of material, and he put that on the brain. It was never in the brain. It was on a piece of fascia or tissue."

"Okay. Was the fascia or tissue ever put down on the brain?"

"Yes, but nothing adhered."

"So how did he get that out?"

"Just wiped off. The floor of the brain in the hole."

"Could you see?"

"No, I didn't see the floor of the brain. I saw the tissue."

"Now how big was the area where he was working, in terms of exposure? Can you remember that?"

"Not very big."

"Can you give the jury your best estimation?"

"Maybe a three-inch area"

"And then where was the microscope?"

"Overhead."

"This event is an event that you approach from your memory versus having a nursing note or some written record of this, is that true?"

"Yes."

"And the only note that you prepared at the time was the operating record, part of which you prepared?"

"Yes."

He then went through the times involved. Nurse B reported the operation started at 2:30, she came in at 3:00, and at 3:30 she was asked to get the Super Glue.

"Now, is it your recollection that this was the first brain surgery that you'd ever been involved with where a surgical adhesive of any type had ever been used?"

"Yes."

"Now when you got there, they were attempting to stop the leak? So, you arrived at 3:00, and then about 3:15 or so you were asked about the Super Glue?"

"Approximately."

"By the way, what's the technical name for Super Glue?"

"I don't know."

"It's 'surgical adhesive' isn't it? You said that in your deposition, didn't you?"

Ms. Kudla immediately said, "Objection, Your Honor; improper use of a deposition." Nurse B was given a copy of the deposition.

"You had a chance to review the operative record and actually talk to Dr. Hartwig (the anesthesiologist for the operation) maybe a month or so before this?"

"Yes."

"And you also went looking in the supplies to see if there was any Super Glue in supply, right?"

"Yes."

"And you read the records. And you were there with a representative, correct?"

"Yes."

"Now look at page 57 of your deposition. 'Question: Do you recall the technical name for it?' And what was your answer under oath at that time?"

"Surgical adhesive."

"Have you looked at the operative record for this procedure?"

"Yes."

"What does Dr. Ogsbury say he used in this surgery?"

"A surgical adhesive was used but did not seem to adhere well."

"Now, all of that comports with your recollection does it not?"

"Yes."

"Have you ever talked to anybody about this procedure?"

"Yes, I talked to a couple of people."

"Okay. Now, some of the details of this surgery have escaped your mind, have they not?"

"Yes."

"So, some of the details stick out, but the request for surgical adhesive stands out in your mind?"

"Yes."

"Have you ever talked to Dr. Ogsbury—about what he used?"

"No."

"You've not talked to Dr. Barron about the kind of surgical adhesive used?"

"No."

"And you've not talked to Nurse Sheran Von Lintel (my surgical technician) about what type of glue was used?"

"No."

"Have you read Dr. Ogsbury's deposition?"

"I have."

"Are you aware of his testimony as to the use or non-use of Super Glue?"

"Yes."

"Would you allow, in your mind, for the possibility that he might have some idea as to whether the surgical adhesive was 'store bought' Super Glue versus something else?"

"Yes."

"The only person—other than hospital representatives—that you've talked to was Dr. Hartwig, about a month before your deposition. You ran into him and the issue of the fact that you've been asked to give a deposition came up, did it not? Was there a discussion between you and Dr. Hartwig as to what he remembered?"

"A brief one, yes."

"And did you tell Dr. Hartwig, 'I don't remember anything about this operation except that it was not out of the ordinary.' Do you deny saying that? "

"No."

"Did you tell him about the Super Glue?"

"I can't remember."

"Now, could you see the area where the leak was coming from? "

"Yes."

"And where was that?"

"On the right side of the brain."

"And so, you're standing there looking into the brain, and you can see the area where the leak is?"

"I looked in the microscope as well."

"Oh, you looked in the microscope and you saw him packing the area?"

"Not under the microscope, but I saw the leak."

"Now, is there, anywhere in the entire St. Anthony chart, any record of the use of this surgical adhesive?"

"No."

"And is there anything noted anywhere about your memory of the surgical adhesive?"

"No."

"How big was this tube?"

"About three inches."

"And what color was it?"

"I don't recall."

"And do you have any recollection as to whether you thought that—that was a tube of Super Glue?"

"Yes."

"And you didn't think that was it or you couldn't say, it was it?"

"I couldn't recall."

"In fact, at the time you thought about this in June of 1989, you had a question whether this was Crazy Glue?"

"I had a question if it was Crazy Glue or Super Glue."

"All right, or surgical adhesive?"

"Well, yes."

"Let's go at this a different way. Do you remember, before you gave your deposition, you looked at Dr. Ogsbury's operative report, right? And he didn't say anything about—anything other than surgical adhesive?"

"Right."

"And then you looked at the discharge summary in your operative record and some other records, in preparation for your deposition, and then you showed up with a copy of the operative report with some notes on it, right?"

"Yes."

"Okay. Do you have that operative report?"

"Yes. It wasn't my writing, though. I obtained it with writing on it."

Ms. Kudla asked to approach the bench and a discussion was held. Judge Peterson said, "We're going to recess for lunch at this time," and the break was called.

The lunch was good. Peter feels Nurse B has been so destroyed that he plans only a few more questions; he does not want to appear greedy. Several surgical dictums come to mind. "Perfect is the enemy of good." "The last bite causes the biggest bleeder." We laughed about Lee flushing his watch down the urinal.

Peter is a little annoyed at Scott. He felt Scott should have asked one more question, the obvious one, of Nurse C. That is, how is it possible that a pneumothorax could not be heard during the six times she listened?

I am concerned that there have been three separate times that the nurses have given testimony that disagrees with mine—first, that I gave permission for the CVP line to Nurse MK after she supposedly chased me into the hall; second, that I was made aware of the CVP line placement; and third, I used Super Glue in the first operation. I realize the nurses were probably coached to place the hospital in the best possible light at the time the hospital was a party, and that their testimony was not directed toward me. I worry, however, that the jurors will think of me as incompetent and simply covering my tracks.

At the end of the break, we called the office to check in and returned to Court. After Court was reconvened, Peter stood up and said, "Your Honor, I don't have any more questions." Judge Peterson said, "I'll send you to lunch more often; any redirect?"

Ms. Kudla stood for a few more questions. She asked Nurse B, "What is the technical name for Super Glue that you described? Is that 'surgical adhesive'?"

"Not in my terminology but it's been referred to as such."

"What were you talking about when you went and obtained for Dr. Ogsbury his request?"

"That would be Super Glue."

"And on the operating record, you indicated to Mr. Pryor that on the note there is no place that indicates Super Glue. Is that correct?"

"That's correct."

"On that record, do you indicate that a pledget of muscle was used?"

"Not on my op record."

"And do you indicate that Surgicel was used?"

"No," Ms. Kudla said,

"I have nothing further," and Nurse B left the stand.

I do think she did briefly look at me as she left. Mr. H stood and called Dr. Krauth. As he went up to the stand, Peter told him to smile. He was asked about his current working situation. He stated that he and I were partners.

Mr. H started right in. "Dr. Krauth, do I understand that in the past years that you have had occasion to treat some number of cerebrospinal fluid leak cases that resulted from nasal surgery? Back last year. I think you had surgically repaired about five, yourself. Is that right?"

Dr. Krauth answered, "Yes that's right."

"And all five of those repairs had been problems that were encountered during ethmoidectomies that were done by ENT doctors, and they were all from different ENT doctors?"

"Yes, that's correct."

"And do I understand you correctly that of all five of those, that you never had to go back in and fix a repair job that you had done initially?"

"Yes, that's correct."

"So, all of your initial repairs, when you did the surgery, had been successful?"

"Yes."

Mr. H continued, "Now were you aware, Doctor, that this CSF repair surgery by Dr. Ogsbury on Sheran R was the very first CSF repair that he had ever done after an ethmoidectomy surgery by an ENT doctor?"

"No, I didn't think I was aware of that."

"Okay. Doctor, would you agree with me that a CSF leak after nasal surgery like this is a treatable problem. It's a problem that neurosurgeons are trained to deal with, and there is literature regarding it in the neurosurgery literature?"

"Yes, I would agree with that."

"And it is the kind of problem that really should present no unique or special difficulty for a neurosurgeon?"

"I'm not sure what you mean by 'unique or special difficulty.'"

"It's within the neurosurgical practice."

"Yes, it's within the neurosurgical practice."

"And would you agree with me, Doctor, that Sheran R should have been able to assume, at least, that Dr. Ogsbury and yourself were competent to treat the problem that she presented with, as neurosurgeons?"

"Yes."

"Now, if a patient is not too sick or severely injured to begin with, it is your opinion, is it not, that most of the time you would expect that patient to recover from repair surgery from this problem without any significant neurologic problems?"

"Yes, most of the time."

Mr. H then went over Sheran R's condition on coming into the hospital. Dr. Krauth agreed that she was a healthy lady whose physical exam revealed no neurologic abnormalities. Mr. H then questioned Lee at length about the issue of meningitis and Lee's opinion that the risk of meningitis is the reason for the need for closure of CSF leaks. He said, "Doctor, a person can exist with a cerebrospinal fluid leak of this nature for weeks or months, can't they? It is not a life-or-death situation to go in and repair a cerebrospinal fluid leak like this just because there is a leak. The concern was here, was it not, that she might get an infection?"

"The concern at the time I wrote the note was that she was already very sick and going down the tubes and that she had an infection."

"And the existence of this infection was your primary motivation to go in and operate so soon, wasn't it?"

"Yes, it was."

Mr. H then turned to the question of the lumbar puncture. "Okay. Now if there is evidence to make a physician feel that she may have had meningitis, what is the classic test that the physician runs to try and determine whether meningitis exists in the patient?"

Dr. Krauth answered, "The classic test would be a lumbar puncture."

"And, Doctor, would you agree with me that if a neurosurgeon has any reason to suspect the presence of meningitis in his or her patient that the standard of care would require that they do a lumbar tap? Get a sample of cerebrospinal fluid, and have it analyzed."

"I wouldn't agree with that whole lengthy thing because there are other ways of obtaining samples of fluid beside a lumbar puncture—like if a person was going to have a cisternogram or another test where spinal fluid was obtained, you could do that. If a person has spinal fluid running out of their nose, you could go through that or check that. So, there are other ways besides doing a lumbar puncture."

"All right, would you agree, Doctor, that the standard of care would require that if a patient was going to have a cisternogram, that spinal fluid be drawn off and sent to the lab for analysis?"

"Yes, that's usually done."

"A cisternogram was done on Sheran R on June 24, 1986, correct?"

"Yes."

"And by necessity is spinal fluid available?"

"Yes, it is."

"Doctor, from your knowledge in this case, was there any spinal fluid drawn at the time of that cisternogram and sent to the laboratory for analysis?"

"I don't think one was done."

"In fact, Doctor, at the time of your deposition in January of 1989, you actually assumed that one had been done. You were surprised when you learned that one had not been done, weren't you, Doctor?"

"Yes."

Mr. H continued to pound the issue, "Now, Doctor, would you agree, in order to make a decision whether or not to do surgery or whether meningitis exists or doesn't exist, that a cerebrospinal fluid analysis would have been very significant?"

"Yes."

"And would you agree, Doctor, under the facts of this case that there should have been a cerebrospinal fluid sample taken and sent to the laboratory before the surgery of June 25, 1986?"

"I hadn't really formed an opinion on that. It's kind of hard to, in retrospect, look at what's been done, but I wasn't involved with the care."

"Doctor, if there is any question about the existence of meningitis in Sheran R, wouldn't you agree, Doctor, that the standard of care for a neurosurgeon in Denver, Colorado, in 1986 would require that a sample of cerebrospinal fluid be obtained, sent to the laboratory?" [It is beginning to appear that Mr. H has chosen to use Lee as an expert against me.]

"If there was a question, I think it should have been done. But in this case, I don't think there was a question in any of the treating physicians' minds that she had meningitis."

"Do you feel, Doctor, that with her clinical picture—the cerebrospinal fluid leak, headaches that you've talked about, the history of nausea and vomiting, and the fever—do you feel there should have been a question in the treating physicians' minds as to the presence or absence of meningitis, under those circumstances?"

"Yes, I think there probably was."

"Doctor, let me refer you again back to Dr. Mason's consultation. Under a section called 'Recommendations' about halfway down, does she not say: 'For the short run, we will continue the Nafcillin and Chloramphenicol' and those are antibiotics 'pending the results of any further cultures obtained at the time of the cisternogram.' Would you agree with me, Doctor, that it's pretty clear that Dr. Mason was expecting cultures would be done at the time of the cisternogram and sent to the lab?"

"Yes, I'd agree with that."

"And would you agree with me that it would be below the standard of care for a neurosurgeon, in light of that recommendation, to not make sure that the CSF was drawn and sent to the laboratory at the time of the cisternogram?"

"No, I don't know whether that's below the standard of care or not." [Yes, he is using him.]

"Doctor, if you go in and do major surgery like a craniotomy, can preexisting meningitis make the risk much greater for the patient?"

"Yes."

"It increases the surgical risk substantially, doesn't it?"

"Yes, it does."

"And if you, as a surgeon, had the alternative, you would want to do that craniotomy without meningitis?"

"Correct."

"If you had an alternative."

"Yes."

"Doctor, you're familiar with a publication called *Neurosurgery*? The primary editor being Robert Wilkins?"

"Yes, I am."

"And that's an authoritative text in the field of neurosurgery, is it not?"

"Yes."

"I'd like for you to look at it. Would you turn to page 1924 to the second column where it says, 'Similar reactive changes'? It indicates: 'Similar reactive changes in the CSF may be found in a variety of other conditions. Postoperative changes or subarachnoid hemorrhage can cause CSF leukocytosis (that's increase of the white count), elevated protein content, and low-grade fever in the absence of infection. In a few of these cases there may be hypogalactorrhea.' Now hypogalactorrhea is lowering of the glucose, right?"

"In the spinal fluid, yes."

"So all of these things that are seen on the 28th cerebrospinal samples—at least the author of this chapter in *Neurosurgery* indicates—those are all consistent with postoperative changes or changes of subarachnoid hemorrhage. Is that correct?"

"Not totally, because you are taking it out of context, and you are not quoting the numbers. The way I interpret this is that basically you can get a slight elevation of the white count, you get a slight elevation of the protein, and you can get a hypogalactorrhea. And since I do tremendous amounts of aneurysm surgery and am very familiar with this, I just don't see this. I've done a hundred aneurysm cases in the last five years and those are not the numbers that we see in our patients."

"Doctor, show me in this article where he puts limits on the numbers. Show me in this article where there are numbers in here that say we can't draw this inference from the article—that if we find increased white count, elevated protein, low grade fever, and low glucose, that that's consistent with a postoperative reaction absent infection."

"I agree with you that those things—when you make them generalized—are all consistent. I'm saying that I am an aneurysm surgeon, and I don't see it, and I talked to many aneurysm surgeons. We just don't see this."

Mr. H paused and continued, "When is the next time, throughout this whole hospitalization, that another cerebrospinal fluid sample was ever drawn or taken from Sheran R through a lumbar puncture or through the brain, or you know what I'm talking about, a pure sample?"

"I'm not totally sure. I seem to reflect from the records that she probably had some cultures done from her intracranial pressure monitoring device. So that would have been around the 5th of July."

"Okay, wouldn't you agree, Doctor, that if a neurosurgeon in charge of this patient was really concerned that meningitis was causing the serious problems that this patient was experiencing, that frequent cerebrospinal fluid samples would be obtained and sent to the lab?"

"No, because they wouldn't grow anything—as evidenced by the fact nothing grew on the ones you did have. She was being treated with maximum antibiotics and there wasn't anything you could change."

"Wouldn't a surgeon want to know if, in fact, meningitis was present so that the surgeon could know if meningitis was causing the severe brain damage the surgeon was seeing, or something else?"

"Well, the point is that he already—is taking the worst-case scenario in assuming meningitis. And he's also treating everything else. So, I don't see what purpose it is to keep doing useless tests." [Lee is hanging in there.]

Mr. H resumed, "Let's talk about something else for a moment. You testified in the past, have you not, that a part of your clinical examination of this area of the cribriform leak in Sheran R at the time of the second surgery, that the graft or patches Dr. Ogsbury had put in the first surgery was lying on top of the hole?"

"Yes."

"And you observed that there was not a water-tight seal?"

"Yes."

"Would you agree, would you not, Doctor, that a water-tight seal is necessary to stop the cerebrospinal fluid leak in this area?"

"Yes, I agree."

"And would you agree, would you not, that if, during surgery, the surgeon was concerned regarding whether or not he was getting a water-tight seal, that the surgeon needs to take steps to make sure that one is accomplished, in other words, a water-tight seal is accomplished?"

"Yes." Mr. H continued to try to hammer me through Lee. He had first tried to show that I had not, at the first operation, obtained a good operative seal of the hole. He then turned to the issue of Super Glue.

"Doctor, with respect to glue, in 1986, it's your testimony, is it not, that the only glues available that a surgeon could use to help accomplish adherence in a procedure like this were not approved by the FDA?"

"Yes, that's true."

"Are you saying it's okay to put a non-FDA approved substance like that into a person's brain?"

"Oh, yes, it's done every day."

"Tell me, Doctor, why do we have approved procedures by the FDA?"

"Well, the main reason why we have FDA approval is so that various pharmaceutical companies and various other manufacturers can get extra protection in their product. But today, I would assume, in every hospital, they're doing Harrington rods and other metal plate procedures and things like that. Those are non-FDA approved procedures. So, FDA approval—it doesn't make it illegal. It's done every day. It's a part of medicine."

"So, FDA approval—if I understand your testimony—is purely for drug companies to obtain some type of legal protection, and it has nothing to do with protection of the general public?"

"I'm not saying it has nothing to do. I can't make a general statement like that. Any time you generalize, you can get into trouble. So, I wouldn't say that."

"Dr. Krauth would you agree that the use of Super Glue or Crazy Glue would not be approved by the FDA in 1986?"

"Yes, I would agree with that."

At this point Mr. H asked if Judge Peterson wanted to call a break and one was called. Fran was here and thought that Lee was doing well; I felt that he had hung in there strongly.

The jury was reconvened after the short break.

Mr. H resumed." Dr. Krauth, on July 1, 1986, you got back from Canada. And that's when you first saw Sheran R, is that right? And Dr. Ogsbury asked you to go with him to see Sheran R, and you went in and saw her and basically, there were two options that were under consideration after you saw her?"

"Basically, there were three or four options available, and each one was weighed, and then they were discussed—and I discussed all of my feelings with regard to each option that Dr. Ogsbury was thinking about."

"Well, Dr. Ogsbury's written a note in the progress notes on July 1 where he says: 'Leak has intermittently occurred, not large volume, much less than before. Options at this point, try repositioning the patient, drain, and reop.' And at that time, he tried repositioning the patient. Do you remember that?"

"Yes, I do."

"And then the next progress note is your note on July 1, where you conclude that the only alternative, in your mind, is to go back and reoperate, correct?"

"Yes."

"Now if I understand it, then, the only two options that you considered before you came to that conclusion the only two options were one, to drain the spinal fluid, or go back in and reexplore the area. Is that right?"

"No. I also considered the options that he had written down. You can either reoperate, number one—and that's a very risky thing to do on somebody who's very sick with what I felt was meningitis and a swollen brain. There was the option that he had mentioned of not operating and trying to see if things would stop on their own. But he had already been doing position changes for three days. And I was also at an advantage. When he saw her earlier in the morning and wrote his notes, in the intervening time she had had another CAT scan that day around, I think, 11:00 or 12:00 during the day. I had the advantage of seeing the new CAT scan. And, when I saw her, she didn't have just a subtle leak. She was literally—when she leaned forward—she was pouring spinal fluid out of her nose. So that was another option—not to operate, to see if it would stop on its own. Another option was to place a drain in her lumbar spinal sac and drain the fluid out continuously, and another option was to put a shunt in or an internalized drain. And I weighed each of those options and I came to the conclusion—my feeling. But my opinion that I offered to Dr. Ogsbury was that I didn't feel that any of the other options in this particular instance were as valuable as going back and stopping the leak."

"Dr. Krauth isn't it true that you only discussed two options with Dr. Ogsbury after you saw this patient?"

"No, that's not true."

"Would you refer to your deposition, Sir, page 47, line 20—were you were asked this question, and did you give this answer: 'What were the options that were discussed?' Answer: 'Well I think the options were one, was to try to put a spinal drainage catheter in her, drain her spinal fluids, and see if that would stop the leak. Another option was to reoperate and reexplore the area that she had explored and look around and see if there were possibly two holes instead of one. So basically, one was to put in a drain and one was to reoperate. I don't know that we really discussed anything else.'"

"Doctor, your reason then, as I understand it, that a second surgery was only to stop the cerebrospinal fluid leak because of your concern about meningitis?"

"Not solely but that was the major concern."

"Was there any emergent neurologic reason why surgery had to be done July 2?"

"I think it had to be done soon because—from the progress notes on the chart, from discussing her case, and from looking at her—she had a remarkable turn of events in the past twenty-four to forty-eight hours, and her spinal fluid had changed to where she now had 2300 white blood cells, and she appeared to be developing a severe meningitis. She had air in her brain. I mean air in the brain, itself, is dangerous. People die from having too much air in their brain—it's recontaminated. She had signs of increased pressure and deterioration, and her level of consciousness was diminishing, and she also had a third nerve, her cranial nerve 3, palsy—which I feel is probably secondary—a combination of the meningitis because cranial nerve palsies appear in ten to twenty percent of the time when you get meningitis. That's telling me that we've got a lady whose brain is getting sicker, despite adequate treatment other than surgery. So, I felt we had to do something to prevent her from dying."

"Now, Doctor, as I understand it you gave no consideration at all to repairing the leak the second time through the nose rather than doing a craniotomy; is that right?"

"That's correct."

"Because you don't do these kinds of surgeries do you?"

"No, I don't."

"You were taught the only way to come in for a leak like this is from, as you put it, I think above; is that right?"

"That's not the only way, but it's the preferred way. And it's the preferred way and recommended way by most neurosurgical authorities."

"You and Dr. Ogsbury did not discuss any approaches other than a craniotomy, is that right?"

"Yes, that's correct."

"Now, Doctor, in the second surgery, you decided—you and Dr. Ogsbury—decided not just to go in on the right side, but to go in on both sides; is that true?"

"That's true."

"And it's true, is it not, Doctor, that you decided to do a bilateral procedure just perchance that there might be two holes?" [Using Lee's words from his deposition.]

"No, not just perchance. There was significant evidence that she might have a left-sided leak that had been missed in the first surgery."

"What was that significant evidence, Doctor?"

"Well, the first thing was that she had had an appropriate operation done, which was technically very good, and it didn't work, and that she continued to leak. So, one has to raise the question that maybe there could have been more than one hole. The second evidence is that—one of the first people who saw her was Dr. Mason. And reading from her consult that she documented in the chart, Dr. Mason documented a significant amount of leak of spinal fluid from the left nostril. Another reason would be that the patient had started complaining of severe left eye—not right eye—but left eye pain and pain behind the left orbit, which was new. And usually, you don't get pain behind the left eye and left orbit from a right sided leak. A fourth reason would be that the patient had air on her CT scan which wasn't there before, and more air was concentrated over the left side than the right. So that's four reasons. And the fifth reason is that I've personally been involved in cases—as you brought up earlier, before that—and every neurosurgeon has to go on his experience—that an ENT had done bilateral ethmoidectomies and he had done both sides and I had to repair it. So, we had five reasons to consider looking on the left side."

Mr. H would not let go. He aggressively challenged each of these reasons and tried to imply that they were not considered at the time of the medical care but only here at trial.

Mr. H continued, "Doctor, would you agree that doing a bilateral procedure is substantially more aggressive than a unilateral procedure?"

"I would agree it's more aggressive, but I wouldn't say substantially more aggressive."

"It was going to require retracting the left side of the brain rather than just the right side, if you did that; is that correct?"

"Yes."

"Now you knew that the right side of the brain had been injured already, from the CAT scan that followed the first surgery. The radiologist was telling you that and you could see it on the CT. There was swelling on the right side, and there was swelling on the right frontal lobe, wasn't there?"

"Yes, there was."

"In fact, there was swelling to the point where the midline that ran down the center of the brain was being pushed from right to left, wasn't it?"

"Yes."

"There was no evidence of any diffuse swelling across the whole brain before the second surgery, was there?"

"I don't think so."

"And that swelling was exactly where the surgery had occurred the first time, wasn't it?"

"Yes."

"Do you agree, Doctor, that that's something the surgeon ought to take into consideration in deciding whether to go back in—the fact that there's already brain damage in there?"

"Yes, and it definitely was taken into consideration."

"You still had the major concern about meningitis, I take it. And that ought to be taken into consideration in whether you go back in as well, shouldn't it?"

"Yes."

"Both of those would be factors that weigh against going back in in the face of their existence—wouldn't they, Doctor?"

"Well, no. One could weigh in favor of or against because the meningitis, I think, is documented as getting worse and in the face of very adequate and impressive medical management. And there are a lot of people that would recommend, in the face of that, when you're losing a battle with an infection, you've got to stop the primary problem. And—she is still reinfecting and recontaminating herself; we had to stop that until we get the leak stopped. So, in order to treat the meningitis, you can look at it as the best way to treat the meningitis is do the operation to stop the meningitis—which was done, and the leak was stopped."

"And you told Dr. Ogsbury that he definitely needed to explore both sides, didn't you?"

"I didn't tell him. I told him my opinion was that I felt he needed to go in, and I would explore both sides. I don't tell him what to do; he makes his own decisions."

"Now, Doctor, when you went in the second surgery, it's true, is it not, that you found the muscle patch and graft on the right side and you found that lying on top of the leak. And it appeared the fluid was leaking around the side of it?"

"Yes."

"And it appeared it was not a water-tight seal?"

"Yes."

"And you recognized at this point, that the original repair had failed, didn't you, Doctor?"

"It appeared to have, yes."

"And Dr. Ogsbury recognized it, as well, didn't he?"

"Yes."

"Would you agree, Doctor, that there was nothing mandating that you go ahead and retract and manipulate the left side of the brain just because you had done a bilateral flap of the skull. When you saw that leak on the right side and realized that the repair failed and it was leaking there again, you could have, you could have stopped and not gone over to the left side, couldn't you?"

"Yes."

"Now, Doctor, after you recognized that the leak was there on the right side that was leaking again, rather than repairing it, you moved, then, to the left side. And did that— and did that entail you retracted the left side of the brain back, correct, the left frontal lobe?"

"We retracted it sideways."

"You retracted it somehow."

"Laterally, yes."

"So, you've looked in the right side; you retract the frontal lobe; you see the leak there. It's leaking. You've probably put the frontal lobe down and moved to the left side."

"Well, your description is very inaccurate in that we do not put the lobe back down. All you're doing is gently compressing the frontal lobe to the side, you don't lift it up or pull it up and down."

"That's what you should be doing, correct?"

"Yes, that's what we do. That's exactly what you do."

"All right, in any respect you took the retractors out and allowed the frontal lobe to move back into position on the right side and then you moved over to the left side of the brain and retracted the frontal lobe on the left side. You retracted all the way back to what's called the tuberculum sella, didn't you?"

"No. What was done is—you're talking about a 3- to 4-millimeter distance, not a football field or something. If you have a retractor and you retract the frontal lobes laterally you are talking about 2 to 3 millimeters of distance. The whole frontal lobe will expose the floor of the cribriform plate back to the tuberculum sella. You aren't pulling it back. You're pulling it to the side and that exposes the thing. It's a linear exposure."

Mr. H continued with the description of the second operation and asked about the technique used to close the hole. "And you took, now, fresh muscle, and you packed in the hole real tight, didn't you?"

"Well, Dr. Ogsbury did, yes."

"Okay. But that was the procedure that you told him about, isn't it?"

"To pack the sinus?"

"To take the muscle and to pack it into the hole real tight. That was the procedure that you told him about, and that was the procedure that you used on virtually every one of the surgeries that you had done that we talked about when we started today. Right?"

"I think, probably, at least four or five, probably, yes."

"And, Doctor, what you did differently than what Dr. Ogsbury had done on the first time around was this packing of the muscle real tightly into the hole?"

"Well, down into the ethmoid the air cell. Actually, down into the—below the level of the cranial vault into the ethmoid air cells into the ethmoid sinus."

"But that hadn't been done in the first surgery?"

"No, it hadn't."

"Based on your review of the records and talking with Dr. Ogsbury, it's your understanding, is it not, that Dr. Ogsbury covered the hole and placed the muscle over it?"

"Well, it's my understanding that what he did is he had a piece of muscle that was attached on top, and he put the muscle on top of the hole so that the muscle was down into the hole but it wasn't packed into it."

"When you opened initially in the second surgery and had an opportunity to look at the site, the piece of muscle was just laying over the hole and was not in it, was it?"

"That's correct."

"One of the advantages of putting the muscle in it is because you were able to get it in so tight, and when it swells and gets tighter, there's no chance of it moving, is that correct, Doctor?"

"Yes."

"You did not use glue in the second surgery, is that correct?"

"That's correct."

"And you didn't suture the muscle because the plug was in there very tight, right?"

"There was nothing to suture it to anyway."

"Doctor, listen to my question. You didn't suture the muscle because it was in there very tight and was not going to move out, isn't that correct, Doctor?"

"Yes."

"And let me ask you again, Doctor. In each of the five procedures that you have done that—where they've all been successful, you've not had to go back in again—every time you've used that procedure, haven't you?"

"I think the answer is yes."

"Doctor plugging the hole with muscle has been known for years, hasn't it?"

"I assume so."

Mr. H turned to the one area he obviously seemed to think Lee himself might be vulnerable, his failure to return a page by the nurses following the CVP line placement. Lee had little difficulty addressing that issue—he simply never received the call for whatever reason.

Finally, Mr. H turned to the issue of the IV lines, the possible need for a central line and the pneumothorax. To my astonishment and chagrin, he through Lee, attempted to demonstrate that my actions led to the pneumothorax and resultant further brain injury by not ensuring a competent

CVP line placement. I cannot believe I am being held responsible for the one procedure that I repeatedly indicated I did not wish would be done. Unfortunately, if one believes the nurses, and despite Scott's attempted objections, he made a pretty good case.

During this questioning he also induced from Lee the admission that Lee did not know Sheran's exact condition at the time of her discharge (not surprising as I had taken him out of the case, after the pneumothorax, to minimize his involvement in the inevitable lawsuit).

With these points made, Judge Peterson called the evening break.

The team stood around in shock. The euphoria of the last few days and even this noon was demolished. The ploy to use Lee as a neurosurgical expert against me was brilliant and well executed.

On major points, Mr. H had obtained from Lee the admission that I was negligent if a certain hypothetical premise were true, placing us in the position of having to disprove each premise he raised. Mr. H is good. I see nothing unethical here, just good tactics, particularly given the obviously ludicrous testimony of Dr. Smith.

It seems amazing that the main issues now seem to be Super Glue and that I should have prevented the pneumothorax. Other issues, the timing and technique of the first operation and the question of meningitis, its diagnosis, and its relevance to the second operation seem less important. We do, of course, emphasize that there is a standard way to perform a CSF leak repair. It did appear that Nurse B was not too damaging, and Nurse C was not convincing despite my continuing concern with their repeated disagreement with me.

Peter, however, was furious. Lee had been well prepared and was not confused by Mr. H's complex questions containing double negatives, several times stating that the question was confusing. Also, he maintained his composure throughout (he said today he was a good dooley—freshman at the Air Force Academy) and firmly maintained his ground. But his admission that he did not know Sheran's condition at discharge made him, and me, appear uncaring, and Peter was angry at Scott for letting him say so.

Peter said, "We could lose the jury over this single issue."

In addition, Judge Peterson apparently has swung back to the Plaintiffs after our initial good impression.

We started to walk out of the courtroom. I am concerned that Scott is doing the rebuttal, not that Scott isn't a good attorney, but he is young and inexperienced, and Lee is now their main witness. If Scott does a great job in countering the ideas that Mr. H left in the jurors' minds, we will be fine. If not, we are in deep trouble. I talked to Peter, and he feels Scott will do fine. I don't feel good about all of this.

I came home, ate dinner, and later that evening the neurosurgical colleague and friend (who had been in the court to see Dr. Smith) called. I felt better after talking to him.

Fran
Tuesday, May 8, 1990, 9:00 p.m.

Resolve is still there, at least to see the week through.

All are shaken by Lee's testimony. When Mr. H makes a direct hit, Peter in turn rises and delivers a sound strike. Not this time. Peter can only watch and hope that Scott is ready to respond. Doubts riddle security. Can Scott be a Boy Wonder tomorrow?

Jay is in shock. Peter is livid. Prep for tomorrow won't stop until the jurors are called into the courtroom. The White Spot Cafe will be in business tonight.

CHAPTER TWELVE

DAY 8
THE CROSS-EXAMINATION OF LEE KRAUTH

Peter
Wednesday, May 5, 1990, 4:00 a.m.

Gut check time. Looked into the mirror this morning, and the bags under my eyes went all the way to my chin. The fatigue which envelopes me is something to accept and try to push away as you enter the courthouse. If only people understood the incredible physical and emotional toll of a trial, maybe we wouldn't be so despised and ridiculed as a profession.

Yesterday started out well and Scott did a "pretty good" job on Nurse C who heard (supposedly) normal breath sounds in a collapsed lung on five different occasions. As an old goat I have an inbred frustration when my co-counsel won't go for the kill (or does not yet know how). Scott is intelligent, hardworking, and presents well, but he's just too inexperienced to smell the blood and go for the jugular. And, while he did well with Nurse C, he now has Lee Krauth, and my compulsive personality features of guilt and hyper responsibility are weighing me down.

Mr. H did a beautiful job on Krauth yesterday, not in attacking Lee's care, but in using Lee's testimony to raise serious questions about

Jay's competence to repair a CSF leak (and the way he packed the leak) and Jay's alleged responsibility for the central line placement based on Nurse MK's bogus story about getting permission to do so the night before. I watched the jury closely, and you can see them teetering toward the Plaintiff, especially Ms. Petit.

Now, I feel bad because Scott has Lee, and I know I could cross Lee and drive the pneumothorax issue right up their butt. Jay and Kathy asked me privately if I thought Scott was up to it and I said "yes," which I believe. Nevertheless, I am carrying around guilt because I am not all things and cannot question all witnesses, and I am feeling bad and a little scared about what I sense in the jury yesterday. I don't think we're tied right now. So, it is time to reach down to find the spirit to come roaring back and smack these people hard. Round 4 is about to begin, and we are behind on points. I am warrior—my spirit is indomitable, and I am not afraid to receive pain to prevail.

All night long I had fitful, symbolic dreams. At one point I was wading in deep water in a fast current with Josh and with my little baby whose name I couldn't remember. I remember fear and guilt, knowing the dream was about the trial, and wonder if the child was Jay. At one point I had forgotten I had the baby until Josh reminded me and I couldn't find him in the dark water. Suddenly, he bobbed up and I got him and saved him but my sense of terror first, and guilt later, was overwhelming. I now find myself becoming calm and focused, and just thinking about my dreams allows me to let anxiety go and begin to work on this jury. I need to let them know and like me, to get to trust me, and to feel my passion for this case. All without getting Judge Peterson on my case. While I like and respect her, I just don't agree with her views on several important evidentiary issues—just one more issue to deal with.

Jay
Wednesday, May 5, 1990

I was unable to sleep well. I dreamt all night about Sheran. After an uneasy drive to the White Spot, I found Peter to be more upbeat than usual. He had been there all night, as usual, preparing for Dr. Cripe, the neuropsychologist. Scott and Lee were working feverishly on Lee's cross-examination. We talked about Judge Peterson. It seems her rulings vary in effect. If testimony seems to indicate the veracity of our care, such as after the debacle of Dr. Smith, the rulings appear to favor our side.

When doubt is cast upon our care, she seems to go for the other. I walked over to the court with Lee. He says he will make me out to be a good guy, a New Age feeling doctor, a kind of Hawkeye Ogsbury. I hope that's how I am.

When we arrived at the court, the other participants were all present, and Lee was called back to the stand to continue his direct examination. Mr. H first questioned Lee about several subjects he had touched upon the day before. He talked about the cultures.

Judge Peterson told Mr. H, "Mr. H, I am not sure the back row has seen what you want them to see. Why don't you move the chair aside and just get up in there." [A statement that seemed quite pro-plaintiff to me.]

Mr. H then resumed his questioning where he left off the day before. He said, "Doctor, when we left off yesterday, we had been talking about this business with putting in the central line on the 4th of July during the early morning hours."

Mr. H continued to try to show that, since the nurses testified that they had asked for a CVP line placement, I should have performed the placement or at least ensured a proper placement and X-ray reading. He further tried to counter the contention that I was angry about the CVP line placement by showing that no incident report or report to the nursing supervisor was filed. Interestingly, I did talk to the nursing supervisor and told her I did not want to know the identity of Sheran's nurse that night as I could never again work with her if I knew.

Mr. H continued, "Doctor, I'm going to be talking about some CAT scan reports."

At this point I left the courtroom and called my office. I am being asked to give a deposition for another matter. The judge in that case was fed up. I came back to the courtroom and talked to Peter. He said Judge Peterson can handle this.

Mr. H was still talking about the CAT scans. He asked Lee to assume that a board-certified neuroradiologist would testify that the CAT scans demonstrated there was evidence of infarction immediately following the first and second operation, then asked, if so, would that not be "directly related to some type of surgical trauma during that surgery?"

Lee again held his ground. "Actually, that statement you just read proves exactly the opposite; because an infarction takes 24 to 48 hours, minimum, to show up on a CAT scan. So, if she had an infarction, if that showed up on the CAT scan, it would have had to have occurred 24 hours before she ever was taken to surgery."

"So, you would refuse to make that assumption. Is that what you are saying, Doctor?"

"I refuse to make that assumption."

Mr. H paused and asked again, as expected, "Doctor, as of the time of your deposition in January of 1989, you had no idea what the condition of Sheran R was and never inquired about the condition of Sheran R, had you?"

Lee answered, "I knew that she went to Craig Hospital. I knew he had flown up to Lander, Wyoming, or Riverton, with her, and basically, I knew that she was very sick and he was still caring for her."

Mr. H said, "I have no further questions, Your Honor" and sat down.

It was Scott's turn for the all-important cross-examination of Lee Krauth. I believe our whole case depends on this day. He immediately addressed Lee's lack of knowledge of her condition at the time of her discharge.

"Dr. Krauth, Mr. H has made quite an issue of the fact that you weren't entirely clear on the neurological condition of Sheran R at the time of her discharge. I would like to ask you, when was the last time you saw Sheran R in the hospital?"

Lee explained, "I saw her one day on the 9th of September, and—prior to that I had not seen her since July 28 in the hospital."

"You continued to cover for Dr. Ogsbury throughout that two-month period while he was off call and you were on call, didn't you? Was it typical for you to see a patient of his while you were on call so infrequently while she was in the hospital?"

"No, this was extremely atypical. And, in fact, it's probably the only time it's ever happened."

"Why was this case different?"

"Well, Dr. Ogsbury was very emotionally involved with this family, and this lady came down and he did the best he could to take care of her. And, she had a lot of complications as has been reported, and she was basically devastated by this disease that she had. The fact that she had done so poorly, and his concern for the family, and his grieving for her condition necessitated for his well-being, that he assumed full, 100 percent care of her case. And because of that, I dismissed myself from following her. And if any calls ever came in, it was directed that the calls go to him; if he was unavailable at the time he received the call, it came to me. I reached him. I had access to Dr. Ogsbury 24 hours a day for the rest of her course. I was not caring for her. Basically, the grief that he was suffering, he needed to work out by his total involvement with her care. And, in order for him to get through this, and me to get through it, as a practice, he had to cancel some cases for a couple of weeks because he was unable, physically and emotionally, to handle the trauma that he had gone through. And so, what I did, is I picked up the practice and I basically took care of everything.

"And, I did some of his cases in surgery that he turned over to me before they went to surgery, and we assumed an entirely different relationship with this lady and her care, where he was the only doctor involved. And that was the way he wanted it. That's the way the family wanted it. He made a trip to Wyoming with the family—he flew up in a plane—and he has never done that before. He was very concerned about the fact that this lady was displaced geographically from her loved ones. He did everything possible, from what I could see, to make her life and the family's life less miserable. He took them into his home; he took them out to dinner;

when they didn't have a place to stay, he arranged for places to stay. His whole life, for two months, was consumed with taking care of this lady. And, so, my role as a physician was really that I—I had no role. My role was to try to support the practice."

At this point, to my amazement, Lee started to cry. He continued with difficulty, "And I'm sorry, but unless somebody has gone through this—you know, we are not automatons; we are not robots; we are doctors; we are human beings; and we have the same emotions that anybody does—that these attorneys have, that Mr. R has. And the point is, Dr. Ogsbury was not capable of functioning for several weeks. And the only way he could work that out was to completely throw himself into her care. And so, my role was to take myself out of her care. I had nothing to do with her care. That's not normal. That's not what we do in our practice, but in this situation, because of the severity of her injury, because of the circumstances and the fact that everything went the way it did, that's the way it worked out. So, I am embarrassed during this testimony to tell people that I don't know everything about her care, but the bottom line is that I didn't have anything to do with her care for the last two and one-half months of her care.

"In fact, I only have seven progress notes in the whole chart. I assisted in the surgery. I covered call a couple of days, and then on the weekend I was on call consecutive days. Every single time I was called, I called Dr. Ogsbury and got his permission to do anything. I did not make any independent decisions because he would not let me. He did not want me to make any independent decisions. He wanted to assume the full responsibility, so I let him have it. So, it's true I wasn't—I don't know a lot about the details of how she was when she left the hospital. I had not seen her. But, that was by design and it was unusual. And it was—it was basically to help three people—it was to help Sheran R, it was to help Dr. Ogsbury, and it was to help The R family."

Mr. Nixon asked, "Dr. Krauth, you have talked about your observations of Dr. Ogsbury. Did you ever, at any time, get an indication that he was acting this way because he felt he had done something wrong?"

Lee answered, "No. He was in practice with me for two years, and he had never had a major tragedy like this, and he was just having a hard time coping with it."

"The jury has heard a lot about consultants so far in the case. Were you a neurologic consultant on this case?"

"Yes, I was. I am a neurosurgeon and am very well qualified, and my opinion was asked, so I gave an opinion."

"In this case, Sheran R had consultants called in in the areas of neurosurgery such as yourself and Dr. Shogan? She had consultants called in from the area of infectious disease, such as Dr. Mason? She had a consultant called in from the area of ear, nose, and throat surgery, and that was Dr. Barron? She had a consultant called in the area of neurology, which was Dr. Yarnell, and perhaps others?"

"Yes."

"I assume you have called in consultants on your own cases. When you call in consultants, do you always do what they tell you to do?"

"No."

"What is your relationship with the consultant when you have one come in and give you an opinion on one of your patients?"

"Well, I have to make the decisions for all of my patients. I am ultimately responsible. I try to gain as much information as I can, and I use people's opinions that I value to help arrive at the most appropriate judgments to make in care of patients."

"Have you and Dr. Ogsbury consulted with one another on your neurosurgical patients?"

"We do that all the time."

"And I would guess, from your answer, that at times you have decided not to do what he recommends or suggests to you?"

"Yeah, a lot—we are both pretty bullheaded, so we listen to each other, we respect each other's opinions, but we are still going to do what we feel is right."

"You said you were partners with Dr. Ogsbury during this period of time. How long had you been associated professionally—as of July of 1986?"

"We had been partners since July of 1984."

"And as far as your office practice with patients, did you see each other's patients?"

"No."

"As far as scheduling surgery, if you weren't available to operate on one of your patients, would you go ahead and schedule your patients for surgery on Dr. Ogsbury's schedule?"

"Never."

"Were you separate?"

"We were totally separate."

"Why is that?"

"Because I don't think it's right to see a patient and have a relationship with the family—then, that would be very inconsiderate. If I develop the patient-doctor relationship, and you don't expect them to just go down the street and have some technicians come in and do it. I mean, it's more than just the technical aspect. So, indeed, when he had some patients scheduled for surgery and he couldn't do it, I saw all those patients again, and I made a relationship, and I counseled them and did that on my own."

At that point Lee completely broke down and asked, "Can we take a break?"

We went out and Lee came out with his closest personal friend who was there in the courtroom for his support. Lee was crying and said he was sorry. Why in the world would he be sorry? I never knew that emotion was in there. I had had the totality of her care for my grieving to the point where I am comfortable with at least my role in her devastation. He, too, was involved in the tragedy but in trying to protect him, I removed him from her care, and he never was given a chance to come to grips with his own grief until today when it came out on the stand for all to see.

I looked around the courtroom. All of the jurors except Ms. Petit and Ms. Huey were crying. I could not talk about them. Mr. H clearly appeared moved by Lee's emotions, yet my impression was that Ms. Kudla and Mr. R were not affected at all. I could not tell about Mr. Schuster. Peter and Scott both had tears in their eyes. I did too—and thought to myself, now I have to tell this story. Lee went downstairs with his friend. Scott said, "We better let Lee talk about his training to start."

The court reconvened. Lee apologized to Judge Peterson.

She said, "The court sometimes does that to you." Mr. H approached the bench and talked to Judge Peterson. I did not hear what he said. Scott resumed his cross-examination. Lee appeared back under control.

Scott said, "Dr. Krauth, from time to time, you were talking about how you and Dr. Ogsbury would consult on cases. Would you also act as surgeon and assistant surgeon on common cases? And, generally, would you, if it was your patient, be the primary surgeon and he would be the assistant? And would the same be true if it was Dr. Ogsbury's patient, that is would he be the primary surgeon and you would be the assistant?"

"That's exactly right."

"Let me ask you, what was your position or your standing in relation to Dr. Ogsbury at the time of the second surgery on July 2?"

"Dr. Ogsbury was the surgeon, and I was the first assistant."

"What did it mean to be an assistant versus a surgeon?"

"Well, the surgeon performs the procedure, and I do what I am told to help him, and I can offer comments or suggestions, and he can deal with those comments and suggestions as he sees fit. Basically, I am there to assist or help."

"Do you know of any reason why this particular operative report was either dictated or typed indicating that you were both surgeons on this case?"

"No, I don't. I didn't dictate it."

"Let me show you what's been marked as Defendant's Exhibit B-168, and let me ask if you can just identify that, please?"

"Yes. This is a copy of my bill to Sheran R."

"Does it indicate your status at the time of that operation on July 2?"

"Yes, it lists me as an assistant to Dr. Ogsbury for the procedure."

"How does the operative record indicate your status at the time of the July 2 surgery?"

"It lists me as the assistant."

"Do you know who prepared the operating room record?"

"The operating room nurses." It was clear that Lee had indeed regained his composure. He appeared softened, assured but not cocky, with his usual academic confidence.

Scott resumed. "Before we talk specifically about your involvement with Mrs. R's care, I would like you to tell the jury a little bit about your training and background in the field of neurology. Where did you go to medical school?"

"I went to Duke University Medical School."

"Where did you go for undergraduate school?"

"I went to the United States Air Force Academy to undergraduate school, and I graduated there in 1972 as a distinguished graduate."

"And you then went to Duke for your medical schooling. And that was a 4-year program?"

"Yes, but I graduated in three years as I validated the first half of my first year." [I thought we are now back to the Dr. Krauth we all know and love.]

He continued. "After I graduated from Duke University, I went to Wilford Hall United States Military Hospital, which is the Air Force equivalent to Walter Reed. It's a thousand-bed teaching hospital, and I did a surgical internship at the U.S. Air Force Hospital, Wilford Hall, in San Antonio, Texas."

"And where did you go after your training period?"

"After Wilford Hall, I came to Denver to the University of Colorado, where I did a neurosurgical residency."

"How long was your residency program?"

"It was four years."

"And describe for the jury briefly what a four-year residency program in neurosurgery consists of."

"Well, it consists of learning the different diseases in the Central Nervous System that we treat, and examining patients under the tutelage of professors and people who are fully trained. And it's kind of like on-the-job training for a neurosurgeon. And, when you complete those four years you are qualified to go out independently and perform neurosurgical operations on your own and take care of neurosurgical patients."

He noted he became board certified in 1983. Following that, the Surgeon General of the Air Force suggested that he return back to the United States to be the primary microvascular surgeon for the Air Force at Wilford Hall.

Scott then asked about his experience with CSF leaks.

Lee reported that he had treated two cases of iatrogenic CSF leaks while at Wilford Hall.

Scott asked him about the procedures for treatment of CSF leaks and he asked did he receive training in those procedures. Lee reported that during the years of residency, 1976 to 1980, he was instructed to open up the skull, expose the cribriform plate, place the muscle over the leak, then layer the fascia over that.

"Was that the same procedure that was used by Dr. Ogsbury, to your knowledge, in the June 25, 1986, surgery on Sheran R?"

"That's precisely the same surgery that he did."

"I imagine you have had an opportunity to review literature from time to time concerning any developments that may have occurred in that surgical procedure. From your review, has there been any change in the reported literature concerning the standard way that residents are taught to repair cribriform plate leaks?"

"No. It's kind of funny, because Walter Dandy was the first one to describe this back in 1926. The literature that I have reviewed basically all starts out with the caveat that nothing has changed much from Dandy's first description, and that's still appropriate today, and basically, Dandy described layering muscle and fascia over a hole."

"Now, that's not the same procedure that you told the jury about yesterday that you had used where you actually stuffed muscle down through the hole and into the ethmoid sinus, is it?"

"It's basically the same procedure, but I have just kind of developed a little quirk of my own that I started stuffing muscle down into the ethmoid air cell. I don't know why I did it, but I felt it seemed like a thing that might work. And, I have done that myself. I have never read about it."

"Would it help for you to explain to the jury with a diagram that shows the cribriform plate area and the ethmoid cell?"

"I think it would help the jury understand." He then went up with the models to the jury and demonstrated how he packed the ethmoid air cell.

Scott asked, "Doctor, you said you picked that up on your own. Did anybody ever teach you or instruct you on that method of packing the ethmoid sinus area?"

"No."

"Have you ever taught that to anyone else?"

"No."

"Have you read about that anywhere?"

"No."

"Are you aware of any other neurosurgeon who uses that same technique?"

"I'm not aware of any."

"Do you have an understanding, Doctor, as to whether or not that is taught to surgical residents currently?"

"My understanding is I do not think it is taught to neurosurgical residents."

Scott next asked Lee to list all of the hospitals in which he had performed brain surgery. When Lee reported he had operated at about fifteen hospitals, Scott asked, "In all of those locations where you performed neurosurgery on the brain, have you used Surgicel?"

"Yes."

"And when did you first learn about the use of Surgicel?"

"The first time I walked into the operating room at Duke University as a medical student."

"Dr. Smith testified that he had never heard of Surgicel being used in the brain in a neurosurgical procedure. Do you have an impression as to the current knowledge of a neurosurgeon who would testify that he had never heard of the use of Surgicel in the brain?"

"Yes."

"And, what's that?"

Mr. H objected. "Your honor, that's an improper question—asking about the knowledge of another witness in the case."

Scott tried to defend his question. "Your Honor, Mr. H has asked a number of questions on direct examination asking for this doctor's impression of statements made by other witnesses." Judge Peterson sustained the objection.

Scott tried again, "Surgicel is commonly used, isn't it? Do you know when it was first developed or used before your training?"

"It's been written about for probably thirty years in the literature."

"And have you seen it used in every single operating room that you have been operating in since the beginning of your medical training?"

"Yes."

"Doctor, looking at Plaintiffs' Exhibit 124, which is a blow-up of the operative report by Dr. Ogsbury, June 25, 1986, he mentions in the description of the procedure that the dura was extensively tented. What does that mean to you, as a neurosurgeon?"

"Tenting of the dura is a technique that we are taught during our first year of residency to put little stitches in the dura. When one does surgery on the brain and opens the skull, you have to peel the dura off the undersurface of the skull. And so, when that is done, it leaves a potential space between the inside of the skull and the outside membrane of the brain. If that space is not obliterated or kept from filling up it could fill up with blood after surgery and you'd have a large blood clot that could press on the brain and cause brain damage. So, what we do when we tent is we put little stitches in the dura and we pull them up to hold the dura back up to the surface of the skull to prevent that complication from happening. That was first described by Harvey Cushing, who is the father of neurosurgery worldwide. That was in 1903."

"And that is something you learned as a first-year medical student?"

"I learned that—actually I learned it when I did my first rotation as a medical student, on the neurosurgery floor at Duke University, with Dr. Odom."

"Something you would expect every practicing neurosurgeon would be familiar with?"

"Something that every practicing neurosurgeon should do routinely with craniotomies." [I thought, Lee is doing great—he is on a roll.]

Scott continued." Now, Doctor, before you saw Sheran R or even knew about her in July of 1986, how many CSF leaks have you treated in patients?"

"Roughly 200."

"And what is the most common type of leak that you have treated in your experience?"

"The most common type of spinal fluid leak is following head trauma."

"If you have a patient that has a leak in the cribriform plate area, do you approach that any differently as a surgeon if it's iatrogenic or medically caused, as opposed to traumatically caused?"

"Yes, you do because, if it is just a fracture, there's a higher likelihood that it would seal off on its own and there is a low likelihood that there are contaminated elements from the nasal contents that have been pushed up into the brain cavity. So, iatrogenically, according to most authorities, it should be dealt with surgically in a more aggressive fashion, with very little delay from the time of the discovery of the leak."

And how many iatrogenic leaks have you treated in your practice?"

"I have treated five."

"And have each of those been surgically repaired?"

"Yes."

"And what approach, extracranially or intracranially—did you use in each of these cases?"

"Well, an intracranial approach is the only recommended approach for an anterior fossa iatrogenically produced leak—that is, doctor-produced leak—through the frontal cribriform."

"Would that be in the same location where Sheran R had her leak in July of 1986?"

"Yes."

Scott and Lee then began to discuss Lee's direct role the care. Lee said he learned of the leak and failed first operation upon his return from a neurosurgical conference and despite the failure said he agreed with the intracranial approach that was used.

When he reported Dr. Spetzler's endorsement of this approach as well, Mr. H objected. "Objection, Your Honor; I am going to request that non-leading questions be used in this examination." The objection was overruled; this was the first in our favor in a while. It appears that Lee has had an effect even on Judge Peterson.

Scott and Lee continued their discussion of Lee's involvement. He felt the lab tests indicated Sheran already had meningitis and that Dr. Mason concurred with that opinion. Scott asked about the CAT scans but soon thereafter the lunch break was called.

The lunch was a good break for everyone. Kathy, Lee, Joneen, Peter, Scott, Lee's friend, and I all went to the Denver Art Museum. Our spirits were up. When Lee went to the bathroom, his friend asked if he could hold Lee's watch. Lee spoke of Mr. R. and his impression that Mr. R. had made an obscene gesture toward him.

During lunch we spoke again of Gerry Spence. Does Peter ever get animated when speaking of him! He told us that he was involved in one of the cases in Mr. Spence's book and said Mr. Spence's description of what happened in that case is quite different than what he remembered actually transpired. Obviously, Mr. Spence is still hanging over our heads.

Before we left the restaurant, we talked about the need to counteract the impression left by Mr. H—that I was inexperienced, particularly in treating this problem.

Walking back to the courtroom, I noticed Mr. R was looking at me.

Scott resumed his cross-examination. He immediately addressed the question of inexperience.

"You mentioned earlier that Dr. Ogsbury was your chief resident during your training. What is a chief resident?"

"The chief resident is the senior level resident in a residency program. He would be the person in his last year of training before being fully trained. A chief resident basically runs the service, does all the major surgery, and instructs and teaches the junior residents on surgical technique and on care techniques of patients."

"Was Dr. Ogsbury, in effect, for a period of time, one of your instructors?"

"Yes."

"Do you have an understanding of his prior experience concerning the repair of spinal fluid leaks in that same area that were caused by something other than a doctor or medical care?"

"Yes, my understanding is that Dr. Ogsbury has personally cared for about ten people who had spinal fluid leaks in the area of the cribriform plate caused by trauma."

"Is there anything different about your decisions on how to approach these intracranially or extracranially when they are caused by a doctor versus caused by trauma?"

"Only that if they are caused by a doctor, it's more of an emergent or urgent situation, you don't want to wait as long. But the surgical repair itself is the exact same technique whether it's caused by a doctor sticking an instrument up there or whether it's caused by a fracture or trauma."

Scott then turned back to Lee's review of the CAT scans that revealed the air on the left prior to the second operation and asked whether the increased leak played into the decision to re-do the repair as well. Of course it had. He then asked, can leaks recur despite good surgical practice? Lee said that it could happen or that an unrecognized leak in another area could show up.

Scott then returned to the issue of surgical experience, "What was your experience in traumatic CSF repairs prior to Mrs. R's case?"

"From a nonsurgical trauma, or iatrogenic as we have talked about, I have repaired two other people that had trauma-induced rhinorrhea with surgery."

"And Dr. Ogsbury had about ten?"

"He had ten not caused by a doctor."

"So, he had actually done this procedure more than you had?"

"That's correct."

Scott and Lee then continued the discussion of Lee's evaluation of Sheran R. Scott asked about the third nerve palsy. Lee discussed the anatomy of the third nerve and felt that the third nerve dysfunction was a complication of bacterial meningitis (where there is reported a ten to twenty percent chance of having this complication). He added that the location of the third nerve is not even visible from a position near the cribriform plate.

Scott then went back to the question of options. "Now, we have talked about the options that were available to Sheran R, in your opinion, at the time of your consult with her on July 1, and I would like to ask you about each of those. One was to wait, correct?"

"Yes."

"One was to reduce pressure?"

"One was to consider some drainage procedure or shunt."

"And the other was surgery?"

"Yes, to re-operate."

"Were any of these options very attractive?"

"No."

"Why?"

"Because they all carry with them significant risks and what you know—the ultimate—the whole purpose of this is that we want to get Sheran R better and want to help her, and so, you have these options, and so you have to kind of do like you do in other things when you are stuck with the bad options. [Scott was nicely getting into the concept of least bad options.]

"So all of these presented risks to her?"

"They all presented risks."

"Let's list the risks that were involved with electing to just wait." Scott had Lee list all of the risks and benefits of each of these options."

Lee felt that re-exploration would have the most benefit with overall least risk. He said, "I felt that the best benefit was an immediate cessation of the leak, to stop recontamination and reinfection and get that under control, and to stop more air from going into the brain."

"And was it your opinion, at that time, to a reasonable degree of medical probability, that Mrs. R—her meningitis could not be treated effectively unless you stopped the CSF leak?"

"I felt as long as the leak was going, we weren't going to be able to cure her of her meningitis."

"So, this is really a situation where you have to weigh some alternatives and decide what is the least worst; would you agree?"

"Yes, you're stuck between a rock and a hard place."

"And that's where your judgment as a surgeon and a physician comes into play in evaluating the risks and benefits of how to treat a patient?"

"Yes."

Next, Scott resumed the discussion of the meningitis. He and Lee talked about taking the gram stain from the ICP monitor. He noted that from the results of that test, Dr. Mason had reported gram negative rods on the gram stain and noted this was a significant finding, noted that it was not growing and then noted further that it was not growing because the antibiotics were sufficient to suppress the growth.

Scott asked, "To you, Doctor, as a physician, is the evidence of gram-negative rods from the spinal fluid taken on the 3rd of July conclusive evidence that Sheran R had bacterial meningitis?"

"Yes, when coupled with everything else, I think it was."

"So that's positive laboratory evidence that she had a bacteria in her spinal fluid?"

"Yes."

"Now, we've heard a lot of talk about whether surgery should be performed in the face of meningitis. That's kind of like being between a rock and a hard place too, isn't it?"

"Yes—a lot of this case is that way. [I thought Lee was on a roll again.] We are already saying that her brain is infected; it's swollen; she has a potentially lethal infection now, and we haven't stopped the problem of the re-introduction of more and more bacteria, so we haven't stopped the underlying problem. And she is recontaminating her brain space and spinal fluid with each breath. So, the question is, well, do you just wait and wait and hope? Or, do you do something and try and stop it? And, if you stop it, hope that by then the antibiotics could ward off whatever is left?"

"So, the fact that she had meningitis, despite being treated for it aggressively, means, on the other hand, that you want to do surgery to stop the continued contamination, right?"

"Yes."

"But, on the other hand, since she has meningitis, you don't really like to operate on a patient who has meningitis."

"You sure don't."

"And it was your opinion at that time, based on your review, that another surgery was the most effective way to treat her meningitis?"

"Yes."

"Was it your decision to do a second craniotomy?"

"No, it was Dr. Ogsbury's decision."

"But that was your recommendation?"

"That was my recommendation."

"He apparently agreed with you and thought that was the best way to treat this patient."

"Apparently."

"Do you know if anyone else consulted with Dr. Ogsbury considering what should be done with Sheran R at that point?"

"Dr. Barron felt that it should be performed."

"And Dr. Barron, as an ear, nose, and throat specialist, you would expect him to consider whether or not this leak should be approached from outside the cranium or inside the cranium. Do you see any indication in the chart that Dr. Barron felt that an extracranial or through the nose approach was advisable on Sheran R at that time?"

"No."

"Now, although you don't mention it in your note, it was your belief that bilateral or both-sided surgery should be considered?"

"Yes."

Now, I want to ask you, with a patient in Sheran R's condition at that time, before the first surgery, do you have an opinion, to a reasonable degree of medical probability, as to whether surgery at that time was within the standard of care without having a CSF culture?"

"Yes. It was within, well within, the standard of care without a culture because you are going to have to fix the leak anyway, and she was being treated with antibiotics—as it turns out, probably would have suppressed the culture anyway—as they ended up doing when they were done."

Scott next turned to the use of Super Glue. Lee reported he had used it in transsphenoidal hypophysectomies and that ENT doctors use it in middle ear reconstruction.

Scott asked, "So, you would agree it's not uncommon for physicians to use medications or surgical hardware or glues that are not approved by the FDA?"

"Not at all."

And would agree that it was within the acceptable standard of care—or would be within the acceptable standards of care—for a neurosurgeon to consider the use of Super Glue in a surgery if he felt it was appropriate?"

"Yes."

"Was Super Glue used in the second surgery?"

"No, no surgical adhesive was used at all."

Scott next asked, "Doctor, I would like to have you go through the surgical report with me now and tell me what happened during the second surgery on Sheran R on July 2, 1986. Now, we have already talked in detail about the indications, haven't we? Now under the 'Operative Procedure' section, I would like to list up here, if I could, the steps of the operation."

Scott began to write down, on the blackboard, the steps of the operation, and Lee, using a model of the skull, explained the operation. He specifically showed on his model the considerable distance from the tuberculum to the anterior cerebral arteries. Furthermore, he pointed out the small distance of retraction necessary to get to the tuberculum.

At this point the jury seemed very attentive. I told Peter that Scott was doing well. Peter said, "He is having fun. He's like a baseball pitcher with five pitches and four speeds, all working."

Scott asked, "The next thing that was done was that there was retraction on the left, correct?"

Lee answered, "I don't remember specifically. But the standard technique that is used is either using a suction or perhaps possibly a ribbon retractor. You would put it in and gently pull it—like I said 2 or 3 millimeters, maybe 4 millimeters at the most—and that would expose the length of the frontal fossa from the front all the way back to the tuberculum. You don't retract backwards, just to the side."

"At any time during the procedure was the brain retracted up and back so that you would look down in and see the tuberculum and the cribriform plate?"

"No. It was retracted sideways."

"At any time was the brain retracted in such a fashion that it was pressed up against the top of the cranial vault above the bone flaps that were opened?"

"No."

Scott continued with the description of the procedure and asked, "When he inspected the floor of the cribriform plate on the left, did he find any type of defect or hole?"

Lee answered, "No, he did not."

"Why did you put the muscle down if there was no hole?"

"Just on the outside chance that you miss something. Again, it would have been a mistake to have gone through all that and not make certain, 100 percent."

Scott then addressed Lee's new trick. "The next thing that happened was you packed the hole on the right. Now, was the procedure used at the second operation one that you had used on other cribriform repairs?"

"Yes."

"And how was that different from the one Dr. Ogsbury had done the first time?"

"It was basically the same procedure. The only twist, if you will, was that I suggested to him that he take a piece of muscle and push it down out of the brain into the ethmoid sinus and fill up the entire air cell. That was the only thing that was different; otherwise, it was exactly the same."

"So, you weren't just laying a piece of muscle over the hole and have it go down a little bit, you were packing muscle all the way into the air cell. Is that a gross description of how you were packing it?"

"Yes."

"And, again, that's a procedure that you had developed on your own?"

"Yes."

"And, then the final thing was you go on to note that it seemed tight and since it was dry, you would expect it to swell and tighten when the wound was closed?"

"Yes."

Scott turned to the morning of July 3. He asked, "Did you call Dr. Ogsbury after you received that call from the nurse?"

"Yeah, immediately."

"At 2:00 or 3:00 in the morning?"

"Yes."

"Where did you call him?"

"I called him at home."

"Why?"

"Because, as I stated earlier, he was in charge of the case. And this was a potentially significant problem. I wanted him to be aware of what was happening so that he could decide if he wanted to treat her, whether he agreed with my orders, and what else, if anything, he wanted done at that time."

"Did you call back the hospital after you spoke with him to give further orders?"

"Yes, I did."

"What was the order you gave when you called back?"

"I asked to have the critical care doctor who was in the hospital to go see her and to check her ventilatory status or breathing status and make sure that her lungs and everything were okay."

"Why didn't you just order that when you got the first call from the nurses?"

"Because I wanted to check with Dr. Ogsbury before I brought another doctor into the case."

Scott then turned to July 4. He asked about changing call and Lee said we usually change call at about 7:00 a.m."

"At any time on July 4 before you saw Sheran R at about 9:00 a.m., did you receive any call or were you notified on your beeper in any fashion?"

"No."

"You heard Nurse C testify that she was never called back. After that call was not returned by you or Dr. Ogsbury, correct?"

"Yes."

"You also heard her testify that she didn't call critical care. She didn't call Dr. M or Dr. D who had both seen her that same evening?"

"Yes."

"She didn't notify her charge nurse or anybody else about a problem that she thought was going on before the end of her shift at 7:00, correct?"

"That's correct."

"You got to the hospital—at St. Anthony Central—at about what time on the 4th?"

"It would be sometime around 9:00."

"What happened when you got into St. Anthony?"

"I walked into the intensive care unit to see a different patient, actually, that I had primary responsibility for—because Dr. Ogsbury told me he was going to make rounds on Sheran R Friday morning."

"So, you wouldn't have routinely, on the morning of the 4th, gone and seen her for Dr. Ogsbury?"

"No, I wasn't planning to. As I walked into the intensive care unit, Dr. Mason was there, and she approached me and explained to me that she had seen Sheran R and that there had been a tension pneumothorax in Sheran R."

The afternoon break was called. The team was fine. Mr. R appeared to be throwing visual daggers at me.

After the break, Scott returned to the issue of Super Glue. "Digressing for a moment, Dr. Krauth, we talked about FDA approval of Super Glue. Are you aware of whether or not the FDA had somehow disapproved the use of Super Glue?"

"No, it is not."

"Now, it's true, isn't it, they allow for the use of a non-approved substance in the brain? Have you seen that in the Yeoman's text?"

"Yes, I have."

"In fact, they tell you how to make it if you want to use it, don't they?"

"Yes, they do."

"Kind of a cookbook for a non-FDA approved glue?"

"That's exactly what they say, yes."

Mr. Nixon turned back to the morning of July 4. "Getting back to where we were, when you came into the hospital on the morning of July 4, after you spoke with Dr. Mason, did you go into Mrs. R's room?"

"Yes."

"Did you see what was going on?"

"Yes, I did."

"What was going on?"

"Dr. Worley and the surgical resident, Dr. M, I believe, were tending to her and in the action of putting in a chest tube to re-inflate her lung."

"What did you do then?"

"Well, I talked to the nurse to try to find out a little more what happened, and then I went downstairs to the Radiology Department to look at the X-ray that was taken at 3:20 in the morning to look at it myself to see what it showed."

"Did you call Dr. Ogsbury?"

"I called Dr. Ogsbury after I found out what had happened to inform him of what was going on—that she was being attended to, that she was stable, and I was going downstairs and look at the X-rays with another physician."

"Was he angry? "

"Yes."

"Why?"

"He was very angry because she was a very sick lady, and she didn't need any complications like this and that he had told them not to put in a central line."

"You are aware that Nurse MK testified that she recalls Dr. Ogsbury giving her permission to place a central line on the evening of July 3, correct?"

"Yes."

"And is it your understanding that the custom, habit, and routine at St. Anthony was for such an order to be written on the chart by the nurse, and signed, and timed, and dated?"

"Yes."

"In your experience, have you ever given such an order to a nurse and had it not entered in the chart by her as an order given to her by a physician?"

"No."

"In reviewing the records, have you seen any indication that Nurse MK recorded the orders she received from Dr. Ogsbury—that she testified about—the evening of July 3?"

"No."

"Do you have any explanation for why there would be no order entered by her in the chart if she received it?"

"Yes. Either she really didn't receive an order, or she didn't do her job in documenting it."

"Now you are also aware that Nurse C testified that she received notification verbally from Nurse MK when she came on shift at 11:00, and that Nurse MK had supposedly received permission from Dr. Ogsbury to place a line, correct? And again, that's the type of thing you would expect as a physician practicing in the hospital, for a nurse to note in the chart as an order?"

"Yes, it was an order."

"Did you see any evidence in the chart, as you reviewed it, of Nurse C recording that she was informed that Dr. Ogsbury had given permission to place a central line?"

"That's not in the chart."

"Do you have any explanation why she wouldn't record an order like that in the chart?"

"Again, either it wasn't given, or she didn't do her job."

"You are also aware that Nurse C testified yesterday that she called Dr. Ogsbury at 4:30 in the morning on the 4th and that she told him about the ICP and the intracranial pressure waveform and that she told him about some drainage from her nose. She also testified that she told him about placement of the central line?"

"Yes."

"Now, in your experience at St. Anthony, when a Nurse Calls a physician with specific information at night that she records in the chart why she called?"

"Yes."

"And she recorded that she told Dr. Ogsbury about the ICP waveform and the drainage?"

"Yes."

"Did you see any indication in the chart that she recorded that she told Dr. Ogsbury about the central line?"

"It's not in the chart."

"Do you have any explanation for why she would note two things that she told him and not the third?"

"I don't think, personally, she told him the central line was put in."

"Now, Nurse C also testified while you were here that she listened to Mrs. R's breath sounds with the stethoscope and that she did so through the morning. Do you recall that?"

"Yes."

"Now you have heard normal breath sounds through a stethoscope. What do they sound like?"

"They sound like what Nurse C told the jury—it's whoosh, whoosh."

"And you have had occasion to hear or listen to a lung with a stethoscope that has a pneumothorax, haven't you? What does that sound like?"

Dr. Krauth lifted the microphone but made no sound. That got the jury's attention.

"You don't hear anything, do you?"

"No."

"Well, now, from looking at the X-ray in the morning, you know that Sheran R had a pneumothorax in her right lung at least from 3:20 a.m. until the end of Nurse C's shift, correct? Do you have any explanation, Doctor, for how Mrs. C could have listened to Mrs. R's lungs on five separate occasions, listened to each lung in five separate places, and compared the breath sounds she heard and thought they were normal?"

"Yes, I do. Nurse C either did not listen to the lungs in five places and compare them like she said, or she is totally incompetent to listen to lungs."

"You also heard Nurse B's testimony yesterday. She testified that Dr. Ogsbury used Super Glue during the first surgery. Do you see any notes in the chart by Nurse B that Dr. Ogsbury used Super Glue?"

"No."

"Now you testified that you went down and looked at the chest X-ray on the morning of the 4th, correct?"

"Yes, I did."

"Was anybody with you when you looked it over?"

"Yes, the chief of general surgery at St. Anthony Hospital."

"Was that Dr. M's supervisor at the time?"

"Yes, it was."

"Now, I think you told Mr. H on his examination that this was an obvious pneumothorax."

"Yes." Lee then explained the pneumothorax and demonstrated its presence on the X-ray.

You are aware that Nurse C testified Dr. D made four or five separate attempts to place that central line. Wouldn't you agree that every time you stick a patient with a needle to place a central line, it increases the risk of pneumothorax? That makes it particularly important to listen to the breath sounds after the line is placed."

"Yes, it does."

"You are aware that Dr. M made no note in the chart when he placed the central line?"

"Yes."

"Dr. D made no note in the chart when he attempted to place a central line?"

"Yes."

"Now you went through the neurologic status sheets with Mr. H, I believe, yesterday. Now, do you see, at 4:00 a.m. on July 4 where Sheran R is shown to be responsive? Does that show she was actually doing a little better?"

"Yes, it does."

"Is that significant to you?"

"It sure could be."

"Doctor, you would agree, from reviewing the chart and the entries at 4:00 and 5:00 a.m. on the 4th of July that it appears that she was doing better neurologically at that time?"

"Yes, I would agree."

"And that was before the pneumothorax was discovered, and the pneumothorax wasn't discovered until 8:30 or 9:00 in the morning?"

"That's correct."

"Now, you have seen from the nurses' notes, haven't you, that at 8:45 it's noted that her color was poor and that she had a decrease in her level of consciousness, and she was not moving in response to painful stimuli. There was no blood pressure palpable with the Doppler, and that her femoral pulse was barely palpable?"

"Yes."

"And you would agree at that time from your review of the record that she was close to death?"

"Yes."

"At the time Dr. Mason found her in the morning, you would agree that if she had not received treatment within a half an hour she probably would have died?"

"Yes, it appeared that way."

"Can you tell from the nursing records how long she had been in that condition?"

"No."

"It's not well documented, is it?"

"No."

"I believe you testified in response to Mr. H's question on cross-examination that a normal person could sustain a low blood pressure of 60/0, as reported, for an hour or so? "

"Yes."

"Sheran R wasn't in the normal condition, was she?"

"Not at all."

"She was critically ill?"

"Yes."

"She had had two brain surgeries, significant edema, and meningitis at that time?"

"Three brain surgeries, if you want to be technical."

"And if another physician who was more familiar with the care of Sheran R than you, from your limited involvement in her care, was of the opinion that this compounded or added to her neurologic condition, you wouldn't have any reason to disagree?"

Mr. H objected to the form of the question. The objection was sustained.

Scott continued, "Is there any evidence in the chart that anybody listened to her lungs with a stethoscope to check her breath sounds between 7:00 when Mrs. C said she last checked her breath sounds and 8:45 when she was found?"

"There is no evidence in the chart that anybody did that."

"Now you understand, Doctor, it's your understanding that Dr. Ogsbury didn't give permission for placement of the central line?"

"That's correct."

"And the records show that just before Nurse MK supposedly asked him for permission, he had been in to see Sheran R—and in fact he was in to see her when she says she asked for permission—and he had examined her, and spent over an hour with the patient and the family?"

"Yes."

"Do you have an opinion, Doctor, based upon a reasonable degree of medical probability, that a physician who has just seen and evaluated a patient as Dr. Ogsbury had and was in a position to determine whether or not a central line was advisable, whether the standard of care requires him to consent for the placement of a central line because a nurse requests it? "

"No, of course not."

"Why not? "

"Because he is a physician, and he is in a better position to determine whether a central line is indicated than a nurse."

"As a doctor, do you expect a nurse will call you before having a central line placed in one of your patients who is critically ill in the middle of the night when there is no written order in the chart giving her permission for such a procedure?"

"Yes, I do."

"Why?"

"Because of what happened to Sheran R. Bad things can happen that way."

"Doctor, you are aware that Sheran R had experienced bilateral infarction of the anterior cerebral arteries, and I think you pointed out to the jury where those arteries are on the right lobe and the left lobe correct?"

"Yes."

"Do you have an opinion, to a reasonable degree of medical probability, as to the cause of the bilateral anterior cerebral infarct in Sheran R?"

"Yes, I do. My opinion is that she had bilateral anterior cerebral infarction due to complication from vasculitis and meningitis."

"Can you explain to the jury why that is your opinion?"

"Because I don't find any other plausible explanation as to why she would have had it. She had evidence of vasculitis by having a third nerve palsy from the meningitis which is a commonly known complication. And, along with vasculitis that can cause a third nerve or cranial nerve palsy, one can see vasculitis in the distribution of other arteries, and I don't have another explanation as to why she had an infarct in that distribution."

"It's been suggested, Doctor, that in this case the brain was retracted up and back, pressed into the top of the cranial vault behind the opening of the craniotomy. Do you have an opinion, based upon a reasonable degree of medical probability, as to whether or not such an action, even if it did occur, could cause such an infarction of the anterior cerebral arteries?"

"Yes. It's hard to even imagine how that kind of retraction could have been done. But, if it had been done, I can't see how it would cause an infarct to the anterior cerebral arteries—which are two inches below the surface, and I also base that on the fact that as an expert in aneurysm surgery, I routinely occlude arteries in the Circle of Willis with aneurysm clips, and could do this up to 45 minutes to an hour—complete occlusion—and I have never had distal infarct in the territory of an occluded artery before, even when it has been occluded that long. Japanese literature and our literature are full of that. It's recommended as a common technique of aneurysm surgery to temporarily occlude the artery."

"It's also been suggested that the brain was retracted back so far during the second surgery and/or the first surgery that it stressed or stretched the anterior cerebral arteries causing an infarction. Do you have an opinion, to a reasonable degree of medical probability, as to whether that happened in this case?"

"Yes, I do. That did not happen."

"And what's the basis for that?"

"The basis is nowhere, at any time, was her brain retracted posteriorly and it was not retracted to anymore distance than a few millimeters, as I stated. When you use the microscope, you have to do very little retraction, as opposed to outdated and antiquated procedures without the microscope where a massive retraction might be necessary."

"Have you performed similar retractions, the same or similar to those performed in the second surgery that you observed in other craniotomy surgeries?"

"Yes—multiple times."

"Have you ever seen bilateral anteriorcerebral artery infarctions as a result of doing a retraction?"

"Never."

"You mentioned that it was your opinion that infarctions in this case were caused by meningitis and vasculitis. How does vasculitis occlude or stop the flow of blood in an artery?"

"If you have vasculitis or an infected blood vessel wall, two things happen. If you look at it under the microscope while the infection is going on, there is a thickening or swelling of the anterior wall, which narrows the artery, and you can get thrombosis or clotting off of the artery, or you can just get the significant narrowing, which impedes the amount of blood that can flow through the areas."

"If the flow is impeded, what is the result?"

"If the flow is impeded enough, not enough blood gets to the brain and the brain cells die."

"And that's infarction?"

"That's infarction."

"And is meningitis causing vasculitis and thrombosis and thrombosis is a blocking of the artery documented in the neurosurgical literature?"

"Yes."

"Is there any other way, Doctor, to a reasonable degree of medical probability, that the bilateral anterior cerebral artery infarctions in this case were caused by swelling from retraction in the surgery?"

"Not that I can see."

At this point Scott sat down.

Mr. H took the stand for re-direct. He stood for a long time. He appeared uncomfortable. [I thought, where can he go?]

He said, "Doctor, if I have understood your testimony, you feel that Dr. N caused the meningitis? Is that right?"

"Yes."

"That the meningitis caused the brain damage; right?"

"Yes."

"That Nurse B was not telling the truth when she said Super Glue was used?"

"Yes."

"That Nurse MK was not telling the truth when she said that Dr. Ogsbury told her that it was okay to put in a central line?"

"Yes."

"That Nurse C was not telling the truth when she said Nurse MK told her that Dr. Ogsbury said she could put in a central line?"

"Well, that one, it's a little hard to answer. She might have been doing that, but she didn't tell Dr. Ogsbury."

"That Nurse C was either—how can I put it?—she either didn't listen for breath sounds or she was totally incompetent?"

"Yes."

"That Nurse C is not telling the truth when she testified that she told Dr. Ogsbury at 4:30 about the central line?"

"Yes."

"That Dr. M didn't look at the X-ray at all?"

"Or was incompetent to read it."

"That Dr. D was incompetent?"

"I didn't say that. I feel that he made a mistake and dropped a lung which caused a pneumothorax."

"So we have Dr. N, meningitis, three nurses, Dr. M and Dr. D, but you don't feel that anything done by you or Dr. Ogsbury in this case was wrong in any way, whatsoever?"

"No, I don't."

"And it didn't cause one ounce of damage to her, anything that either of you did?"

"I think if we had not done what we did, she would not be alive today."

"Your answer is that nothing that you did caused one ounce of damage to Sheran R?"

"Yes."

Peter turned to me and said, "And that's why we're here."

"Doctor, let me ask you: Nurse MK—you said that Dr. Ogsbury was angry when you talked to him on the phone and said that he had not told them they could put in a central line and yet, no incident report was filed and no nursing supervisor was talked to, to your knowledge. Nurse C—all of the things you felt she didn't do, that she was lying—you didn't file an incident report or go talk to a nursing supervisor at all, did you?"

"No, I didn't, but I didn't find out about this until now."

"To your knowledge, not one thing was done with respect to these nurses to bring to the attention of the hospital these alleged acts of misconduct and telling untruths, is that right? Was anything done by you or Dr. Ogsbury?"

"I can't speak for Dr. Ogsbury. I did not do anything."

"Do you have any knowledge that Dr. Ogsbury did anything to arrange for discipline or bring to the attention of the hospital these acts of misbehavior of the nurses?"

"No. I haven't discussed it with him."

"Now, you have testified that this pneumothorax was obvious. I think you said that yesterday, and from what I have seen in this chart, virtually every X-ray that was ever taken of Sheran R was read by a radiologist, but during the night, there is no radiologist at St. Anthony?"

"That's correct."

"And so, it fell upon Dr. M in this case and Dr. D. There is no indication that Dr. D stuck around and looked at the X-ray is there?"

"No, there isn't."

"There has been testimony that Dr. M did, right?"

"Yes."

"Now, Dr. M is still or at that time was still in his medical training. He was a resident, right?"

"Yes."

"I think you indicated—maybe it was this morning—this pneumothorax was something that if Dr. Ogsbury had looked at it that you are certain he would have recognized the pneumothorax on the film?"

"Yes, I am."

"So, if Dr. Ogsbury, while he was there at the hospital that evening, had stuck around with no radiologist present in the hospital—and whether he put in the central line or not—if he had stuck around and read the X-ray, he would have recognized it, wouldn't he?"

"Yes." [But I didn't want a CVP line placement in the first place, so why would I be around for an X-ray?]

"Mr. Nixon and you talked about the neural assessment and if I heard correctly, at 4:00 a.m., you thought she was more responsive, and at 4:00 to 5:00 you thought she was appearing better. That's after the pneumothorax has occurred?"

"Yes, it is." [But obviously before the hemodynamic effects became significant.]

"Mr. Nixon asked whether the standard of care would require that if a Nurse Came and asked for a central line that it would be incumbent upon Dr. Ogsbury to do it if he had been with the patient. Now, Doctor, when a doctor goes into a room on an evening like this, the doctor generally doesn't do an examination and assessment of IV lines do they? That's generally left up to the nursing staff. As far as the status of the IV lines, doctors rely upon the nurses?"

"Yes."

"And wouldn't you agree, Dr. Krauth, that a nurse who had been with a patient since 3:00 in the afternoon, constantly, and who had been managing her and watching those IV lines and also who had cared for her on previous days, would be in a better position to assess the status of the IV lines than Dr. Ogsbury?"

"Probably."

"Now, Doctor, the meningitis, are there characteristic signs that you can see on a CAT scan of meningitis?"

"Yes."

"And they include diffuse brain swelling?"

"Yes."

"Now, Doctor, prior to the second surgery, would you agree with me that there was not any evidence of diffuse brain swelling on any of the CT's—CAT scans of Sheran R?"

"Yes."

"And, Doctor, would you agree with me that if the meningitis is severe enough to cause this vasculitis that you have talked about, that there ought to be diffuse brain swelling present?"

"No, not at all."

Mr. H continued.

"You wouldn't agree?"

"No."

"Doctor, I want to go back to some of your earlier testimony with Mr. Nixon when you talked about a plug that was put in the second surgery. Doctor, yesterday you testified that the use of muscle to plug or pack a hole for a cerebrospinal fluid leak had been known for years. Now is that true or not?"

"I don't remember saying that."

"Doctor, yesterday I asked you a question. I said, 'wouldn't you agree, Doctor, that packing a hole with a cerebrospinal fluid leak with muscle, that procedure has been known for years?' and didn't you indicate, yes, you would agree with that?" "I think you said, 'covering a hole and putting the muscle into it.'"

"I'm talking about packing muscle down into the hole."

"Didn't you say yesterday that that had been known for years as a procedure that could be used. Are you saying now, that's not the case?"

"I'm saying that placing muscle into a hole and layering it has been known for years. If you are talking about packing it into and occluding an air cell, I have never read about it before, and I have testified to that consistently all the way through to trial and deposition."

"And you indicated, Doctor—if I heard you correctly—that in your training, that you weren't taught this—the packing, the plugging; that you were taught to just lay the muscle across the top of the hole. Did I hear you correctly?"

"Yes."

"And yet, Doctor, in every one of these procedures that you have done—I believe they total five, if I recall correctly—every one of them, you have plugged the hole by pushing and packing muscle down into that hole. Is that true?"

"That's true."

"All right, Doctor. You indicated—my notes indicate you said—it's never been reported in the literature to use muscle plugs or packs in the form you have talked about. Did I hear you correctly?"

"I'm not aware of it."

Mr. H then took out an article in the handbook of Clinical Neurology and another article written by Dr. Bronson Ray, the professor at Cornell under whom I briefly trained, and asked if in these cases were not the air sinuses filled?"

Dr. Krauth said no. He then brought out an article written by neurosurgeons at the Mayo Clinic which indicated they used a muscle plug.

He then said, "Now, Doctor, you have had great success with this method you have used by plugging the hole."

"Yes—of filling up the ethmoid air cells."

"Correct."

"And you testified that you have never read about this procedure anywhere in the medical literature?"

"That's correct."

"Have you shared your success with your colleagues in the neurosurgical community by writing an article reflecting your experience with this procedure for addressing cerebrospinal fluid leaks in this cribriform plate area?"

"No."

"Well, understanding the problem that's associated with getting good watertight seals on leaks in this area, Doctor, don't you think that that would be something that would be very, very valuable to neurosurgeons throughout the United States to know about your unique experience?"

"It might be and maybe I should write a paper about it."

"But you have been doing it—well, what ten years?"

"Yes."

"The fact is, Doctor, the reason you haven't written about it is that there are already numerous mentions of this procedure in the medical literature. Isn't that true?"

"Not at all."

"Doctor, let me talk about the glue for a moment. You indicated that you have used Surgicel, right?"

"Yes."

"Did I hear you say that you have in fact used Super Glue or Crazy Glue, or something similar to that?"

"Yes."

"Is this Super Glue that you had purchased at a hardware store? "

"Yes."

"Are you aware, Doctor, that it has been reported in the medical literature that glues of this type have been associated with actually creating a barrier for making watertight seals?"

"Yes."

"And finally, Doctor, are you aware that it's been reported in the literature that glues like this have been associated with causing meningitis?"

"No."

"Are you familiar with the book entitled *Operative Neurosurgical Techniques, Indications, Methods and Results* by Schmidek and Sweet?"

"No."

"You're not familiar with that, Doctor?"

"No, I'm not."

"Let me refer you to page 66, Doctor, and does it say, 'Unfortunately, the first generation of acrylic tissue adhesives has proved disappointing. In addition to carrying a risk of meningitis and of neural toxicity, and particularly to the optic apparatus, they form a barrier between layers of tissue inhibiting granulation, preventing fibroblastic proliferation from fusing one layer to the next. With time, tissue adhesives become coarse and can result in recurring leaks.' Now, what they are saying there, isn't it, Doctor, that they inhibit the tissue growing together—the growth process together?"

"Yes."

"You disagree with the statement in there?"

"Taken out of context, no."

"How did I take it out of context, Doctor?"

"I mean—what you just read to me, I don't, but in individual cases where I have used it I am gluing bone, and that isn't a problem."

"You said yesterday, Doctor, if there was a question at all whether or not all of the glue was removed after Dr. Ogsbury decided he didn't want it in there, and if there was any question at all whether it would impede a watertight seal, that the surgeon should take out the graft, harvest a fresh graft, and use that rather than the one that might be contaminated by glue. Do you still stand by that?"

"Yes."

"Doctor, would you agree with me that if there had not been a recurrence of this leak, there wouldn't have been a need for a second surgery, would there?"

"That's correct."

"And, in fact, Doctor, he indicated in the operative report that the patch that he had put in the first surgery actually had moved, hadn't it?"

"Yes."

"There is no indication that he harvested a fresh patch and placed it in the first surgery is there?"

"No."

"Now, Doctor, if I heard your testimony correctly earlier, you indicated an opinion that the meningitis in this case was caused by Dr. N's surgery and you relied upon the language out of Wilkins that we talked about yesterday. And that language and Wilkins indicated bacterial meningitis was the important potential complication to many neurosurgical procedures. Now, in fact, what Dr. N did was not exactly a neurosurgical procedure. It was an ENT procedure, correct?"

"The only thing is he punctured the plate. He got into the brain and the cranial cavity."

"There is no indication he touched the brain, is there?"

"I think that there was when Dr. Ogsbury went in and saw that there was—I think he saw some injury."

"All right, and it went on to say, 'pre-disposing factors include submission to more than one surgical procedure,' had she had a surgical procedure before Dr. N's surgery?"

"No."

"But she did have a surgical procedure before Dr. Ogsbury's first surgery, didn't she?"

"Yes."

"And when it went on to say: 'early infections occurring within the first seven days of a craniotomy'—they are not talking about what Dr. Ogsbury did, are they?"

"Yeah. Dr. Ogsbury did a craniotomy."

"All right, the first, Dr. N, his surgery was June 16, right? And Dr. Ogsbury's was June 25?"

"Yes."

"Now, from the 16th to the 23rd of June would be seven days. If the language in this article is correct, for this to apply, she had to have had meningitis when she was admitted to the hospital on the 23rd?"

"Not necessarily. Because I don't think, if you ask the authors, that anything in medicine is cut and dried. This isn't engineering. 'Seven days' could be ten days."

"Now the first documented laboratory results that were even consistent with the meningitis occurred on June 28. Where in the time span did the meningitis occur?"

"Sometime between June 16 and June 28."

"Within a reasonable degree of medical probability, can you tell me where it occurred, can you tell me that it was more likely to occur over here than over there?"

"Yes, I think so."

"All right, tell me what your basis is for being able to tell this jury that it was more probable that it occurred over here than over there on that surgery?"

"Because I feel that she had a contaminated operation done on the 16th, that with every breath she took she recontaminated herself, for seven days. I feel that the most likely cause of meningitis, within a reasonable degree of medical probability, was contamination through the nose, and not through a sterile field that Dr. Ogsbury would have done through a craniotomy."

"Doctor, based upon the picture that existed, wouldn't you agree that you are not able to say, within a reasonable degree of medical probability, that this lady had meningitis when she came into this hospital, any more likely than after the 25th? You are not able to say, are you, Doctor, within a reasonable degree of medical probability, that she had meningitis anytime from the 23rd to the time of her surgery?"

"No, I cannot say that within a reasonable degree of medical probability."

At this point, the afternoon recess was called.

After the Plaintiffs' team left, we went over our plans. Lee needs to adjust his schedule because he will need to come back for further cross-examination by Mr. H. Lee went back to his office to see patients for two more hours. Peter was in an upbeat mood. He said, "I think it was when I yelled 'f*** you' this morning that did it."

Scott did a marvelous job of onion-skinning, going through point by point all of the issues raised yesterday. Mr. H really took a chance when he summarized the defense posture near the end. I suspect that may work against him.

Today was amazing. Lee set out to show me to be the New Age man, and, lo and behold, he did it to himself. Peter feels we are running neck and neck again. Judge Peterson now seems to be back on the middle of her judicial fence. Peter's back up in the clouds and Scott's like a little boy with a new bicycle. Oh, what a difference a day makes.

Fran
Wednesday, May 5, 1990, 9:00 p.m.

The pendulum swings, first crashing you into depression and despair, then the swooping ride into hope and elation. The flame of passion is never extinguished in the transition. Such is the life of a trial attorney and all those in the midst of it. Surprise, surprise, surprise. It's expected, but you never know when it's going to come, you just know it's coming. Yikes!! Where are the jurors in all of this—remember them?

Keep juggling Peter, keep juggling Scott.

Today, Lee is someone we'd never seen before. The steely man I had met months ago melted on the stand, recalling the pressure he was under while Jay was taking care of Sheran R. In Jay's words, "It was awesome." There were few dry eyes in the courtroom that day. Another turn.

Whether the turn is for or against you, it always takes a toll. Lee laid down a burden he had been carrying for years, or maybe it was just because he had accidentally flushed his watch down the toilet in the men's room.

CHAPTER THIRTEEN

DAY 9
LLOYD CRIPE & MORE LEE KRAUTH

Peter
Thursday, May 10, 1990, 4:00 a.m.

If I feel this bad, it must be Thursday. Thinking about how I try to keep relationships and friendships and family afloat during trial last night after debriefing Jay and Kathy (yet another way of bonding and giving them my energy). I stop by the end of Josh's soccer game to take him home and to let him know I love him. I called Kay and Pete just to stay in touch and, sinful as it seemed at the time, stole off to a B movie for a few hours of brainlessness. And as each evening break flashes by, I find myself here again preparing, preparing, preparing.

Yesterday was incredible, as Lee, the automaton, the angry and cold neurosurgeon (at least as I saw him) fell apart on the stand (when asked to explain Mr. H's charge he knew nothing about Sheran's poststroke course, with the implication Lee was inhumane and didn't care). He sobbed through an explanation of how this result had devastated Jay, how the Rs became Jay's life, how it affected him (Lee), how devastated doctors are when a tragedy like this occurs—"we are not automatons" he proclaimed, tears streaming down his face (and mine as I watched and listened to this poor man grieve this tragedy for the first time for all to witness). This consummate, compulsive, skilled, and seemingly detached neuro machine, with all of his ego defenses, his shame and guilt because he could not and did not cure, was brought to this emotional watershed for all to witness. I care not whether or how the jury was offended or affected by this poor man's agony; I only hope it will help relieve him of his terrible burden.

After a break, when Lee got a chance to compose himself (Jay was crying too), Scott and Lee just moved through the Plaintiffs' claims and theories like a lawnmower through wet blades of grass. The jury is relaxed and loves to be taught and visually educated. We are still in the hunt; we are about sixty percent of the way through their liability case, and their theories, although simplistically and superficially appealing, are transparently thin. Like true fighters, we came roaring back—the hard and fighting spirit of the peaceful warrior. Fear and uncertainty are my enemies, and I will not allow them to enter me lest they drain me of my energy and conviction. On to Dr. Cripe, the stuffy neuropsychologist hired to help bring in the "top dollar." Pretty soon Jay will arrive. I wonder if it is reassuring for him to see his lawyers laboring so hard, how we try to make him part of the team so that our energy and enthusiasm vitalizes him; hope he writes about it.

Jay
Thursday, May 10, 1990

I slept an additional fifteen minutes this morning. I must have felt a little better. I arrived at the White Spot at 7:15 and Scott and Peter were there. Everyone seemed more relaxed and upbeat than yesterday. Today is the day of Dr. Lloyd Irvin Cripe, the neuropsychologist. In his curriculum vitae he reported a talk under "L. I. Cripe, *The Role of the Neuropsychologist in Determining Personal Damages*," a paper presented at the Washington State Trial Lawyers Association Top Dollar Damages Seminar in Seattle,

Washington. Of course, Dr. Cripe will be Dr. Top Dollar to us. Peter will have fun with that; he certainly is in a mood again to hammer someone. I talked to Lee on the telephone; he will be in at noon.

We went to the courtroom. Mary and Peter were there. The attorneys are in a variety of clothes. Today appears to be a small day. There was a delay in getting started, but the jurors finally came in. The Judge apologized. I thought I heard one of the jurors say, "No problemo"—could that have been Narcisco?

Today was a day of great humor. Mr. Fitzgerald took part in the proceedings for the first time, and, after he called Dr. Lloyd Cripe, Dr. Cripe answered in a very slow, controlled way. Mr. Fitzgerald and Dr. Cripe immediately reminded me of the Bob and Ray skit about the "Slow Talkers of America." With his slow delivery, Dr. Cripe took a long time describing the role of a neuropsychologist. He then took an even longer time to discuss what has been known all along, that Sheran R had a severe injury to the front part of her brain and suffered the loss of executive function that that injury can cause. But it wasn't until he was handed a note from Mr. H that Dr. Cripe finally pointed out that executive functions are what separates humans from more primitive forms of life, and summarized the limits that this loss has, and will, create for Sheran R.

After lunch, Peter immediately pointed out that Dr. Cripe had traveled 1,200 miles from Spokane to Riverton to perform tests that had already been performed by multiple physicians, and at Craig Hospital. Peter had difficulty containing himself when Dr. Cripe said he was nervous in the trial, because he wanted to do well to please his parents. Then, on a roll, Peter addressed Dr. Cripe's resume which included the history that Dr. Cripe had given a presentation to the Washington Trial Lawyers Association meeting, titled as the Fourth Annual Top Dollar Seminar. And while Dr. Cripe insisted that his purpose in attending the meeting was simply to explain the role of a neuropsychologist in assessing brain-injured patients, even Judge Peterson smiled, understanding that it was very clear that his purpose in attending the conference was to drum up legal business for himself. He will forever be "Dr. Top Dollar" to our team.

During a break Peter said he was a little upset with himself. He said he went a little too far. He could have stopped at the ludicrousness of the top dollar seminar and felt he lost a little by going on.

After the break, Mr. H took the lectern and called Lee (Krauth) back to the stand. He began by challenging Lee's opinion that both he and Dr. Mason definitely felt that Sheran had meningitis. Lee remained firm. "I still think she had meningitis, and I think Susan Mason thinks she had meningitis."

"Would you leave room in your mind for the possibility, Doctor, that, in fact, Dr. Mason on the 29th, felt that while the cerebrospinal fluid values were consistent with meningitis, they were consistent with other things as well. And as late as the first, she still wasn't certain that this lady had meningitis. Would you leave room for that possibility?"

"No, I wouldn't. I can't."

He next asked Lee, again, to assume that experts would say that there as early indication of infarction on the CT scan following the first surgery and further suggested, "Wouldn't you agree that, in all likelihood, that probably was the result of the surgical procedure done on the 25th?"

"Yes."

Mr. H next addressed again the issue of the failure to obtain a spinal fluid analysis before the first operation.

"Doctor, yesterday, also you indicated that you had an opinion after the first surgery that this third nerve palsy was caused by vasculitis, secondary to meningitis. Did I get that right?"

"Yes."

"This kind of vasculitis, I take it, is one of the reasons you don't like to do surgery in the face of meningitis? "

"Yes."

"Now if I've heard you correctly yesterday, you indicated an opinion in response to Mr. Nixon, that you felt it was within the standard of care to do the first surgery without obtaining a spinal fluid sample before you did the surgery?"

"Yes."

"And your reasoning for that was because it probably would have been normal anyway?"

"That's one of the reasons, yes."

"Now with the spinal fluid sample as far as your reasoning that it would have been normal—your reasoning there was because she had been on antibiotics and because you feel the culture wouldn't have grown anyway?"

"It wasn't going to change anything. She still needed surgery."

"Now besides the culture, Doctor, there are certain values that as a physician you can look at these values to try to decide whether meningitis is present, don't you? If there is an elevated white count that indicates to you—at least when you looked at the 28th, the results on the 28th—you felt that was rather diagnostic to you that she had meningitis, right?"

"Yes."

"But as I understand it, it was okay because it wouldn't have changed anything; that is your analysis?"

"Yes. She still needed an operation."

Finally, Mr. H turned back once more to the second operation, the reason for going in on both sides, and particularly to the apparent change in Lee's testimony.

"Doctor, you testified yesterday that on the decision to go in with the second surgery and to do it bilaterally was based upon you and Dr. Ogsbury discussing this before the surgery, right? And your reasoning was that there was a leak on the left side—there was pain over the left eye; there was air on the CAT scan on the left; and based on your experience. Did I get all of them?"

"Yes."

"Now, it's true, isn't it, Doctor, that back in actuality, before the surgery when you and Dr. Ogsbury talked about this, your decision was based on you, you personally wondering if perchance there just might be two holes because Dr. N had done a bilateral nasal surgery? Isn't that what your decision was really limited to?"

"That wasn't limited to that; that entered into it."

"Doctor, isn't it true that these factors that you have described to this jury have been things that, since this lawsuit was filed, you've gone back in the chart and you've listed to try and support that in your deposition. Is there anywhere in there mention of anything about a left leak? Is there anything mentioned in there about pain over the left eye or pain over the left side of her head? Is there anything there mentioned about air in the CAT scan being indicative of a leak on the left side?"

"No. After reviewing the records, I've gone over and explained everything as honestly and straightforwardly as I can, and I have testified to that for you. And I definitely considered the CAT scan. We discussed the air. We discussed the leak. Dr. Barron had multiple references in the chart as to the left eye pain, and after refreshing one's memory and going over everything, you can get more detail."

"Wasn't it your experience, Doctor, that whenever you did one of these surgeries, that you always did it bilaterally?"

"I think that's been my experience."

"Did that have some influence on this decision?"

"That probably had some influence on that decision, yes."

"And, Doctor, you testified that, by July 1, you were absolutely convinced she had meningitis?"

"Yes, I was."

"And, Doctor, if there was any way to avoid manipulating half of a brain that had meningitis, as a surgeon you would like to try to do that, wouldn't you?"

"Yes. But not at the risk of not repairing the main problem that is still unrepaired."

"And then you got into the second surgery, and you went down to the right side, and you found the leak. Repair failed and yet you continued to suggest to him, even at that point, that he definitely needed to go over to the left side, even though you had found the leak that occurred on the right?"

"At that point in the operating room I don't think I definitely said he needed to go over there, no."

"Did you tell him not to go over to the left side?"

"No, I don't think I told him not to."

Mr. H then said, "That's all I have, Your Honor."

Mr. Nixon took the stand once again, "Dr. Krauth, you just answered some questions about whether the fact that a CSF culture wasn't done on the 24th wouldn't matter in the decision to do surgery on the 25th. Why didn't it matter? Why wouldn't that have mattered in the decision to do surgery?"

"Because she had a leak that wasn't stopping. She had air in her head on the CAT scan. She had a persistent leak. She had a contaminated wound. And with an iatrogenic injury, according to the literature and the literature quoted by the expert witness, Dr. Frank Smith, there are indications in that textbook that that is an absolute indication for surgery."

Do you recall yesterday, when Mr. H quoted using language from the operative neurosurgical techniques text by Schmidek and Sweet?"

"Yes. In the textbook it says, 'In contrast, there are three classical criteria for surgical intervention: (1) a bout of meningitis; (2) pneumocephalus (for the jury, pneumocephalus is the air inside the cranium); and (3) an active leak (persistent or recurring).'"

"She had air in her head before both surgeries by CT?"

"Yes, she did."

"She had meningitis or the second surgery?"

"Yes."

"She may have had it before the first surgery?"

"She might have."

"This doesn't say you have to have all three of them?"

"No, any one of the three would be a classical indication."

"Do you agree those are the three classical indications for surgical intervention and cerebrospinal fluid leak?"

"Yes, I do."

"So if she had meningitis, the surgery still would have been indicated on the 25th?"

"Yes."

"And if she had—if she had meningitis, that is really an indication for surgery, isn't it?"

"Yes, it is."

"You were also asked some questions about the fact that meningitis places the brain at somewhat increased risk of damage from manipulation and retraction at the time of craniotomy. Nevertheless, you recommended the second surgery be performed when you knew she had meningitis on the 2nd of July?"

"Yes, I did."

"If you didn't do surgery because she had meningitis, what do you think, to a reasonable degree of medical probability, would have happened to Sheran R in her condition at that time?"

"I felt that she would have gone on to develop a superinfection, which would have been probably life ending, or at least severely debilitating, disabling to her. And I felt that the leak wouldn't stop."

"So, if you weighed that risk against the risk of increased possibility of damage from manipulation, it wasn't a difficult decision for you, was it?"

"No, I think it was a difficult decision. It's always—I don't think you take decisions for operating on people's brains lightly at any time, even if they don't have any infection.

When they have an infection—I think the mere fact that Dr. Ogsbury struggled with this, that he had four or five consultants involved, tells you that it's a difficult decision. If it wasn't a difficult decision, he wouldn't have consulted anybody. He would have just done the surgery or not done the surgery. But in this case, he sought out all kinds of consultants and help because it was a difficult decision."

Scott continued, "Now, also in the Schmideck and Sweet test, Mr. H quoted some language about the use of acrylic tissue adhesive?"

"Yes, he did."

"Have you had an opportunity to review that since yesterday?"

"Yes"

"And what did you find out when you looked at those references?"

"Well, it was very interesting. The first reference referenced an article written by a Dr. A. N. Martens. Dr. Martens is—I would call him a close friend. But he was the Chief of Neurosurgery at Walter Reed for about twelve or thirteen years. I was very well acquainted with him. As a matter of fact, he operated on my wife. He did brain surgery on my wife. And Dr. Martens, I know, as he does brain surgery, he used an acrylic surgical adhesive on my wife, and we talked about that. If I felt that was dangerous, I wouldn't have allowed him to do it on a family member.

Mr. Nixon continued, "Now there was a lot of talk yesterday about the packing—the ethmoid sinus that you do, and the packing of the hole used by Dr. Ogsbury at the time of her surgery."

Mr. Nixon asked if he could use the overhead projector. Lee had found in one of their articles a great picture of the head and sinuses. A transparency was made to be projected onto white paper which could be written upon. Scott asked Lee to demonstrate the difference between the two procedures.

Lee started, "The method that I was taught as a resident and Dr. Ogsbury was taught as a resident because we were in the same program, and that is described in most articles, is to lay fascia and muscles and actually put a plug of muscles like this. So, if you put this thing over the hole and push down the muscle, it will plug up and fill the hole like that. And then you layer stuff on top of this. And the brain comes down and it plugs the hole and that's how it works. The plug can be dislodged if the patient sneezes or coughs or vomits or breathes. The operation I did was basically the same operation. The difference is—and the thing that hasn't been written about, I have still never read it, the article didn't show it—this air cell right here. We took a big muscle—what I've done in the past, what Dr. Ogsbury did in the second operation was take a big piece of muscle. Since this is a tiny hole, you couldn't get a big piece of muscle to fill this thing up.

"So, you had to enlarge the hole, take a big piece of muscle, and you pack this whole area like this. This is outside the skull. This is not in the hole. Here's the hole. It is actually below the hole. This muscle was outside the brain, if you will, in this air cell. And on top of that you layer the other. So, the difference in the two operations was—this is a standard operation that's been read about, that I've been taught as a resident. The only thing I did different—and after yesterday I think I am going to write an article about it—is to take the air cell and pack the whole air cell. And that's the difference. That's the critical difference. Because if the air cell is packed solid, even if she coughs or sneezes, you've got this bony compartment, and it can't get dislodged. That's the advantage."

Finally, Scott asked Lee about the difficulty in stopping CSF leaks by any procedure. Lee noted the reported failure rate in the Mayo Clinic article to be forty percent and in the Dr. Ray article to be greater than twenty percent; obviously failure with this procedure is in and of itself not evidence of negligence.

The jurors appeared to be impressed with Lee's demonstration. They seem to understand his procedure was indeed fundamentally different than packing the actual hole. I even noticed Mr. Saline put down his notebook, sat back, and crossed his arms; clearly his questions have been answered. Mr. H had attempted to show that the two procedures were the same, indicating an incompetent first operation. He obviously placed great emphasis on that issue and when the answers to his questions were convincing, there was an obvious change in the mood in the courtroom. With this, Mr. Nixon said there were no further questions, and the court was adjourned for the day.

Following the adjournment, we all felt quite good. Peter said we're running neck and neck, all we can hope for in Plaintiffs' case. We laughed as Peter mimicked Dr. Top Dollar. With his quaint little bow tie, perfect coat, and half-framed glasses, Dr. Cripe is a caricature. He complained of Mrs. R being rigid—he is Mr. Rigidity himself. Even at this time of stress, there is indeed incredible humor. We laughed about the names, Dr. Fossil, Dr. Top Dollar. We laughed about the Plaintiffs' attorney repeatedly introducing articles that worked in our favor. Had Mr. H not introduced the Schmidek article, we would not have been able to mention that the wife of one of the Defendants had undergone a brain operation in which Super Glue was used. The jurors listened, and I hope the Super Glue issue has finally died an ignominious death. And the failure rate reported in their two articles emphasize just how difficult it can be to stop these leaks. Also, while Mr. H came back hard, he merely rehashed the same points. We continue to relish the difficulty the Plaintiffs are having with their theory of the case.

Apparently, I'm being held negligent for not getting the tests for the meningitis that they say she didn't have. It seems that they are working both sides of the fence; either we're wrong for saying that she had no meningitis or for claiming she did. I'm amazed by the process and the ingenuity of the attorneys. When our defense is solidified on one issue, they raise another—often one directly opposite to that which they claimed before, so it is difficult to stay the course of defending ourselves when their theory of the case keeps changing as we keep answering their questions. This is, however, a problem we can happily endure.

We also continue to note the difficulty Mr. H has experienced with the legacy left to him, the witnesses chosen by Mr. Spence and his team. Dr. Smith was so unconvincing that Mr. H was forced to use my partner as the primary neurosurgical expert against me. Dr. Cripe, with his precise scientific description of the effects of a bilateral anterior cerebral artery infarction, managed to fail to convey to the jury, until reminded otherwise by Mr. H, the essence of Mrs. R's injury, the loss of the single most human part of our being. And, because of their repeated charting failures, even the nurses who were chosen did not seem credible.

On the other hand, Lee made such good sense that the jury is beginning to recognize that we may have an answer to every question. Indeed, Peter and Scott feel that the jurors are starting to swing our way. Peter said he thinks that Mr. Saline has already made up his mind; he, too, noted that Mr. Saline put down his book when Lee convincingly demonstrated the difference between the two procedures. Peter also caught Mr. Saline wiping a smile from his face when Dr. Cripe confessed he was nervous in court because his mother and father had always wanted him to do well. I noted that Mrs. Petit looked at me and smiled.

Today, I also noticed that for the first time Judge Peterson looked at me. Prior to today, whenever I looked toward the bench, I never found her looking toward the defense table. Today she frequently moved her head around a reading lamp that sits between our positions to look my way. It was strange. Her look was neither friendly nor unfriendly, she just looked. It does appear she is at least back to neutral. Finally, in the midst of all this, I heard from my office that I was being subpoenaed to appear for a deposition that had already twice been cancelled by the attorneys involved. Peter said he would handle that.

Tomorrow, we face Dr. Melvin Greer. He is clearly a pro and would be dangerous if he were a neurosurgeon. As we left the court, Peter walked by Lee, hugged him, and said, "I think we are where we want to be."

Fran
Thursday, May 10, 1990, 9:00 p.m.

Peter was in the mood to hammer someone today, according to Jay. It was a good day in trial for Peter. Straight forward, points to be made, yet not too emotionally charged. Peter's exhausted, but he doesn't stop scanning, his radar stays on and he responds to any blip on the screen. Lifting a lagging spirit, disarming an expert witness, touching base across his broad universe, whatever is there, he attends. It's all important to him.

Jay's riding off of yesterday. He likes Peter's humor. I think Peter is the first to make Jay laugh from his belly. These guys are becoming quite a pair.

CHAPTER FOURTEEN

DAY 10
DR. MELVIN GREER

Peter
Friday, May 11, 1990, 4:00 a.m.

I am a little distracted today but confident I can handle Dr. Greer, Plaintiffs' last standard of care expert. Yesterday was a good day, but I had an off day, mostly because I was so tired that I was detached from what was going on, and I lost my rhythm.

Dr. Cripe, or as we later labeled him, "Dr. Top Dollar," proved to be an obsequious, uptight, neuropsychologist who had spent an inordinate amount of time running a battery of unnecessary neuropsychological tests to establish what everyone had agreed to from the onset—Sheran has significant frontal lobe brain damage.

On cross, I challenged him on his attempts to ingratiate himself to the jury. ("I'm so nervous." "Why?" He claimed he was a seasoned witness but "nervous" because "Mommy and Daddy told him to do his best," not because he was uncomfortable in the courtroom.) I challenged him on his participation in a "Top Dollar Damage Seminar" in Washington (which he claimed he didn't know was a "top dollar" damage training session for Plaintiffs' attorneys until he got there and that he didn't participate in hoping to drum up some business, even though sixty to seventy percent of his work comes from attorneys). The jury and the Judge were smiling as I gently teased him, asking him if he'd come all the way to Denver to tell us what we already knew, he was "Dr. Top Dollar." I've been so hot for most of the trial. I was disappointed in my cross for two reasons, one legitimate and the other esteem oriented.

The cross was a little ragged and was not art form, leaving me chagrined because it wasn't as good as the other stuff I had been doing. Invalid reason to worry, so I'm letting that go; I simply can't hit high C every time I sing. But I should have stopped on the high note of "Dr. Top Dollar" part of the cross instead of going on, only to get bogged down over extraneous points.

A few observations: one, Jay is a trooper. He was and is bright-eyed and enthusiastic and is hanging on every word—the jury has got to be noticing that. This is not some frightened, shamed, and guilty man cowering in the corner of the courtroom but an enthusiastic, proud, involved man whose conviction radiates from within.

Two, Lee was almost giddy yesterday, proud of his performance on the stand, doubtlessly relieved to know that he is essentially done and at peace, too, because there has been some resolution of all the emotions he has kept locked up since Sheran had her stroke.

Three, there is a prisoner's mentality developing between the lawyers. All the attorneys are cordial and operating on a high ethical plane, in turn allowing us to relax and enjoy the trial. And, because the trial is so long and taxing, we become like enemies thrown together in some prison camp forced to get along together. Yesterday, Mr. H and I wore the same outfits, and we checked at the end of the day to make sure we didn't do the same today (they showed up as the "suits" the first day, but quickly became "sport coats and slack guys" the very next day after getting a look at us in our casual, warm colors and dress style).

Four, although trying to read the jury is always a risky business, one has to try. They seem warm, relaxed, and open to me. They have found humor in the things I have found humorous, have enjoyed my occasional bunglings (some to let them know I'm human, most just natural klutziness) and for the most part seem receptive. I "weathervaned" a little yesterday on the humor front, trying out little jokes and then watching for positive and negative responses. Since the case is still tied, I'm just trying to see if their humor is still there, their minds are open, and they're still laughing with me.

I have the sense that Mr. Saline was impressed by Lee's defense of the care and has begun to tilt our way. We'll see, as we've got to keep their minds open through the emotional part of the week next week. If we're wounded, I'll open our case with Jay; if not, I will save him until the last. If we're lucky, I'll do the first part of his testimony at the beginning and maybe be able to pop him in and out over an extended period of time. I need to see if there's a way to put him on in two parts, as although here is a law of recency, I am concerned that with a trial this long, the jurors will be bored and worn out by the time we get to the end and devoid of the energy and emotion to listen to, care about, and relate to him.

Jay
Friday, May 11, 1990

Day ten started better than the days preceding. I had slept well, and the drive in felt good. I met with Peter at the White Spot. He was very busy; there were many points that I could see from Dr. Greer's deposition that might be relevant. Dr. Greer, while obviously skilled and sophisticated as a witness, does not, as a neurologist, seem to understand many of the neurosurgical issues. There was a delay of twenty minutes before we started. Mr. H is here in a suit. This is a power day for him.

Mr. H took the stand. He introduced Dr. Melvin Greer. Dr. Greer reported he is the professor and chairman of the Department of Neurology at the University of Florida, Gainesville. His education included graduation from NYU, residency at Belleview, two years in the Navy, and one year fellowship at Columbia in 1961. He went to the University of Florida as an assistant professor and has ultimately become the chairman of the department. He further stated that neurology encompasses an understanding of the state of health of the brain, the spinal cord, and nerves with focused study on nonsurgical diseases. He spends about fifty percent of his time treating patients, the other training residents and medical students. He was asked, "Do neurologists and neurosurgeons work together in the management and treatment of patients?" He reported, "Yes, we have joint conferences; we discuss cases often. It's a very close relationship, particularly in our institution." This was certainly not the impression we had from his apparent lack of knowledge of neurosurgical problems.

Dr. Greer reported that he was board certified. He also was involved in multiple professional associations including the American Academy of Neurology of which he was president from 1985 to 1987. He reported that he had been elected to speak at neurosurgical meetings. [I thought that was interesting. I had talked to the American Academy of Neurology meeting last year.] He had produced professional publications and was on the editorial board of one. He had written two textbooks, two dozen chapters, and about eighty articles.

Mr. H then asked, "Let me ask you specifically, does the diagnosis and treatment of cerebrospinal fluid leaks fall within the field of neurology?"

He reported, "Yes, I have cared for patients with that problem." [I disagree; since surgery may be necessary, the treatment of CSF leaks is generally thought to be the domain of neurosurgeons, not medical neurologists.]

"And does the diagnosis of the disease process called meningitis fall within the specialty field of neurology, Doctor?"

He said, "Yes." [That, of course, is the truth.]

Dr. Greer reported that he examined Sheran R, traveled to Wyoming, saw the medical records, and read the depositions. His answers were quite cryptic. He noted there were volumes of materials, and he said he had spent sixty to seventy hours in evaluation. He stated that if he had known the amount, he would not have become involved in the case. He said that he did review malpractice and injury cases averaging twenty-five cases per year and five to six hours per week.

He reported further that two thirds of the cases were for the doctors, one third for the plaintiffs. When asked if he charged for his time, he said he had the Dean's permission to charge $375 per hour.

He was offered as an expert in neurology. Mr. H then said he would testify on the issue of causation only. [This came as a total surprise as he had originally been offered as an expert on the subject of negligence, as well.]

Mr. H began, "Have you after your review of this case and after your examination of Sheran R, formulated some opinions in this case about the causation of Sheran R's neurologic problems?"

"Yes."

"And will you in expressing your opinions today express those opinions only if you can do so within a reasonable degree of medical probability?"

"Yes."

"Thank you, Doctor. Doctor, do you have an opinion about—within a reasonable degree of medical probability—as to the cause of the brain injury to Sheran R?"

"Yes."

"And what is that opinion, Doctor?"

"Sheran R suffered brain injury initially as a result of the perforation of the ethmoid sinus and then the subsequent surgical treatments that were undertaken. She has suffered bilateral strokes in the distribution of the anterior cerebral artery as her area of deficit."

"Okay. Doctor, do you have an opinion as to whether any part of her brain injury was caused by bacterial meningitis?"

"Yes, it was not."

"Doctor, do you have an opinion as to whether or not Sheran R had bacterial meningitis before her surgery of June 25, 1986?"

"Yes. She did not."

"And, Doctor, do you have an opinion as to whether or not Sheran R had bacterial meningitis at any time after June 25, 1986?"

"Yes, she did not."

"And, Doctor, do you have an opinion as to whether the pneumothorax that she suffered on July 4, 1986, caused any neurologic injury to Sheran R?"

"Yes. It did not."

Mr. H began Dr. Greer's analysis by asking him to describe the disease entity called meningitis.

Dr. Greer said that meningitis is an inflammation of the meninges or lining of the brain, the most common type is viral, sometimes called aseptic, the other type being bacterial. He discussed the clinical findings. [I noted during this time he was talking directly to the jury.] He explained that this process initially involves the lining of the brain and then the brain tissue becomes infected and the whole brain swells.

He was asked, "In diagnosing meningitis, other than looking for the clinical signs that you talked about—the chills, headaches, tiredness, you mention confusion and convulsions—are there tests that can be done radiographically by X-rays to assist the physician in trying to diagnosis whether meningitis is present?"

"In this day and age, the test that's called the CAT scan. The brain in general we say has gray matter and white matter. In a typical case of bacterial meningitis, you'll see that the junction between the gray and white is obliterated because of swelling."

Mr. H asked, "Why does the disease process, bacterial meningitis, involve the whole brain?"

Dr. Greer answered, "That's the nature of the meninges. It's freely communicating. If you have an infection that comes into one place in the meninges, it would be all over the place."

"All right, anything else in the CAT scan? You said something about the bottom of the skull?"

"The patient is sitting in an erect position lying down or looking up at the ceiling. Characteristically the inflammation, which turns into pus as time goes on, sort of settles at the base and you can see this with the CAT scanning sometimes. [Of course—this is why she developed a third nerve palsy.]

Dr. Greer then described the laboratory tests of the spinal fluid, noting that increased cells, increased protein, decreased glucose, and a positive gram stain are the characteristic findings of meningitis. He said the gram stain was not too reliable, was too full of contaminants, germs from the environment. He said the most important test is the culture which shows the bacteria that might be present.

Mr. H then asked if there was any other meningeal reaction which gives the same features. When Dr. Greer said reactive or aseptic meningitis can give a similar picture, Mr. H asked him to describe reactive meningitis.

Dr. Greer said, "You're not going to see all of those features. He noted you could get many of the same symptoms and changes in the spinal fluid with aseptic meningitis as with bacterial meningitis but "no organisms."

Next Mr. H asked about the period of time from the surgery in Wyoming to the first surgery in Denver. Mr. H said, "You've indicated earlier that you didn't feel she had meningitis between the 16th and the time of the first surgery. Let's start out talking about your reasoning that leads you to believe there was not bacterial meningitis in that period."

Dr. Greer explained, "Although the patient in Wyoming prior to the first operation in Denver did have headaches, did have low grade fever, did have some questionable stiff neck, these were all certainly something that can be seen following what happened in Wyoming where the ethmoid was perforated and the patient developed free air inside the head. So, although some of the features that one sees in meningitis were present, she did not have meningitis, at least as identified by the tests that we talked about."

He gave multiple reasons for that opinion: normal blood white count, negative blood cultures, normal spinal fluid, normal CT scan, and a normal exam.

"Doctor, would taking the presence of a headache and a low grade fever upon presentation to the hospital and existing right up to the 25th, in the face of all this other information, could one possibly make a diagnosis of meningitis just on the patient that walked in with a headache and a low grade fever?"

"No."

Mr. H continued, "Okay. Doctor let's turn our attention to the 25th. And purely from the perspective of the causation issue in this case, what do you understand occurred in that operation that would be relevant to your opinion about the causation of her brain damage?"

"There are two issues. One is the obvious mechanical activity involved in moving the brain to get at the operative field. And there's reference made to a posterior retraction. The second is the fact that the operative undertaking itself included the use of a substance—"

Peter abruptly objected and a break was called.

Peter sent me for coffee. He obviously wanted me out of his hair while he quickly researched the legal issues. I could feel something was up. I brought some coffee back to Peter and Scott. I had the impression that Dr. Greer does not wish to be here. I think he has changed his mind. I basically agree with what he has said so far except his assertion that there cannot be meningitis; with antibiotics and continuing contamination, one can never know even with a negative culture.

Peter talked to Mr. H about using Dr. Greer only on the issue of causation, not on the question of negligence. Peter told him, "You've gutted all our fun."

Mr. H said, "I knew what you were going to do to him."

Peter said, "Gee, and we had learned all the surgical anatomy."

The court was reconvened without the jury, and with Dr. Greer out of the courtroom at Peter's insistence. Peter asked for the court reporter and said he once did three minutes without a court reporter. Mr. H said he had once done that as well.

Peter continued, "Your Honor, so this won't be much ado about nothing, I'll tell you what I said at the bench and repeat the conference in terms of what Mr. H said, then he can disagree. I objected about halfway through his response with Dr. Greer, anticipating an argument—that he would say Super Glue is an irritant and would be an explanation for some of her meningeal-consistent picture which existed between June 25 and the time of the second surgery. I asked to come to the bench, told the court that this had never been disclosed, and Mr. H indicated that he was going to ask Dr. Greer opinions concerning the use of—alleged use of—Super Glue, and I assume if it were used it would be an irritant. And I chatted with him during the break to make sure again that I wasn't jumping up about nothing, and he has indicated that through Dr. Greer that they would talk about the Super Glue and the use of Super Glue and it is Dr. Greer's—or will be—his opinion and testimony that this would at least be a partial factor or explanation for her course in terms of meningeal inflammation or irritation after June 25. Is that a fair statement?"

Mr. H answered, "I think that's fair."

Peter continued, "Your Honor, quickly, then I can go back through this just in terms of our position on this and that is the first time that we knew of this, even by way of informal disclosure, was as that answer started to come out of Dr. Greer's mouth. Now, I served Interrogatories way back at the beginning of this case, and in these Interrogatories that we served back in November of 1988, as I always do, I notified counsel of our position of their duty to supplement imposed on Rule 26D. We also served a request for supplementation on September of '89, specifically with request for expert witness opinions, and nothing has ever been said about this. Now there's also been filed in this case an Affidavit by Dr. Greer which we received on August 28, 1989, and he discussed his opinions that he has concerning both causation and negligence as he was, I think—I think as you know he was endorsed apparently until recently—was going to talk about both. He was then asked on page 9 of his deposition, 'Do you have any other causation opinions that were not contained in your affidavit?' and he answered, 'No.' Now briefly the law on this, and there is law, Your Honor—and a very strong law—that indicates there is a duty to supplement right up to trial. It doesn't stop at some point, but right up until a jury trial. The first case is Smith v. Ford Motor Company. This involves Mr. Spence and his firm. This is a case where a doctor was endorsed on the issue of care and treatment."

At this point Peter paused, offering a copy of the case to Judge Peterson.

Judge Peterson turned to Peter and said, "Mr. Pryor let me ask you a question, since you're pausing. Why would you not think they would bring the Super Glue issue in with Dr. Greer?"

"Why would I not think?"

"Yes. That's the big issue with them. Why would they leave that out with Dr. Greer?"

Peter continued, "Your Honor, the Super Glue issue has taken on proportions far beyond my imagination. I never thought for a moment they would bring this up with Dr. Greer. Let me just go on and I ask your indulgence, Your Honor, because I think this is an important issue. The man has a substantial resume, he's triple boarded, he certainly has qualifications, and for him to be allowed to get into an area such as this, I think is improper. Now, in a nutshell, what Smith v. Ford Motor Company says is in that case they brought a treating doctor in, and then, during his testimony, although he'd been endorsed as to his care and treatment, he began to testify as to opinions that the injuries were consistent with a defective seat restraint mechanism or system. The objection was disallowed at the trial court level, and there was a verdict for the plaintiff, and this was reversed on appeal for, among other reasons, the failure to allow the doctor—or prohibit the doctor—from testifying as to an area that had never been disclosed until the time of trial, and this case says very specifically that the duty to supplement continues up to and including the time of trial.

"Now, as to the Court's question—and I understand the Court's concern as to whose duty is it. Is it our duty to anticipate that each expert will talk about everything, or the Plaintiffs' duty of disclosure?"

Judge Peterson said, "I think Rule 16 is clear that the opinions of the experts are to be disclosed."

Mr. Pryor continued, "Right, so I will tell the Court, I was taken aback and surprised by the fact that they didn't call him on the negligence issue. That's a tactical decision, and I salute them for whatever they want to do in that regard. I will tell you that I was taken by surprise and that my client is prejudiced, and there has not been disclosure, and there was ample request for that disclosure. And I say that's improper, and I say that I shouldn't be required under these circumstances to deal with that issue at the time of trial when I wasn't told about it beforehand."

Mr. H answered, "Your Honor, I don't question the duty to disclose. I mean that's always a problem on both sides. There's always a question of how detailed you get as far as the opinions on that disclosure. I would just bring to the Court's attention that this issue was brought up before Judge Carelli before the first trial."

Judge Peterson asked, "Was it brought up in response to Dr. Greer testifying or just generally?"

Mr. H answered, "Dr. Greer wasn't mentioned by name, but let me read to you what was said. 'Our expert will say that falls below the standard, that the use of it could cause damage, and certainly it's evidence in any event of the attitude, the approach, the skill of this neurosurgeon.' Now, Dr. Greer's name, I could see, was not mentioned there, but this issue was. And Mr. Pryor was there. And this issue was certainly brought to the attention of all the defense counsel at that time that we intended to put on expert opinion testimony on that—that Super Glue could cause part of the injury in that situation that existed here. Now if I could look back on it, and if I had to do it over again, I would be the first to concede that a lot of times I'd like—I wish I did more complete disclosures and more detailed answers to Interrogatories. Unfortunately, Mr. Spence didn't say the expert's name, and I don't know about any inquiry or discussion after that. From my understanding of what his testimony is, is that the Super Glue helped explain some of what appeared after the first surgery, and I think that was covered here. So, I don't mean to cause anybody any prejudice, but I think the issue has been out both before Judge Carelli—and Judge Carelli denied that motion right after that, but I think the issue has been on the table, certainly it has been in this case—or in this trial—as it was before Judge Carelli."

Judge Peterson was obviously upset. Her voice quivering, she began her discourse. "We have spent twenty minutes on this issue. I don't know how much time we spent on the other Rule 16 issues that have come up so far. I'm going to tell you that I have come to hate Rule 16, because the reason for which it was implemented is not for what it's been used and as it's being used now and putting this Court in the position that wasn't meant to be done under Rule 16. Rule 16 states—and it's very simple, and if people would follow the Rule, we wouldn't find ourselves in this type of problem. On the other hand, the trial occurs in the courtroom. That's supplemental procedure, and unfortunately we've gotten the feel that depositions are some kind of dress rehearsal, and it has to be repeated verbatim in trial or else there is some violation of disclosure.

"Concerning the disclosure experts, Rule 16 states, paragraph IX, that in the disclosure certificate, the expert witness is identified together with a statement as to each expert witness, which sets forth the substance of the opinions to which the expert is expected to testify. Now, that states that we must disclose the opinions, not just disclose the area in which the opinions are going to be given.

"The endorsement of Dr. Greer filed in the disclosure certificate on April 6, 1989, states that it is expected that Dr. Greer would testify that the surgical procedures of June 26, 1986, and July 2, 1986, fell below the applicable standard of care and that insufficient opportunity was provided for the CSF leak to spontaneously repair. It is expected that Dr. Greer will testify that a cause for Sheran R's injuries was the negligence associated with the surgeries of June 25, 1986, and July 2, 1986. He will testify concerning Sheran R's significant neurological deficits that existed prior to the development of the pneumothorax, as well as his opinions concerning the nature and cause of the damage to Sheran R. Nowhere in there does it give any substance of what his opinions will be, only the area in which he is going to testify. Now probably the endorsement up to that point is sufficient because then you just supplement eighty days before trial, and the supplement must set forth the opinions of the expert and the basis for each opinion.

"Now there does not seem to be anywhere that the opinion is known, even after the deposition, that Dr. Greer is going to testify as to causation with the Super Glue. Now, if this disclosure would just be made and be made sometime other than during the trial and during testimony, then we wouldn't be in this position for the opposing side then to bring up a very technical objection which is taking a substantial amount of time on an issue that is inconceivable to me that they would not have expected the Plaintiffs to go into. The Super Glue issue has always been an issue with the Plaintiffs. It was—and the Defendants knew that. It was the subject of at least one, perhaps other motions, that were filed in limine before trial, and it was so important to the Defendants, that knowledge in addition to the written motion, that just prior to the trial, it was brought up again orally, and there was substantial discussion about it again.

"If I seem frustrated in this respect, I am because I don't think that this is the purpose of Rule 16 to place the Court in this type of position. As I stated, I think it's inconceivable that we would think that an expert such as Dr. Greer playing the role that he's playing in this case as an expert witness would not be asked about the Super Glue. On the other hand, if it would have been disclosed, then we wouldn't be in this position." Judge Peterson paused and said, "The objection is overruled. Let's bring in the jury and let's bring in Dr. Greer."

It seemed obvious to me that after weighing both positions, Judge Peterson made her final decision only just as she said it.

The jury was brought back, and Mr. H continued. "Dr. Greer, I think before the break I was asking you what you understood occurred in the first surgery that was of significance to you in your opinion regarding the cause of the brain damage to Sheran R. And you talked about the retraction of the brain posteriorly. What else was significant to you in your opinion concerning causation that you learned occurred in the first surgery?"

Dr. Greer answered, "The nature of the means by which the tissue was to occlude the area where the leak existed employed the use of a substance that was initially described as adhesive, a surgical adhesive. I was made aware of the information in a deposition that the material used was Super Glue. This is a type of substance that does have an effect upon brain tissue, which is rather significant, and it is this more so than anything else that I read in this material that would lead me to believe that it's the use of the Super Glue which I felt was the cause of the mechanism for the subsequent problem which Sheran R experienced—more than any mechanical retraction, although that always is to be considered in any intracranial operation."

Peter turned to me in shock and said, "He has changed his entire opinion."

Mr. H asked, "After the first operation, what do you feel happened with Sheran R?"

Dr. Greer replied, "There was the beginnings of a vascular response, namely, the blood vessels at the base of the brain were reacting to the Super Glue that was used, giving rise to the beginnings of a change in the blood vessels' ability to feed blood into the brain. This Super Glue also induced a reaction, the meningeal reaction, that we spoke about before, as a foreign substance, and then subsequently additional problems involving a vasculature were evident."

"Doctor, from your review of his deposition, was Dr. Ogsbury—did he indicate an awareness of the potential toxicity of the problems that could occur with glue and its use in the brain like this?"

"Yes."

"Doctor, in your opinion, first of all, would you relate to us what clinical picture essentially occurred after the first surgery and before the second? Neurologically is what I'm talking about primarily?"

"What basically did happen initially was the patient recovered from the operation, but the following day she began experiencing indications that the nerve that leads to the right eye which moves it and opens the lid was not working the way it should. My interpretation for this is that this probably reflected the effect of the surgery, the Super Glue causing ischemia, which means a temporary shuttage of the blood flow to that nerve."

She was somewhat able to follow simple commands only on the 28th, but then on the 30th she improved somewhat; the eye began moving better; and she was described as being bright and alert. July 1, she's once again febrile, and the infectious disease identified no obvious cause."

Peter went to the bench, obviously angry, and had a discussion with Mr. H and Judge Peterson. The jury was removed from the room.

Peter began, "Your Honor, I'm just stunned what's happened in the last ten minutes and by representations to counsel on the records before this man took the stand, and I go back to the Court. I have made—and Mr. Nixon—we made a couple of motions before trial. We've made maybe a dozen objections, but I think the Court will know that we've pretty well sat in our chairs and listened and have not been obstructive to the evidentiary process. I do not think we've asked for a lot of the Court's time, and when I objected, I objected in good faith. Now on the record, we were told that Mr. H—there was just kind of a little record where he told us and you that the basis of this ruling that the doctor was going to say that this explained the meningeal or meningitis course, that is, the elevated white count and these other laboratory pictures and the clinical course, and then he asked Dr. Greer—he said, 'Doctor, do you have an opinion as to the role of the Super Glue?' and now he's said, 'I have changed my opinion that retraction was the cause of this stroke, and I now am of the opinion that this was the use of the Super Glue in the first operation.' This was a total departure from anything that has ever been disclosed to me, and now I'm supposed—not only is it improper, I don't even know where to start in terms of how to prepare for this type of cross-examination, and the jury is sitting here writing away furiously now that Super Glue caused the stroke when there was not even disclosure to the Court that that was going to be his opinion. And I don't know—I don't even know what to do about this. I have to talk to Dr. Ogsbury now about the issue of mistrial, whether we need to talk to the Court about that problem. This is a serious transgression of the Court's discovery procedures.

"Now you may think that this is emotional and reactive, but I'm sorry. This is not a technical objection anymore—when they changed their theory of the case and what happened midstream with a witness two weeks into the trial and he's had that deposition for two weeks—and I'll bet you Mr. Schuster met with him all day yesterday, and you weren't told, and I wasn't told, and nobody was told until those words came out of his mouth, and I do resent that, I really do resent that." Peter slammed down his notes and sat down.

Mr. H stood up. He too was angry, visibly trembling. He stated, "Your Honor, I resent something, too. I resent the accusation that I would make a misstatement to this Court, and I resent Mr. Pryor saying that. And I have dealt with this Court before, and I have dealt with Mr. Pryor before, and I have never done that, and I didn't do it today.

"Now first of all, what the witness said was—he didn't say he was retracting his opinion—what he said was that he thought that the glue 'more so than mechanical traction contributed to'—and I don't have the language after that, but he didn't say that mechanical traction wasn't involved here. He said 'more so.' Now I represent to this Court that what I understood he was—his opinion was just what I represented to you—there was certain things in the clinical picture of this lady that were explained by a toxic reaction to the Super Glue. Now I don't—I may be wrong—but I don't think he's necessarily gone beyond that. I think what he—what he is saying is that there was a toxic reaction. He's talked about the literature that's said that the experiments show that you can have a toxic reaction. I think he said that there was a vascular response. I think that's as far as he's gone, and he's related the vascular response to the Super Glue.

"Now I will—I will represent to this Court that what I expected to come out—first of all when I asked the question, 'What do you feel happened after the first surgery?' and what I expected him to talk about—very honestly, very honestly—I expected him to talk about the neurologic condition. And I was going to come back with the meningitis and take him through—here are my notes right here—I was going to take him through the cerebrospinal fluid, the gram stain. He was going to explain how the glue came into the picture and affected that. I didn't represent anything to this Court, and I didn't do anything I'm ashamed of here, and I resent Mr. Pryor implying that."

Judge Peterson said, "Well whether or not this was done intentionally or not, I think it has developed into a significant problem." She almost appeared to be crying but continued, "I agree with Mr. Pryor on that. Now we have the record available if we need to refer back to it, but my notes say, the 'use of Super Glue was a causal connection' and I underlined the words causal connection, and while I was writing that and underlining it, I was pretty surprised to find out that this testimony, which is opinion which had not been disclosed, was—has turned out to be—a very, very important opinion, and as far as this expert goes, maybe, I mean, causal connection of the subsequent problems. That's a pretty important opinion. Now that has turned out not to be disclosed. When I ruled before, I was under the impression that he was going to mention Super Glue and say that yes, this was another element of the cause or a possible—element of the cause, but I didn't think he was going to testify that this was going to be a—*the* causal connection, and I think there's a problem here. I also have a note on the side that he testified on that causal connection for ten minutes of his testimony. That's pretty significant."

Mr. Pryor asked, "If I may make a suggestion, Your Honor."

Judge Peterson said, "Yeah."

"I would ask if the reporter, if this would not insult her or the Court, that if we could just get the transcript for that ten-minute part after the session, then there's no debate as to what was said. I think that might help everybody in terms of how strongly he stated this."

Judge Peterson turned to the court reporter and asked, "Can you do that?"

The reporter said, "Yes."

Mr. Pryor continued, "You know if Mr. H didn't elicit that on purpose, then I accept his word as an officer of the court. But it doesn't change the fact that the man has just jumped out with an opinion that totally changes the complexion of the case."

Judge Peterson said, "Well, at the very least, Mr. Pryor, I'm not going to make you proceed this afternoon without further preparation, if that's necessary."

Peter asked, "So I don't need to spend the lunch hour trying to scramble and put something together?"

Judge Peterson answered, "To do cross-examination, you do not."

Peter continued, "I'll also need to counsel Dr. Ogsbury as to his options in terms of any positions that we would take with the Court."

Judge Peterson answered, "All right, let's take our recess until 1:30."

After the break Mr. H came up to Peter and said he would never do that. Peter said he accepted that from Mr. H.

We took the break for lunch. I was happy. I had been concerned about meningitis and my mistake in not ensuring the testing of the spinal fluid. Dr. Greer was credible on that issue, but I'm obviously totally comfortable with the Super Glue issue. This will blow Dr. Greer and his testimony out of the water.

Peter is charged beyond belief. Mary laughed and said, "Here we go juggling again. First you say you will, then you won't; extracranial versus intracranial—gone, retraction—gone, meningitis—gone."

I called Lee about checking with Dr. Al Rhoten, the Chief of Neurosurgery at the University of Florida, about Dr. Greer and the glue. We came back into court and Peter talked to Mr. H.

Scott talked to Ms. Kudla, and the two Wyoming attorneys talked together behind their table. I have to admit that as the case has gone on, Ms. Kudla has become more open. Peter was given the copy of the transcript. Dr. Greer's testimony was exactly as we heard and remembered it. Mr. H looked very distressed at the bench talking to Peter. By then Mr. Schuster was talking with Mr. R, and Mr. Fitzgerald had his head in his hands.

The court was called back into session. Peter asked Judge Peterson, "I have an initial suggestion and a request. I would like Dr. Greer to come in, and I would like to ask him about three minutes worth of questions, maybe eight or nine in number, concerning the timing of this knowledge and information, just so that we have a record on that. Would that be permissible with the Court?" Judge Peterson said, "Let's do that."

Peter took the lectern and turned to Dr. Greer. He stated, "Dr. Greer, I'm Peter Pryor. I represent Drs. Ogsbury and Krauth, and I have about ten questions in terms of some information gathering. When did you originally read Dr. Ogsbury's deposition? Can you give me an approximate time frame?"

Dr. Greer answered, "Spring of '89."

"All right. And in connection with your review of his deposition, did you know at that time that he was questioned at some length concerning the possibility that he had used Super Glue in connection with the first craniotomy on June 25, 1986?"

"I don't remember that detail with regard to Super Glue. I remember the event that I described to you when he mentioned the glue as something that entailed a double-edged sword effect."

"There's a lengthy discussion here concerning, do you know if Super Glue has since been approved, and the discussion about has the Super Glue that you were thinking about using today been approved? Were you aware at the time, or would you have been aware at the time that you read that deposition, of the possibility that he had used Super Glue?"

"Yes."

"Did you ever read Dr. Smith's deposition, the neurosurgeon expert in this case?"

"Yes, I read his deposition."

"And were you aware, from Dr. Smith's deposition, that he testified that even though he was under the assumption that Super Glue was used, that he did not think that this had any significant effect on the outcome?"

"I don't accept that, but I'll accept what you said."

"All right. Now when did you receive Nurse B's deposition?"

"In the past three weeks or so."

"Was there an occasion where you had a conversation with Mr. Schuster or any attorney representing the Rs?"

"Yes. There was a discussion that dealt with the neurosurgeon who testified in Dr. N's trial or at least was involved with Dr. N's trial where Super Glue was incriminated as the cause of the problem."

"And to let him know your thoughts about if Super Glue was used, whether that played a role in her course?"

"I think it was in conjunction with other material that I requested that he send anything that he could get on the topic of Super Glue and the nervous system."

"All right. What other material did you request that he send? Did you receive a series of articles or some articles and texts concerning the use of or the potential toxic effects of Super Glue?"

"Yes."

"All right. When did you receive that material?"

"It's about the same time or shortly thereafter."

"Was there at that point—at that point, did you form an opinion concerning Super Glue and any role that it may have played in Sheran R's stroke?"

"Yes."

"All right. Did you form this opinion, then, approximately three weeks before trial?"

"Two to three weeks before trial, yes."

"And when did you first share that opinion with Mr. Schuster and—and/or any other attorneys for the Rs?"

"This was Thursday, the day, yesterday."

"So, you're telling us that the first—even though you've had this opinion for three weeks—that the first time you discussed this with Mr. Schuster was yesterday?"

"That's right."

"All right. Now, how long did you meet with Mr. Schuster yesterday?"

"Well, Mr. Schuster and subsequently with Mr. H. It was pretty much—I would suspect eight hours or so."

"And did you discuss first with Mr. Schuster your opinion, as you've expressed at trial, that the cause of the stroke, at least a significant part of it, was the Super Glue?"

"I discussed this as a causal mechanism—the topic was, as you guessed, was there—meningitis or not, and I felt there wasn't."

"But did you, yesterday, tell Mr. Schuster that your opinion was that the Super Glue was the causative factor—a significant factor in the stroke?"

"Yes, Mr. Pryor."

"Did you tell Mr. H of that opinion?"

"Yes."

"And did you come to Court today expecting to express that opinion based upon your conversations with them as to testimony that you would be covering at trial?"

"Yes."

"So that the attorneys for the Rs were well aware of your opinion in that regard when you were asked this morning as to the role of Super Glue in the patient's outcome, specifically the stroke that resulted in bilateral anterior cerebral artery infarct?"

"Yes, that as well as other things."

"Have you discussed this theory or your new theory as to what happened with any other neurosurgeon or physician or health care provider?"

"No."

Peter said, "Your Honor, those are the questions that I have at this point," and sat down.

Judge Peterson said to Mr. H, "Do you have any follow up questions you wish to ask Dr. Greer?"

Mr. H said, "Yes I do," and took the lectern. "Dr. Greer would you agree that at least your discussion with me when we talked about Super Glue was limited to the effects of Super Glue and the issue of presence or absence of meningitis in Sheran R?"

"It had to do with that in part and what the interpretation of what the spinal fluid was, what I said was Super Glue rather than meningitis."

"You discussed the literature you reviewed indicated it had a toxic effect?"

"Yes, on blood vessels in the brain."

"But you didn't express to me yesterday that you—that you were disregarding the theory of excessive retraction used in this case and replacing it with a theory that all the damage done here was done by the Super Glue?"

"The concept that I had when I gave my first deposition was that something happened at the time of surgery, and I used the word 'surgical manipulation' as the general scheme of what was going on. Now I have something else to go with that appears more plausible and that Super Glue was the cause of the difficulty."

"The point that I want to make, though, is that when you talked to me yesterday, you didn't convey to me your opinion that it wasn't the retraction that caused the vascular problem but rather it was the Super Glue that caused the vascular problem?"

"I don't know whether I spoke of this in so many words. We used both concepts together in terms of what was going on at the time Super Glue was being looked upon as the causal mechanism."

"Doctor, if I represented to this Court that my understanding was that your testimony about Super Glue was going to be that it effected certain evidence of laboratory results as far as the presence or absence of meningitis, would I have been making an accurate statement?"

"No, that's accurate."

Mr. H said, "That's all I have, Your Honor."

Peter stood up and said, "I have one other question if I may, Your Honor," and came back to the lectern.

Peter asked, "Did you and Mr. Schuster discuss during your meeting yesterday the understanding that, if you were asked about the effects of Super Glue, that you would tell the jury, if permitted, that it was a significant cause of the stroke? What I'm getting at—Mr. Schuster was aware of your opinion that Super Glue played a role to a medical probability in the stroke?"

Mr. Schuster stood up, "Your Honor, I want to be heard."

Mr. H said, "I'm going to object, too—it's getting argumentative."

Judge Peterson said, "It's getting beyond questions."

Mr. Schuster said, "And I resent the—innuendo of Mr. Pryor, Your Honor. I resent him using leading questions to lay those innuendoes that are false."

Peter said, "I would still like an answer to that question, but I have no further questions."

Mr. H retorted, "And I object to those questions."

Judge Peterson suggested, "Why don't you rephrase it? Phrase it as a factual request instead of an argumentative statement."

Mr. Pryor answered, "He's already answered that question once before. I withdraw the question."

Judge Peterson said, "Mr. Schuster, do you have any questions to ask of Dr. Greer?"

Mr. Schuster said, "No Ma'am, I needed to vent on Mr. Pryor."

Mr. Pryor stood up and asked that Dr. Greer be excused. He said, "Your Honor, I have a suggestion. We do not obviously waive our position that the Court should not have allowed any of this to begin in the first place. I mean you overruled our objection to any discussion, and we accepted that and then it got to a different level."

Judge Peterson said, "Mr. Pryor, just let me say about that—I wish it was 11:00 again."

Mr. Pryor continued, "I do, too, Your Honor, because then we wouldn't be doing this. Now, without waiver of that position, I will tell the Court, and this is obviously for the record—rather for my benefit—and I've discussed the issue of asking for a mistrial with Dr. Ogsbury, and Dr. Ogsbury emotionally could not, I don't think, go through this again, so he has absolutely no desire, even if he were entitled to one, and I'm not even asking that you hint either way. It's just we're not—we're aware of that right. He has been advised of that right. It is not his desire—in fact he is adamant that we go forward even if this is harmful to our case."

Judge Peterson answered, "Well, I think there are other remedies we can fashion."

Mr. Pryor continued, "I've also discussed with Dr. Ogsbury and Mr. Nixon the possibility of a curative instruction but, Your Honor, the testimony has been extended and it's so strong and this jury is taking notes and it's in their notebooks and in their minds even if the Court were to strongly admonish them, so I wouldn't see that a curative instruction is the answer.

"I've told the Court that I'm not prepared to cross-examine on this theory. So my suggestion is to the Court that he finish his direct examination today, that he be excused to return Monday, and I be provided the literature that he was provided by Mr. Schuster and that I be allowed to prepare for his cross-examination to meet this new theory or opinion, and, under the circumstances, I think that that—at least at this point—that is the best solution that I can propose to the Court."

Judge Peterson asked, "Do you want to take his deposition on this issue?"

Peter answered, "No, Your Honor, I don't want to let this sit. I think if, for example, he were to come back in a week or ten days—that would be extremely prejudicial and unfair to Dr. Ogsbury. I think that we should have the right to deal with this on Monday. I have a conference in Colorado Springs before the American College of Surgeons that I'm a participant in tomorrow, and if I were to take his deposition, the only time I could do that would be Sunday, and I would prefer to use that time for his cross-examination. I would be ready to go with him Monday morning without a deposition. I think that I would rather focus my energies on reading this material and preparing to deal with these opinions than I would deposing him, so my suggestion is that if I get the material, I do not request a deposition under these circumstances.

"And I would rather—I want him back soon, that's the main thing, and I—the only time that I'll have to prepare for his testimony will be Sunday. So I'll go without deposition, and obviously I'm waiving that option offered by the Court, and I've discussed that with Dr. Ogsbury, and he understands my position on that point."

Judge Peterson said, "Will Monday morning give you enough time or would you prefer Monday afternoon?"

Mr. Pryor answered, "Monday afternoon would probably be better."

Judge Peterson turned to Mr. H, "All right, Mr. H?"

Mr. H answered, "Well I have to tell you this. Mr. Pryor mentioned this to me that this was going to be his position. I had someone ask Dr. Greer if he could be available, and he indicated he could not be because he had patients scheduled but that he could be the following week.

"Now, Your Honor, I understand that if I was sitting where you are how I'd feel about that, but I don't have control over the docket. I hope that the court appreciates and believes that what happened here wasn't done by design and it wasn't done with any intent. I've shown Mr. Pryor my notes of my examination and I think it's—it should be clear that that wasn't supposed to be what came out. Now I will tell you I asked a follow-up question after it came out, and if I could go back in time like you said, if you could go back to 11:00, if I could go back in time, I would go back and withdraw that question, but it still happened. But it wasn't done with any intent of misleading the Court or to bring anything improper into this hearing. And if he says he can't come back because of his patients he's scheduled—well, I suppose you have the powers to make him do it, but it puts—as Dr. Ogsbury's been put in the situation—that puts the Rs in a bad situation also. I don't know what the answer is."

Judge Peterson said, "Well we know one thing. Whether it was intentional or inadvertent, it was not caused by the Defendant, and Mr. Pryor's request is much milder than the remedy I would have fashioned. I was ready to order a deposition on Monday at the Plaintiffs' expense to pay the defense attorneys' fees during that deposition and have Dr. Greer return for testimony. This is a substantial deviation from the requirements of disclosure. This transcript shows he is now placing this as the main cause, and if not the main cause certainly a significant cause. And as I stated before, I had no idea that this was the type of testimony that was going to come out regarding the Super Glue."

Judge Peterson was visibly upset. "And whether it was intentional or not, I think that if his testimony was known, it should have been disclosed. This is substantial. This is major. This isn't just a small expansion of someone's testimony which we originally thought it was, or which I originally thought it was. This was an ambush, that's what this was. Intentional or not, this is an ambush. So, I'm going to grant Mr. Pryor's request. I think under the circumstances, it's a very reasonable request. If the doctor has any problems returning for testimony at 1:30 on Monday, then I'll order him to do so."

Mr. H talked to Dr. Greer and said, "Your Honor, for the record, I've spoken with the doctor. He will be back. We will be ready to go 1:30 on Monday. I talked with Mr. Pryor, and he feels we can have the doctor out of here Monday afternoon, and he's indicated as long as I don't have a lengthy redirect—he felt comfortable he could leave me half an hour on Monday, and that's fine with me, and the doctor's willing to come back."

The jury was brought back, and Mr. H resumed.

At this point, I was paged by Lee. I went out of the courtroom; it felt strange to walk out of my own trial. Lee wanted to know the questions he should ask Dr. Rhoten. When I finally returned, Mr. H and Dr. Greer were discussing the positive gram stain from the 3rd of July.

Mr. H went on, "Now, Doctor, I believe it was suggested yesterday by Dr. Krauth that perhaps there were just these few gram-negative rods floating around, and they were dead. Does that make any sense to you?"

Dr. Greer answered, "Well I don't accept that concept. The body has the ability to destroy organisms of the gram-negative rods."

"Doctor, what about the argument that Sheran R was receiving antibiotics and that the antibiotics were killing the organisms so that they wouldn't grow in the culture, but at the same time there was an ongoing active meningitis occurring within her brain or in her skull?"

"That's inconsistent. If you're going to have an ongoing, active-producing substance, then you should see growth, particularly if you see the rods."

[Mr. H was still showing no fire. Peter said, "I think their camp is in disarray."]

Mr. H proceeded, "Now, Doctor, as indicated yesterday, there is a theory by the Defense in this case that meningitis was present on June 25 and caused the vasculitis of the anterior cerebral artery and subsequent infarction. If meningitis were present to a sufficient degree to cause this kind of vasculitis, would you expect to see other evidence of the meningitis, both clinically and radiographically, to be present?"

"Yes, I would."

"Even if meningitis was present and surgical trauma somehow caused a local reaction because of the presence of meningitis, would you still expect to see evidence of meningitis throughout the brain?"

"Yes."

"If meningitis was present, was it active enough to cause this vasculitis, what would you expect to see on cultures even in the face of antibiotic therapy?"

"Well, if it's an active meningitis, then it's going to cause significant changes and you would expect to have a positive culture."

"And the cultures were all negative?"

"Yes."

"Did you ever see a positive culture at any time for meningitis, bacterial meningitis, in Sheran R, in any of the records?"

"No."

I told Peter that Dr. Greer is now subdued. Peter laughed and said that he is no longer the big dude. He is now subdued, Dr. Subdued.

"Doctor, on the morning—during the early morning hours of July 4, do you understand that Sheran R suffered a pneumothorax?"

"Yes."

"And have you reviewed the records regarding this event?"

"Yes."

"Doctor, do you have an opinion, within a reasonable degree of medical probability, as to whether or not the pneumothorax caused or contributed to any of Sheran R's neurologic damage?"

"Yes, I have an opinion."

"And what is that opinion, Doctor?"

"It did not contribute to any of Sheran R's neurologic damage." [Is that all? This is a major issue. Mr. H obviously wants to get through this.]

Mr. H continued, "Doctor, I want to move now to your examination of Sheran R. Could you tell the jury, if you please, summarize your findings with respect to your examination of Sheran R? First of all, where did you examine her?"

"At her home in Wyoming."

"And would you relate to the jury, please, what you found to be of significance as far as your neurologic examination of her injuries suffered in this hospitalization?"

"The two main areas are related to behavioral problems as well as other features that are called frontal lobe manifestations of behavior. She had inappropriate types of actions."

"Of what, Doctor?"

"Actions. Her interpersonal relationships with people were inconsistent. She would do things that were out of keeping with the real situation. While my testing of her on the basis of frontal lobe insult confirmed this—where she was inattentive, was unable to continue with the type of activities in testing that indicate an intact frontal lobe—in contrast to this, the rest of her brain function from the standpoint of cognition and intelligence appear to be all right. Her memory was fine, calculations, and so forth."

At this point, Lee called with a report from Dr. Rhoten. He reported he had been kept on hold for over a half an hour waiting for the secretary to put through the call to Dr. Rhoten but finally was put through. Lee reported Dr. Rhoten said that the use of Super Glue was not malpractice; he uses physiologic glue now, but in 1986 a variety of adhesives were used including the acrylics. He never saw meningitis; he never saw bilateral anterior cerebral infarctions. He can't come to Denver because he's giving the neurosurgical boards, but he's willing to confirm his opinions on the telephone. I came back in with that information. The trial had been recessed for the day.

After the trial was recessed, our side was upbeat to say the least. The other side was in disarray. We now have only one issue to fight—that is the Super Glue that wasn't used. Peter is charged. He came prancing back into the courtroom and reported an offer for $400,000 but said he could probably get it down to $250,000. This is quite a bit different than the initial offer of $1.8 million, and Peter's estimate that it would likely take $1 million to settle.

I will see Peter Sunday to prepare him for Dr. Greer. It certainly has been a strange day. Dr. Greer has been more and less than we expected. His concise, well-focused style was consistent with his obvious stature, yet his abrupt and highly improper change of position has apparently helped our side more than any other single factor. And his confident, almost arrogant demeanor and affected English-like accent of the morning gave way to a much more passive style and New York accent after lunch.

The attorneys also surprised me. Mr. H seemed to be as angry as Peter when the change of opinion appeared to be sprung unannounced upon him as well as on us. I'd always thought that the only rule for attorneys was to do whatever they could get away with—not for these two men. There is a very strong legal ethic here.

Yet, even despite the upbeat finish to the end of the week, I thought as we left the Court at the end of the day, I'm still not going to volunteer for this job again.

Fran
Friday, May 11, 1990, 9:00 p.m.

It is day ten. We made it this far and we're still walking around. Jay is feeling gooooood. I like seeing him like this, just smooth not arrogant, solid and positive. The jurors were open, alert, and still in sync with the trial. Another turn today. Dr. Greer had changed his tune. Peter was on fire with this. Mr. H was equally shocked. The Judge used the word "ambush."

Noises were being made about settlement. The Plaintiffs have presented their expert witnesses and it's time for the Defendant to shine. The moment we have been striving for, waiting for, is at hand. Jay's ready to go another week. No ambivalence, no settlement.

Jay
Friday, May 11, 1990, 11:55 p.m.

After the excitement of the day's events, I found myself lying in bed wide awake.

As a neurosurgeon, in the night before any major surgery, I am awake going over the myriad of potential danger points in the procedure and the steps that will be necessary to address those situations.

Now, as a defendant in a malpractice trial, I am concerned about the next part of the trial and my role in it. Also, and perhaps more stressful, I have heard talk of a potential settlement offer coming from the Plaintiffs. If the offer is not reasonable, then, of course, we will proceed as planned with the defense portion of the trial. My main concern is my possible reaction to a reasonable settlement offer.

In surgery, we rarely complete an operation with only part of its goal satisfied. Here in the trial, after being emotionally prepared to carry this battle to its completion, I am afraid that, no matter how reasonable the settlement offer appears to be, I will be unable to respond without feeling let down and considering the settlement to be a loss that I will regret for the rest of my life.

With all of those issues circling about in my mind, it took more than an hour for me to finally fall into a dreamlike sleep....

CHAPTER FIFTEEN

THE DREAM

Cross-examination of Dr. Greer

We came to the courthouse much later than we had previously because of Judge Peterson's stipulation that Peter's cross-examination of Dr. Melvin Greer should commence at 1:30 p.m.

During the drive to the courthouse, I wondered about how Peter would approach his cross-examination of Dr. Greer. I met Peter at the courthouse at about 1:00 p.m. and walked with him up the steps to the entrance without asking about his plan.

I took off my jacket, placed all my items in a basket for X-ray, and walked through the metal detector. This is my moment, my daily moment. Once I'm cleared of the metal detector, I'm transformed to another reality. It becomes a feeling of unreality, disorienting. I'm here, yet I'm not. My mind shifts to getting on my virtual mask and following my ironclad rules of showing nothing, but responding appropriately. It is a surreal life as we entered Courtroom 9, our ephemeral trial home for the past two weeks. Mr. H, Ms. Kudla, Mr. Schuster, and Mr. Fitzgerald, as well as Mr. H's paralegals, who, again, we had dubbed Frick and Frack, were already present at the Plaintiffs' table. Peter and I joined Scott, plus Mary and Sam, Peter's paralegals, at the defense table. Kathy and Fran took their place behind the defense team.

Once in the courtroom, I realized that, for the first time, Peter seemed remarkably eager to proceed. Like an athlete who senses weakness on the part of an opponent, Peter clearly was looking forward to his cross-examination of Dr. Greer.

Obviously, things went well late last week with the change of testimony by Dr. Greer. In addition, he had the weekend to prepare for the encounter. While superficially appearing relaxed, it was clear to me that Peter had prepared for the cross-examination of his career. He would later tell me that circumstances such as these, where witnesses have opened themselves to nearly complete vulnerability, rarely present themselves in the courtroom. Dr. Greer had made himself and the Plaintiffs vulnerable by dropping the nuclear bomb of changing his expert opinion in open court, in front of the jury.

In all games, there are rules. Peter had told me that in a civil trial, there are Rules of Civil Procedure. There is simply no deviation from these rules. Ever. They are sacrosanct. If extensions of time are granted, including for discovery, only the judge has the power to grant them. In a civil case such as this one, an expert like Dr. Greer and the R's attorneys had the obligation to disclose precisely the opinions about which he was to testify, at a certain time before trial. The purpose of the rules is to create a level playing field to the extent that is possible. Only in black-and-white Perry Mason episodes is there supposed to be trial by ambush.

Advance disclosures have an added incentive; if all parties have the opposing party's evidence, there should be a greater likelihood of settlement. Dr. Greer has disregarded that code. In doing so, he has disrespected the Rs, Judge Peterson, the rule of law, and even Mr. H, who obviously was not made privy to the change in opinion before Dr. Greer's testimony began.

Precisely at 1:30 p.m., Judge Peterson and the Bailiff entered the courtroom. We all stood and then sat at the Bailiff's direction. The jury was brought in and seated.

Judge Peterson paused until all was quiet and everyone was in their place. We were all ready to proceed. She looked down from the bench at Dr. Greer, who had returned to the witness box. "You're still under oath," she said curtly, barely able to hide her frustration for the near mistrial this expert had caused. She then turned to the jury and said, "Today is the day for Mr. Pryor to direct questions to Dr. Greer regarding his testimony last week."

Judge Peterson first turned to Mr. H and asked if he had any questions for Dr. Greer prior to Mr. Pryor's cross-examination. Mr. H indicated he had no questions at this point, but, as agreed to previously, he would likely have a few further questions after the cross-examination had been completed. Judge Peterson then turned to Peter and asked, "Are you ready for your cross-examination of Dr. Greer?"

Peter stood. He somehow seemed taller than usual this morning. His shoulders square, he replied with a calm resoluteness that could only be described as a foreshadowing of the storm that was to come, "Yes, Your Honor." Pleasantries purposefully ignored, Peter looked at Dr. Greer directly and went straight to business. He said, "Dr. Greer, since we met for your deposition, you had met with the Plaintiffs' attorneys, correct?"

Dr. Greer answered, "That's correct."

"Several times?"

"That's right."

Peter added, "They are paying for your time?"

Dr. Greer answered, "Yes."

"They are paying for your expertise?"

"Yes."

"You estimated previously that you are paid about $375 per hour."

"That is correct."

"And you estimated you spent sixty to seventy hours in your evaluation."

"That is correct."

Finally, Peter asked, "And they are paying for your travel expenses?"

"That's right."

Peter added, "Did you fly first class?"

Dr. Greer hesitated; he knew what effect this might have on a jury.

"Uh, yes." And thus, the point was made clear that Dr. Greer stood to significantly benefit financially from this trial, a benefit that potentially could lead to bias.

Peter then asked, "Dr. Greer, you are a neurologist, correct?"

Dr. Greer answered, "Yes, that's right."

"You are not a neurosurgeon, is that true?"

"No, I'm not a neurosurgeon."

"Neurologists do not perform surgeries, correct?"

"That's correct."

"In contrast, primarily what neurosurgeons do is brain surgery. Would you agree with that, Dr. Greer?"

Dr. Greer answered, "I would agree."

"Neurosurgeons like Drs. Ogsbury and Krauth?"

"Uh-huh."

"Is that a yes?"

"Yes."

Peter went on, "So when Dr. Ogsbury performed the transcranial dural repair on the Plaintiff at the time of the first surgery, that is not a surgery you have ever performed, isn't that right, Dr. Greer?"

"That's right, but—"

"Peter stopped Dr. Greer from finishing and said, "Nor have you ever received any training for the surgery, have you, Doctor?"

Dr. Greer answered, "That's right, but I can explain—"

Peter countered, "You will have a chance to explain on redirect should Mr. H choose to do so, but for now, I am just asking you to answer yes or no." Peter asked the court reporter to read back the last question.

Dr. Greer answered, "No, I have not been trained for the surgery."

Peter went on, "Thank you, Doctor. And when Drs. Ogsbury and Krauth performed the ethmoid packing procedure, the second surgery, that is not a surgery you have ever performed either, correct?"

"Correct." A barely perceptible expression of irritation appeared on Dr. Greer's face. He knew the direction this was headed.

Peter asked, "Nor have you received any training or education on how to perform this surgery, have you, Doctor?"

"No, I have not."

"In fact, Dr. Greer, you have not performed brain surgery of any kind."

It was not phrased as a question, but Dr. Greer answered, "Well, no, but I work with neurosurgeons on cases every day."

Peter countered, "But that wasn't my question, was it, Doctor?" Dr. Greer said nothing. Peter continued, "The question was whether you have ever performed brain surgery of any kind, and the answer to that question is no, is it not?"

Dr. Greer answered, in a voice barely above a whisper, "No, I have not." His expression and tone began to portray frustration.

Peter insisted, "I apologize, Doctor, but I didn't hear your answer." I realized that, of course, Peter had heard.

Dr. Greer answered, "No, I have not."

Peter continued, "Thank you. So, in preparation for your testimony here today, it is my understanding that one of the documents you reviewed was Dr. Ogsbury's deposition, is that right?"

Dr. Greer answered, "I did."

"You are well aware that Dr. Ogsbury is, in fact, a neurosurgeon?"

"Yes, I'm aware."

"And you reviewed his background. You also know that Dr. Ogsbury has been a neurosurgeon for thirteen years."

"I am aware."

Peter concluded, "So forgive me, Doctor," Peter looked up in mock puzzlement and continued, "You are not a neurosurgeon, have never performed the operation that was performed in the first operation by Drs. Ogsbury and Barron, have never performed the operation that was performed in the second operation by Drs. Ogsbury and Krauth, indeed have never performed brain surgery of any kind, so please enlighten this jury on how it is that you believe you are qualified to give an expert opinion about Dr. Ogsbury's professional performance to a reasonable degree of medical probability?"

Mr. H shot up like a bullet, and said, "Objection, Your Honor. Argumentative." He had to try to do something to stop the locomotive that Peter had become, but it was no use—the damage was done.

Peter said, "Withdrawn." Peter knew the question was one step too far. Dr. Greer sighed, resigned, glancing at Mr. H as if to say, "Do something, help me out up here, can't you see this guy is cutting me to pieces?" I don't think the jury saw his glance, but our team sure did. Peter paused and looked at the jury. He had been standing fairly close to Dr. Greer in the witness box.

Peter walked back to us at our counsel table and glanced at his notes. He was pausing on purpose to show the jury he was moving to his next area of inquiry. You could almost see the tension, like a fog, in the courtroom. Was that a bead of sweat on Dr. Greer's forehead? Remaining at counsel table, but now looking at the jury, Peter closed his eyes briefly as if to recenter himself and resumed his questions.

Peter said, "Let's now discuss some of the opinions that you gave to Mr. H in his direct examination. You indicated to him that it was your opinion that neither meningitis nor the pneumothorax suffered by Mrs. R caused her significant brain injury. So, let's talk about your opinions as to what actually did cause the brain injury. And let us clarify the timing of your opinions." When I took your deposition some time ago, I asked you many questions about what, in your expert opinion, had caused Mrs. R's brain damage, didn't I?"

Dr. Greer answered. "Among other things, yes."

Peter went on, 'It's fair to say, Dr. Greer, that you told us in your deposition that, essentially, the main cause of Mrs. R's brain damage was Dr. Ogsbury's excessive posterior retraction of the brain."

Dr. Greer answered. "I think that oversimplifies it a bit, but yes."

"At no point during your deposition did you testify that Super Glue was, in your opinion, the primary cause of Mrs. R's brain damage." Dr. Greer paused too long for the jury not to notice. He blinked several times and shot another disappointing glance toward the Plaintiffs' table.

They were supposed to be protecting him, but they were leaving him flapping in the wind like a sheet on a laundry line.

He stammered. "I didn't but... but... but I wasn't aware at the time this was an issue."

Peter paused and then asked, "Now, Dr. Greer, much ado has been made about the alleged use of Super Glue in this case. Is that a fair statement?"

Dr. Greer answered, "That's a fair statement. I wouldn't say 'alleged'—but okay."

"It is also fair to say that, from your perspective, the Super Glue, above all, is driving Mrs. R's injuries here, fair?"

"Fair."

"So, let's break that down here together right now so that we can learn when this became a significant issue for you." More than one of the jurors sat forward in their chairs. Judge Peterson even leaned forward a bit.

Peter continued, "Dr. Greer, you have carefully reviewed the entire medical record. Let's start with that, isn't that true?"

Dr. Greer answered, "Yes, that's true."

"And nowhere in the medical record is there evidence that Super Glue was used in any surgery, is that so?"

"Well, yes, but, I believe an error was made in the records."

"But let's be clear, Dr. Greer. That's not the question I have asked you, was it?"

"Um... wow... um, I suppose not."

"The question I asked was what is stated in the medical records."

"Fair enough."

"So please, for the court record, please answer my question. In the entirety of the medical records, **nowhere** (Peter emphasized "nowhere") in any medical record or note does it state that any physician used Super Glue on Sheran R."

"Okay, that is true."

Peter continued, "You would also agree, would you not, in the importance of keeping complete and thorough medical records?"

Dr. Greer answered, "Yes, of course I would."

"You would also agree that keeping thorough and accurate medical records is vital when a lawsuit is anticipated?"

"Absolutely."

"But you still believe that an error must have been made in the medical records?"

"I do."

Peter paused and said, "Dr. Greer, in addition to the medical records, you have reviewed other records including depositions, is that not true?"

Dr. Greer answered, "That is true."

"You testified last week that you met with Mr. Schuster the day before your testimony in this court, and shared with him that, about three weeks before the trial, you read a deposition which led you to come to the conclusion that Super Glue was used during the first operation and was the main cause of the brain injury. Is that correct?"

Dr. Greer answered, "That is correct."

"That document was the deposition of Nurse B, correct?"

"That is correct."

"In Nurse B's deposition, she testified that she believes Super Glue was used in the first surgery, right?"

"That's right."

Peter continued, "At that time, you changed your opinion as to the main cause of Mrs. R's brain injury, is that true?"

Dr. Greer answered, "That's true."

"You changed it essentially from retraction to Super Glue, is that a fair description of the change of your opinion?"

"That is fair."

"Because it is your belief that Super Glue might cause damage within the spinal fluid, and then to the brain?"

"I would agree."

Peter asked, "By the way, at about the same time, you also met with Mr. H, but your discussion with him was solely regarding the issue of the changes Super Glue might cause within the spinal fluid."

Dr. Greer answered, "I would agree."

Peter then added, "And you have met with Mr. H and Mr. Schuster in person, before the trial today, is that right?" Peter outstretched his arm and pointed to the opposing counsel.

Dr. Greer answered, "We have, yes."

Peter continued, this time quite slowly, "There have been many months between when I spoke to you under oath during your deposition, and now under oath on this witness stand."

Dr. Greer said, "Again, as I have said, I have only recently become aware that Super Glue actually was used."

Peter countered, "This awareness is in the face of Dr. Ogsbury's testimony in his deposition, which you also have read, which indicates, to the contrary, that Super Glue was not used in the first operation."

Mr. H jumped up and said, "Objection, Your Honor, argumentative. Mr. Pryor is putting words in the witness's mouth."

Judge Peterson responded, "Sustained. Be careful, Mr. Pryor."

Peter then briefly turned to our table and smiled. He turned back to Dr. Greer and said, "Dr. Greer, you have rendered many opinions during your testimony. I would like to address those opinions and will ask you to confirm whether or not my interpretation of each of your opinions is true."

Peter began what I bet will be the height of the storm. He asked, "Dr. Greer, you are a neurologist, not a neurosurgeon, and thus have never performed an operation on the brain. Is that correct?"

Dr. Greer answered, "Yes, Sir, that is correct."

"For that reason, you cannot be considered an expert on the techniques of brain surgery. Is that correct?"

"Yes, Sir, that is correct."

Peter paused and continued, "It is your opinion that Sheran R did not have meningitis before or after the operation of June 25, 1989. Is that correct?"

"Yes, Sir, that is correct."

"It is your opinion that you believe that even if Sheran R did have meningitis, that meningitis would not have caused the serious brain injury that she suffered. Is that correct?"

"Yes, Sir, that is correct."

"It is also your opinion that, while Sheran R suffered a pneumothorax on July 4, 1989, that pneumothorax had no impact on the condition of Sheran R; indeed, specifically, it is your opinion that pneumothorax did not cause the brain injury suffered by Sheran R. Is that correct?"

"Yes, Sir, that is correct."

"Next, you believe, from prior testimony, that the procedures performed by Drs. Ogsbury and Krauth were negligent. Is that correct?"

"Yes, Sir, that is correct."

"Also, at the time of your deposition under oath many months ago, it was your opinion that the negligent posterior retraction of the brain was the primary cause of the brain injury. Is that correct?"

"Yes, Sir, that is correct."

"Finally!" Peter spread out his hands widely from left to right indicating a wide expanse of time, from the time of that deposition under oath, through the many months between then and now. Peter walked up to the jury box as close as he dared without drawing an objection and whispered slowly, "Now... now... now, you are telling the jury that the use of Super Glue, as you said, and I quote, 'more than any mechanical retraction' was the primary cause of the brain injury suffered by Sheran R. Is that correct?"

Dr. Greer answered, "I suppose that's right."

Peter turned to the Defense, and then back to Dr. Greer, and asked, "Dr. Greer, you indicated you were able to read Dr. Ogsbury's deposition as part of your preparation. So, you understand that Dr. Ogsbury testified in that deposition, under oath, that he did not use Super Glue, is that not true?"

"That is true."

"Were you also able to read the deposition of Dr. James Barron?"

"Yes, I read Dr. Barron's deposition as well."

"Therefore, you understand that Dr. Barron, who assisted Dr. Ogsbury at the time of the first surgery, also testified in his deposition, under oath, that Super Glue was not used in the first operation, is that true?"

"Yes, that is true."

Peter paused and asked, "So it remains your opinion, despite the testimony of these two surgeons, that Super Glue was used in the first operation, is that true?"

"That is true."

Peter then asked, "Why is that?"

Dr. Greer answered, "Because the nurse who had all of the equipment and medications on her operating room table testified that it was."

"Did she testify she was able to look through the microscope to see the actual procedure?"

"I do not believe she did."

"And would a nurse in the operating room typically be able to assist while viewing through the microscope?"

"As you know, I am not a surgeon and would therefore not know the positions of the surgeons and scrub nurse in the operating room."

"Of course. Thank you, but what about the opinions of the two doctors?"

"I believe they were mistaken."

"Both mistaken?"

"Yes. Both mistaken."

Peter paused, with an incredulous look on his face, and said, "You are testifying under oath that it is your opinion that two experienced surgeons were mistaken in describing the actual operation they were performing together under the microscope?"

Dr. Greer slowly answered, "That is my opinion."

Peter responded, "And you, Sir, were not in the operating with them, were you, Dr. Greer?"

"I was not."

Peter left a long pause in the courtroom to let Dr. Greer's last answer hang in the air for a moment. He resumed, "Are you still confident to a reasonable degree of medical probability?"

Mr. H stood up and said, "Objection. Asked and answered. Mr. Pryor is badgering the witness."

Peter quickly responded, "Withdrawn. At this time, I have no further questions for Dr. Greer, Your Honor. However, I will be calling three witnesses tomorrow, including Dr. Barron. Dr. Barron will testify as to his reasons for believing that Super Glue was not used. I would like to keep Dr. Greer as a possible rebuttal witness to testify after Dr. Barron's testimony."

Judge Peterson turned to Dr. Greer to confirm that he would be available tomorrow. Dr. Greer agreed to be available.

On his way back from the witness stand to counsel table, Peter looked at me. No one else noticed but he winked, gently smiled, and sat down.

Wide-eyed, unable to hide her admiration for Peter Pryor, Judge Peterson waited a moment and then turned to Mr. H and asked, "Redirect, Mr. H?"

Mr. H stood, thought for a short while, and indicated he had only one question for Dr. Greer. He asked, "Do you believe that at least some significant portion of the brain injury may have been caused by the posterior retraction of the brain during the operations?"

Dr. Greer reported that was indeed his opinion.

Mr. H indicated he had no further questions for Dr. Greer, and Dr. Greer stepped down from the witness stand.

Judge Peterson turned to Peter and Mr. H and said, "I believe we have accomplished what we set out to do this afternoon. Let's adjourn for the day. The jury is dismissed for the day. Let's reconvene at 9:00 a.m. tomorrow morning."

The defense team met briefly in the courtroom, then quickly went home to prepare for the defense arguments and the rebuttal of Dr. Greer.

Defense Case

The day of the defense case is at hand. I met Peter at the nearby White Spot where he was comfortably surrounded by the hum of the people who frequent the White Spot at night. I sat across from him, marveling at his ability to focus with the sounds of silverware clanking as the waitresses seated customers, as well as the sounds from the people recovering from their late nightlife. Sharp, abrupt bursts of laughter punctuated the white noise hum. It startled me, but Peter didn't seem distracted. I sat back in my chair as he looked up from his notes. Peter said he was cautiously optimistic about our chances.

Again, things have gone well with the change in testimony by Dr. Greer late last week and then Peter's cross-examination of Dr. Greer yesterday. However, Peter emphasized that, while we challenged their witnesses during the Plaintiffs' case, they could equally challenge our witnesses during the defense case.

His strategy is to be very judicious in his choice of witnesses. Indeed, he has chosen to utilize only Dr. W to express his opinion that my operation fell within standards of care, Dr. Barron to confirm that Super Glue was not used, and Dr. Mason for her testimony about meningitis, and for her experience of unexpectedly finding Sheran R in extremis, and the measures that took place after that. I agreed with him. It was still unsettling to not be the decision-maker. It was time to go. Anxiety began its slow creep into my chest. We gathered our notepads and briefcases. As we walked out the door of the White Spot, I was hoping this was the last time I would smell the mix of coffee, eggs, bacon, and cigarette smoke.

We walked up the steps of the courthouse, entered the courthouse door, walked through the metal detector and down the hallway, and again entered Courtroom 9.

Mr. H, Ms. Kudla, and Mr. Fitzgerald, as well as Frick and Frack, were already present at the Plaintiffs' table. Notably, Mr. Schuster, who played such a prominent role during the Plaintiffs' case, was not present.

Peter and I joined Scott, Mary, and Sam at the defense table. Kathy and Fran again took their place behind the defense team. I nodded to Kathy. I don't want to think about what this is doing to her. I have to focus.

The Bailiff and then Judge Peterson entered the courtroom. We all stood and then sat at the Bailiff's direction. The jury was brought in and seated. She paused until all was quiet and said, "Today is the day for the Defense to present their witnesses, and for the Plaintiffs to ask questions of these witnesses from their perspective."

Judge Peterson turned to Peter and asked, "Are your witnesses present and prepared to testify?"

Peter answered that yes, they were and said, "I would like to call Dr. Susan Mason." Dr. Mason came up to the stand, was sworn in, and sat down. Peter asked about her field of expertise, and Dr. Mason indicated that she is an internist with specialty training in infectious disease. Peter then asked about her training. Dr. Mason indicated that she went to medical school at Tufts University School of Medicine, graduating in 1979, had an internship at the University of Colorado Medical Center from 1979-1980 and a residency from 1980-1982. Peter then said that be had only two questions for Dr. Mason.

First, he said, "The record indicates that the CSF lab values indicated to you that, as early as June 28, 1986, Mrs. R had findings consistent with meningitis." He asked, "Is it your opinion that, as of that date and thereafter, she did indeed have meningitis?"

Dr. Mason said, "Yes, that is my opinion."

Peter added, "As you have become aware, Dr. Greer testified that, in his opinion, Mrs. R did not have meningitis based on the absence of positive cultures for meningitis. How would you explain the lack of positive cultures?"

Dr. Mason stated that it is her experience and training that patients who have the clinical signs of meningitis, and have all lab values consistent with meningitis, but who were on therapeutic doses of antibiotics prior to the testing, will frequently have a negative CSF culture, presumably because of the antibiotics.

Peter then said, "My second question involves your experience finding Mrs. R on the morning of July 4, 1986. The record indicates you entered the room of Sheran R while making standard rounds, found her to be much less responsive than previously reported and close to having a cardiac arrest, recognized what had occurred, and the chest X-ray was read, which confirmed the presence of a tension pneumothorax. Is that a correct summation of your experience?"

Dr. Mason answered, "Yes, Sir. That is correct."

"Is it your opinion that her condition that morning represented a dramatic change, in contrast to her condition on July 3, 1986?"

"That is correct; that is my opinion."

Mr. Prior then said, "Dr. Mason, those are the only questions I have for you."

Judge Peterson turned to Mr. H and asked if he was ready for cross-examination. Mr. H indicated that he was ready and came to the lectern. He turned to Dr. Mason and asked, "Dr. Mason, you indicated this morning that it was your opinion that the patient had meningitis at least as early as June 28, 1986, and that Mrs. R had findings consistent with meningitis. Is it your opinion still that, as of that date and thereafter, she did indeed have meningitis?"

Dr. Mason said, "Yes, that is my opinion."

"And you understand that Dr. Melvin Greer, a noted professor at the University of Florida, disagrees with your opinion, based on the lack of a positive culture?"

"I understand that was his opinion, but I have to disagree with his opinion."

Mr. H insisted she again report the reason she disagreed with Dr. Greer. She repeated her previous reasoning. Mr H then said, "Okay, we heard that you entered Sheran R's room while making routine rounds early in the morning of July 4, 1986, and unexpectedly found her nearly or completely unresponsive, with no palpable blood pressure. Is that your testimony?"

Dr. Mason indicated that it was. Mr. H asked, "Would you agree that, basically, the patient was then in an extremely dangerous condition from which she likely would have died had she not been promptly treated?"

Dr. Mason answered, "That would be my opinion."

Mr. H then asked, "Indeed, is it not true that it was you that initiated the review of the X-ray and the treatment of the pneumothorax which saved Sheran R's life?" Dr. Mason confirmed that was probably true.

Mr. H. then asked, "Given all of the above, would it not be your opinion that the untreated pneumothorax caused the stroke from which Mrs. R never fully recovered and therefore would be considered the cause, or at least a main cause, of her current condition?"

Dr. Mason paused for a moment and then answered, "You have to understand that I was not her primary physician, but mainly a specialist on her case involved with the treatment of the meningitis. That being said, while clearly the untreated pneumothorax could not have been good for her and may well have contributed to her ultimate condition, I am not in a position where I can render an opinion as to whether or not the untreated pneumothorax was the cause, or even a primary cause, of her ultimate condition."

Mr. H thanked Dr. Mason for her candor and indicated he had no further questions for her.

Judge Peterson turned to Peter and asked if there were any questions raised by Mr. H's cross-examination for redirect. Peter indicated he had no further questions, and Dr. Mason stepped down from the witness stand. Judge Peterson then indicated that she would like to have a short 15-minute break and left the courtroom.

After the short break, Judge Peterson returned to the courtroom and asked Peter, "Mr. Pryor, is your next witness ready for testimony?"

Peter said, "Yes, Your Honor, he is. I would like to call Dr. James Barron."

Dr. Barron was sworn in and confirmed that he was an otolaryngologist. Peter then asked about his training. Dr. Barron reported that he went to medical school at the University of Colorado Medical School, graduating in 1974, had an internship at the University of Colorado Medical

School from 1974 to 1975, and had a residency in otolaryngology at the University of Colorado Medical School from 1975 to 1978. Peter then indicated that he would address with him only the operation performed on Sheran R at St. Anthony Hospital on June 25, 1986, and the possible use of Super Glue during that operation.

Peter said, "The records indicate that you assisted Dr. Ogsbury on that operation. Is that correct?"

Dr. Barron answered, "Yes, Sir, that is correct."

Peter then indicated that the records showed that Dr. Barron was asked to assist because the original operation in Wyoming, an ethmoidectomy, was performed by an otolaryngologist. That operation was complicated by a spinal fluid leak which persisted, and for which she was sent to St. Anthony for a presumed repair. Dr. Barron confirmed this information.

Peter then indicated that it was his understanding that Dr. Barron was asked to assist because the perspective of an otolaryngologist might be useful during and following the operation. "Is that correct?"

"Yes, Sir, that is correct."

Peter then said, "Dr. Barron, my question then, is very simple. Was Super Glue, which was present on the operative table, utilized during that operation?"

"No, Sir, it was not used during that operation."

"And why was that?"

"Dr. Ogsbury indicated that since a serious complication had occurred from the ethmoidectomy, a future lawsuit was likely, and the use of any nonstandard treatment would likely be implicated in that lawsuit. Therefore, after initially considering its use because of the twenty to thirty percent reported failure rate with the standard operation for the repair of a CSF leak, but since the use of Super Glue was not FDA-approved for use during the repair of a CSF leak, Dr. Ogsbury decided that it would be unwise to use Super Glue during the operation from a medical-legal perspective. A standard surgical adhesive, and not Super Glue, was used during the operation."

"Did you agree with that decision?"

"Obviously, the decision was for Dr. Ogsbury to make, but I certainly understood his perspective."

"So therefore, you are testifying that you are certain that Super Glue was not utilized during the intracranial CSF repair on June 25, 1986?"

"That is correct, Sir. Super Glue was absolutely not used during that operation."

"By the way, has Dr. Ogsbury subsequently made any mention of that decision? "

"Yes, Sir, he has."

"And what was that mention?"

"Dr. Ogsbury subsequently indicated that he was almost sorry that he had not used Super Glue during that operation—that he chose to follow a medical-legal perspective rather than a pure medical perspective. He believes that its use during the first operation might likely have led to a successful result not requiring the second operation and all of the problems that occurred thereafter."

Peter then said, "Dr. Barron, thank you for your very important testimony. Those are my only questions."

Mr. H. then went back to the lectern and said, "Dr. Barron, I have several issues to discuss with you. First, I noticed that you and Dr. Ogsbury trained at the University of Colorado Medical Center at the same time. I have learned that you shared an office space with him. I gather you have worked with him frequently, and obviously he asked you to assist him on this case.

Clearly, you are colleagues. But my question is, are you also friends?"

Dr. Barron responded, "You are correct that Dr. Ogsbury and I trained together and have worked together for many years. I have great respect for Dr. Ogsbury, and I would hope he has the same for me. With regard to friendship, I do not think that we have socialized together other than perhaps during holiday festivities at the hospital, but even with that, I would consider him a friend."

Mr. H answered, "Thank you for that. Next, and more importantly, you indicated this morning that you are completely sure that Super Glue was not used in the operation of June 25, 1986? Given that the nurse at the operating room table on the day of the surgery testified that it was her opinion that Super Glue was used during the operation, how can you be completely sure that Super Glue was not used during the operation?"

Dr. Barron answered, "There are two reasons. First, before the operation, Dr. Ogsbury and I discussed the fact that he had decided not to use Super Glue, and I would have been most surprised had he asked for it. Indeed, I likely would have challenged him as to the reason for his change in plans. Second, Dr. Ogsbury and I were both in close proximity while working under the microscope. Had Super Glue been used, I would have both heard a request to the nurse for the Super Glue and would have witnessed the measures that one would take when using Super Glue in that location, such as making the field entirely dry, and walling off the area of its use from the spinal fluid and brain. Neither occurred. Dr. Ogsbury asked for the standard surgical adhesive which is different from Super Glue, and the techniques while using standard adhesives are obviously somewhat different than when using Super Glue.

Mr. H then said, "Okay, lastly, I am interested in your comment that Dr. Ogsbury bad subsequently indicated that he was, if I may, almost sorry that he had not chosen to use Super Glue. What did he mean by that?"

Dr. Barron explained, "Dr. Ogsbury initially planned on using Super Glue, as it is an excellent tissue adhesive, but then, understanding that there was no literature supporting its use in this operation and therefore no knowledge of what might happen if even the smallest amount entered the CSF, he decided he should stay with the tried-and-true standard surgical adhesive which, unfortunately, failed to adhere to the tissue and was removed thereafter. There was always the slight worry in his mind that the medical-legal aspect of the situation may have influenced his decision, and had Super Glue actually been used, perhaps it would have been successful in maintaining a good closure. Obviously, we will never know that answer, but it has been a bother for him."

Mr. H then asked, "And what do you, Dr. Barron, think of that decision? Was that decision appropriate in your mind?"

"Again, as I said before, I was not the operating surgeon, and the decision was for him to make, but I can assure you that being cautious and avoiding the use of procedures or materials that are not supported in the literature cannot be considered a bad thing. So, I indeed continue to support that decision."

Mr. H thanked Dr. Barron and returned to the Plaintiffs' table.

Judge Peterson turned to Peter, and asked if there were any issues for redirect that were raised by the cross-examination. Peter answered that he had two further questions he needed to address to Dr. Barron, and Judge Peterson agreed that he could do so.

Peter said, "Dr. Barron, you agreed with Mr. H that you have worked with Dr. Ogsbury for many years, there is mutual respect between you two, and perhaps, to a degree, you are also friends. Has that situation in any way colored your testimony?"

Dr. Barron answered, "Of course not."

Peter then asked, "So it remains your testimony that you are sure that Super Glue was not used during the operation of June 25, 1986?"

Dr. Barron answered, "It remains my testimony that I am absolutely sure that Super Glue was not used during the operation of June 25, 1986."

Peter turned to Judge Peterson, and reported he had no further questions and Dr. Barron stepped down from the witness stand. Judge Peterson then paused and said that this would be a good time to take a one-hour break for lunch, to let each attorney prepare for further possible witnesses in the afternoon.

During the break, we left the courtroom and went to a local cafe for a small lunch.

Peter was upbeat, stating that he saw very little that can be challenged by the Plaintiffs' team. He also said that, as planned, he intended to call only one more witness, Dr. W, who was one of the three neurosurgical experts supportive of my care. I was surprisingly relieved to witness Peter's upbeat mood. I felt a little lighter and optimistic but still felt the creep of tightness in my chest. I couldn't fully trust to being optimistic. I don't know how to prepare for the worst. I can't describe these feelings. All I know is I wish them on no one.

We returned to the courthouse, going through my transition point of security and metal detector. Once again, I was leaving this world to the surreal world of the courtroom. We took our seats at the defense table. Our demeanor shifted to "courtroom demeanor." Our light conversation ended. We were now back to serious work. Soon thereafter, the Bailiff and Judge Peterson returned as well.

Judge Peterson turned to Peter and asked if the next witness was ready for testimony. Peter confirmed that the next witness was ready and called Dr. W to the witness stand. The afternoon begins and Peter is visibly prepared to be a warrior. I get the sense that he respects and honors this transformation from the world we all know to the courtroom. My trust in him surges through my body. I am not a victim, yet here I have no voice. I have Peter.

My thoughts return to Dr. W. I have known Dr. W for years, and he is certainly an immensely respected neurosurgeon in the Denver region. Can I anticipate his views to confirm our working relationship as professional only, as I have thought over the years? Has he seen our interactions as something more than cordial and mutually respectful?

I'm not particularly religious, but I said a prayer, then sat back anxiously to watch the afternoon unfold. Dr. W was sworn in, and Peter first asked him about his training. Dr. W indicated that he attended medical school at the University of Tennessee College of Medicine, graduating in 1963; had an internship in general surgery at Methodist University Hospital in Memphis, Tennessee, from 1966 to 1967; and underwent neurosurgery training at the University of Michigan University Hospital, Ann Arbor, Michigan, from 1967 to 1971. Peter then immediately addressed the issue of possible bias.

He asked, "Do you know Dr. Ogsbury?"

Dr. W said he did.

"Have you ever worked with Dr. Ogsbury?"

Dr. W reported that he had not.

"And why is that?"

"Because we work with different groups in different parts of the city. There would be no opportunity for us to work together."

"Have you ever socialized with Dr. Ogsbury?"

Dr. W indicated that he had not socialized with me at any point.

Peter then pointedly asked, "Would you consider Dr. Ogsbury a friend, or have some sort of personal relationship with him?"

Dr. W strongly indicated that we are not friends, but simply neurosurgical colleagues in the same town. Peter then asked, "Well, how do you know him then?"

Dr. W confirmed that we had worked together as leaders in the Colorado Neurosurgery Society, "But that has been our sole interaction."

"So, you can be sure that you have no bias one way or other regarding Dr. Ogsbury."

Dr. W confirmed, "That is absolutely the truth."

Peter then indicated that he would ask questions of Dr. W only about the operation of June 25, 1986. He asked, "Have you read the operative report regarding that operation?"

Dr. W reported that he had carefully reviewed the operative report.

"Could you summarize your interpretation of the operation as it was performed by Dr. Ogsbury?"

"Certainly. Dr. Ogsbury performed a standard, right-sided craniotomy, gently retracted the brain posteriorly and to the side, and the exposure revealed a 4- to 5-millimeter hole leading into the location of the ethmoid sinus."

Peter asked, "What happened next?"

"Dr. Ogsbury took a small piece of muscle and fascia from the right side of the scalp, placed the muscle flap over the small hole, muscle side down, and gently pushed some of the muscle into the hole. He then attempted to increase the chances of the muscle flap staying in place by using a standard issue adhesive."

Peter asked, "Why did he do that?"

Dr. W answered, "We all know that this operation, as it has been performed, has a significant failure rate, presumably caused by slippage of the muscle flap, and I would assume he was attempting keep the muscle flap in place by using the adhesive."

"Did that work?"

"No. Dr. Ogsbury evidently found that the adhesive would not adhere to the tissues, and therefore removed the adhesive."

"And what did he do next?"

"He laid the brain down on top of the muscle flap, which hopefully would assist in keeping the muscle flap in place, particularly with the patient in the supine position."

Peter then indicated, "My question, then, is whether or not you consider the procedure performed by Dr. Ogsbury to be within the standard of care."

Dr. W indicated that, "It is my opinion that, not only was the operation, as he performed it, within standard of care, but that was the standard procedure utilized at that point, was how he was trained to perform the procedure, and indeed is the way I perform the procedure myself."

Peter then asked, "Why did Dr. Ogsbury, and why do you, not suture the muscle flap to keep it in?"

Dr. W reported that in that area, the dura is plastered up against the bone and is very thin, making it essentially impossible, in his opinion, to place a stitch even at the most superficial end of the muscle flap.

"As I am sure you have subsequently learned, Dr. Ogsbury considered using Super Glue which then was in some limited use as a tissue adhesive but, given the nature of the case, elected to proceed with the use of the standard surgical adhesive. What do you think of the idea of using Super Glue?"

"Now we know more about the use of Super Glue, but at that point I don't believe it was ever being used in that location."

"Have you ever used Super Glue in that location?"

"I have not, but I am sure, by now, a neurosurgeon has tried to use that material but, unfortunately, there is no literature about that."

Peter asked, "In summary, is it your opinion that the procedure performed by Dr. Ogsbury fell well within the standard of care as of the time with that operation, and to not use Super Glue was reasonable, as well?"

Dr. W responded, "It is my strong opinion, for the reasons I have already given, that the procedure performed by Dr. Ogsbury on June 25, 1986, fell well within the standard of care in neurosurgery. Indeed, it was the standard procedure of that date. Also, given the known failure rate, to at least consider other options such as the use of Super Glue, was reasonable, but given that there was no history of its use in the literature, I would agree that it was a medically wise decision not to use Super Glue."

Peter indicated that he had no further questions for this witness.

Mr. H resumed his position at the lectern and indicated that he would like to first address the issue of possible bias.

He asked, "You and Dr. Ogsbury are both neurosurgeons in the Denver area, is that not true?"

Dr. W indicated that was indeed true.

"Have you and Dr. Ogsbury ever performed any surgery or any treatment together?"

"We have not."

"How is that the case?"

"Dr. Ogsbury works in hospitals on the west side of town, and I work in hospitals downtown. To the best of my knowledge, I have only been in one of the west side hospitals on one occasion, when I performed a second opinion for a patient of a different neurosurgeon, a patient who was not a patient of Dr. Ogsbury. Otherwise, to the best of my knowledge, I have not been in his hospitals, nor has he been in my hospitals."

"Next, have you had any social interactions, for example, dinners or other social occasions, with Dr. Ogsbury?"

"As I said, my only interaction with Dr. Ogsbury has been at the Colorado Neurosurgery Society meetings which, of course, did involve dinners, but most of which were strictly scientific or business meetings. Occasionally, the Christmas meeting was somewhat social but it was scientific with a speaker. Dr. Ogsbury and I were both past presidents of the Colorado Neurosurgery Society, and we certainly interacted on neurosurgical matters during those meetings. Otherwise, we have had no interactions."

"So, you can say, without equivocation, that you were neither a neurosurgical associate (that is partner) or friend of Dr. Ogsbury?"

"I can say that, without equivocation."

"Next, I would like to address your role in this case. Were you asked to review the case and by whom?'

"I was indeed asked to review the case, and the request came from Mr. Pryor."

"And what questions were you asked to address?"

"I was asked to address the quality of the decision-making regarding, and particularly the performance during, the operation of June 25, 1986."

"Were there any statements or questions which you feel might have been leading in nature?"

"No, I was asked simply to address the issue of standard of care regarding the decision to perform the operation, and the performance of the operation itself—nothing more, nothing less."

"And it was your opinion at the time of your initial review, and remains your opinion, that Dr. Ogsbury's decision to perform the operation, the type of operation he chose to perform, that is intracranial versus through the ethmoid, and actually the performance of the operation, fell within the standard of care for a neurosurgeon for that operation as of that date?"

"It is my opinion that his decision, his choice to perform an intracranial repair of the post-ethmoidectomy CSF leak, and the performance of the operation, fell well within the standard of care for a neurosurgeon. Indeed, the type of operation that was chosen, and manner in which the operation was performed, were exactly the way I was trained and perform the operation myself."

"So, you don't attempt to suture the graft in to keep it from slipping?"

"No, I do not. It is simply not feasible to suture the graft deep within the intracranial cavity, and the only way one could suture a graft would be to place a large graft and suture it at a more superficial location. I know of no one who does that."

"What about the use of Super Glue which, as you know, has been an issue in this trial?"

"Because, as I'm sure has been testified, there is a substantial, perhaps as much as thirty percent, at least, failure rate with the standard operation, the neurosurgery community, in that circumstance, is always looking for different methods to improve the result. However, I think most neurosurgeons are quite uneasy with using Super Glue in a location for which contamination of the CSF could occur with unknown consequences. Therefore, I do not use Super Glue in this location."

Mr. H concluded, "Finally, you were afforded the entire hospital chart, were you not?"

"I read the entire hospital record."

"Did you read the report of the subsequent operation which was performed by Dr. Ogsbury and Dr. Krauth, the operation that successfully treated the CSF leak, but was followed by a tension pneumothorax following an attempted CVP placement?"

"Yes indeed, I read the report of that operation."

"What did you think of that particular operation, that is, was it not really just a subtle deviation of the original operation, but better performed?"

"My feeling was that an operation involving enlarging the already present hole, and packing the entire ethmoid sinus from above was an interesting innovation, certainly not one that I had ever performed, or even read about. It is an operation that Dr. Krauth, as a military surgeon, may have learned in the treatment of military injuries. In my opinion, its use was totally appropriate when the standard operation had failed, as, again, it sometimes does, but I know of no other surgeon that performs that operation, that is the filling of the ethmoid from above, particularly as a primary treatment. Therefore, it remains my opinion that the operation performed on June 25, 1989, was appropriately chosen, and appropriately performed."

Mr. H then said, "Even so, would you not agree that other neurosurgeons might have a different opinion about that?"

Dr. W answered, "I would agree other opinions are at least possible."

Mr. H then indicated that he had no further questions. Judge Peterson turned back to Peter, and asked, any further questions for redirect?"

Peter answered, "I have just one question in response to Mr. H's last question."

Judge Peterson suggested he proceed.

Peter then asked Dr. W, "Other than what you called the standard procedure as performed by Dr. Ogsbury, what might be alternative procedures that would be possible?"

Dr. W smiled and answered, "First, of course, would be the closure from below through the ethmoid sinus, as advocated primarily by some otolaryngologists, but rarely by neurosurgeons. Another possibility would be an attempt to place sutures to stabilize the graft but, as I said, attempting to place sutures deep in this hole is very difficult because of the thin dura up against the bone. Finally, of course, would be the unusual procedure, possibly learned in the military by Dr. Krauth. Otherwise, I know of no other procedure advocated by neurosurgeons in this circumstance."

Peter indicated he had no further questions for redirect, and as Dr. W exited the stand, my muscles released the tight contractions I hadn't been aware of. Dr. W did experience our relationship as I had. Relief washes over me. I exhale.

Judge Peterson asked Peter if he had any further witnesses, and Peter stated that he had no further new witnesses to call. However, as he mentioned to her at the end of the cross-examination of Dr. Melvin Greer, he now wished to call Dr. Greer back to the stand as a rebuttal witness. Dr. Greer was called to the stand and sworn in again.

Peter looked at his notes, turned to Dr. Greer, and said, "Dr. Greer, as you remember, you testified yesterday that it was your opinion that Super

Glue was utilized in the first operation. Your opinion was based primarily on the deposition testimony of Nurse B who, as you said, had the equipment and medications for the operation on her operating room stand, although you admitted that you did not know whether Nurse B had actually witnessed the operation through the operating microscope. As you know, since your testimony, Dr. Barron has testified that it remains his opinion that Super Glue was definitely not used in that operation for a number of reasons, which he discussed with the jury this morning. You have been given a copy of his testimony, and my question for you is, Dr. Greer, after reading Dr. Barron's testimony this morning listing his reasons that he is convinced that Super Glue was not used in the first operation and knowing that Dr. Ogsbury previously testified in his deposition that Super Glue was not used in the first operation, do you continue to be of the opinion, to a reasonable degree of medical probability, that Super Glue was used in the first operation and was the primary cause of Mrs. R's tragic brain damage?"

Dr. Greer paused for a long lime, and finally replied, "Based on Dr. Barron's compelling testimony, to be honest, I must admit that I can no longer be sure that Super Glue was used in the first operation, to a reasonable degree of medical probability."

Peter concluded by asking, "Then you must no longer be convinced, to a reasonable degree of medical probability, that Super Glue was the primary cause of Mrs. R's severe brain injury?"

Dr. Greer answered, "I guess that would be correct."

"That is, yes?"

"That is yes."

Peter turned to Dr. Greer and rather quietly said, "Thank you very much, Dr. Greer, for your honesty and integrity." He turned to Judge Peterson and said, "I have no further questions for this witness."

Judge Peterson then said, "I have decided that we will adjourn until tomorrow when we will hear the closing arguments from the Plaintiffs and defense attorneys. The court is now adjourned for today."

Peter, Scott, Mary, Sam, and I hung around the court to discuss the day's activities. Peter indicated he was very satisfied with the way things had transpired today. He felt that Drs. Mason, Barron, and W had made their points strongly and convincingly and that their statements and opinions were not significantly challenged by Mr. H. This is not surprising, as Peter had already predicted there was little to challenge. Peter did indicate that his closing summary will be interesting to develop, given that the opinion regarding the essential issue of the case, that is, what primarily caused the severe brain injury to Sheran R has progressively changed during the case. With a smile, Peter listed some of the issues that he will have to address, many of those raised by Dr. Smith. For example, there was initially criticism by Dr. Smith of the choice to perform the intracranial closure, rather than an extracranial closure. Dr. Smith also indicated that the need for two operations was caused by an incompetent first operation.

Finally, Dr. Smith also raised the issue of the effect of what he felt was excessive surgical retraction on the brain during the operation(s), particularly the second operation. There was also a question by other witnesses as to whether or not meningitis was present, and, if so, it's a possible cause of part of the brain damage.

In addition, the Plaintiffs' witnesses suggested that the use of, or even the consideration of the use of Super Glue during the first operation, was negligent. Dr. Melvin Greer, initially in his cross-examination, was of the opinion that Super Glue was used in the first operation and, rather than any other potential cause that bad been discussed, was the primary cause of the majority of the severe brain damage. However, during his rebuttal testimony, after reading Dr. Barron's convincing reasons for confirming that Super Glue was not used in the first operation, Dr. Greer admitted he was no longer convinced that Super Glue was used in the first operation and therefore that Super Glue was a significant cause of the brain injury. Indeed, Dr. Greer revealed that he was no longer even sure of the exact cause of the brain injury.

Finally, a major issue was made of my supposed approval to the nurses for the placement of the CVP line. Interestingly, the effect of the pneumothorax and near cardiac arrest following the placement of the CVP line seemed to have been minimized by all of the Plaintiffs' witnesses, including Dr. Greer, but the fact that the physicians involved in the placement of the CVP line had already settled with the Plaintiffs may have played a role as well. Given all of these factors, Peter indicated that it will actually be challenging to predict what Mr. H will be able to say and to which he will need to respond. In addition, Peter reported he and Fran have been carefully following the jury. They feel that a number of the jurors, particularly Mr. Saline, who Fran thinks will be the leader of the jury, seem to have gotten beyond the simple presence of the horror of the injury to Mrs. R and have carefully listened to the testimony. The difficulty will be in maintaining a compassionate tone in deference to Mrs. R, while pointing out the obvious inconsistencies in the Plaintiffs' case.

My main concern is whether or not this jury, which includes a complete lack of professionals, will be able to understand the complex medical issues involved in this case. Peter indicated that, in his opinion, the majority of this jury already understands the basic issues, which he will then have to carefully, but not overly, emphasize. All in all, we left the courtroom still feeling cautiously optimistic about the outcome. I leave with my thoughts again spinning. At home, I go straight to my office, close the door, and rest my head with my spinning thoughts in my trained, surgical hands. I hurt, and I don't understand. I look at my hands with wonder. How can I be in this morass? Tomorrow will come.

Plaintiffs' Closing Arguments

The morning dawned on what was going to be the final day of the actual trial. It has been nearly two years since I first received the stinging accusation of malpractice. Now with the first trial, forestalled by the Plaintiffs' caused mistrial, and this, the second trial, approaching its conclusion, I feel like a marathon runner who finally sees the finish line. Seeing the finish line and crossing it are two different animals. Ask marathon runners, running on fumes in their tanks. I am feeling some relief knowing that the trial is soon to be over. What will it be like to not be in this reality? I want to go home. I want to go back to my life. I want this nightmare to be over.

As much as I understand that the Plaintiffs' witnesses were bought and paid for, it has remained difficult for me to hear the repeated criticisms of my care.

Each time, it stung like the first time. Why can't I be numb to the continued attacks? I cannot help but be anxious, both because I understand that one can never fully predict a jury's verdict, no matter how good or bad things seem to be going, but also I have come to worry that this trial, no matter the outcome, will forever change what medicine has meant to me over all these years. This verdict, my identity, my life as a neurosurgeon is in the balance. I'm waiting for the impending tsunami. Anxiety and fear are familiar bedfellows these days. In the operating room, no matter the crisis, I had the confidence I could respond as the best of the best. I was in control and confident I could succeed.

With all of these thoughts swimming in my head, Kathy and I drove in silence to the courthouse.

I did my best to feign a cheerful outlook with Peter when I met him at the White Spot, where he was hovering over his closing argument. He again mentioned he would have to be agile, because he was not sure exactly what the Plaintiffs' attorney was going to say in his closing argument.

This feigned cheerful outlook I learned from my patients before surgery. They were scared, yet mustered the courage to communicate their hope, faith, and belief in me. They were willing to put their lives in my hands. They instinctively knew, and now I instinctively know. Putting your life in the hands of another requires a grand leap of faith. It's important to communicate that to the one that holds your life in balance. Peter had become my trusted brother and protector, my brother-in-arms. I have to show I have complete confidence in him to be ready for any approach the Plaintiffs' attorney might try. His broad smile and confident demeanor reassure me. I trust him, and for a moment I feel strangely peaceful.

We arrived at Courtroom 9 and found that Mr. H, Mr. Schuster, and Mr. Fitzgerald, plus Frick and Frack, were all huddled around the Plaintiffs' table. They were evidently completing their strategy for the Plaintiffs' closing arguments. Ms. Kudla was curiously absent.

For the Defense, as usual, Peter, Scott, Mary, Sam and I all sat down at the defense table. Kathy and Fran were in the gallery. Fran chose to be available, such that she might be able to read the jury responses to the Plaintiffs' attorney closing argument, in the event Peter needed to modify his arguments. The Bailiff, and then Judge Peterson, entered the courtroom, and called the jury back to the jury box. Judge Peterson turned to the jury and indicated that today was the day for closing arguments from both parties. The arguments again were not evidence, but what they believed the evidence showed.

She turned to Mr. H and said, "Closing arguments for the Plaintiffs?" Chills ran through my body. I braced myself for now, for the duration of this day. Judge Peterson fired the starting shot. It's on. I'm filled with hope and dread.

Mr. H stood. The courtroom was silent. All eyes were upon him. His brow was furled, and he took a deep breath.

He took one last look at his notes, looked up, and said, "May it please the Court, Mr. and Mrs. R, and ladies and gentlemen of the jury? As I said before, this case is about a tragedy to Mrs. R, who was a vibrant, active woman, loving wife, and mother of three, who entered St. Anthony Hospital in June 1986 in excellent health, and in September 1986, she left the hospital essentially comatose, unable to walk, unable to talk, paralyzed, in a more or less vegetative state with extreme brain damage. That was a terrible tragedy." Mr. H paused. "But the real tragedy is that it should not have happened. How do we know this should not have happened? Throughout this trial, we have shown you that both Dr. Ogsbury's and Dr. Krauth's lack of reasonable medical care caused Mrs. R's brain damage in June of 1986 that will last the rest of her life. Through the testimony of our witnesses, we have proved by a preponderance of the evidence that these men caused this tragedy."

When Mr. H said, "These men," he raised his hand and pointed to me. [It was all I could do to remain composed. I have never had to muster this much effort over my feelings of outrage.]

"This tragedy has involved many diverse medical issues, but I would like to respectfully submit to you that there are only two issues you need to consider. The first is whether or not Drs. Ogsbury and/or Krauth were negligent during the care of Sheran R. During her jury instructions, Judge Peterson will give you a definition of negligence in this context. She will tell you that a physician is negligent when that physician does an act that reasonably careful physicians would not do, or fails to do an act that reasonably careful physicians would do. The second is whether or not that negligence caused Mrs. R's brain injury. Judge Peterson will also read to you that causation is deemed as the existence of a causative link between the Plaintiffs' injuries and the Defendant's negligence. Then, if you believe that negligence on the part of Drs. Ogsbury and/or Krauth did occur, and further that the negligence was the main cause of the brain injury, we will ask you to render your opinion as to the financial responsibility for that negligence, based on the long-term impact on the life of Mrs. R, and the future medical and nonmedical needs for her.

"Ladies and gentlemen of the jury, we have proven to you by a preponderance of the evidence that Drs. Ogsbury and Krauth breached the standard of care they owed to Sheran R in the operating room, and in the days and months that followed. Their negligence caused her injuries. They made her the person you see here before you today. They have created long-term future medical and nonmedical needs for Sheran R. How do we know that? We know that from the testimony of our eminent witnesses.

"We know that from Dr. Frank Smith, a prominent neurosurgeon who was the Professor and Chairman of the Department of Neurosurgery at the University of Rochester for twenty years. Dr. Smith testified that a radiologist had seen no leak and that the fluid in Mrs. R's nose was a sinus reaction. What does this mean? It means that the operations these men performed may not have been necessary. He testified that, if there was a leak, nonsurgical alternatives were available, with the strong possibility that the leak would stop. He indicated that, if surgery proved to be necessary, the preferable operation was an extracranial approach, with packing of the sinus through the nose, rather than the intracranial operation. He further testified that the right-sided brain retraction during Mrs. R's first operation was excessive and below the standard of care, and that the bilateral approach at the second operation fell below the minimum standard of care.

"Dr. Smith also testified that the right-sided retraction and compression at the time of the first operation, and compression from both sides at the time of the second operation, caused Mrs. R's brain injury. With his past experience, Dr. Smith testified that he did not believe the pneumothorax contributed significantly to the brain injury." [I thought, this is astonishing because I have always believed that the pneumothorax and near cardiac arrest was the single most important factor in producing the stroke and brain injury.]

"Dr. Smith also testified that he did not believe Mrs. R had bacterial meningitis, but that even if she did have meningitis, that meningitis did not contribute to her brain damage. Thus, Dr. Smith concluded that it was his expert opinion that the actions of Drs. Ogsbury and Krauth definitely fell below the standard of care, and also that those actions caused Mrs. R's permanent brain damage.

"We know that these doctors were negligent from the nurses at St. Anthony Hospital. One nurse testified that she ran down the hall to talk to Dr. Ogsbury to find out if it was acceptable for a CVP line to be placed, and that Dr. Ogsbury stated that he didn't care. A second nurse testified that she was sure that Dr. Ogsbury used Super Glue on Mrs. R's brain during the first operation, despite Dr. Ogsbury's assertion that it was not used during that operation.

"We know that these doctors were negligent from Dr. Melvin Greer, Chairman of the Department of Neurology at the University of Florida, Gainesville. Dr. Greer testified that the bilateral strokes in the distribution of the anterior cerebral arteries occurred as the result of the surgical retraction and the use of Super Glue during the operation. He indicated that he believed Mrs. R did not have meningitis prior to her surgery of June 25, 1986, and further testified that he did not believe the pneumothorax caused any neurologic injury." [I thought, "Again astonishing."]

"We even know that from Dr. Krauth, Dr. Ogsbury's partner, Dr. Krauth himself testified that he performs the operation differently than

Dr. Ogsbury did, and, had there not been a recurrence of the leak after the first operation, there would not have been the need for a second surgery.

"Expert after expert has told us in this courtroom that both Dr. Ogsbury and Dr. Krauth fell well below the standard of care for a neurosurgeon. Their lack of care, and only this lack of care, directly caused Mrs. R's stroke.

"We learned from Dr. Lloyd Cripe, the neuropsychologist, the horrible impact that this stroke will have upon Sheran R. Because of the brain damage and loss of so-called executive functions, she can no longer work; she cannot play sports or be involved in recreation; she cannot read or understand what is happening on television; she can no longer have relations with her husband; she can no longer feel the love and joy watching her children grow up, graduate from high school, get married, and enjoy her grandchildren. It's as if, while her body is mostly still alive, her complete life has been taken from her and very likely will never return.

"Now, please allow me to talk with you for a moment about the credibility of the witnesses you heard during this trial. Judge Peterson will instruct you that it's your job to judge the credibility of each witness's testimony. What I submit to you is that the opinions Mrs. R's experts gave you from the witness stand were based solely on their extensive experience. You have also heard from the Defense's expert witnesses. One of their expert witnesses is a friend of Dr. Ogsbury, and the other had worked with him during Colorado Neurosurgery Society meetings."

[As the Plaintiffs spoke of bias, I thought, "Only I had that scalpel in my hand, Sir. Only I had that woman's life in my hands. Only I had the weight of Mrs. R's future lying before me on the operating table, and that is something you will never know. You will never, ever know. My rage boiled beneath my mask of calm.]

Mr. H paused and said, "I understand what you have heard from the witnesses, and what I have just said sounds like a bad television movie in which a patient is injured by an incompetent doctor. Unfortunately, this story is real and worse than any fiction that could be imagined. Obviously, if I were a magician, I would make the brain injury go away, and Mrs. R could resume her normal life. You, the jurors, would do the same if you could. Unfortunately, neither you nor I are magicians, and the terrible effects of the brain damage are likely to be permanent." [I thought, unfortunately, I have to agree with Mr. H's compelling conclusion.]

"None of us are magicians." What powerful words. I was pulled in by this display of emotion. Would the jury be impacted by his moving words? My throat tightens, holding back my urge to protest.

Mr. H slowly turned back to the jury and said, "Ladies and gentlemen of the jury, I understand there have been many complex medical issues brought up during this trial. However, when hearing all of the points that have been raised by our witnesses, as I said at the beginning of this trial, we believe that you, the jury, will have no choice but to come to the conclusion that, absent the negligence by Drs. Ogsbury and Krauth, Mrs. R would today be happily in her home in Riverton, Wyoming, raising her wonderful family.

"Therefore, Drs. Ogsbury and Krauth are responsible for her condition as you see her today. As you have heard, Mrs. R and her family will have extensive long-term physical and emotional needs. And while no amount of money will ever restore what has been lost, Mrs. R and her family will also have extensive long-term financial needs. We respectfully ask you to support those needs. We ask for this financial support, not to punish Dr. Ogsbury or Dr. Krauth, but rather to bring at least some degree of dignity to Mrs. R, and to her family. We thank you for your attention."

His closing arguments completed, Mr. H sat down at the table. I was struck by his words, "not to punish Drs. Ogsbury and Krauth." The only way to obtain her financial need is to punish us. I am fearful the jury won't understand. I'm terrified they will be swayed by his closing argument. My thoughts are jumbled, spinning like balls in a lottery basket. I have to focus.

Judge Peterson turned to the jury and said, "Jury members, we have now heard the Plaintiffs' summary of their case, their closing arguments. Next will come the Defendant's summary of their case. However, before the Defense begins their closing arguments, we will take a one-hour recess for a quick lunch. We will return at 1:00 p.m. and when we return, you will hear the Defense's closing arguments. Then, if there is time, I will give you the instructions for your deliberations." With that, she and the Bailiff left the courtroom.

After Mr. H completed his closing arguments, I felt a sense of ambivalence about what had just happened. Clearly, he had given an eloquent and believable recounting of the Plaintiffs' case. He cleverly mixed an accurate description of the devastation Sheran R suffered with a summary of the events of the hospitalization, mentioning only his experts' opinions, while totally ignoring the changes in these opinions that occurred under Peter's intense cross-examinations.

However, unlike his witnesses, at no time did he seem to stretch the truth as he saw it from a plaintiff point of view. Even I had to agree with much of what he said because it was true. For this, I felt a grudging admiration for his role as an advocate. More importantly, for the first time, I felt a sense of true trepidation. If I as the Defendant, admired his closing argument, I was concerned that the jury might respond to his eloquence by simply ignoring Peter's verbal destruction of the testimony of the Plaintiffs' witnesses, and find for the Plaintiffs. I am not sure exactly how Peter will address this in his closing arguments, but I have to trust him to find a way to do so. Trust does not come easily for me. My mask is becoming more challenging to maintain.

Finally, Scott, Mary, Sam, Fran, Kathy, and I left for lunch. How do I eat, walk, or move when a part of me feels dumbstruck and paralyzed? I remind myself to keep my mask firmly on, not flinch. Not surprisingly, Peter indicated that he wished to remain in the courtroom to complete his closing arguments. As I left the courtroom, I looked over my shoulder to see Peter alone in an empty and silent courtroom, hunched over a stack of papers containing my future. I am like my patients' families, sitting for hours, silently waiting, anticipating—no control, but fear and hope, wondering again will I have back the life I knew. How will I reconcile with the outcome?

Defense's Closing Arguments

Scott, Lee, Mary, Sam, Fran, Kathy, and I returned to Courtroom 9. Scott, Lee, Mary, Sam and I took our seats at the defense table, and Fran and Kathy took the seats behind the Defense. I sat quietly with no discourse. I wondered what Kathy was thinking. I glanced at Peter who was still working on his closing argument, so we did not bother him, but he seemed much more relaxed than when we left. Mr. H, Mr. Schuster, Mr. Fitzgerald, Frick and Frack entered soon thereafter and sat down at the Plaintiffs' table. I looked briefly at them and felt conflicted. Did they honestly believe Lee and I were at fault or are they simply performing their commitments? A lot goes through my mind. A plethora of questions never to be answered.

Sometime later, the Bailiff entered, followed by Judge Peterson. We stood, and then sat at her direction after the jurors had been seated. Judge Peterson turned to Peter and said, "Closing arguments for the Defense?" It was our turn, our final best shot. I was nervous and anxious, silently hoping Peter would knock it out of the park. The jurors appeared to be attentive. The decision will be in their hands at the end of Peter's closing argument.

Peter walked to the lectern and began, "May it please the Court, Mr. and Mrs. R and ladies and gentlemen of the jury. We would agree with Mr. H's statement that this is a case about the tragedy to Sheran R who entered St. Anthony Hospital in June 1986 in excellent health except for a CSF leak from an ethmoidectomy, underwent two operations at St. Anthony, and left the hospital with severe brain damage. That is where our agreement ends, ladies and gentlemen, for one simple reason."

Peter paused for what seemed like a long time. He looked every single juror in the eye while saying, "Mr. H stated that Dr. Ogsbury and Dr. Krauth were negligent in their medical care and that this negligence caused Mrs. R's brain damage. In short, that is simply not what the evidence showed. So, let's talk about that evidence.

"But first, let's talk about the credibility of the witnesses. Mr. H raised the issue of bias of witnesses and suggested that the witnesses who testified on behalf of Dr. Ogsbury and Dr. Krauth were biased because they had relationships with these neurosurgeons. Now, Judge Peterson will instruct you that sizing up the credibility of each witness is entirely up to you, the jury. You decide the weight to give each witness's testimony. In doing so, when you retire to the jury room, I would ask you to keep one question in mind: who is in a better position to tell you about the care Dr. Ogsbury and Dr. Krauth gave Mrs. R? People who have (Peter held up his hand and started ticking off a list finger by finger): 1. Never met Dr. Ogsbury? 2. Never met Dr. Krauth? 3. Are utterly unfamiliar with them as colleagues and neurosurgeons? And 4. Have only reviewed pieces of paper before appearing before you to give their testimony?

"Or physicians who (Peter held up his other hand and again began to raise each finger): 1. Physicians who knew the specific care Dr. Ogsbury and Dr. Krauth gave to Mrs. R? And 2. Were in this courtroom to testify to you about it?

"I ask you to keep these considerations in mind as you assess the credibility of the witnesses in reaching your verdicts."

Now I'm already completely enthralled by Peter's words. He was succinct, straightforward, specific. He made it so simple for the jurors to compare witnesses for each side. He made it so simple for me. I was mesmerized by his narrative. It was so clear yet delivered with eloquence.

Peter then went on, "Ladies and gentlemen of the jury, from the testimony during this trial we have come to know Sheran R as well as the horror of what happened to her and the impact the stroke will have for the rest of her life. However, while you did not hear from him through direct testimony throughout this trial, we have also come to know Dr. Jay Ogsbury." [I thought, I don't understand why he used my informal name, but it felt right.]

Peter continued, "As testimony has shown, Mrs. R was transferred to his care for the repair of a CSF leak. Thereafter, he was her primary physician and operating neurosurgeon through two operations, the development of meningitis, and the beginning of improvement, at which point it looked like she might fully recover. But then, soon thereafter, she suffered a severe stroke from a tension pneumothorax, a collapsed lung following the placement of a CVP line. You will remember that Dr. Krauth testified that, from there on, Dr. Ogsbury assumed her total care, assisted the family in many ways, and even flew to Wyoming with her and her family on the governor's plane, taking her home after her discharge from the hospital."

Peter paused and then said, "So let's take a look at that for a moment. Mrs. R was not Dr. Ogsbury's only patient. He has a full neurosurgery practice. And, of all of his patients, he took the time to personally fly her home to Wyoming to make sure she would be properly cared for."

"Peter again looked directly at the jurors and said, "I submit to you that Dr. Ogsbury performed this procedure the only way he could, consistent with his training, extensive experience, and well within the reasonable standard of care. Also, Dr. Barron testified under oath that Dr. Ogsbury did not use Super Glue, which was not approved by the FDA, during Mrs. R's first operation. Dr. Krauth testified about how angry Dr. Ogsbury was when he learned that a CVP line had been placed against his orders just as Mrs. R was beginning to improve. Dr. Ogsbury realized that the pneumothorax from the CVP line caused a near cardiac arrest, which he believes was the primary cause of Mrs. R's brain damage, and, but for the pneumothorax, Mrs. R would not have had a stroke and would not be sitting before you as you see her with brain damage today. Ladies and gentlemen, Dr. Ogsbury and Dr. Krauth did everything that they were supposed to do as competent, experienced neurosurgeons during the care of Sheran R. Tragically, she still suffered severe brain damage."

Peter paused and walked over, stood behind Lee and me, and put his hands on our shoulders. He uttered words slowly and deliberately. "Under the law, just because Mrs. R was injured, because Dr. Ogsbury and Dr. Krauth acted as competent and reasonable neurosurgeons, and the evidence showed this, does not mean they are liable for her injuries."

I was struck by this sudden, unexpected move by Peter. He was standing behind Lee and me. Throughout the closing arguments, all eyes were on Peter. At this moment, Lee and I were now sharing the spotlight with him. Now eye to eye with the jurors, I was unnerved, finally slowly exhaling as Peter moved to the center of the courtroom. [Did I blush? Was I visibly perspiring?]

Peter again paused and then began his recommendations for the jury. He said, "We are asking you, the jurors, to assess the credibility of each of the witnesses, that of the Plaintiffs as well as that of the Defendants. We understand that this is particularly difficult for this jury, in that multiple complex medical issues were addressed.

"However, your obvious attention during the trial makes me believe that you recognize the clear differences that are present here. I submit that the testimonies by the defense witnesses were direct and to the point. For example, the correct standard technique was utilized in the first operation; Super Glue was not used in either operation; and clearly Dr. Ogsbury felt that the placement of the CVP line was something that he wished done only in the most extreme of circumstances. Also, Dr. Krauth's testimony dispelled any implication that Dr. Ogsbury and Krauth were not caring physicians.

On the other hand, the curious answers from the Plaintiffs' witnesses, to questions regarding their multiple criticisms of Drs. Ogsbury and Krauth, seem at best difficult to understand. Despite the implication by Dr. Smith that the CSF leak might have stopped without surgery, the need for the surgical treatment of the CSF leak was obvious, given that she was sent to Denver only after a significant period of time had been taken in Wyoming to allow the leak to stop spontaneously. The intracranial technique used by Dr. Ogsbury makes logical sense, given that closing any leak, be it CSF from the brain or air from a tire with a hole, rarely works well when the closing is performed from the outside. The testimony that Mrs. R did not have meningitis, but if she did, it would not have impacted her condition, seems unlikely. And, particularly, the testimony that the tension pneumothorax leading to an absent blood pressure and near cardiac arrest, played no role in the development of a stroke in a critically ill patient, makes no medical sense whatsoever. These widely divergent opinions between the Plaintiff and defense witnesses expose the Plaintiffs for what they are—blatantly incorrect.

"They were not present for Mrs. R's care. They were in no way involved in Mrs. R's surgeries or aftercare. Some have not even met Sheran R. They were not in the operating room and yet profess to know about the standard of care Dr. Ogsbury and Dr. Krauth gave to Mrs. R. I submit to you, ladies and gentlemen, that the reason the Plaintiffs' experts' opinions run so far afield from the testimony of Dr. Krauth is because Dr. Krauth was there, and the Plaintiffs' experts were not."

Peter turned to the jury and concluded by saying, "I think no one would disagree with the obvious fact that Mrs. R was, and remains, a wonderful woman, full of life, who, during a series of tragic events at St. Anthony Hospital from June 24, 1986, through July 4, 1986, suffered a severe brain injury from which, unfortunately, she did not, and likely will not, recover. We realize that it is difficult to get beyond the devastation suffered by Mrs. R. However, we ask you to thoroughly look at the issues that have been extensively addressed during the testimony. When you do, you will come to the conclusion that neither Dr. Ogsbury nor Dr. Krauth were negligent in their medical care of Mrs. R, nor did either contribute significantly to the brain injury. Indeed. I believe you will conclude that Drs. Ogsbury and Krauth did everything in their power to protect her, as much as they humanly and medically could, from the tragic series of events that befell her, and you can understand what it must mean to these men that they were unable to do so. And while you saw, on the stand, the impact that this tragedy had on Dr. Krauth, I believe his words also described the effect this tragedy has had on Dr. Ogsbury, who, as a neurosurgeon, completely understands the full magnitude of what the brain injury has meant, and will mean, to Mrs. R."

Peter paused, slowly turned around toward Lee and me and gently smiled. [I thought, "Is this not unlike a father offering reassurance to his two frightened sons?" It was a fleeting moment. I relished this moment.]

Peter turned back to the jury and continued, "The law says that even though doctors follow the accepted standard of care, as these neurosurgeons did, sometimes terrible things still happen to people. Something terrible happened to Sheran R. No one is disputing that. The obvious question is what actually caused the terrible injury. Plaintiffs' witness, Dr. Melvin Greer, dismissed all other causes when he believed that Super Glue was the primary cause of the brain damage. However, once he became aware of the testimony of Dr. James Barron, who convincingly discussed his reasons for being confident that Super Glue was not used in the first operation, Dr. Greer concluded that he himself was no longer convinced that Super Glue was used in the first operation and was the cause of Mrs. R's severe brain damage. He had to admit that he saw no obvious cause for the brain damage and certainly saw no cause that could be related to Drs. Ogsbury and Krauth.

The evidence shows that Drs. Ogsbury and Krauth brought to bear every day of their decades of medical training and experience to care for Mrs. R. They weren't thinking about the law in that operating room. They weren't thinking about the accepted standard of care. They were thinking about saving her life. And when you transport that care from the operating room to the courtroom, I ask you, ladies and gentlemen, to submit your verdict in favor of Dr. James Ogsbury and Dr. Lee Krauth."

Peter paused and, once again, he looked directly at the jurors and said. "While, the actual tragedy can never be undone, it is now our sincere hope that there will not be any further victims of this horrible tragedy. Mr. and Mrs. R, Judge Peterson, and jurors, we thank you for your attention during this difficult case."

Judge Peterson turned back to Mr. H and said, "Rebuttal, Mr. H?"

Mr. H stood silently for quite some time and finally said, "No, Your Honor, thank you."

Judge Peterson then looked around and said, "I think our best course of action is to end the day here. I will call a recess, and the Court will come back in session at 9:00 a.m. tomorrow for my instructions to the jury. The

Bailiff left the courtroom with the jurors. We all stood as Judge Peterson exited the courtroom and then sat back down.

At this point, neither the Plaintiffs nor the defense team moved for quite some time, exhausted by what had just transpired. Finally, it was the defense team that first moved to exit Courtroom 9. As we were about to leave the courtroom, Peter turned back to Mr. H and the two attorneys shook hands. Thereafter, even Peter had little to say, not surprising given the emotional impact that the trial has had on each of us. His closing argument was powerful. I suspect it had drained him mentally, emotionally, and physically.

I, too, found myself to be completely drained. I was surprised by Peter's decision to introduce Lee and me as the good guys, almost heroes. My feeling is that we were simply physicians trying our best to do the right thing for a patient caught in the web of a tragic series of events. I truly do not know how the jury will respond to Peter's closing argument.

Peter and I agreed that, while we had often ridden the Washington Park circuit together following each day's events, neither of us felt like riding today. We all rather silently walked away to our cars and went home. This was it. Now a time to show up tomorrow and begin the painful wait. I am an impatient man. The remaining time I know will be interminable. Another sleepless or at least restless night awaits Kathy and me—silently, separately counting the hours until tomorrow.

Jury Instructions and Deliberations

The day of the final stage of the trial dawned bright and clear, hopefully a good omen. While driving in, I was not sure how I felt, never experiencing anything exactly like this before in my life. Good omen. What am I thinking? Has the stress of the trial, my fear, triggered some magical thinking? Maybe so. Maybe my inability to stop thinking about the trial is part of that. If I keep thinking about it, I can control the outcome. It reminded me of the childhood phrase, "Step on a crack, break your mother's back."

No, I'm not losing my mind. I'm absolutely clear this unfamiliar and terrifying trial experience has me locked in its grip. Fran pointed out during trial prep that unremitting stress can play with your thinking. Given this is the second trial, I'm beginning to understand what she meant. Today is bright and clear. I feel somewhat optimistic. I'm not going crazy. It's the first time I've looked up in weeks.

My experience with my role in the actual trial is not totally dissimilar from the feelings one experiences during a difficult brain operation. We review and re-review the surgical plan, the critical time, anticipating as many unforeseen possibilities as possible as well as plans to take care of each possibility. We always question ourselves. For us, the surgery begins days or weeks before the act of surgery. There is no room for rigidity in surgery. One must be prepared for unanticipated complications. That preparedness means remaining flexible. Training as a neurosurgeon prepares one to rely on protocol, standard procedure, and that knowledge keeps a steady hand. We are at the helm from start to finish. However, with this trial, from here on in, we have absolutely no control of the outcome, something that we neurosurgeons rarely, if ever, experience at the operating room table. Today the judge will issue her instructions, and then my life, really our lives, will be in the hands of the jury. I can do nothing, speak no words, or influence the outcome. Feeling helpless is the most excruciating feeling. All I can do is control my thoughts. It's like leaving the operating room without knowing the outcome. It's unthinkable for a surgeon. It's unthinkable for me.

We came to the court but were told by the clerk in the hall outside of Courtroom 9 that Judge Peterson had an urgent matter she needed to address, and there would be a short delay. She said we should all wait there in the hall, and she would let us know when Judge Peterson was ready to resume our case.

During our wait, Peter took the time to describe once again exactly what happened when Dr. Greer unexpectedly raised the issue of Super Glue. Peter said he immediately objected, but when Mr. H indicated that Dr Greer's testimony regarding Super Glue was simply to be with regard to findings within the spinal fluid, Judge Peterson denied the objection. However, when Dr. Greer resumed his testimony, it became completely clear that he had changed his entire theory as to the primary cause of the injury and specifically that Super Glue was the primary cause of the stroke.

Peter said he was furious and said Judge Peterson appeared angry as well, probably because she was likely embarrassed by her initial ruling. Judge Peterson then allowed Peter to address specific questions to Dr. Greer. Dr. Greer indicated that the idea had been raised about three weeks prior and discussed extensively with Mr. Schuster the day prior to his testimony. Dr. Greer admitted that he had also discussed the issue of Super Glue with Mr. H but only with regard to the CSF findings. I understood Peter's anger given his role as an attorney.

He said, "You probably know that one of the foundations of the legal system is that each side in a disputed case must make available to the other side their primary opinions and the major points that were to be made. If this were not true, the fairness of the trial would always be suspect."

Peter added that an obvious breach of this ethical standard occurred in this case and that the breach was of sufficient severity that a request for a mistrial likely would have been granted.

However, I was equally interested in the response from Judge Peterson. She was clearly personally upset, after trusting the initial explanation by Mr. H only to find out that Dr. Greer had an additional opinion in mind. It was only after extensive discussions with the attorneys that she became convinced that Mr. H himself was undermined by another member of the Plaintiffs' team, a declaration of a mistrial was not necessary, and moving forward with the trial was reasonable. I have known all along that Mr. Pryor and Mr. H are highly skilled attorneys who have each other's respect. I also realized that Judge Peterson trusted the ethical standards of each of them and was aghast when it appeared, at least initially, that one of them might be a party to an ethical breach. Then, I believe I could sense her feeling of relief when she realized that a mistral was not necessary, and apparently further, that her opinions regarding both of these attorneys were still valid. At no time did she directly verbalize her personal feelings about this series of events, though she did seem to express her anxiety through a series of rulings and statements.

Peter explained that we should understand that while judges frequently explain their rulings, rarely, ever, do they explain their internal response to a case. This is so that they can be, or at least appear to be, in control of their courtrooms and completely neutral in the cases that occur in them. Peter said. "If a judge explained his or her feelings about a situation in the courtroom, that itself could be grounds for a mistrial." What is clear to me, however, is that Judge Peterson has, herself, very high ethical standards but, in addition, a very personal response, not able to be expressed, to what is going on before her. My own personal impression was to begin to understand that judges, or at least this judge, have their own humanity, and, for once, that humanity was brought out in the courtroom for all to see.

After a short while, the clerk came out into the hall and reported that Judge Peterson was ready to proceed with the trial. Both teams entered Courtroom 9. Peter, Scott, Mary, Sam, and I took our seats at the defense table. Kathy sat behind us as did Fran although her task assisting the jury team was completed. This time the entire Plaintiffs' team, Mr. H, Ms. Kudla, Mr. Fitzgerald, and Mr. Schuster, as well as Frick and Frack, took their seats at the Plaintiffs' table. Finally, the Bailiff and then Judge Peterson entered the courtroom and took their seats.

Judge Peterson first apologized for the delay. [To me another example of her sense of propriety.]

Prior to coming to court this morning, she had met with Peter and Mr. H, and the jury instructions to be used had been determined.

After a pause, Judge Peterson turned to the jurors and said, "This morning is the time for me to give you the instructions about the trial and how you should proceed with your deliberations." She then carefully read in detail the chosen jury instructions.

After Judge Peterson had completed reading these formal jury instructions, she swore in the Bailiff and said, "The Bailiff will now escort you to the jury room to begin your deliberations." She then handed the stack of jury instructions, the law from which the jury will decide my fate, to the Bailiff who will distribute them to the jurors. The Bailiff escorted the jury to their deliberation room, and Judge Peterson left the courtroom.

Once Judge Peterson had left, the Plaintiffs' team quickly exited the courtroom. As was usual, the defense team, as well as Fran and Kathy, stayed around for a while longer. I guess Courtroom 9 had become a second home for all of us. Peter again said that he truly believed that Mr. H had not been informed about the change in opinion regarding what caused the brain injury, as testified to by Dr. Greer. Indeed, he suspected that Mr. Schuster may possibly have played a role in this, but since he could not prove it, that was not something that was relevant to pursue. Scott said he agreed.

I felt we all agreed. We then talked about the prospects from here on in. Fran indicated that she felt that, at this point, at least four of the jurors (of the eight on the panel including the two alternate jurors) had either decided, or were close to deciding, in our favor. She also noted, however, that two have not, so far, seemed to be open to our arguments, even after Dr. Greer's change of opinion during his rebuttal testimony. And while four to two seems like a good starting point, she emphasized that, in her experience, one strong-willed juror can affect the whole panel, and that one can never be sure about the outcome with a 6-person jury. She did again point out that Mr. Saline seems to be the strongest member of the jury and is reasonably likely to be chosen to be the jury foreman. He appears to be clearly in our camp. Fran again pointed that out Mr. Saline dramatically closed his notebook after Lee convincingly demonstrated the significant difference between his procedure, and the standard procedure that I performed. Hopefully, he is picked to be jury foreman, and his opinion carries significant weight in the jury room. Those points made, the six of us left the court but, before we left, Peter and I made plans to ride our bike route in Washington Park early in the afternoon. Peter is confident that the jurors will not come to a very early decision, given the complexity of the case, and that it is safe for us to ride soon after we leave the courtroom.

The good thing about riding in Washington Park is that we can complete a ride and get back to the court quickly, which obviously would be necessary if the jurors come to their decision while we are on our bikes. We both think it is important for us to be able to relieve some of the energy that has built up since we last rode. I felt a sense of relief. I had something to do. For me when riding and riding fast, my brain completely focuses, nothing else exists. I knew I had the opportunity for my mind to turn off from the trial, a much-needed break. I was exhausted from my thoughts, but my body felt like a racehorse in the starting gate too long—restless, fidgety, irritable, and ready to snap at anyone. I needed to ride.

After driving home with Kathy, Peter and I met at Washington Park at about 1:00 p.m. Peter brought his beautiful white Kestrel carbon bike, and I brought out my Tom Kellogg-built titanium bike, a wonderful machine that I bought used from the Denver Spoke after the Spoke obtained that bike for Robert Forney to ride in the Race Across America. The sun was bright with deep azure-blue skies. I realized I hadn't looked up until this morning when I had a moment of hopefulness. I reminded myself I needed to look up more often.

Peter and I rode repeatedly around Washington Park at speeds that probably were not legal, but I did notice there were some riders, much younger than us, occasionally passing us on the circuit, so we did not get into trouble. All I needed now was a bike fine for speeding with the trial not yet complete. Ludicrous thoughts. I'm now silently laughing at my thoughts. I'm not crazy, just intensely and chronically stressed. The wind on my face from our speed felt like a salve for my mind. The pain in my calves and thighs were a familiar welcome feeling, pain unlike the pain of the trial. I was getting back into my body. I realized how tightly I was gripping the handlebars. Releasing my grip to a soft, gentle grip felt familiar, like holding a surgical tool. After many loops, finally we reached our limit. The ride was exhilarating. I was smiling and felt a surge of energy I hadn't felt in a long time. Peter was smiling too. We were dripping wet with sweat, and it felt so good. I looked around for a moment, noticing the people walking and jogging in the park, as well as the stately homes surrounding the park. This is a beautiful place to heal. The people and the homes are innocent as to what I'm feeling. That's okay. They don't realize they are silent witnesses for me. A squirrel darted across the path. I looked north across the park and saw the geese and ducks leisurely floating and feeding on the shimmering lake. I thought to myself. This is the healing of nature Fran spoke about. She would say, Jay, you have been given knowledge from animals. The squirrel is like your monkey mind, dashing from place to place, chattering incessantly, directionless with no particular destination, full of anxious behavior. The water birds are calm and peaceful, hardly disturbing their water home. I think about this. I know her words come directly from her Native American heritage.

We had not been called. As we were both drenched with sweat, we both went home to shower. I stood under the shower head feeling the sharp water jets dislodge any remaining feelings of apprehension. I met Peter at the courtroom to wait out the verdict. At this point, there was little to say, and even less to do, as we just sat, and sat, and sat. Later, Scott came by, but other than voicing encouragement, also had little to say. These hours proved to be the most difficult of all for me, as I guess neurosurgeons are used to being in some form of control, and obviously here there is none to be had. I wondered how trial attorneys, such as Peter, are able to do this over and over without going crazy. I chose not to ask about it and my thoughts returned to Peter as the warrior. He knew how to be still and unmoving. He could hold a silent posture with steady eyes, alert to everything around him. He could not be disturbed. That's how he does it. Five p.m. arrived, and we were told that the jury had completed its deliberations for the day and would resume at 9:00 a.m. tomorrow. We left. It was another silent drive home. At home, it was difficult for me—and I'm sure equally for Kathy—to eat, and even more so to sleep.

I've lost weight over the last couple of weeks. I eat, but it all tastes like cardboard. I eat anyway.

The hours took forever to move forward, and the television was no respite for either of us. The dawn arrived, and Kathy and I drove to the court at about 9:00. When we arrived, we found Peter and Scott were already present, and, to my surprise, Mary, Sam, and Fran were there as well. Fran, always the most sensitive to everyone's needs, had arranged that the entire trial family be there for our support. After making rounds, Lee arrived somewhat later, and I hope he, too, felt somewhat reassured. Peter spent a significant amount of time talking to Kathy and hopefully that helped her, at least a bit. I had no idea what they spoke of, but I hoped it was more than I could speak of with her. I had kept her at a distance because I was afraid she wouldn't understand it. If you weren't in the trenches, there was no possible way anyone could comprehend what I was experiencing. She was my life partner, and previously I had shared everything with her. Not now. Finally, we all ran out of things to say and again just sat and sat in deafening silence.

We then heard that the jury had taken a lunch break, which was arranged by the Bailiff, and then returned to their deliberations. To all but the attorneys, the time seemed interminable, but by the jury's noon break, there had been only about seven hours of deliberation by the jury, four hours yesterday and three hours this morning. As expected, the jurors had asked a number of questions during this time. At about 1:00 p.m., we heard that the jury had returned and resumed deliberations. Time began to move at a snail's pace again. Then, at about 4:00 p.m, to at least Peter's amazement following what was, for him, a very short time of deliberations, we were told that the jury had reached a decision.

I was both excited and fearful. Would I walk out of the courtroom a free man, or would I leave with a scarlet letter on my forehead? We gathered and entered the courtroom and took our respective seats. Soon thereafter, the Plaintiffs' team also reassembled. We waited for what seemed like a long further period of time, but finally the jury was called back to the jury box. We noted that some of them were looking at us, but others were not, and we were not sure what that meant. Finally, the Bailiff and Judge Peterson entered the courtroom. Again, we stood, and then sat, and waited for her to speak. Ever in control, she waited until the courtroom was entirely still, and then turned to the jury and asked, "Has the jury reached a verdict?" Mr. Saline, as we expected, stood and handed a slip of paper to the Bailiff who handed it to Judge Peterson. She read the slip of paper, asked that Lee and I stand, and said "Please report your verdict." Mr. Saline took back the paper, stood up, and read "In the matter of Sheran R and Scott R versus Drs. James Ogsbury and Lee Krauth, we, the jury, find for…."

CHAPTER SIXTEEN

WEEKEND BREAK FROM THE TRIAL

Jay
Saturday, May 12, 1990, 12:05 a.m.

I awoke from what I thought was a long dream and found that only ten minutes had transpired. I was keenly disappointed to realize that the dream did not allow me to come to an end of this experience or to even predict how it might end. Obviously, we will have to go to the second weekend of the trial with the defense case to start on Monday.

Peter
Saturday, May 12, 1990

Back from the Springs and my talk to the American College of Surgeons. A few thoughts about the trial yesterday, as the imperial and haughty Dr. Greer ("Dr. God") armed with his impressive professional resume and an even larger ego, arrived to proselytize that Sheran never had meningitis.

When Mr. H tried to direct him to the Super Glue issue, I raised a big ruckus pointing out the indisputable fact that we had never been told

"Dr. God" was going to discuss Super Glue. Judge Peterson, having been told by the Rs' lawyers that Super Glue was going to be discussed by this witness only as it affected to certain laboratory test results and caused certain symptoms he would relate to "meningeal irritation secondary to Super Glue," overruled my objection, mildly chiding me for making a "technical" objection that put her on the spot. But, as soon as the jury was brought back in and "Dr. God" was asked about Super Glue, he promptly blurted out his brand new, hot-off-the-press opinion theory that Super Glue, not overly aggressive surgical retraction, had caused Sheran's stroke. I listened to this for about a minute in my initial shock, unable to object. Through this highly paid and willing foil, the Plaintiffs, without a word of notice and directly contrary to what they had told Judge Peterson moments before, changed their theory of what had caused Sheran's stroke right on the stand.

Finally I rose and asked to be heard at the bench, telling the Judge in shouted, animated whispers I was angry and shocked at this major change in Plaintiffs' theory of what happened (denying me the opportunity to prepare for it) without any forewarning to Judge Peterson or to us, and improper, especially after we had been told on the record what his testimony was going to be.

She was furious at Mr. H, later characterizing this new theory as an "ambush." Mr. H was in shock too but loudly proclaimed his innocence; Schuster sat quietly in the background, nary a peep from him as he sat silently while letting Mr. H tell the Court what the doctor would say about Super Glue (but knowing full well, having spent the whole day preparing "Dr. God" the day before that "Dr. God" was going to say Super Glue caused the stroke). Ironically, all of this came on the heels of yesterday's journal entry where I was reveling in the fact that the case was being tried on such a "high ethical plane." I don't believe Mr. H was part of this sham and don't want to believe that, but deceit and slippery tactics aren't a problem when it comes to others. How pathetic—the win-at-all-costs mentality.

Country boy Fitzgerald and Schuster: "Well, shucks Mr. H, you sho have got yoself some strange bedfellows." Judge Peterson has ordered "Dr. God" to be back at 1:30 Monday so that I can prepare for him over the weekend. When I'm done, he will be ground chuck; everyone in the courtroom knows what's coming. I told Jay what Plaintiffs had done was so bad we could easily get a mistrial. But that meant starting over and we were way ahead—probably why someone thought he could get away with this outrageous stunt. I tell Jay to "forge on" and get ready to watch me chop "Dr. God" in little pieces. He's loving it, bright eyed and alive. I will nurture and care for my body and mind this weekend and will destroy this black knight. Amid all the chaos on Friday afternoon the Rs, they dropped their demand from 1.8 million to $400,000, my sense being they might drop as low as $250,000 or $300,000. Jay doesn't want to settle, nor do I.

Peter
Sunday, May 13, 1990

Sunday, after eighteen hours away from the wars, in the company of my sweet girlfriend, Casey. 'Tis a beautiful, warm summer day and the birds are chirping happily—a perfect kind of Mother's Day, and I in my van, fresh from my brief slice of R&R am about to leave this bliss to go inside to prepare for my assault on Dr. God. I feel good, calm, relaxed, and ready to slay this man.

Jay
Sunday, May 13, 1990

Nothing much happened on Saturday. I made rounds and that felt foreign. I did not feel like exercising even on the bike. I simply felt like doing nothing, so I read my deposition for a while and did little else for the rest of the day. Today, Sunday, I felt somewhat better. I rode my usual circuit and then started into PC&J for trial preparations.

On the way, I was called to the hospital for a patient with a subarachnoid hemorrhage and subdural hematoma. I arrived as the initial testing was starting, agreed with the diagnosis, and helped Lee get started with the operation. Once that was done, I called home and found to my surprise that a settlement offer had been made for $100,000 with no attorneys' fees. As I drove back toward the PC&J law offices, I once again considered the various factors. One, the defense of medicine—Lee had done that. Two, the challenge of Mr. Spence is gone and therefore there is no longer the feeling of his challenge. Three, not wishing to lose—I remembered Fran's words, "This is not about winning, it is about not losing." Any settlement is a settlement on the record, but the low numbers are taken into account by the Board. The settlements have taken care of Sheran's needs and anything more would be a windfall. I do not wish the attorneys, particularly Mr. Spence, to benefit, but I do not necessarily wish to win either. Mr. H is strangely a concern given the ethical way he has approached the case. I decided I might consider a contribution by the insurance company.

When I arrived at PC&J, Peter himself came to the door, let me in, and reported that while he personally wished to continue, from a legal point of view he advised me to take the offer, though he said he could probably get it somewhat lower. I told him my concerns, that the exact amount was not important, but that any settlement with the family still felt like losing.

He then startled me with the suggestion that a donation be made to a charity, presumably an Indian charity, for that amount and began to explain its advantages. I interrupted his discussion to tell him that this suggestion was appealing, that somebody would finally benefit from this tragedy. He called Mr. H, Mr. H called Mr. R, and Mr. H called quickly back with the agreement: $100,000 given directly to a tribal council in Mr. and Sheran R's name, no attorneys' fees, the settlement would be open.

Peter told Mr. H about the book, and Mr. H was not unreasonably concerned that I might be vindictive. Peter suggested I talk to him. I told Mr. H that I appreciated his professionalism and the way he had presented his side, particularly given the little time he was given to prepare his case. I said further that we understood he felt badly about the episode Friday and reiterated that neither Peter nor I felt that he knew of the change in testimony by his witness. I told him that the reason for the book was simply to describe the experience from all of our positions and that we in no way look to embarrass anyone, particularly him. Finally, I told him that indeed I had not used Super Glue, that the nurse was mistaken. He said that he, too, had come to this conclusion; it is unlikely I would have gotten permission for its use in the second operation if it had been used and failed at the first operation.

Peter and Scott both feel very good about this. It's a win/win circumstance. Everyone wins in some way. Scott gets to go on vacation. I defended the medicine. The attorneys finished the case. The Defense came up with a creative settlement. The insurance company paid less than the attorneys' fees for the next three weeks. Peter called Fran—she likes it too, and she will come to court with her tape recorder to interview the jury. I called Kathy and she alone is not happy; she feels like it is a loss. I called Lee and he said he is happy as long as I am happy. And, as much as I was prepared for the full fight, I guess I'm glad it's over without embarrassment to either side. The strange irony is that if Mr. Spence had been here, I doubt that he would have accepted this reasonable solution, but I know I would not have. Mr. H challenged my medicine; Mr. Spence challenged my integrity.

Fran
Sunday, May 13, 1990

It's Mother's Day and I'm working in the midst of my vegetable garden. Mother me and mother earth, seeds and seedlings, happy as a clam when Peter calls. There's no happier place in the world for a Snapping Turtle than to have all four appendages planted in the cool earth.

Peter called to talk about a settlement. No! No! No! Damn! Now sitting in the dirt and listening to Peter in the role of wise counselor.

I guess I better listen. Money given to Indians, not to the Plaintiffs or their attorneys. A creative, graceful, last, and final movement from the warrior in this trial. He couldn't have come up with this without his own deep appreciation and respect for a people punished for simply being who they are. Ahh, the seeds germinated from months ago finally yield their fruit.

It's harvest time. Peter knows Jay has been getting to know Snapping Turtle. Peter's mind plays tricks on him. He thinks he is still a clever white man. His act was a gift from his heart that freed us all. In this, there were no victors and there were no vanquished. The outcome served us all, healing ointment on our wounds. It was a right action. Aho.

CHAPTER SEVENTEEN

DAY 11
THE SETTLEMENT

Peter
Monday, May 14, 1990, 10:05 a.m.

"God, give me the serenity to accept the things I cannot change, the courage to change things I ought to, and the wisdom to know one from the other." How drastic, how quickly things change. It's 10:05 Monday morning and here I sit all alone with my thoughts, listening to Sinead O'Connor and basking in the bittersweet peace of a settlement. Early Sunday afternoon, Mr. H called to talk more about what happened Friday. He then announced that if it would do any good, the attorneys would waive attorneys' fees as to any money paid on behalf of Jay.

When I pressed him, he also said while he had no authority, he thought the Rs would accept as little as $100,000, yet another catastrophic drop in Plaintiffs' demand. And while I liked the way the case was going and was looking forward to the opportunity to beating up on Dr. God, we had finally gotten a figure so low that Jay had to consider it.

When he arrived at the office around 2:30 or 3:00 p.m., he balked at any settlement, seeing this as a concession or admission of guilt. He had won! But how could I communicate that or the fact that it wasn't necessary for him to have a verdict as his final vindication? When I came up with the idea of donating the $100,000 to an Indian charity of Mr. R's choosing, I knew it would appeal to Jay's humanistic side, to Fran, and, most importantly, place the responsibility of going forward squarely on the back of Mr. R. Also, with the Indian culture so much in the forefront, I needed a device to allow our vanquished foe to leave the arena with dignity intact.

By the end of the afternoon, the case was over, more than three years after I first attempted what I then thought was the ingenious ploy of trying to settle with the Rs before they even had an attorney representing them. It took little time to write the details of the settlement.

After a call to Mr. H to confirm his agreement, I went to a local restaurant and, while waiting for Kathy and Jay, worked on my journal. When lawyers for the Rs made money, as did my firm, unfortunately, Sheran and Mr. R received substantially less than they would have had they just trusted me, going through three years, parts of two trials, and untold stress to get less than what we would have paid to begin with. Mr. R, drawn by siren's call of big money, turned to his high-powered attorneys. Sadly, they turned away from the opportunity to resolve this conflict quickly and quietly and for the family, what would have been lots more money.

Today I awoke with rising of the sun, a real sadness and emptiness in my heart. I will miss you, Jay, the trial, the rush of adrenalin each morning as I charged through the black of night on my way to the White Spot. I will miss those times the trial lawyer dreams of when there is nothing else alive in the moment and your senses. At the podium, there was only me and my enemy on the stand—me oblivious to all but the battle, the clicks and the whirrings of my brain, having no idea what I'm doing but flowing with intuition knowing it would be good.

Moments of pure concentration, pure ecstasy, being alive and on fire. But when they surrendered, I realized in my heart I could no longer make this my battle, that the time had come to lay down our weapons and to allow the Rs and their attorneys to walk from the arena with some shred of dignity. I did the right thing. Why then do I feel so bad? Because my warrior's spirit, my fire, still burns brightly—it is so hard to turn away from that and become a peaceful man again.

As for Jay, he remains a man of character, conviction, and concern. He took the Rs into his heart and home. Sheran R was devastated through no fault of his, and in allowing this settlement without a loser, he once again showed his humanism, a remarkable gesture for someone who has been to hell and back many times since the time he first laid eyes on Sheran R on June 23, 1986.

Jay
Monday, May 14, 1990

I awoke with an emptiness but mainly simply feeling let down. Kathy is still unhappy. She is worried that this is a loss, and that Peter has manipulated me to accept it; hopefully, he will be able to reassure her.

We met Peter at a restaurant where he was working on his journal. He seemed genuinely happy and talked of other creative settlements. I still feel fine about the outcome, as at least someone will benefit. Kathy is still very unhappy, but Peter works his magic on her too. He is indeed a master manipulator. He would, of course, rather have it called negotiator; he calls it the counselor part of his practice.

Scott came in and reported that one of our experts, Dr. Mason, was not sure regarding the meningitis—that 10 percent of gram stains are in error. Therein lies the difference between surgeons and internists. Surgeons act on a 90 percent chance; internists worry about the 10 percent.

We returned to the court. Only Mr. H and Ms. Kudla were present at the Plaintiffs' table. Scott, Peter and I were on our side. Fran joined Kathy and Joneen in the gallery. We then met in the judge's chambers. Judge Peterson stated that she understood there was a development in the case. Peter said, "Your Honor, I talked to you this morning, and I think Mr. H has talked to you. I have told you, in no uncertain terms, about my feeling about what happened Friday, of the fact that Mr. H had nothing to do with that. I will say it again on the record, nothing further need be said. That's number one."

"Number two, we have reached a settlement. Mr. and Mrs. R agreed to dismiss any and all claims arising out of the care at any time, and specifically with respect to the St. Anthony hospitalization in 1986 at the hands of Drs. Krauth and Ogsbury. And it is agreed that upon our carrying out our side of the agreement, that the Rs will sign a stipulation for dismissal of this case with prejudice."

Peter then showed Judge Peterson the details of the settlement:

> "COPIC Insurance Company, on behalf of Dr. Ogsbury, with Dr. Ogsbury's express consent, will pay the sum of $100,000 to a nonpolitical Indian organization, program, charity, what have you, of the R's choosing. And it will be shown only that the contribution and payment is in the name of the Rs—that is, Dr. Ogsbury has nothing to do with it, COPIC has nothing to do with it—it will be in the R's name only.
>
> It is agreed that the parties will pay their own costs and attorneys' fees. I have been assured by Mr. H that in light of the unusual nature of this settlement, involving a contribution, that the Rs will not be charged any attorneys' fees from this $100,000 contribution—which is a specific part of the settlement negotiation in terms of Dr. Ogsbury's ultimate willingness to consent. Finally, there is an unusual provision in that it is understood, from our standpoint, that the parties and the attorneys shall be free to discuss and/or write about the facts, terms, and conditions of the settlement, the negotiations, and the details of the lawsuit, the care insofar as is of public record and has been discussed as part of the trial, and treatment, and the trial."

Mr. H said, "That's my understanding, Your Honor. They are acceptable to the Plaintiff. I have talked with Mr. R and discussed the details, and he has given authority for the settlement."

Judge Peterson then talked about the episode of Friday and said, "Well, I should place on the record, too, that I never had any doubt, Mr. H, that what happened was planned. I know I used the word 'ambush' but I also used the word 'inadvertently.' I am not sure how all that came down, but I have no doubt that there was nothing planned on your part. You have complete credibility with me. If you came in here on the 15th of July and told me it was snowing outside, I wouldn't even look out the window—I'd ask if you'd put up the top of my convertible."

Mr. H answered, "I appreciate that."

Judge Peterson continued, "I don't know how that happened. You looked as stricken as everybody else did in the courtroom."

On our way out from her chambers to the courtroom, I spoke briefly with Judge Peterson. I told her that I had talked to Mr. H and that the book was not intended to embarrass anyone. She joked that, if a movie was to be made, she wished to play herself.

Judge Peterson called in the jury and simply said, "You're probably wondering why we are not up to our ears in files and documents, as we usually are. The case has been settled over the weekend. Now before I excuse you from jury duty, I want to thank you very much for corning in. We did want you to come down here and explain to you that it has been settled rather than just giving you a telephone call. I want to thank you very much for your time and attention in the two weeks that you have put into this case. One of the reasons that it did reach a conclusion without having to reach a verdict is because you were very attentive and gave your time to this case. Sometimes that happens; it's just having a jury present that brings about a resolution that couldn't have been brought out before." She instructed the jurors that they may talk with whomever they want, as much or as little as they wished about the case. She noted if anyone persisted in talking to them over their objection, that they should let the Court know immediately. She thanked them once again for their time.

Peter, Fran and I went out and talked to the jurors. Mr. Saline, much more open than we had imagined, came back into the courtroom and shook my hand. He reported that he believed in our case and said that if he needed medical care, he would choose us and that if he needed legal care he would choose Peter. He talked happily about once being a Santa Claus.

After the trial, Narciso ran up to Peter and said, "Good job, Dude." He also told Peter, "Them dudes was laying some heavy shit on the Ogs" and he "wasn't going to let it happen." He then added, "Like old Ogs here, you wouldn't stop now, would you, just because they come up on this stuff?" Then Narciso turned to me and said, "Let me say something. Who do you live for, for what they say about you or do you live for you? You tried. There was nothing more you could have done. You are already scarred, don't let it go over this." Later, I thought, I am honored to be counseled by that man.

Most of the others were equally open as only Miss Garcia did not wish to discuss the trial. Mrs. Holmes said that most of the jury had made up their minds in our favor, and Mr. Quintana said that he was in our favor as well. Mrs. Petit, however, said that she had wished to wait. Mrs. Huey, the consummate juror, felt the same, wishing to delay her decision until the trial was completed.

Mrs. Romero was impressed that we had taken care of Mrs. R's family but probably best expressed the tragedy when she said, "I'm not even a doctor and I know that—she was caught up in the system and paid a big price."

I took one final look around Courtroom 9. The chairs were still in order but now with no one filling them. A few exhibits were the only evidence of the activities of the last two weeks. We left the court. I rode in Washington Park with Peter and Scott, the trial over.

Peter
Monday, May 14, 1990

By the end of the day, we had talked to the jurors who were for the most part leaning strongly towards Jay, and, at 3:30, Scott, Jay, and I went for a bike ride, pounding around Washington Park as fast as fast can do. Time again to begin letting go. I dropped Jay off and went to get my boys knowing that the sun was already beginning to set on this experience. Soon this will fade away—the long hours, the anxiety, the laborious debriefing sessions each night in court, the incredible bursts of energy, the oneness of the time, the love, laughter, fear, and the fire will quickly fade. Like leaves in the brisk fall winds, we will each be blown in our separate directions. Soon it will seem like it never happened; God, it was good while it lasted.

Fran
Monday, May 14, 1990

It's funny, the place of beginnings is often the place of endings. I suppose one could assume I am referring to Courtroom 9, but I'm not. The faces I probably will never see again, except in dreams and faint memories. *Ga li e li ga* (I am thankful). No other words come.

CHAPTER EIGHTEEN

POST-TRIAL

Jay
Tuesday, May 15, 1990

I awoke this morning. The letdown is obvious. The sun rose, the world looked the same, but felt different.

No early morning drive to downtown Denver thinking of today's tactics on the drive in.

No meeting at the White Spot with Peter who had been there all night.

No going through depositions word by word to arm Peter and Scott with ammunition for the day.

No walk to the courthouse with these men laughing over past humors.

No arrival at Courtroom 9, my home for two weeks.

No Mary and Sam battling Frick and Frack for the desired front row seats behind the Defense.

No Dr. Berman with her amazing sense of personality.

No Mr. H, Ms. Kudla, Mr. Schuster, and Mr. Fitzgerald at their table in clothes especially designed for that day's encounter.

No Peter, Scott, and me always in friendly sport coats and slacks.

No Judge Peterson, always gracious, sometimes human, sometimes humorous, but always in complete control of her domain.

No jurors—each unique, each different, each assumed but not known to represent a certain perspective, but all holding all of our lives in their hands.

Most of all, no feeling of both the thrill and the fear of having to place all that you stand for in front of all these people. Not knowing what else to do, I climbed upon my favorite bicycle and took a fast 35-mile ride. The high and low points of the past weeks, months, and even years came welling back.

But, at the end of the ride, I simply could not dismiss the disquieting thought that, without these extraordinary circumstances and people, that is, appropriate medicine in the middle of a tragedy, the honorable response by the agents and directors of an insurance company throughout, the extraordinary lawyers on both sides, but particularly ours, and the remarkable jury chosen by our skilled psychologist, this result might not have happened. Hopefully someone, someday, will discover a process that serves the same goals, justice, and the appropriate care of the injured, without the immense financial, professional, and personal toll that this process took on all of us.

<h1 style="text-align:center">Jay</h1>
May 21, 1990
One Week Post Trial

The day broke warm and clear, a far cry from the trial weeks. The events which came to a climax one week ago with the formal settlement are already becoming a blur of memory, the only accuracy lodged in these words.

I made the decision to return to work rather than take time off, hopefully to put as much of this behind us as soon as possible. Practice for the first few weeks proved to be predictably unrewarding. The faces of Sheran, Mr. R, Mr. Spence, Peter, Mr. H, and to a greater or lesser degree all of the other players, friend and foe, simply will not go away. Fortunately, my colleagues were helpful in not asking me to share the memories. Other than the surprise at seeing me back by those who did not know the outcome, little mention was made of the trial. Either they respected my desire for privacy or perhaps they entertained the hope that they would not somehow be touched by a similar action if they simply avoided talking about it. In any case, happily little was said as they went on with their daily lives. Hopefully at some time I will be as divorced from these proceedings as they.

Peter
September 22, 1992

It's Sunday afternoon and I'm sitting in Jay's living room in Vail after two intense days of poring over and editing the manuscript, a tedious yet rewarding task which so vividly brings back the incredible experience we shared—without the manuscript the experience is almost gone; with it, I again feel and relive the fear, fatigue, camaraderie, laughter, and exaltation that mark a big- stakes trial. Tears, chills, and laughter mark my revisit to Jay's ordeal through the trial manuscript.

Jay remains my friend, but the intensity of our friendship has changed. Now he seems a little different—a little less bounce in his step, not quite the same sparkle in his eyes.

The words of someone who knows keep running through my mind as I spend this time with him, "A lawsuit is like a fast current in a river which picks you up and sweeps you away to be deposited at another point, never to be the same." Jay has changed—he won but he lost; some part of his spirit has been taken from him in the process. Or maybe Jay saw a life so different than his, a lawyer's life—the warrior, vital and alive, on fire with its cause—fire and ice—so incredibly different, yet for that one glorious period of time together as warriors.

And, as the warrior away from the battlefield, peaceful and content, I wonder if anyone will ever understand the incredible toll of a trial. I have a certain sadness as I finish this job—a distant longing for the rush of legal combat, the love and camaraderie that go with it. But as I sit here watching and listening to Jay, I sense part of my sadness comes from knowing the toll may have been too high.

Fran
November 1992

The trial gave to Jay a taste of emotions, a feel of passion for life that in its own strange way had nothing to do with medicine or law. He was involved in his trial out of anger and indignation. It took this energy, the energy of one star, to move him through the self-doubt, the fear, the humiliation. In the midst of this chaotic experience, it gave back to him moments of true being. The range and spectrum of emotions, whether it be joy, sadness, anger or rage, he experienced and expressed. Moments of realness, whether it was a flash in the pan laugh filled with mirth or sputtering indignation. These were the micro-moments burned in my memory. But those moments are foreigners to him, retreating to his depths as he moves back to his familiar life. Those moments cannot exist safely there. There cannot be this union of true self and work in our present medical system, so in a sense he must remain separated from himself. And for this, it is a loss, not just for Jay, but for all of us.

Jay
January 1993

Sitting late at night in front of a winter fire in my Colorado mountain home, I find myself once again reflecting on the events of the past six years. The ordeal, which brought together three unlikely people, began in June 1986 with the terrible medical tragedy that befell a lady loved by all who knew her and culminated in the malpractice trials of November 1989 and April 1990. Now, some three years after the trials, as Peter, Fran and I finally complete our project of trying to describe the experience of being involved in those trials, I am struck by the impact that this experience has had on us and those around us.

Peter remains an incredibly successful attorney in the Denver area, his energy and aura unchanged. Yet he no longer limits his practice to malpractice defense and indeed sometimes seems most excited when he describes his representation of clients in other areas. He has said that the move away from malpractice defense occurred strictly for business reasons. I do not question those practicalities played a role in that decision, but I wonder if his experience in the legal disposition of Sheran's tragedy somehow played a role as well. I have always felt that, after his attempt to arrange for Sheran's care for the rest of her life was forestalled by the filing of the lawsuits, Peter seemed to be on a mission far greater than the usual defense of a malpractice defendant.

Could it be that part of his zeal was due to his feelings about the role he felt his own community played in preventing an honorable resolution to this tragedy? And while he was successful in being the warrior that Fran trained him to be, I sense he also now has a very personal feel for that which happens to those involved in a trial, including himself.

Fran continues to amaze. For many months she resisted my entreaties to complete her part of the story from her notes and tapes taken at the time. Her words show us why. I had, of course, known of her ambivalence in opposing our Indian adversaries. But her painful description of her Indian background and the difficulties encountered even today by Native Americans in our society give testimony to the depth of her feelings. I hope all of us can learn from Snapping Turtle.

I trust also that she understands that, without her, neither the result of the trial nor the manuscript describing it would have been possible. Because of her help and especially her caring, I will remain forever in her debt.

It is obviously most difficult to look at oneself. However, it is clear to me now that the character known as Jay no longer exists. Prior to 1986, he had a passion for medicine that was a central focus of his being. When his medicine was challenged, his very essence was challenged, and the Defense became the passion. He saw only the Defense and excluded all around him, except those involved directly in the trial. Only now do I understand the torment that that exclusion created for his family and friends who wished, but were not allowed, to be with him. He did it his way, selfishly and a bit crazed I guess, but really the only way for him and the immediate result was good.

But now, with the trial over and the manuscript completed, the passion, and with it the love of medicine, is gone. I considered retirement at one point, but like most physicians, am ill-equipped for any field but medicine. Indeed, several colleagues who have tried retirement—and failed—have advised against that plan. So, I have joined, without bitterness, the growing group of physicians who look to medicine as a vocation, a job, not an avocation. Our years of training provide the discipline to still do the job well, and experience has produced the wisdom to recognize and avoid the medical situations that involve risks we no longer wish to take.

Unfortunately, I fear the present generation of physicians will be the last to experience medicine as I knew it. I know for me, and I suspect for others, that the current economic, political, and legal pressures will no longer allow us the joy of being true physicians, that is, the ability to be concerned solely with the needs of a patient and the courage to carry out that which needs to be done.

Fran

I continue my Earth walk. Jay is no longer a part of my surroundings. It's like someone cut down the shade tree in my front yard. A familiar piece of my landscape is gone. Peter will always be on the path with me showing up and vanishing, until I become a sky walker. Maybe he'll learn how to walk the sky too.

EPILOGUE

Sheran R died at her Wyoming family home in 2005.

Dr. Krauth left the partnership soon after the trial. He continued to practice neurosurgery for many years, retired in 2000, and lives near his family home in Western Colorado. He has a continuing interest in the Air Force Academy where his son is now enrolled, and he is a member of The Association of Graduates' Board of Development.

Dr. Barron and I remain friends, and he has agreed to let me use his name. He is happily retired from the practice of otolaryngologist.

Dr. Mason recently passed away, ironically from an immunologic-caused infectious disease.

I have not been able to locate the neurosurgeon (Dr. W) who was to be the one expert witness chosen from the three neurosurgeons who were supportive of my care. For that reason, I have used his initials.

Jay
January 2023

It has now been almost exactly thirty years since Fran, Peter, and I met in the mountains to edit the manuscript. It was a process which Peter described as "a tedious yet rewarding task, which so vividly brings back the incredible experiences we shared." However, it has only been in the last year, since my retirement one year ago, that I have had sufficient time to relive the experience and reconsider the long-term impact that it has had on me and, indeed, on all of us.

Even after thirty years, the memories keep flooding back, as if the events of June and July 1986 occurred yesterday. I still clearly remember my first encounter with this beautiful lady, loved by all around her. I particularly remember her surprise at the consent process, to which she said I was treating her as an enemy, not a friend, and that she knew I would do my best. My compassion for her started then, but could only be exposed later, much later. It was there, always there, hidden, camouflaged, but ever-present. I remember every event of her hospitalization which led to the devastating stroke with permanent brain damage. I remember flying to Wyoming in the governor's plane in September, finally taking her back to her family home in Riverton. I remember Peter, at my request, making the arrangements with the malpractice insurance company to make funds available for Sheran, and then pride when that company agreed to pay $1.5 million for the lifelong care of her and her family. I remember the disappointment when this honorable resolution became no longer possible after a medical malpractice action was filed by Sheran's husband through Gerry Spence, the well-known Wyoming attorney.

I remember the first trial when Gerry Spence, large in stature, large of ego, and skilled at storytelling, was possibly surprised when he found that he was aggressively opposed by Peter, smaller in stature, smaller of ego, but at least equally skilled in the courtroom. Peter was clearly passionate about his client and the medical issues to be addressed. He was laser focused as if nothing else existed. He was the warrior Fran trained him to be. I remember the feeling of letdown, particularly for Peter, but also for me, when the declaration of a mistrial meant that we would likely no longer be facing Mr. Spence. Finally, I remember Peter making the unusual request, probably to keep me out of his hair during the second trial, to write a diary describing the life of a defendant during a malpractice trial. I took this dictum to heart. I wrote and wrote.

I now understand that the horror of what happened in 1986 led to the challenge of my medical care during the malpractice trials in 1989 and 1990. Then, the creation of a manuscript describing that experience from the point of view of three separate people became a substitute for the passion of medicine that was taken because of the trials. The process of finishing the manuscript was accomplished in January 1993.

Unfortunately, because of the abrupt ending of the trial by the settlement (and therefore the story written about it), the manuscript was never published—a keen disappointment because of the energy and care that was poured into the project of producing it. Each of us, Peter, Fran and me, reluctantly accepted the loss. Each of us moved forward, wounded that this story would never be told. We lost touch for years.

Following the trial, I continued to practice within the field of neurosurgery. Not surprisingly, the passion for medicine never returned. I was left searching for something—anything—to fill this void. Initially, that passion was replaced by a significant concern to avoid taking a risk that might lead to the occurrence of a similar situation. The comment "We treat plaintiffs, not patients, and anyone who thinks otherwise is naïve" never left my mind, a disquieting perspective for a physician to have. Because of this, the joy and fulfillment that comes from neurosurgical practice also never returned. Finally, in 2006, after sustaining a broken hip on a bike ride, I decided not to return to surgery, and, for some years, functioned as a neurosurgical consultant. The broken hip had finally exhausted my attempt to resume living in the operating room as a healer.

Thinking back, maybe it's true. We neurosurgeons don't have the ability to relate to others or even ourselves. We certainly don't have stellar bedside manners. I was trained to heal, not to relate. What our patients don't understand is our mindset. Failure is not an option. That's the trained mindset. This mindset leaves many neurosurgeons ill-prepared to deal with any unexpected failure.

During this time, in the absence of time spent in the operating room, I became interested in healthcare reform, and, with a colleague, developed a computer-based program for the treatment of acute low back pain called the Colorado Low Back Collaborative. With the incredible support of the wonderful local director of United Healthcare, the program was rolled out to national acclaim in 2011. Unfortunately, after four months, the primary care physicians, for whom the program was developed, decided that the generous program remuneration was not worth the small amount of extra work and exited the program, causing its demise.

Also during this time, I was offered the opportunity to become a contract physician to another insurance company. Then, about one year ago, after more than thirteen years, my position as a contract physician with the company was abruptly terminated. Of course, I was not given a reason for the decision, but I surmise that my insistence on performing thorough reviews focusing on patient safety and outcome led to the elimination of my position, another key disappointment given the pride involved in being a patient advocate in a company that needed one. Fran was right. As she taught us during the trial, white men break treaties. Profit is the prize, not the outcome of the people they serve. I then decided to fully retire.

Now, in the year since my retirement, I finally have had the time to mull over these many stages in my life. I have come to realize that each of the major events—the trial and defense of my medicine, the manuscript, the Colorado Low Back Collaborative, and even the position as a consultant in an insurance company—were really surrogates for the passion for medicine that was taken by the trial. Like the passion, each of these surrogates has failed in its own way, and I realized that a neurosurgeon without a passion is, or at least should be, an oxymoron. At the same time, however, I also realized that a failure which closes a door in one direction almost always uniquely opens a door in another. An open door offers hope. A loss occurs only when one fails to walk through the newly opened door to see what is on the other side.

So, some months ago, I reconnected with Fran, who, thankfully, is still functioning as a practicing psychologist in the Denver area. I was happy to learn that, since the trial, she has maintained her contact with her Indian heritage and her identity with her tribe. Hopefully, our reconnection has allowed the shade tree, metaphorically lost to her after the second trial, to retake its proper place in her front yard.

I realized that the introduction to the simple beauty of her Native American culture, which she taught us so well during the trial, has remained with me over the years. Finally, after talking to her at some length, she suggested that I create an avatar. I initially declined, perhaps not knowing the full implication of that word. However, one morning about three months ago, I awoke following a dream about the trial, which I have had multiple times since the trial. Each time the dream unfortunately ends just as the jury foreman is about to announce the verdict. I have come to understand that the abrupt ending to the actual trial has left a significant mark on me that needed to be addressed, a hole asking to be filled.

Therefore, on awakening from the dream three months ago, I decided to try to fill the hole by somehow re-creating the dream. I fully realize that the primary narrative of this book is purely experiential and true to actual events. At the same time, the dream chapter at least tries to recapture the essence of an actual dream and is, therefore, not purely fiction either. Thus, it is consistent with the original goal of the book which was to document the trial and its effect on those involved in the trial. Interestingly, I have noticed that since the writing of the dream sequence, I have not had the actual dream once in the past three months.

During this endeavor, I have had significant help from others. I am a physician neurosurgeon who is certainly not privy to all of the subtleties of a trial. Therefore, I asked Heidi Ray, a wonderful attorney friend who once was a litigator but more recently chose to become involved in the educational aspect of the legal system, to look at the plausibility of the dream sequence which I wrote. She immediately found multiple passages that needed to be reworded or eliminated altogether. Without her help making these changes, I would not have been able to develop a legal story. Fran, of course, has also been a great help, repeatedly insisting that I step out of the safety of a purely medical focus to understand and address the personal impact that each step creates. A project attempting to re-create and properly interpret a dream is clearly not consistent with a neurosurgical personality and just might not have been possible without Fran's encouragement and sometimes stern admonitions. She was able to describe emotions that I might have felt but never could have put into words. Thus, without Heidi and Fran, who were, in essence, co-writers, I would have been a neurosurgeon without the tools to embark on this project.

In addition, I was able to reconnect with Peter, who happily has retired. He no longer has a desire to return to, as he said before, "this crazy process of emotional, psychological, physical, and intellectual warfare we call trial by jury." However, his energy and aura remain intact, just as it was three years after the trial. He has kindly agreed to look at "The Dream" chapter. Hopefully, he will find it plausible, and appreciate my description of his created trial performance.

While I realize it is unusual to produce a chapter written thirty years after the rest of the manuscript was completed, it is now my hope that the addition of "The Dream" chapter will create a plausible sense of completion to a neurosurgeon's personal story about not losing and, particularly, his appreciation of the two extraordinary people who shared his journey.

Jay
April 2024

The story began as a description of a medical malpractice trial which resulted from a catastrophic medical occurrence. The manuscript was written as the trial occurred from the perspectives of the neurosurgeon Defendant, the defense attorney, and the team psychologist. The expectation was that the manuscript would document the effect that the experience of the trial would have on each of the three. Clearly that expectation was realized. However, equally clearly, a more significant dynamic became progressively apparent, that is the friendship and emotional interdependence that developed between these three very disparate people.

Peter, the attorney, had been trained by Fran, the Native American psychologist, how to oppose a brilliant Native American plaintiff's attorney. In addition, Peter was involved in the initial attempt for the medical system to take care of the tragically injured patient. When that failed, it seemed, at least to me, he had a passion for the issues raised by the lawsuit well beyond that of a standard defense attorney. I will never forget the many images of the diminutive Peter standing up to his very large adversary during the first of the two trials that occurred. When I met him again in January 2023, his energy, aura, and passion were undiminished.

However, subsequent hints from his wife to me and then from one of his colleagues in the spring/summer of 2023 indicated that he may not have been well at that point. Since that time, he has not responded to many calls from a previous partner and me. Unfortunately, both of us have had to conclude that he may no longer be with us, that perhaps he has become the "sky walker" that Fran poignantly predicted he might ultimately become.

Fran continues to have an active psychology practice. However, between the ongoing "encouragement and stern admonitions" which I have come to expect from her, I have noticed a subtle respect for at least the medical and legal aspects of the white man's world, a grudging acceptance of the strong ethical boundaries in those fields, in contrast to the white man's corporate world which she finds so troubling. I hope I can assume that Peter and I played a role in this. I do know that Fran has had an enormous impact on both Peter and me. Even after the trials, Peter seemed to frequently think in Native American homilies. Like Peter, I, too, came to appreciate the Native American culture, and that appreciation has remained with me since the trials. Also, I was pleased that Fran was willing to lend her voice to the description of the dream which I experienced for years after the trials. The dream sequence is strongly imbued with Native American overtones, as it should be.

For me, the practice of neurosurgery is a distant memory, but the love for my field remains strong. About this, Fran recently commented, "Passion has once again found its way home." I hope, somehow, Peter is proud.

Therefore, now, there lives a part of each of us—in the other of us, which comes from the understanding and appreciation of our differences. Each of us, even Peter from wherever he now resides, would hope that this rediscovery could be a model for others during difficult times.

And in the end,
It's not the years in your life that count.
It's the life in your years.

Frequently attributed, without verification, to Abraham Lincoln

www.ingramcontent.com/pod-product-compliance
Lightning Source LLC
Chambersburg PA
CBHW050418170426
43201CB00008B/449